Communication Networks: A First Course

The Aksen Associates Series in Electrical and Computer Engineering

Principles of Applied Optics
Partha P. Banerjee / Syracuse University
Ting-Chung Poon / Virginia Polytechnic Institute and State University

Software Engineering
Stephen R. Schach / Vanderbilt University

Introduction to Applied Statistical Signal Analysis
Richard Shiavi / Vanderbilt University

Communication Networks: A First Course
Jean Walrand / University of California, Berkeley

Advisory Editors

Jacob A. Abraham / University of Texas at Austin

Leonard A. Gould / Massachusetts Institute of Technology

Frederic J. Mowle / Purdue University

James D. Plummer / Stanford University

Stuart C. Schwartz / Princeton University

Communication Networks: A First Course

Jean Walrand
University of California at Berkeley

Aksen
Associates
Incorporated
Publishers

IRWIN
Homewood, IL 60430
Boston, MA 02116

Project Supervision: Business Media Resources
Electronic Compositor: Ocean View Technical Publications
Cover and text designer: Harold Pattek
Developmental Editors: Marjorie Singer Anderson and Thomas Woolf
Copyeditor: Bob Klingensmith
Proofreader: Christopher Bernard
Technical Illustrations: Jean Walrand and George Jardine
Indexer: Alexandra Nickerson
Printer: R. R. Donnelley and Sons

This book was produced from the author's troff files with pagemakeup in Xerox Ventura Publisher®. Typefaces are Times Roman and the Univers families. Illustrations were rendered with Aldus Freehand®.

Library of Congress Cataloging-in-Publication Data
Walrand, Jean.
     Communication networks : a first course / Jean Walrand.
          p.   cm.
     Includes bibliographical references and index.
     ISBN 0-256-08864-0
     1. Computer networks.   I. Title
     TK5105.5.W35   1991
     004.6--dc20   91-12891
                                                              CIP

Printed in the United States of America

1 2 3 4 5 6 7 8 9 0 DOC 8 7 6 5 4 3 2 1

About the Author

Jean Walrand is Professor of Electrical Engineering and Computer Science at the University of California at Berkeley. Dr. Walrand received the *ingenieur* civil degree in electrical engineering at the Université de Liège in Belgium and his PhD in electrical engineering from the University of California at Berkeley. From 1979 to 1981, he taught at Cornell University in Ithaca, New York and then joined the faculty at the University of California at Berkeley.

His primary research interests are in queueing networks, communication networks, stochastic control, stochastic simulation, and stochastic processes. He has published numerous technical papers and is the author of *An Introduction to Queueing Networks* (Prentice-Hall, 1988) for which he was awarded the Lanchester Prize from the Operations Research Society of America. Dr. Walrand has served as an Associate Editor for the *IEEE Transactions on Automatic Control* and for *Systems & Control Letters* and is currently on the editorial board of *Queueing Systems* and *Probability in Engineering and Information Sciences*.

To Annie, Isabelle, and Julie

Contents

Contents

Contents

Preface

A universal revolution is underway in telecommunications. The changes taking place are having a dramatic impact on how individuals and institutions communicate and do business with one another. Government at all levels, retailing and finance, health care, education, and entertainment are among the areas of human activity profoundly affected by the technological advances now underway.

In order to adapt and contribute effectively to these changes engineers and computer scientists need to acquire a solid foundation and understanding of communication networks. The purpose of this text is to help both students and practicing professionals master the background knowledge necessary to participate in and influence ongoing developments in telecommunications.

This book has been written and designed to be accessible to junior-level engineering and computer science students as well as advanced undergraduate and graduate students with no prior knowledge of communication theory or computer networks. Several of the chapters make use of elementary probability concepts and calculations, which are explained in an appendix. The last chapter of the book uses results from queueing theory, derivations of which are included in another appendix. Throughout the text, to the extent possible, descriptions of communication networks have been separated from their mathematical analysis to accommodate differing levels of reader comprehension and preparedness.

Many of the implementation details of current networks are transistory; only a few basic principles are likely to survive the current changes in telecommunications technology. This text has been organized and written with a focus on principles—such as the management of complexity, standardized connectivity, and resource sharing—which will continue to guide the development of networks. These principles motivate the layering of software, standardization, hierarchical addressing and routing, and the multiplexing and switching methods implemented in networks. Although many specific networks are discussed in the book, a continuous effort has been made along the way to emphasize the underlying structure of the field.

Organization of the Book

The plan of *Communication Networks: A First Course* is as follows:

Chapter 1, "Introduction to Communication Networks," introduces communication networks and reviews their history. The chapter explains circuit-switching and packet-switching, as well as the store-and-forward and channel-sharing methods used by networks to transport information. Packet-switching, the decomposition of information into packets of bits that are then transported along links of the network before being reassembled at the destination, is the procedure that makes efficient and reliable networks possible. The historical overview is designed to provide a sense of the rapid pace of evolution of network technology.

Chapter 2, "Design Principles for Communication Networks," describes the general operating principles of networks and explains how network functions are organized. The chapter presents the open systems interconnection (OSI) model and explains the switching and multiplexing techniques used by networks to achieve connectivity and share resources. This chapter also discusses a number of widely used networks. The general decomposition of the network functions discussed in Chapter 2 serves as the framework for the rest of the book.

Chapter 3, "Physical Layer," explains how bits are transported as electromagnetic waves in optical fibers or transmission lines. The chapter discusses the characteristics of communication links, modulation and demodulation methods, the framing of packets, and the methods used for controlling errors. A few important aspects of communication theory—such as the sensitivity of optical receivers, the Fourier analysis of transmission lines and filters, and the synchronization of receivers—are emphasized.

Chapter 4, "Data Link Layer," shows how packets are transmitted reliably over a noisy communication link. The basic method used to achieve reliable transmissions is to retransmit when errors are suspected. Implementations of this method differ in how the packets are numbered by the sender and how their reception is acknowledged by the receiver to identify transmission errors. Three widely used methods—the alternating bit protocol, the selective repeat protocol, and GO BACK N—are explained and their characteristics are analyzed. The verification of protocols using finite state machines or Petri nets is also discussed. These verification procedures are becoming increasingly important as more complex network software is designed.

Chapter 5, "Local Area Networks," describes the most widely used local area networks—IEEE 802.3 (Ethernet), IEEE 802.4 (token bus), IEEE 802.5 (token ring), IEEE 802.6 (DQDB), and FDDI—and explains their operating principles and performance characteristics. FDDI will probably replace Ethernet for high-performance workstations and for larger installations. DQDB may become the standard for interconnecting LANs across wide geographic areas. The discussion of countless multiple-access protocols has been deliberately omitted; while ingenious and mathematically interesting, they have little practical import.

In the OSI model terminology, the IEEE 802.3–6 standards specify the physical layer and part of the data link layer of local area networks. The remainder of the data link layer of local area networks is covered by the IEEE 802.1 standards. Thus, Chapter 5 reviews some topics already discussed in Chapters 3 and 4. The treatment of certain aspects of local area networks has been separated because these networks share communication links; this sharing necessitates procedures that are not required in the networks of point-to-point links addressed in Chapters 3 and 4.

Chapter 6, "Network Layer," explains how networks control the progress of packets and discusses addressing, routing, and flow control. We illustrate the main features of routing and flow control with simple examples, explaining window flow control, the potential instability of distributed routing algorithms, and the possible unfairness of optimal routing algorithms. The spanning tree and shortest path routing algorithms are also analyzed.

Chapter 7, "Transport, Session, and Presentation," discusses the end-to-end transmission of messages between users. The chapter explains how connections are set up, how the dialog between users is supervised, and how the network recovers after a failure. Translation between different syntaxes and compression of data are also discussed. In addition, the chapter explains encryption methods and systems for electronic signatures. The main ideas of the transport and session layers are rather elementary and do not require detailed elaboration.

Chapter 8, "Applications," discusses some widely used protocol suites, including TOP, MAP, and the Internet suite. In concluding the presentation of the OSI layers, this chapter reviews important aspects of the previous chapters and provides applications of the various layer functions.

Chapter 9, "Integration of Services," discusses networks that transmit voice or video in addition to data. These integrated services networks include the

ISDN being implemented by the telephone companies and the future BISDN networks, in addition to some integrated LANs.

Chapter 10, "Performance Evaluation," is an introduction to performance evaluation methods. After discussing SNMP and CMOT, the chapter covers some simulation and analysis methods. Network engineers use performance evaluation methods to analyze and also to design networks. These methods help identify sections of a network that should be upgraded and can also be used to design the least costly network modifications that will meet user requirements.

Appendix A, "Probability Theory," is a self-contained introduction to the concepts and methods of probability theory applicable to our topic. For instance, the calculation of average delays of packets subject to retransmission after a time-out is explained. Appendix B, "Queues," is an elementary introduction to queueing theory. This appendix explains the analysis of simple queues and networks of queues used mostly in Chapter 10. Appendix C, "Communication Theory," provides some elements of communication theory for readers with no background in that subject.

Each chapter concludes with problems selected to help readers test their understanding of the material in the book. Each problem section includes some more challenging problems, which are marked with an asterisk (*). Selected references are listed at the end of each chapter and a compilation of all references previously cited appears in Appendix D.

Acknowledgements

I am grateful to many students and colleagues for their suggestions and their help with this textbook. In particular, N. Bambos (University of California, Los Angeles), D. Browning (Georgia Institute of Technology), A. Fawaz (Teknekron Communication Systems, Berkeley), B. Hajek (University of Illinois, Urbana), T. Hsiao (Purdue University), P. Lapsley (University of California, Berkeley), N. McKeown (University of California, Berkeley), B. Mukherjee (University of California, Davis), K. J. Pires (University of California, Berkeley), P. Varaiya (University of California, Berkeley), S. Verdu (Princeton University), all have provided valuable comments on the text. P. Konstantopoulos (University of California, Berkeley) formulated the problems in the last four chapters. Part of the text was written when I was enjoying the warm hospitality of F. Baccelli at INRIA in Sophia-Antipolis, France. Marjorie Singer Anderson was an invaluable developmental editor responsible for the final style of the text.

Finally, this book would not have been written without the encouragement and the help of Howard S. Aksen, who is the most graceful, competent, and supportive publisher and editor a technical author can hope for.

Jean Walrand

Introduction to Communication Networks |1

1.1 What Are Communication Networks?

Communication networks are arrangements of hardware and software that allow users to exchange information. This very broad definition will help you begin learning about one of the fastest growing areas in electrical engineering. Once we examine some common communication networks, we will develop a more precise definition of communication networks. In this chapter we will elaborate on the importance of this field and review its evolution.

The telephone network is the most familiar and ubiquitous communication network. It is designed for voice transmission. An office computer network is a communication network used by organizations to connect personal computers so they may share programs and data and to link those computers to printers and, possibly, to some other peripherals (e.g., file servers that provide mass storage or plotters). Computer networks also are used in manufacturing plants to connect machine tools, robots, and sensors. Some computer networks cover the United States and have connections to networks in Europe and Japan. They allow users to exchange messages and computer files. Some experimental networks transmit video and audio signals as well as data.

Although all these systems are communication networks, they are quite different in the information that they transmit and in the way they are used.

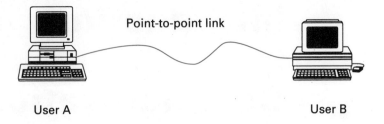

Figure 1.1 Point-to-point connection between users A and B.
A dedicated link can be used to connect two users permanently.

Nevertheless, they operate on similar principles. The unifying characteristics of all networks help us to develop a definition of communication networks that describes the arrangements of hardware and software that we study in this text. Each system described is designed to exchange *information*, which may be voice, sounds, graphics, pictures, video, text, or data, among *users*. Most often the users are humans, but they also can be computer programs or devices. Before the information is transmitted, it is converted into bits (zeroes or ones). Then the bits are sent to a receiver as electrical or optical signals (electromagnetic waves, to be more precise). Finally, the information is reconstructed from the received bits. This transmission method, called *digital transmission*, reduces the transmission errors.

The transmission from some user A to another user B can take place over a *point-to-point* communication link, i.e., over a link that permanently connects A and B. (See Figure 1.1.) The physical medium that supports this communication may be a cable, copper wires, an optical fiber, or a radio link.

A network is a broader arrangement than a single point-to-point link; it connects a large collection of users. A network is almost never built by laying out one point-to-point link between each pair of users, because the cost would be prohibitive and resources wasted. Instead, a network is organized so as to have different information flows *share* communication links. (See Figure 1.2.) One of the main network design problems is to find efficient ways of sharing communication links. Typically, the sharing of links means that an information flow may have to wait for a link to become free. Quantities that measure that aspect of the behavior of the network are important network design and selection parameters.

From this description we can define a communication network:

A communication network is a set of nodes that are interconnected to permit the exchange of information.

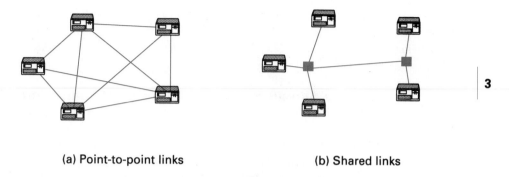

(a) Point-to-point links   (b) Shared links

Figure 1.2 Point-to-point links (a) versus shared links (b).

Two solutions are possible for connecting users. In solution (a), each pair of users is connected by a dedicated link. This solution is not feasible for a large number of users. In solution (b), some links are used by different pairs of users, not simultaneously. That solution achieves significant savings in link length.

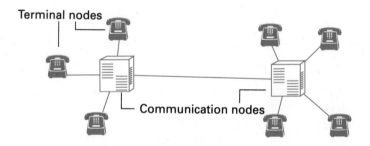

Figure 1.3 Terminal nodes and communication nodes.

A communication network is a set of interconnected nodes. Some nodes are *terminal nodes*, such as the telephone sets in this figure. In other networks, terminal nodes may be computers, printers, file servers, or video monitors. The other nodes are *communication nodes*, such as switches or other communication devices.

The nodes in the definition can be terminal entities, such as phone sets, computers, printers, file servers, or video monitors. They can also be communication devices, such as telephone exchanges (switches), gateways, or repeaters. (See Figure 1.3.) Thus there are two types of nodes: *terminal nodes* and *communication nodes*. The terminal nodes generate or use the information transmitted over the network. The communication nodes transport the information but do not generate or use it. Note that terminal nodes perform some communication functions: at the very least they have to receive or transmit information.

Our new definition of communication network is still rather general. But it is accurate enough for our purpose now in introducing the subject and our goals in this book. In Chapter 2, we discuss concrete examples of networks.

4

1.2 Why Should You Learn About Communication Networks?

The design, manufacture, and maintenance of hardware and software for communication networks are among the fastest growing engineering areas. This growth is fueled by the rapid progress in computer and communication technologies and by the substantial increase in productivity generated by improved communications. This section discusses the impact of communication networks and future applications, emphasizing the expanding opportunities available in this field.

Computers and workstations have had a dramatic impact on the work place. When these machines are organized as a computer network, their capabilities are extended, increasing even further the range of applications available to users. Computer networks offer immediate cost benefits by allowing many computers to access the same expensive peripherals (a high-quality color printer, for instance). Beyond this benefit, computer networks make efficient communications possible through electronic mail and file transfers. Such communications can improve productivity by reducing the time needed to disseminate information throughout an organization.

Future communication networks will merge the capabilities of the telephone network and of computer networks, enabling the simultaneous transmission of voice and data. This merging will make new applications possible, such as voice-mail, in which a voice message is stored on the disk of the destination workstation. The workstation will serve as an answering machine controlled by the caller from his or her phone keypad. Users will be able to annotate typed texts or graphics with spoken comments. Speech recognition and speech synthesis systems will provide convenient interfaces for visually-impaired or for hearing-impaired users. The combination of telephone and computer networks will make existing services more convenient. For instance, the workstation can find and dial phone numbers automatically. The phone-computer combination will require a single hookup and a single "address" instead of a telephone number and a computer address.

Under development are high-speed networks that transmit high-quality, full-motion video. These networks will make connections with video and audio channels economical and an effective alternative to many business trips. The entertainment industry may use high-speed networks to distribute digital audio or video programs. Other services can also arise from these networks:

instant access to news, to libraries, to help services (medical information, auto and appliance repair, cooking, gardening, quantum mechanics, movie theater schedules, restaurant menus and reservations), and video dating.

The possible applications of the future communication networks are so numerous that they will affect most sectors of society. The impact of the future communication networks will be comparable in magnitude to that of the telephone network. All this translates into a range of opportunities for those responsible for working to construct such networks and to apply them to new tasks.

1.3 What Should You Learn About Communication Networks?

A general understanding of the way network operations are organized and of the telecommunication principles on which networks rely helps everyone working with communication networks use them more effectively. This book is intended to provide you with that understanding, which can form the foundation for the more specific knowledge that you may need as a network user, manager, buyer, or designer.

To benefit from a network, the user must understand the capabilities of the available hardware and software as well as the way the information flow should be structured to improve work productivity. Often, a company must reorganize its work procedures to take advantage of the communication facilities created by the network. For instance, for the network to be an efficient tool, department managers must convince all employees to use electronic mail instead of paper mail and to maintain an up-to-date schedule on the network calendar for automatic appointment scheduling.

The network manager must understand the network facilities to update the software and hardware and to perform the necessary file backups. The network manager should also monitor the network performance to identify problems quickly and to initiate repairs.

The network buyer faces the complex task of assessing the potential benefits of a network. Before selecting equipment, the buyer should analyze the information flows in the company, determine how new communication channels would affect existing procedures, and assess the value of electronic communications with other company branches or with professional data bases. Criteria for selection of hardware and software composing the network are ease of use, ability to be upgraded, and cost.

A network designer must be familiar with the possible services of existing networks and of forthcoming enhancements. The designer cannot construct an adequate system without understanding the needs of the users and the added value provided by new services.

The author of any textbook on communication networks faces a dilemma in presenting details about specific network implementations. As you will see, communication networks are all based on relatively few simple principles. However, an actual implementation has to follow a set of detailed specifications that are, to a large extent, arbitrary. Those detailed specifications are required to guarantee the compatibility of products from different vendors. The details are not necessary to understand how the network operates. For instance, the precise format of the information units being transmitted is important mostly to engineers who will design new software or hardware for a given network. To obtain the background, the engineer facing such a task will need to consult official network standards and product documentations. It is not our intention to reproduce that information in this book. However, some details are useful for making the descriptions of networks realistic. For example, knowing the number of address bits used by a network allows the reader to consolidate his or her understanding of related size parameters of that network. As a consequence, we have opted for providing enough details to give you a thorough understanding of network operating principles but have avoided the tendency to drown important concepts in a sea of inessential facts.

As background for the current and future technology and applications of communication networks, we now briefly review how networks evolved and describe some of the major trends that affect those systems.

1.4 Evolution of Communication Networks

The telegraph was developed by Samuel Morse in the 1830s and the telephone by Alexander Graham Bell in 1876. The original point-to-point telephone lines connecting pairs of users in the first telephone systems gave way in the 1880s to lines switched by human operators. Electromagnetic switches appeared in the 1890s. Computerized switches started being deployed in the 1970s.

Two developments in telephone networks paved the way for modern networks: *digital transmission* and *common channel signaling*. Digital telephone transmission transmits the voice signals as bit streams. Such transmissions have low noise levels. Moreover, digital transmissions facilitate the switching of signals and the simultaneous transmission of many signals on the same line. Common channel signaling transmits connection control information among telephone switching equipment. This control information permits efficient implementations of many services, such as call forwarding, credit card calls, and 800 numbers. It also leads to better utilization of the network lines by providing better control over how the lines are selected to carry the phone calls.

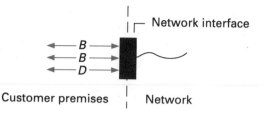

Figure 1.4 Basic ISDN access.

The *basic ISDN access* is intended for use by most residential customers.
It consists of two *B* (for "bearer") channels and one *D* channel. Each *B*
channel is a full-duplex digital channel at 64 kbps. The *D* channel is a full-
duplex channel at 16 kbps.

Digital transmission and common channel signaling form the basis of
the *integrated services digital networks* (ISDNs) now being implemented. The
basic ISDN connection (called *basic access*) provides a subscriber with three
full-duplex (e.g., two-way) digital connections: two with a rate of 64,000 bits per
second (called the *B* channels) and the third with a rate of 16,000 bits per second
(called the *D* channel). (See Figure 1.4.) The *B* channels can transmit voice or
computer data. The *D* channel can transmit alarm, monitoring information, control signals for lights and such appliances as air conditioning and heating units, or
network control information as needed in services offered by the ISDN. The
common channel signaling system controls the ISDN connections. It is being
expanded to carry some of the user data transfers.

Computers were born in the 1940s and began to multiply in the 1960s.
The need for standardized connections of a computer to such peripherals as tape
drives, keyboards, printers, disk drives, and terminals led to the publication of the
specifications of the connection RS-232-C by the Electronics Industries Association (EIA) in 1969. This connection allows transmission rates of up to 38,400 bits
per second over four to 12 wires for distances of up to 15 meters. The RS-232-C
connection still is widely used. Data transmitted over this connection are sent and
received character by character. Specifically, one character is sent at a time, and
two characters must be separated by a minimum time interval. A character is
represented by a group of seven or eight bits, depending on the code being used.
This type of transmission is called *asynchronous* because successive characters
can be transmitted at arbitrary times, other than for the minimum separation.
Standards for faster asynchronous connections (RS-449, RS-422-A, and RS-423-
A) followed in the late 1970s. Also, in the 1960s, *modems* (*mo*dulator-*dem*odula-
tors) were developed to permit the transmission of bits over telephone lines. The
modulator of a modem converts bits into sounds in the frequency range transmitted by telephone lines, and the demodulator converts such sounds back into bits.

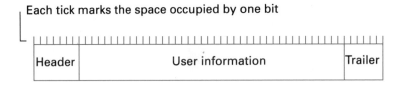

Each tick marks the space occupied by one bit

| Header | User information | Trailer |

Figure 1.5 Typical packet.

A typical packet consists of a header, user information, and a trailer. The header and the trailer contain control information used by the network to transmit the packet and to verify its correct reception. The header usually contains the addresses of the destination and of the source of the packet. The header may also indicate a sequence number used by the destination to verify that all the packets were received. The trailer contains error control bits that are used to verify the correct reception of the packet.

To implement a long-distance connection between a terminal and a computer, one can connect the terminal to a modem, the modem to a telephone line, and the other end of the line to another modem that is connected to the computer. By dialing different phone numbers that access different modem-computer hookups, a terminal connected to a modem can access different computer services.

Computers were first interconnected with point-to-point links in the mid-1960s. The need for fast connections with automatic error control led to the development of a set of procedures called *data link protocols* known under the abbreviations SDLC, LAPA, LAPB, and HDLC. These connections are *synchronous*: They transmit the information in the form of *packets*. A packet is a group of bits, typically from a few hundred to thousands, that are transmitted at precise times. (See Figure 1.5.) There is a minimum separation requirement between successive packets instead of between successive characters, as was the case for asynchronous transmissions. This difference makes synchronous transmissions faster than asynchronous transmissions: The amount of inserted idle time per transmitted bit is smaller for synchronous transmissions than for asynchronous transmissions. Synchronous connections also can be implemented over telephone lines with a modem at each end.

The development of data link protocols led to the idea of indirect connection of computers. Consider Figure 1.6: If computer *B* is connected to computers *A* and *C* by two point-to-point links, it is possible to send messages from *A* to *C* by sending them first from *A* to *B*, then from *B* to *C*.

This idea is called *store-and-forward transmission*. A store-and-forward transmission from *A* to *C* via *B* is more efficient if the transmission from *B* to *C* can start before that from *A* to *B* is completed. In order to do this, one must decompose the messages into relatively small packets. This decomposition allows the transmission from *B* to *C* to start as soon as *B* has received one packet from *A*

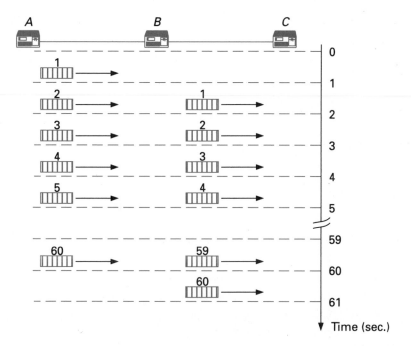

Figure 1.6 Indirect connection of A and C through B.

Packets are sent from A to C via B. A packet may be sent from B to C
while another is being sent from A to B. If the transmission of a packet
from A to B or from B to C takes one second, then 60 packets can be sent
from A to C in 61 seconds: one second for the first packet to reach B,
another second for the second packet to reach B and for the first to reach
C, and so on. This method is called *store-and-forward packet-switching*.
If a block of 60 packets was sent in 60 seconds from A to B and then
from B to C in another 60 seconds, the full transmission would take two
minutes instead of 61 seconds when store-and-forward packet-switching
is used.

instead of having to wait until B has received a complete message from A. To
make this idea precise, assume that A wants to send a long message to C and that
the transmission of that message on a direct link takes one minute. If A sends the
complete message to B (which takes one minute) before B sends it to C (which
takes another minute), then it takes two minutes before the message is received
by C. However, if the message is decomposed into 60 packets that take one
second each to be transmitted on a direct link, then during the first second packet
1 is sent from A to B, during the next second packet 2 is sent from A to B and
packet 1 is sent from B to C, and so on. After one minute and one second, the
complete message is received by C. The saving achieved by this decomposition of
the messages into small packets increases with the number of intermediate nodes:

if there are N intermediate nodes, the transmission of the undivided message takes $N + 1$ minutes while that of the 60 packets takes only one minute and N seconds. The transmission of messages as small packets is called *store-and-forward packet-switching*.

10

When many computers are connected by point-to-point links in a meshlike network, the network designer must resolve a number of questions to ensure effective use of the network resources:

- *Routing*: What paths should the packets follow in the network?
- *Flow Control*: How can one regulate the flow so as to avoid parts of the network becoming congested?
- *Addressing*: What is a convenient way of specifying the addresses of the terminal nodes?
- *Security*: How can the privacy of the information transmitted over the network and the integrity of the nodes of the network be maintained?
- *Standards*: How can the characteristics of the nodes be described so that vendors can build compatible hardware and software?
- *Presentation*: How can one enable many different types of terminal equipment to communicate?

In order to study these questions and to develop solutions, the Department of Defense initiated the development of the ARPANET network in the late 1960s. ARPANET was the first large-scale store-and-forward packet-switched network. It has evolved into the Internet, a collection of interconnected networks that are used today by hundreds of universities and research institutions worldwide.

Many companies developed store-and-forward packet-switched networks in the mid-1970s. IBM introduced its Systems Networks Architecture (SNA) in 1974, Digital Equipment its DECnet in 1975, Sperry-Univac its Data Communications Architecture in 1976, Siemens its TRANSDATA in 1978, CII-Honeywell-Bull its Distributed Systems Architecture in 1979, etc. These networks differ in how they solve the routing, flow control, addressing, and other problems and also in the way these functions are organized. Standards for *public data networks*, networks that can be accessed by any subscriber, were published in the 1970s by the *CCITT* (Consultative Committee for International Telegraphy and Telephony). They are known as the X.25 standards.

The store-and-forward networks that we have discussed are classified as *wide area networks* (WANs). WANs can cover very large areas (hundreds or thousands of miles), and they typically use telephone lines leased from phone companies. The transmission rates usually are of a few tens of thousands of bits per second.

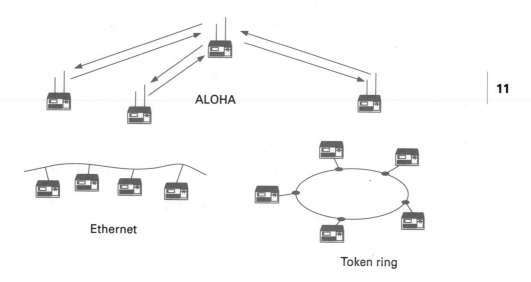

Figure 1.7 Multiple-access networks.

ALOHA is a packet-radio network developed at the University of Hawaii
in the early 1970s. A variation of the protocol used by ALOHA is used by
Ethernet, developed in the mid 1970s at Xerox PARC. The token ring uses
a token passing protocol to regulate the access to the channel; it was
developed by IBM in the early 1980s.

In parallel with the evolution of store-and-forward networks that send
information over a mesh of point-to-point links, the 1970s saw the development
of networks in which nodes share a single communication channel. These networks are called *multiple-access* networks. (See Figure 1.7.) An early example of
a multiple-access network is ALOHA, which was developed to connect computers situated on different Hawaiian islands. The computers of the ALOHA network
transmit on the same radio channel whenever they have a packet to transmit.
When two or more computers try to transmit simultaneously, the information is
"garbled." Thus, the computers transmit their packets, then check whether the
transmissions were garbled; if so, they wait for a random time before trying
again.

An idea similar to that of ALOHA was used in the early 1970s by
researchers from the Xerox Palo Alto Research Center to connect computers with
a single coaxial cable. The resulting network—Ethernet—differs from ALOHA in
that the transmitters interrupt their transmissions as soon as they detect simultaneous transmissions. This detection may occur long before the packets are transmitted completely (at least, if the cable is not too long). Consequently, Ethernet is
more efficient than ALOHA. The development of Ethernet coincided with the
explosion in the use of personal computers. It is the most widely used *local area*

network (LAN), i.e., network for computers that are geographically close. Another popular LAN is the *token ring*, developed in the early 1980s by IBM. Other LANs that were also introduced in the 1970s and 1980s include the *token bus*, the *slotted ring*, *AppleTalk*, *DataKit*, and *StarLan*. The LANs have high transmission rates, typically a few million bits per second; geographical ranges limited to a few miles; and short delays, usually fractions of a second, before the start of transmissions.

An important development is a class of networks that take advantage of new electronics and opto-electronics technology to transmit at rates of a few hundred million bits per second over optical fibers. These networks are being designed to be able to carry two types of traffic: *asynchronous traffic*, which is very irregular in rate, such as computer data traffic, and *synchronous traffic*, which has a fixed rate for a long duration, such as voice or video traffic. Asynchronous traffic and synchronous traffic have different requirements: Asynchronous traffic can be delayed somewhat but does not normally tolerate errors; synchronous traffic has some tolerance for errors but cannot usually be delayed. The *fiber distributed data interface* (FDDI) and the *distributed queue dual bus* (DQDB) are examples of these new networks. Some will be used as LANs, whereas others are designed to cover areas of a few dozen miles and are called *metropolitan area networks* (MANs).

Research is being conducted on *broadband integrated services digital networks* (BISDNs). One tentative specification is that a BISDN will provide subscribers with three incoming channels at 150 million bits per second and with one outgoing channel with the same rate. These channels are fast enough to carry *high definition television* (HDTV) signals that have been suitably processed (compressed). They can also transmit many digital high-fidelity sound channels (about 100 each). BISDN is viewed by many in the telecommunications industry as the network of the future. BISDNs may be deployed by the end of the 1990s. Work is also progressing on wireless methods for accessing a BISDN. A solution that will probably emerge is a digital cellular network in which a geographical area is divided into small cells that are each monitored by a central station. Users would be equipped with portable terminals that would communicate with the cell centers with low-power, wireless transmitters and receivers. Such portable terminals could serve as videophones and as terminals for powerful computers attached to the BISDN.

1.5 Organization of the Book

Our objectives in this text are to explain the principles that guide the design and operations of networks, to describe some of the popular networks, and to identify important trends.

The topics in this text fall into two categories. Some discussions are conceptual. They describe the determination of rules for identifying and comparing feasible network designs. Other sections are descriptive. They discuss existing or proposed networks. You should attempt to master the general concepts explained in the conceptual discussions and to see how they are implemented in the networks that are described. You should also learn to appreciate the impact of design choices on the behavior of networks.

Chapter 2 explains general operating principles of networks and how network functions are organized. In particular, it introduces the *open systems interconnection* (OSI) model. In this model, which is commonly accepted for computer networks, the functions implemented by a network are divided into seven layers with precise interfaces. The layers can, at least in principle, be designed independently of one another and then put together to form the network. ISDN and BISDN networks are organized according to models that are based on the OSI model. Chapters 3 through 8 are devoted to the discussion of the OSI layers. Chapter 5 revisits some elements of Chapters 3 and 4 to explain how they are implemented in LANs. Chapter 9 deals with the integration of services in networks; it covers ISDN and BISDN as well as integrated LANs. Chapter 10 is devoted to the evaluation of measures of networks' performance, by monitoring analytical methods, simulations, or emulations.

Appendix A reviews some basic probability theory which is useful for most of the text. Appendix B covers elements of queueing theory which are needed in Chapter 10. Appendix C is a review of communication theory for readers with no training in that field. It is useful mostly for Chapter 3.

Summary

- A communication network is a set of nodes interconnected to permit the exchange of information.
- Communication networks are a rapidly growing engineering field which will significantly affect our personal and professional lives.
- The text will provide you with a general understanding of the operating and design principles of networks.
- The evolution of networks began with digital communications, followed by the introduction of store-and-forward and of multiple-access packetized communications.
- The ISDNs and BISDNs are important developments for future networks.

Problems

1. Consider the network in Figure 1.2. Assume that there are N users which should be connected by point-to-point links, with one link between any two users. How many links are required? How many links are connected to each user? Assume now that shared links can be used. How would you draw the links which require the minimum total length of wires to connect all the users? (*Hint:* Try first with three users and consider progressively larger numbers of users.)

2. Consider four users located at the four corners of a unit square, as indicated in Figure 1.8(a). Figure 1.8(b) indicates one possible connection which uses two communication nodes and a total length of wires equal to three units. Find the connection with the smallest total length of wires, assuming that communication nodes are free. Assume now that the communication links are free but that a communication node costs $n\log n$ if n links are attached to it ($\log n$ denotes the logarithm of n, in base 10). Thus, the cost of the network of Figure 1.8(b) is equal to $6\log 3$ since it requires two communication nodes attached to three links each. Find the network with the minimum cost.

3. One is given a communication link that transmits 10,000 bits per second. The objective is to transmit a file of B bits. A synchronous transmission is used. The bits are sent in packets of P bits. Each packet contains 16 extra bits which are used for error control. Two packets must be separated by at least 10 ms (1 ms = 10^{-3} second). Find the total time taken to transmit the file as a function of P and B.

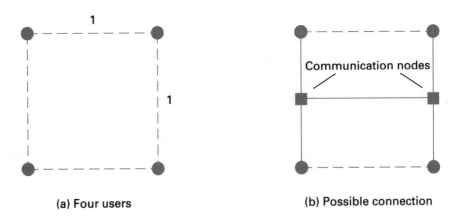

(a) Four users   (b) Possible connection

Figure 1.8 (a) Four users in a square; (b) a possible connection.

4. Consider the connection in Figure 1.6. One file of $K \gg 1$ bits must be sent from A to C. That file is decomposed into packets of P bits each. Each packet contains 16 error-control bits and 32 bits of address and sequence number, in addition to the P data bits. The transmission rate is R bits per second. Each packet is first sent from A to B and then from B to C. Find the value of P that minimizes the transmission time from A to C, neglecting the propagation times. (*Hint:* First assume that the best value of P is such that $K/P \gg 1$ so that one can approximate the number of packets of P bits required to transmit K bits by K/P. Then justify your assumption.) Repeat the same problem when the file must go through N communication nodes between A and C.

5. This is a simple network optimization problem. The network is as indicated in Figure 1.9. The terminal node A transmits λ bits per second for terminal node B and also λ bits per second for terminal node C. The network is built with a link with rate 2λ from node A to the communication node S and with one link with rate λ from S to B and also from S to C. The cost of a unit length of link with rate α is assumed to be equal to $K \times \alpha^{0.5}$. Thus, the cost of a link grows more slowly than its rate. This reflects the economy of scale of faster links. Assuming that S is free, find the value of x, i.e., the position of S, which minimizes the cost of the network. Assume now that the node S costs some amount J. For which values of d is it less expensive to use a switch S instead of two direct links from A to B and from A to C?

6. Each of two links fails one day per month, on the average. The failures of the two links occur independently. How often do the two links fail on the same day?

7. Comment on the ethical questions raised by communication networks. Should unauthorized access to a computer account be considered ille-

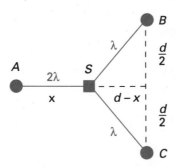

Figure 1.9 Network optimization problem.

gal or does the responsibility for security lie with the owner of the
account?

References

General descriptions of computer networks can be found in Comer
(1988), Halsall (1988), Martin (1990), Meijers (1983), Schatt (1987),
Stallings (1988), and Tanenbaum (1988). Popular computer magazines, such as *Byte* and *PC Magazine*, frequently carry descriptions of
computer network software and hardware. Integrated networks are
discussed in Bocker (1988) and Stallings (1989).

The IEEE journals *Communication Magazine* and *Networks* publish
descriptive papers on current developments in networking.

More technical references will be indicated in subsequent chapters.

Bocker (1988). Bocker, P., *ISDN—The Integrated Services Digital
Network: Concepts, Methods, Systems*. Springer-Verlag, 1988.

Comer (1988). Comer, D, *Internetworking with TCP/IP: Principles,
Protocols, and Architecture*. Prentice-Hall, 1988.

Halsall (1988). Halsall, F., *Data Communications, Computer Networks and OSI*. Addison-Wesley, 1988.

Martin (1990). Martin, J., *Telecommunications and Computers* (3rd
Ed.) Prentice-Hall, 1990.

Meijer (1983). Meijer, A. and Peeters, P., *Computer Network Architectures*, Computer Science Press, 1983.

Schatt (1987). Schatt, S., *Understanding Local Area Networks*. Howard W. Sams & Company, 1987.

Stallings (1988). Stallings, W., *Data and Computer Communications,
Second Edition*. Macmillan, 1988.

Stallings (1989). Stallings, W., *ISDN: An Introduction*. Macmillan,
1989.

Tanenbaum (1988). Tanenbaum, A., *Computer Networks* (2nd Ed.).
Prentice-Hall, 1988.

Design Principles for Communication Networks

2

Our goals in this chapter are to describe the general operating principles of networks and to explain how network functions are organized. In particular we focus on the *open systems interconnection* (OSI) model because it is widely used and because it provides a useful framework for understanding network organization. Our approach in this chapter is to learn about network structure through its function. Thus we begin by examining the services provided by networks. We start by learning about the characteristics of the services required by different applications. We then learn that complex services are built from simpler components. Most communication networks use a layered construction of services in which services of one layer are built on top of those of the layer immediately below. Services require information to be transported in a network. We learn that information is converted into bits and that the bits are transported as electrical or optical signals. There are two central features of information transport in networks: *connectivity* and *resource sharing*. Connectivity refers to the capability of exchanging information among many users. Resource sharing is the utilization of common equipment—hardware and software—by a large number of users. We will learn how networks implement these two features. Building on the information about the structure of services and about information transport, we then examine the OSI and related models to see how most networks are organized.

In addition to giving you an overview of network structure, this chapter is the background for the next six chapters. In this chapter, you will see how the tasks required to provide services are divided. In the six subsequent chapters, we examine those tasks in detail.

18

2.1 Network Services and Architecture

The goal of a communication network is to provide *services* to users. The services include *information transport*, *signaling*, and *billing*. For example, you can lease a T1 line between two office buildings. This line enables you to transmit 1.544 megabits per second. This is an information transport service. The *plain old telephone service* (POTS) permits the connection of a telephone set to any other telephone set in the world. POTS combines information transport and signaling services: the called telephone set rings to announce the call, and the caller is informed when that set is busy. The 800 numbers service provides a routing of the calls which varies according to the time of day and the day of the week as specified by the subscriber. Call forwarding, three-way calling, and call waiting are other services provided by telephone companies. Data networks provide information transport and other services. For instance, electronic mail is a service which enables users to exchange text messages among networked computers. File transfer services make it possible to move files between computers. Printer servers allow the computers on a network to share a common printer.

Although network services can be widely different, they share similar structures. We will explore these structural similarities in order to understand how services are constructed.

A service is the execution of a sequence of basic actions on network resources. Resources include links, dial tone generators, registers, recording and playback devices, timers, data bases, and switches. Basic actions are activating a dial tone generator, connecting two links with a switch, and timing some events. Consider the following simplified description of POTS:

1. wait for handset to be "off-hook"
2. allocate a register to off-hook handset
3. send dial tone to off-hook handset
4. store dialed digits in register
5. determine route of call from dialed digits
6. set up the connection between the two parties
7. verify that the called party is not busy
8. ring the called party

9.   wait for off-hook

10. start the billing timer

11. transfer the voice signals between the two parties

12. detect termination by "on-hook"

13. stop the billing timer

14. release the links used in the connection

The above sequence is only one of many possible executions of the service. If the called party is busy, then steps 8–14 are modified.

Thus, a service is the execution of a *script*; that is, a program where the basic steps are actions on network resources. You will notice that the service script is executed jointly at many locations. For instance, the dial tone and the ringing are generated by different pieces of equipment. The service script itself is distributed in a number of devices: steps 1 and 7 are executed by two pieces of code that run in different locations.

Conceptually, a script is executed by a number of communicating *entities*. An entity is the abstraction of a device which acts upon inputs by performing some actions and by producing some outputs. When the output of an entity A is the input of entity B, we say that entity A communicates to entity B. We will call *messages* the inputs and outputs of entities. Thus, entities communicate by exchanging messages. An entity can be a physical device, such as a bell. When a given voltage is applied to the bell, it rings. The bell performs an action (ringing) in response to the input message (applied voltage). An entity can also be an active program in a computer. An active program is called a *process*. A process acts upon inputs by performing a set of instructions and, possibly, by producing outputs.

A possible implementation of POTS is then as follows: Step 1 is performed by a process which runs in a processor connected to the subscriber telephone line. When that "wait for off-hook" process detects that the phone set is off-hook, it sends a message to the process in charge of allocating registers. That process performs the register allocation (step 2) and sends a message to the process in charge of sending dial tones. The latter process sends a dial tone to an entity in the telephone handset: the headphone. The other steps are performed similarly.

The advantage of the entity abstraction is that it unifies the elements which compose a service: processes and physical devices of various types. The unifying view is that of activities that interact. We will see that the entity abstraction is central to the construction of services in communication networks. We view a service, then, as a collection of communicating entities. This view is illustrated in Figure 2.1.

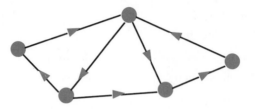

Figure 2.1 Entities and messages.

Circles represent entities. Arrows indicate the flows of messages
between entities.

Most services require complicated programs. A modern telephone
switch is controlled by several million lines of code. The specifications of the
manufacturing automation protocols, used to control the flow of information in
some local area networks, take up about 2,000 pages. Such complex programs
can only be written and verified if they are decomposed into manageable *modules*. A module is a block of code which is specified by the action it performs and
by the way it interacts with other modules. These specifications leave the pro-
grammer free to design the implementation of the module. That is, the module
can be constructed independently of the rest of the software, as long as it respects
the interaction and functional specifications. In addition to making the testing and
writing of complex programs manageable, a modular construction has three
important benefits. First, it makes it possible to reuse portions of the code for
different applications. Second, it enables the upgrading of parts of the code without necessitating a global rewriting. Third, the specifications of modules can be
standardized to permit interoperability of components provided by different
groups or vendors. The decomposition of a service into communicating entities
permits the software engineers to decompose their programs into modules. For
instance, if an entity corresponds to a process, the code of the program executed
by the process can be decomposed further into smaller modules.

The advantages of software modularity are shared by physical entities.
For instance, the phone set specifications may call for a bell which consumes 0.2
watt of electrical power and rings with a specific loudness when a voltage of 5
volts is applied. Those specifications let the designers choose an efficient implementation of the bell. The specifications are sufficient to guarantee that the bell
will work with the rest of the equipment. Different designers can then compete to
produce the most reliable and cost effective bell which meets the specifications.
As another example, we all take for granted the possibility of replacing the turnta-
ble of our stereo system with a compact disc player. This possibility is due to the
standardization of the mechanical and electrical characteristics of the connections
to a stereo system. The decomposition of services into entities with well-defined
interactions provides similar benefits.

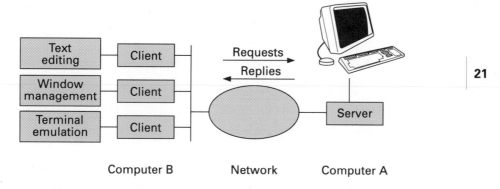

Figure 2.2 The X Window System.

The decomposition of X Window into clients and servers that can communicate over a network enables users to run remote applications as if they were executed locally.

We will see that, in addition to being composed of communicating entities, complex communication services are also composed of simpler services. For instance, setting up a three-party call between Tom, Dick, and Harry is implemented by setting up a call between Tom and Dick and then setting up a call between Dick and Harry. These last two steps are simpler services which are decomposed into the 14 basic actions described earlier. The general principle for decomposing a service into simpler services is that a service is executed by a set of communicating entities and therefore such a service can be based on simpler "interentity communication services." Thus, if a network provides the capability of transferring information between processes that run in different computers, services can be constructed as if the processes were running in the same computer.

Many implementations of communicating processes are based on the *client-server* model. A client is a process which makes a request to a server and then waits for the request to be executed. A server is a process which is generally designed to be able to handle simultaneous requests from many different clients. A simple server can be a process which gives the time of day upon request. A more complex client-server system is the *X Window System*. X Window is a set of facilities for building graphics on computer monitors. The central feature of X Window is that it is decomposed into a server attached to the monitor, keyboard, and mouse, and clients attached to various applications, such as text editing, window management, and terminal emulation. (See Figure 2.2.) The clients and the server can communicate across a network if they are located in different computers. This decomposition makes it possible to use the mouse, keyboard, and monitor of computer A to run applications on computer B. The inputs at A are

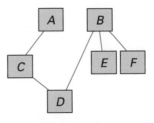

Figure 2.3 Decomposition of services into simpler services.

The boxes symbolize services. Box *C* is located above box *D* and is connected to it. This indicates that service *C* makes use of service *D*.

sent to the applications processes in B and the application processes send their messages to A. Everything appears to the user of computer A as if the applications were running in computer A.

Let's illustrate the decomposition of a service into simpler services by discussing one specific service: *TALK*. TALK is available on networked UNIX computers; it enables a computer user to dialogue with the user of another computer. When TALK is started, the screen of each computer is divided into two parts. The first part displays the messages that are typed locally, and the other part displays the messages typed by the remote user. In this example, there is one TALK process active in both computers. The TALK process in one computer gets the messages that are typed on the local keyboard, and that process sends these messages to the remote TALK process, which displays them on its monitor. (In actuality, a monitor displays the local messages only after they have been sent back by the remote TALK process.) Thus, TALK relies on the information transport service provided by the computer network. TALK must know how to initiate the information transport, in what format the information to be sent to the other TALK process should be presented, and the format of the received information. TALK need not know about other aspects of the information transport. For instance, TALK does not know whether the two computers are connected by a phone line or by a satellite link. As far as the two TALK processes are concerned, everything appears as if messages were being exchanged directly. Thus, the two TALK processes are engaged in a *virtual communication*. The communication is virtual in that it only *appears* as if the communication were taking place directly between the two processes. In fact, the exchange of information involves many complicated steps which result in the illusion of a communication between the processes.

Figure 2.3 illustrates the decomposition of services into simpler services. The decomposition evoked in Figure 2.3 requires some elaboration. Consider the two services *C* and *D* in Figure 2.3. Both services are executed by communicating entities. The services themselves can be viewed as entities: they act upon input messages by performing actions and by producing outputs. Thus, the line between boxes C and D corresponds to flows of messages between entities.

Let us summarize the above discussion:

Network Services

- A communication network provides *services* to users.
- A service is the execution of a distributed service script by communicating entities.
- The decomposition of services into entities with specific actions and interactions makes their construction manageable; it enables the reuse and upgrade of entities, and it permits interoperability across developers.
- Complex services are built from simpler services.

The general organization of services into simpler services is called the *network architecture*. A few different architectures have been defined for *data networks* and are being defined for *telephone networks* and *integrated services digital networks*. In the next section we will discuss the widely used *layered architecture*.

2.2 Layered Network Architectures

Many network architectures are possible. Figure 2.3 illustrates a general decomposition of services into simpler ones. Most of the network architectures are *layered*. In a layered architecture, a service of layer N uses only services of layer $N - 1$. (See Figure 2.4.)

Typically, a service of layer N is executed by *peer protocol entities* in different *nodes* of a communication network. A node is generally a computer or a controller board. The messages exchanged by peer protocol entities of layer N are called *layer N protocol data units* (N_PDUs). The messages exchanged by a service of layer N are also called *layer N service data units* (N_SDUs). Thus, the $N + 1\_PDU$ is an N_SDU.

There is a standard terminology used to describe the communication between successive layers. That terminology is illustrated in Figure 2.4. Assume that a protocol entity of layer $N + 1$ in A wants to send an $N + 1\_PDU$ to a peer protocol entity in B. The protocol entity uses a *service primitive* of layer N called an *N.request*. This request is placed by sending some *interface control information* (ICI) to layer N. The ICI specifies the request type as well as some parameters, such as the addresses of the nodes, and of the protocol entities inside the nodes and, possibly, a description of the desired quality of the information transfer service. The ICI also contains a *pointer* to the $N + 1\_PDU$, i.e., the location of that data in the memory of node A. The service provided by layer N, called the $N\_SERVICE$, eventually sends an *N.indication* to the protocol entity in layer $N + 1$ of B. At that time, the protocol entity normally receives the $N + 1\_PDU$. The protocol entity in B later sends an *N.response* as a reply to the *N.indication*. The *N.response* is another $N\_SERVICE$ primitive which contains parameters that describe the reply to the *N.request*. This response eventually gets back to the protocol entity in layer $N + 1$ of A as an *N.confirm*.

24

Layered Architecture

- The *network architecture* is the organization of services into simpler services.

- In a *layered architecture* a service of layer N uses only services of layer $N - 1$.

- A *layer N protocol* is the distributed service script of a service of layer N; the layer N protocol entities exchange N_PDUs via the layer $N - 1$ services.

- The communication between layers proceeds by exchanges of *requests*, *indications*, *responses*, and *confirms*.

The following analogy may help further clarify the definitions above. One business executive in San Francisco is negotiating a contract with a colleague in Tokyo. The negotiations are done via the exchange of letters. The executive in San Francisco tapes her letters with a cassette recorder. Her secretary types the letters and sends them by facsimile to Tokyo. These letters are translated into Japanese by a secretary, who then gives the translation to the Japanese executive. A reverse procedure is followed from Tokyo to San Francisco. One can view the two executives as performing a service of layer N (for some N) for the companies. That service is a contract negotiation. The executives are layer N protocol entities. The executives are *peer entities* which are jointly executing a specific protocol. The executives exchange messages: the letters. These letters are N_PDUs. Notice that the two executives are engaged in a virtual communication. The exchange of information is essentially equivalent to a direct communication, even though it involves many complicated steps: typing, facsimile transmission, translation. The two secretaries are performing a layer $N - 1$ protocol: preparing the letters for transmission and making sure that the executives get these letters. These secretaries are engaged in a virtual communication. They provide a service of layer $N - 1$ to the executives: exchanging the suitably typed and translated

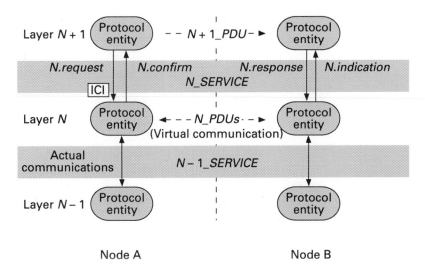

Figure 2.4 A layered architecture.

The script of a layer *N* is called a layer *N* protocol. The entities which execute the layer protocol are protocol entities. Protocol entities exchange messages called *layer N protocol data units* (*N_PDUs*). The *N_PDUs* are exchanged via the services provided by layer *N* – 1. The messages exchanged by a layer *N* service are called *layer N service data units* (*N_SDUs*).

messages. If one facsimile transmission does not take place satisfactorily, then the secretaries repeat the transmission. The executives are not made aware of the transmission difficulties. The facsimile machines perform a service of layer $N - 2$: the electronic transmission of the letters.

Notice the following features of the above example. Even if the facsimile transmissions are not fully reliable, the service provided by the secretaries is. The secretaries know how to use the facsimile machines, but they need not know how the machines work. That is, the protocol performed by the secretaries is independent of the specifics of the protocol performed by the facsimile machines, and also of the contract negotiation protocol. Only the interactions between layers need to be defined carefully, not the internal implementations of these protocols. Observe also the simplification brought about by layering the protocol as opposed to using a more general structure: Each layer need only know how to interact with the two adjacent layers. In our example, the executives need to know how to interact with their secretaries and their bosses, not with the facsimile machines. Finally, you should note that the actual path followed by the messages is very different from the paths of virtual communications. Messages go from one executive to her secretary to the facsimile machine to a telephone line to the other facsimile machine to the other secretary, to the second executive, and

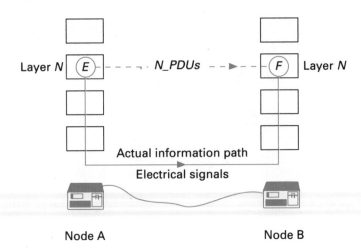

Figure 2.5 Actual path followed by information.

The information travels from one entity *E* down through all the layers in node *A* until it reaches the bottom layer. The information is then physically transported to the bottom layer of node *B*, where it goes up through all the layers to entity *F*.

conversely. The virtual communications are between *peer entities*: the two executives, for instance.

As the business executives in the above example, peer protocol entities of layer *N* in different nodes of a communication network are engaged in virtual communications. In this virtual communication, the entities exchange *N_PDUs* that are used to implement a protocol. In turn, this protocol is the script of an *N.SERVICE*. The actual path followed by the information from one protocol entity *E* of layer *N* in node A to a peer protocol entity *F* of layer *N* in node B is indicated in Figure 2.5. The figure shows that the information is transported physically between successive nodes as electrical or optical signals. By successive nodes we mean nodes connected so that signals can move between them. Information can also be transmitted between node A and node B via a sequence of intermediate nodes.

The selection of the transport mechanisms and of the actions performed by the layers depends on the ultimate use of the information transferred by the network. That is, the design of the network layers is based on the services provided to the users of the network. Therefore, in order to appreciate the designs of networks, we must discuss the characteristics of the information transfers required by users. These characteristics depend on the type of information to be transmitted, the information communication services that are performed by networks, and how such services are implemented. These topics are covered in sections 2.3 through 2.6.

2.3 How Information Is Transmitted in a Network

End users exchange information of various types. You will learn that all information is transported and stored in networks as bits. Thus, a network is a complex bit mover. It is this realization that *a bit is a bit is a bit* which enables the fusion of telecommunications and computer technologies.

Images, sounds, text, graphics, and data are all transported in a network as electrical signals in copper wires or cables, as radio waves in free space, or as optical signals in free space or in optical fibers. Thus, before being transported in a network, the information must be converted into electrical or optical signals. Network designers select the specific conversion of information into such signals on the basis of the fact that a signal is never received exactly as it was sent. A signal is always corrupted during its transmission. Moreover, the exact form of the received signal is not fully predictable. That is, if the same signal is transmitted many times, it is received differently every time. Communication engineers describe the unpredictable corruption of the signals by saying that the transmission adds *noise* to the signal. You are familiar with the noise that disturbs the reception of radio and television programs.

Noise can be reduced with *digital transmissions*—by sending the information in the form of a string of *bits*. (A bit is a *binary digit*, i.e., a 0 or a 1.) By transmitting the bits 0 and 1 as two very different signals, one can almost guarantee that these signals are distinguishable even after being corrupted by the transmission. Thus, bits can be transmitted reliably even though the corruption of the signals cannot be avoided. Moreover, error-control bits can be added to the information bits to reduce transmission errors even further. Digital transmission and error control will be explored in detail in Chapter 3.

The type of information to be transmitted determines the way we organize the bits representing that information. A *static* piece of information, such as a page of text or a picture, is converted into a *bit file*, i.e., a finite number of bits. For instance, a typewritten page of text corresponds to about 16,000 bits. That is equivalent to 16 kbits (1 kbit = 1 kilobit = 1,000 bits), which is equal to 2 kbytes (1 byte = 8 bits and 1 kbyte = 1,000 bytes = 8,000 bits). A source generates *dynamic information* when it contains quantities that change over time. Dynamic information, such as audio or video information, normally requires the continuous transmission of bits at a given rate. For instance, the transmission of voice by the telephone network requires the transmission of 64,000 bits per second. In the case of voice, the continuous transmission of bits is needed to indicate the variations in the air pressure that create the auditory impression. For video, the transmission of images in rapid succession is required to create the impression of motion. Generally, the faster the information to be transmitted changes, the more frequently bits must be transmitted to communicate those changes.

A *bit stream* is a sequence of bits that follow one another at a given rate continuously. Thus, voice is transmitted digitally by a bit stream with a rate of 64 kbps (1 kbps = 1 kilobit per second = 1,000 bits per second).

Note that a bit file can be used to represent a finite duration of dynamic information. For instance, a voice-mail message of 30 seconds corresponds to a file of $64,000 \times 30 = 1.92 \times 10^6$ bits = 1.92 Mbits = 0.24 Mbyte (1 Mbit = 1 megabit = 1 million bits and 1 Mbyte = 1 million bytes = 8 million bits). As another example, a 60-minute compact disc contains approximately 5 billion bits = 635 Mbytes. This quantity of information is equivalent to about 300,000 pages of text, which require roughly 20 meters of bookshelves. As you may know, compact discs known as CD-ROM (read-only memory) are used to store text, data, and figures. The books and technical journals in my office, with all the text and the figures, could probably be replaced by fewer than 10 CD-ROMs.

We can then summarize the conversion of information into bits as follows:

Conversion of Information into Bits

- Signals are corrupted during their transmissions.
- Information is sent as bits to reduce the effect of signal corruption.
- Static information is transformed into bit *files*.
- Dynamic information is transformed into bit *streams*.

Thus, information is transmitted as bits. What are the end-to-end characteristics, i.e., the characteristics seen by the users, of this information transmission? The end-to-end characteristics depend on the many steps of the information transmission, possibly through many successive nodes. In the next section, we will see that different classes of end-to-end communication services are provided by networks.

2.4 Classes of Communication Services

Users exchange bit streams or bit files over a communication network. Depending on the application, the transfer of bits may be required to be more or less reliable and to take more or less time. Thus, the error and delay characteristics of the bit transmission depend on the application. These different requirements are implemented by a few different *classes* of communication services. It is

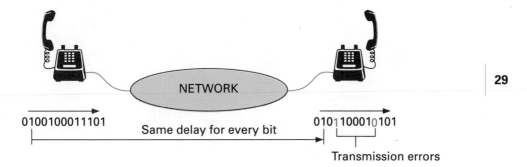

Figure 2.6 Synchronous communication service.

A synchronous communication service delivers a stream of bits with a fixed delay.

important for you to appreciate the differences between the classes of service because those differences determine how these services are implemented.

We will classify *end-to-end* communication services—as seen by the users—as either *synchronous* or *asynchronous* communication services.

A synchronous communication service delivers a bit stream with a fixed delay and a given error rate. That is, every bit in the stream reaches the destination after the same delay; some bits may not be received correctly. In an incorrect transmission certain 1s are received as 0s and vice versa. (See Figure 2.6.) Some bits may also be inserted or deleted. If a voice signal is converted into a bit stream that is transmitted synchronously, then the voice signal will be reconstructed at the receiver with a fixed delay and with an error rate that will be heard as background noise.

In an asynchronous communication, the bit files or the bit stream to be transferred are divided into packets. (See Figure 2.7.) The packets are received by the destination with varying delays, and a fraction of them may not be received correctly. An asynchronous communication service is evaluated by its *quality of service*. The quality of service consists of parameters, such as the packet error rate, the delay, the throughput (rate of transmission), the reliability, and the security of the communication (difficulty of interception).

Notice that our characterization of a communication service is based on its end-to-end properties, not on how the bits are transported. For instance, the synchronous delivery of a 64-kbps voice bit stream can be implemented by dividing the bit stream into packets which are received with random delays and are stored in a buffer which holds the bits until their delivery time comes up. (See Figure 2.8.) This implementation of a synchronous transmission service is called *packet-voice*. Thus, in packet-voice, a buffer is used to absorb the random fluctuations in the packet transmission delays. Another implementation of the synchro-

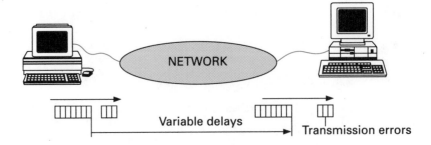

Figure 2.7 Asynchronous communication service.

An asynchronous communication service delivers packets with variable delays.

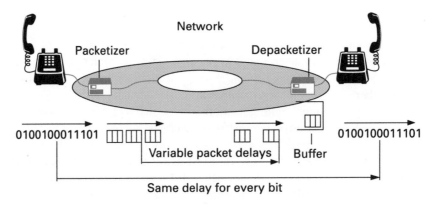

Figure 2.8 Packet-voice transmission.

The voice bit stream is divided into packets. The packets are transmitted asynchronously. The random-packet propagation delays are absorbed by a buffer at the receiver where the bit stream is reconstructed.

nous transmission of the bit stream is to use a dedicated coaxial cable that propagates the bits one after the other, all with the same delay.

Thus, the *communication service* characterizes the transfer of information between users. Many different *implementations* are generally possible for a given service. To emphasize the distinction between the service and its implementation, we shall use the terms *communication* and *information transfer* for the service and *transmission* or *transport* for the implementation.

There are two classes of *asynchronous* communication services: *connection-oriented* and *connectionless*. A connection-oriented communication service delivers the packets in sequence, i.e., in the correct order and confirms the delivery. Depending on the quality of the service, the delivery may be guaranteed to be error-free. (See Figure 2.9.) Thus, a connection-oriented service looks from

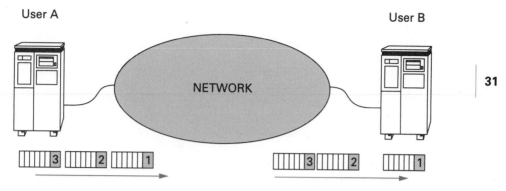

Figure 2.9 Connection-oriented communication service.

A connection-oriented service delivers the packets in the correct order.

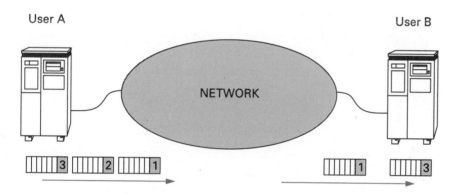

Figure 2.10 Connectionless communication service.

A connectionless communication service delivers the packets in a random order and without guarantee of correctness nor of delivery.

end to end like a dedicated link, which may be noiseless or noisy. A connectionless service (Figure 2.10) delivers the packets individually. The packets can be delivered out of order, and some may contain errors and others may be lost. Some connectionless services provide an acknowledgement of the correctly delivered packets. Hence, connectionless services are similar to the mail services provided by the post office: Letters may be delivered out of order; normal mail delivery does not guarantee nor acknowledge the delivery, whereas certified mail acknowledges the correctly delivered letters.

Another class of communication services is also used in some applications. It is called *expedited data*, and it corresponds to a potentially faster delivery of packets, usually by making them jump to the head of the queues of packets that are waiting to be transmitted. (See Figure 2.11.)

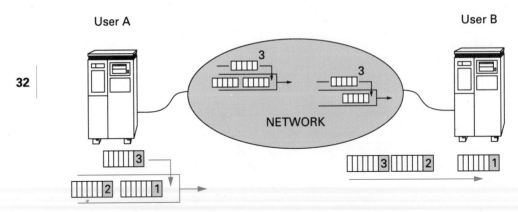

Figure 2.11 Expedited-data communication service.

An expedited-data communication service speeds up the delivery of the packets by jumping to the head of the queues of packets that are waiting to be transmitted.

Let us summarize the above discussion of the different classes of communication services:

Classes of Communication Services

- A communication service is either *synchronous* or *asynchronous*.

- An asynchronous communication service can be *connection-oriented*, *unacknowledged-connectionless*, *acknowledged-connectionless*, or *expedited data*.

- The *quality of service* of an asynchronous communication service specifies the delays, error rate, throughput, reliability, and security of the communication.

The application determines the class of the communication service. Applications such as audio and video transmissions require synchronous communication services. Applications that require a dialogue between remote machines usually use connection-oriented communication services. When the delay and the sequences of packet deliveries are not critical, or when only a few packets are transmitted, a connectionless communication service is used. This is the case for electronic mail or news-distribution applications.

Having discussed the properties and the general organization of communication services, we now turn to the *implementation* of the transport of bit files and bit streams composing communication services. The economic constraints of communication networks require the sharing of transmission resources among the users. You will learn that *switching* and *multiplexing* are the basic bit-transport techniques that make such sharing possible. Switching and multiplexing are two methods that permit an efficient utilization of the hardware used to transport bits.

2.5 Switching

Communication services are implemented by transporting bits over the network. One essential objective of the bit transport is *connectivity*: One network user should be able to exchange information with many other users. Thus, it should be possible to *route* the bits of one user to any one of a large number of other users. This property of being able to vary the path followed by the bits is called *switching*. In this section you will learn the three basic methods that are used for switching bits in communication networks:

- Circuit-switching
- Virtual-circuit packet-switching
- Datagram packet-switching

These three switching methods have different characteristics that make them preferable for different communication services. The objective of all these methods is to achieve connectivity while permitting many users to *share* hardware resources. It is important to understand these three methods because they are implemented in networks with very different characteristics. We first look at why sharing of network resources is necessary and then look at the three switching methods.

Bits are transported over *communication links*. A communication link is a set of physical devices used for the transmission of bits. A communication link consists of a *transmitter*, a *receiver*, and a *transmission medium*, such as a coaxial cable, copper wires, optical fiber, or free space in the case of radio or of nonguided optical transmission. (See Figure 2.12.) This section explains why it is necessary for communication services to share communication links.

Consider the telephone network and its millions of telephones. It would not be possible to lay down one phone line between every pair of telephones. Instead, the telephones are connected to switches. These switches are connected together. To appreciate the savings that are possible with this arrangement, consider the simplified network model of Figure 2.13. In this network, 100 telephones are connected to each of three switches, and each pair of switches are connected by ten pairs of wires. To make the situation more concrete, we will assume that each switch is in an office building and that the average length of wires between a telephone and the switch in a building is 0.1 km. Moreover, we will assume that the wires between office buildings (i.e., between the switches)

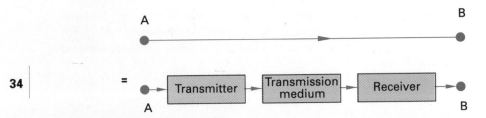

Figure 2.12 A communication link.

A communication link consists of a transmitter, a receiver, and a transmission medium.

are 1 km long. The total length of wires is therefore equal to $(300 \times 0.1) +$
$(30 \times 1) = 60$ km. If the telephones were connected in pairs, then each telephone
would be connected to 99 other telephones in the same building with wires of an
average length of about 0.1 km and to the 200 other telephones with wires of an
average length of about 1 km. Thus, each telephone would be connected to about
210 km of wires, so that the total length of wires required would be about
$150 \times 210 = 31,500$ km. (The computation is 150×210 and not 300×210 since
only one telephone should be counted in every pair.) This spectacular savings
(from 31,500 km to 60 km) has a cost: the number of simultaneous communications between any two different office buildings cannot exceed ten. If a user
attempts to place a call when all the lines are busy, the call is *blocked*: the switch
indicates that situation to the user by means of a special tone.

Thus, a substantial reduction in the amount of wire can be achieved by
sharing communication links. The sharing is made possible by switching. The
price paid is a limitation on the number of possible simultaneous calls. How does
the network designer select the number of communication links between
switches? Going back to the example, the designer must estimate the likelihood
of more than ten simultaneous conversations between any two buildings. If this
likelihood is very small, then the designer may decide that ten links between the
buildings are sufficient. If it is not very small, then the network needs more links.
Similar principles apply to the design of the telephone network. In a large network, because of the large number of possible paths that can be taken by a phone
call, it is difficult to determine how likely it is that a call will be blocked. This
likelihood is called the *call blocking probability*.

Important network design decisions are: How many switches should
be used? Where should they be located? How many links should be used to
interconnect them? Which path should be used for a given call? We will address
some of these questions in Chapter 6.

To summarize, instead of connecting users with point-to-point links, it
is more economical to use a different *topology*, i.e., a different configuration of

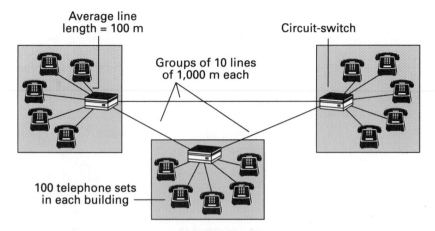

Figure 2.13 A simple telephone network.

This network connects three buildings. Each building contains 100 phone sets. By connecting the telephones via switches, instead of with point-to-point links, the network designer saves more than 31,000 km of links.

links. A typical topology is one where users are connected with a meshlike network which consists of switches and links. The switches connect links to establish circuits between telephones. This technique is called *circuit-switching*. The telephone network is *circuit-switched*.

Thus, circuit-switching is a technique for *sharing* links in a meshlike network. The term *sharing* refers to the fact that transmissions of information corresponding to different communications can use the same communication links—though not at the same time. Links are monopolized by users for only the duration of the communications; they are then released and made available to other users. Circuit-switching achieves substantial savings in total link length at the cost of a small blocking probability.

A *packet-switched* network uses another method for sharing links in a meshlike network. Consider the network in Figure 2.14. The nodes of the network, *packet-switching nodes* (PSNs), play a role similar to that of switches in a circuit-switched network. In a packet-switched network, the transport of information proceeds as follows. The information bit stream or bit file is first decomposed into packets. As we saw in Chapter 1, a packet is a string of a few hundred to several thousand bits, depending on the network. Each packet is labeled with the address of the destination and with a sequence number. Each PSN uses the packet destination address to determine the next PSN to which it should send the packet. The packet sequence numbers are used by the destination to reconstruct the information bit stream or file from its fragments contained in the packets. Consider the transmission of information from node *A* to node *B* in Figure 2.14.

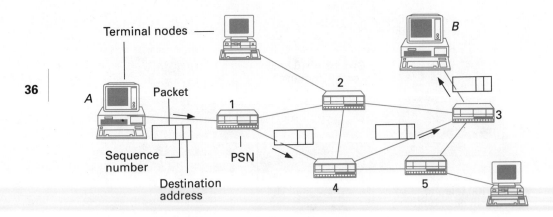

Figure 2.14   A packet-switched network.

Packet-switching decomposes the bit stream of the bit files into packets.
The packets are then transported by transmitting them from node to
node along a path to the destination.

The packets are sent one at a time by node *A* to the PSN that it is attached to
(node 1). Whenever node 1 receives a packet, it looks at the destination address of
the packet. It then transmits the packet to a communication node, say node 4, that
node 1 selects from the destination address and from information about the congestion in other network nodes. You see in Figure 2.14 that the packets are sent
one at a time and that they are stored and then forwarded by successive communication nodes. This type of transport is called *store-and-forward packet-switching*.
This is similar to the way letters are sent to their destinations by the post offices.
Each letter is labeled with its destination address, and the delivery proceeds step
by step from one post office to the next until the letter reaches its destination. A
post office sends letters to a second post office, where they are *stored*. After
further sorting and routing decisions, the second post office then *forwards* the
letters to the next post office, and so on. This is a store-and-forward transmission.

Packet-switched networks can use two different methods for selecting
the paths followed by packets: *virtual-circuits* and *datagrams*. In a virtual-circuit
transport, the different packets that are part of the same information transfer are
sent along the same path: the packets follow one another as if they were using a
dedicated circuit even though they may be interleaved with other packet streams.
Some implementations of virtual-circuits perform an *error control* on each link
between successive nodes. That is, not only are the packets delivered in sequence
by each node to the next node along the path, but they are also transmitted
without errors. This is implemented by each node checking the correctness of the
packets it receives and by asking the previous node along the path to retransmit

incorrect packets. Nodes verify correctness by using an *error-detection code*, as we will see in Chapter 3.

Two different *link error-control* procedures are used by the nodes to determine which packets they must retransmit. In the first method, called *negative acknowledgements*, a node requests explicitly the retransmission of the packets that it did not receive correctly. In the second method, *positive acknowledgements*, a node acknowledges the correct receptions of packets. A node retransmits the packets that have not been acknowledged within a specific time.

Virtual-circuit transport is illustrated in Figure 2.15(a). In contrast, in a datagram transport the successive packets are sent independently of one another. It is therefore possible for different packets from the same file to follow different paths in the network and for those packets to arrive in an order that differs from that in which they were transmitted. A datagram transport is illustrated in Figure 2.15(b).

We summarize the switching methods:

Switching Methods

- In *circuit-switching*, switches connect links to set up circuits between users for the duration of the communication.
- In *datagram packet-switching*, the bits are grouped as packets. Each packet is labeled with the address of its destination. The packets are routed independently of one another.
- In *virtual-circuit packet-switching*, the packets of the same communication service are transported along the same path, called the *virtual-circuit*.
- Error control is implemented by retransmitting erroneous packets.

How do these three switching methods compare? We can make a few simple observations that justify the existence of networks using the different switching methods. Circuit-switching has the advantage over packet-switching of not requiring any processing of packets, such as storing or forwarding, once the circuit is set up. Such processing delays transmissions. This makes circuit-switching ideally suited for long-lasting transmissions of signals that should not be excessively delayed. It is the method of choice for audio and video transmissions. However, circuit-switching is not efficient if the traffic is *bursty*, i.e., if the transmissions are short and occur irregularly. Indeed, in that case, the time taken to connect the users for every short transmission would be an important overhead, while keeping the connection open between transmissions would waste a large fraction of the capacity of the links. In this case, packet-switching offers more efficient use of network resources.

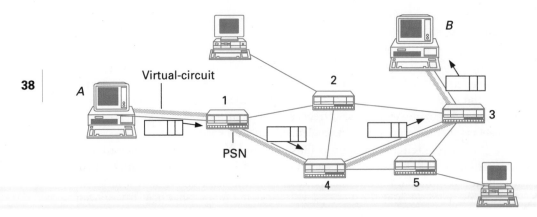

(a) Virtual-circuit transport

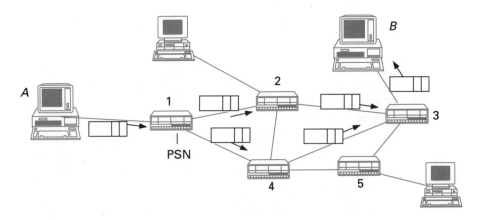

(b) Datagram transport

Figure 2.15 Virtual-circuit (a) and datagram (b) transport.

In a virtual-circuit transport, the packets of a given communication service follow the same path from the source to the destination. In contrast, in a datagram transport, the packets are sent individually and may follow different paths.

Once the designer selects packet-switching, he or she must weigh the benefits and costs of virtual-circuit and datagram transmissions. Virtual-circuit packet-switching requires the selection of a path that will be used for the duration of the file transmission. The packets of that transmission are labeled with a virtual-circuit number which designates the path. The routing decisions are made when the virtual-circuit is set up. Each node stores these routing decisions in a

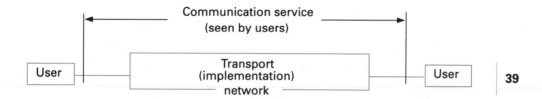

Figure 2.16 Communication service and transport.

The transport of information implements a communication service seen by the users.

routing table that indicates the path to be followed by a packet from the virtual-circuit number. After the virtual-circuit is set up, the node determines the path to be followed by a packet by looking at the routing table. As a result, the node does not have to make complex routing decisions for each packet. In addition, since all the packets of a file are transported in the correct sequence, one can expect the reassembly task to be simple. These properties make virtual-circuit packet-switching advisable for fast transmissions of relatively long duration. Interactive services, such as data base queries/replies, are such applications.

One advantage of datagram transport is that it does not require any set up. It is therefore ideal for short transmissions of a few packets. Another advantage is that, when datagram transport is used, the selection of paths is made for each packet; that selection can therefore react quickly to changing conditions, such as node or link failures.

We have just seen that the three different switching methods have different end-to-end characteristics that make them preferable for different applications.

Comparing Switching Methods

- *Circuit-switching* is best suited for synchronous traffic.
- *Packet-switching* is preferable for bursty traffic.
- *Virtual-circuits* are efficient for long transmissions.
- *Datagrams* are suitable for short transmissions.

Thus, there are different methods for switching bits. The switching methods are used to implement a *communication service*. (See Figure 2.16.)

A specific communication service can be implemented with different switching methods. For example, one can implement an error-free connection-oriented communication service with a datagram transport. This can be done by having the receiving terminal node ask for retransmissions when packets are delivered incorrectly and by re-sequencing the packets that arrive out of order. A more natural implementation of a connection-oriented communication service is based on a virtual-circuit transport with or without link error control.

The three switching methods that we have discussed provide connectivity while enabling different users to share communication links. This sharing of resources allows the designer to achieve substantial savings in the cost of the network. What is the price paid for these savings? We saw earlier that in a circuit-switched network the savings in total link length are achieved at the cost of a blocking probability. In packet-switched networks, blocking occurs when a PSN runs out of buffer space to store packets that happen to arrive faster than they can be transmitted. Such blocking may occur because of temporary fluctuations in the flows of packets. However, *flow-control* procedures that prevent buffer overflow reduce the blocking probability, as we will see in Chapter 6. The real cost for achieving the savings in link length in a packet-switched network is the *delay* faced by packets that have to wait for their turn to be transmitted at the successive PSNs. The size of such a *queueing delay* depends on the characteristics of the traffic transported by the network. In turn, this traffic depends on the number of users and on the applications. We will discuss the determination of packet delays in Chapter 6.

In addition to the switching used to share links in a mesh, it is also possible for *a given link* to be used by different transmissions. This is done by means of a procedure called *multiplexing*, the subject of the next section.

2.6 Multiplexing

Multiplexing is the transmission of different flows of information on the same physical link. By *flow of information* we mean a sequence of packets or a bit stream sent by one user to another user.

One simple way to implement multiplexing of sequences of packets, called *statistical multiplexing*, is to store in the same buffer all the packets that need to be transmitted over a given line. (See Figure 2.17.) The packets can then be transmitted in some order which may depend on when they arrived in the buffer and also on some priority index. Statistical multiplexing has the advantage of using the physical link efficiently: the link is never idle as long as there are bits to transmit. There are three costs to this efficiency: first, each packet must contain some extra information—a label that indicates the information stream to which it belongs; second, the packets face a variable queueing delay; third, the transmitter and the receiver are rather complex and must process each packet to determine its information stream.

Another form of multiplexing is implemented by a communication link that is divided into independent *communication channels*. A communication

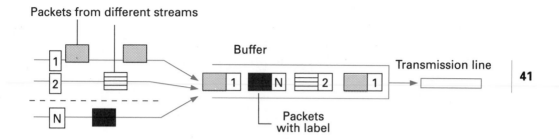

Figure 2.17 Statistical multiplexing.

In statistical multiplexing, the packets to be transmitted are stored in a common buffer and are then transmitted according to some specified scheduling rules. The advantage of this approach is that the transmitter is never idle as long as there are packets to transmit.

channel is a communication service. For instance, a cable TV system can transmit a few dozen TV programs simultaneously on the same cable. The different TV programs do not interact. Thus, the communication *link* (the coaxial cable and its associated electronics) is divided into a number of communication *channels*: one per TV program. This division is done by *frequency-division multiplexing* (FDM). The basic idea, indicated in Figure 2.18, is that the different TV programs are modified so that they lie in different frequency bands. This is also why radio programs do not disturb one another even though they are received by the same antenna. The details of FDM are covered in Chapter 3.

Another method for dividing a communication link into independent communication channels is *time-division multiplexing* (TDM). In TDM, time is divided into time slots of equal duration. (See Figure 2.19.) For instance, if three different transmissions A, B, and C are to take place simultaneously on the line, then transmission A takes place during time slots 1, 4, 7, etc.; transmission B takes place during time slots 2, 5, 8, etc.; and transmission C takes place during the remaining time slots, 3, 6, 9, etc.

Going back to the example of Figure 2.13, we see that the ten pairs of wires between any two office buildings can be replaced by a single pair of wires that is multiplexed by FDM or TDM into ten different communication channels. This allows us to replace 30 km of wire pairs with 3 km of wire pairs, plus some electronics to perform the multiplexing.

How do statistical multiplexing, FDM, and TDM compare? Statistical multiplexing is the most costly procedure of the three. TDM and FDM have equivalent costs. We will see in Chapter 3 that FDM is used to adapt the signal to the characteristics of the transmission media. A familiar example of this is radio transmissions. For antennas to be efficient radiators and collectors of electromag-

42

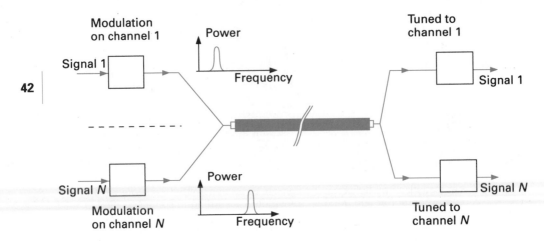

Figure 2.18 Frequency-division multiplexing.

FDM divides the bit transmission rate of the communication link into
a set of independent channels. The different channels use different
frequencies.

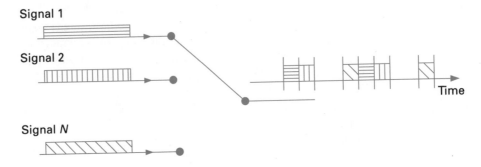

Figure 2.19 Time-division multiplexing.

In TDM, the division of the transmission link into independent channels
is performed by dividing the time into slots. The successive time slots
are allocated cyclically to the different channels.

netic energy, they should have a length comparable to the wavelength of the
electromagnetic wave that they transmit or receive; for instance, a 1-meter-long
antenna is efficient for frequencies in the 100-MHz range, which is the range used
by FM radio stations. The original radio program, i.e., the audio signal, lies in the
range from 0 Hz to 15 kHz; it is moved in the 100-MHz range by the transmitter.
Thus, in addition to enabling multiplexing, the modification of signals used by
FDM to place them in chosen frequency bands can also facilitate their physical
transmission.

There is an important difference between statistical multiplexing and both FDM and TDM. FDM and TDM divide a communication link into communication channels with fixed transmission rates; these transmission rates are reserved for some information streams which may not need them all the time. In contrast, in statistical multiplexing, the information stream uses the communication link only when it has a packet to send. As a consequence, FDM and TDM are less efficient than statistical multiplexing for irregular flows of packets. In such cases, the average packet delay is larger in TDM and FDM than in a statistical multiplexing system, as we will see in Chapter 6.

Let us summarize our findings:

Switching and Multiplexing

■ Replacing point-to-point links by shared links leads to substantial savings.

■ The sharing of links is achieved through *switching* and *multiplexing*.

■ Three forms of multiplexing are *statistical*, *FDM*, and *TDM*.

There is an important variation on the statistical multiplexing idea that we should discuss now because it opens up a range of network designs. This method is known generally as *multiple access*. Multiple access is a method that enables a number of nodes to share a common transmission channel. We will describe the multiple-access method in Figure 2.20.

Figure 2.20 shows N stations $S_1, S_2, ..., S_N$ connected to a common coaxial cable. The coaxial cable is terminated at both ends by a resistor which absorbs completely any signal that reaches it. Thus, when a signal is transmitted by one of the stations, it propagates in both directions over the cable from the station to each end, where it is absorbed. The other stations can listen to the signal. There is the possibility that at least two stations transmit at the same time. When that happens, the signals corrupt one another and the transmissions are *garbled*. One says that a *collision* occurs when transmissions take place simultaneously.

Consider then the situation in which the stations get information to transmit at unpredictable times. How can one prevent these transmissions from occurring simultaneously and garbling one another? A possible method is to use time-division multiplexing, as we have seen previously. That is, one could divide the time axis into intervals that are reserved for different stations. However, as we discussed earlier, this method is not efficient when the stations have to transmit at unpredictable times. For instance, a station might not need its reserved time slots, while another station might need more than its allocated time slots. A multiple-

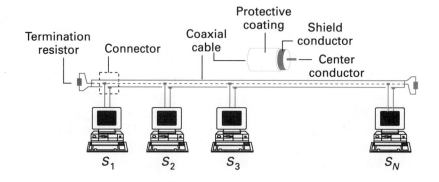

Figure 2.20 A multiple-access system.

In this system, a number of stations use a common transmission channel. The design problem is to select a rule for regulating the access to the channel by all the stations. A good access rule should be efficient; that is, the rule must limit the time wasted because of collisions and idle periods.

access solution is as follows: The information is divided by each station into packets; when a station has a packet to transmit, it does so; if the transmission of the packet collides with a transmission from another station, then the station waits for some random time and repeats the procedure. Eventually, if the random delays are suitably selected, the stations choose different retransmission delays and the packets can be transmitted without colliding. This is the procedure used in the ALOHA network discussed in Section 1.4. The variation used by the Ethernet network is that a station must wait until the channel is idle, i.e., there is no signal on the cable, before attempting to transmit. Also, a station must stop transmitting as soon as it detects a collision. Thus, the Ethernet stations are more "polite" than the ALOHA stations. This politeness pays off: The Ethernet network makes better use of the transmission channel than ALOHA—at least if the cable is not too long—as we will see in Chapter 5.

Another method for sharing the cable in Figure 2.20 is to use a *token-passing* protocol. A token is a special string of bits with a label. One example of a token protocol is the following: Station S_1 transmits a packet of information; it then transmits a token with label S_2. The stations are listening to the cable and can receive the information packet sent by station S_1.

After the token with label S_2 is sent, only station S_2 can transmit an information packet, which is then followed by a token with label S_3. After that, station S_3 sends an information packet followed by a token with label S_4. The procedure continues until station S_N transmits its information packet followed by a token with label S_1. The procedure then repeats. Notice that for this protocol to work, it is not necessary for the token labels to be in the order $S_2, \ldots, S_N, S_1$, as

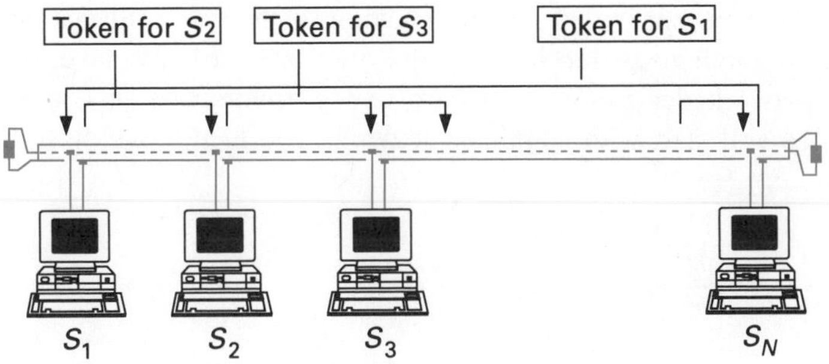

Figure 2.21 Token bus protocol.

The stations take turns transmitting. The succession of transmissions is enforced by having the stations pass a token to one another. Only the station holding the token is allowed to transmit a packet. That station then transmits the token to the next station.

long as they are all used periodically. Moreover, some stations may not transmit information packets. This method is called the *token bus* protocol. The token bus protocol is illustrated in Figure 2.21.

You can see that the token bus protocol may be more efficient than the Ethernet protocol because it eliminates the time wasted by collisions and by random delays. A protocol similar to the token bus was also developed for stations connected in a ring topology; this protocol is then called the *token ring* protocol.

Multiple Access

- Multiple-access methods enable stations to share a transmission channel efficiently even when they transmit at irregular times.

- ALOHA is a multiple-access method. Stations transmit whenever they have packets. If a collision occurs, they retransmit after a random delay.

- Ethernet is a polite variation of ALOHA: The stations wait until the channel is idle before transmitting. If they detect a collision, they stop immediately and they retransmit after a random delay.

- The token bus protocol is a multiple-access method. It regulates the transmissions by having the stations send a token (permit) to one another in turn. The token ring is a similar multiple-access protocol for stations connected in a ring topology.

We will explore and compare ALOHA, Ethernet, token bus, token ring, and a few other multiple access protocols in Chapter 5.

We have concluded our introduction to the way information is transmitted and the implementation of communication services. We have the building blocks for network design. We now turn to the architecture of communication networks. We will start with computer networks and then move on to the ISDN and BISDN.

46

2.7 The OSI Model

As we saw in Chapter 1, a number of companies developed computer networks in the 1970s. Not surprisingly, each company used a different structure for its network, or architecture. The reason for the variations in architecture is that there are many different ways in which network functions can be organized. Despite all their differences, the various architectures used in early networks share a number of similarities. First, all are layered (see Section 2.2). Second, the layers tend to follow a similar pattern: The bottom layer transmits bits; the next layer transmits packets on one link between two nodes; the third layer supervises the end-to-end transmission of packets in the network; and a few layers on top of the third layer use the end-to-end transmission of packets to implement end-to-end communication services and to make them available for user applications.

In the late 1970s, to promote the compatibility of network designs, the *International Organization for Standardization* (ISO) proposed an architecture model called the *open systems interconnection reference model* (OSI model). The OSI model is a layered architecture with seven layers. It shares the similarities of the architectures used previously: The bottom three layers respectively deal with bit transmission, with packet transmission on one link, and with the end-to-end packet transmission; the top layers construct communication services for user applications.

The OSI model is illustrated in Figure 2.22. It is intended for packet-switched networks, and it can be used to model store-and-forward networks as well as multiple-access networks. In addition, the model can describe the interconnections of different packet-switched networks. As we will see later, most popular networks have an architecture similar to that of the OSI model. Figure 2.22 shows a store-and-forward network with two host computers that are connected via two packet-switching nodes (PSNs). Think of Figure 2.22 as illustrating one path in a larger network. As we saw in Section 2.2, the network nodes execute distributed service scripts with peer entities in the same layer in neighboring nodes executing a protocol of that layer. To do this, they exchange *protocol data units* (PDUs) by using the services provided by the layer below. We will examine each of the seven layers in Chapters 3–8. As a background for those chapters, we now present a general description of what the layers do.

Functions of the Seven OSI Layers

- Layer 1 (physical): Transmission of bits
- Layer 2 (data link): Transmission of packets on one given link
- Layer 3 (network): End-to-end transmission of packets
- Layer 4 (transport): End-to-end delivery of messages
- Layer 5 (session): Setup and management of end-to-end conversation
- Layer 6 (presentation): Formatting, encryption, and compression of data
- Layer 7 (application): Network services (such as e-mail and file transfer)

In order to make these functions more concrete, let us examine what happens in the network of Figure 2.22 when computer *A* is used as a remote terminal for computer *B*. In this application, the key strokes typed on *A*'s keyboard are sent to *B* and messages from *B* are sent to be displayed on *A*'s monitor. Successive key strokes from *A* are placed in different packets, and long messages generated by *B* are typically divided into smaller packets for transmission to *A*. Each packet contains its destination address so that the PSNs know where to send it. Thus, information from *A* is placed into packets with destination address *B*; the packets are sent from *A* to PSN1, where they are first stored, as they are received, and then forwarded to PSN2; packets received by PSN2 with destination address *B* are then sent to *B*; computer *B* extracts the pieces of information that it receives from the packets to reconstitute the messages in their original form. The same procedure is followed from *B* to *A*. As we discussed in Chapter 1, packets can be sent from PSN1 to PSN2 at the same time as other packets are being sent from *A* to PSN1.

What actions must be performed for this remote terminal application? One possible scenario is as follows. First, computer *A* calls computer *B* and informs it that it wants to be connected as a remote terminal. Second, *B* determines whether it accepts the connection and informs *A*. Third, assuming that *B* accepts the connection, *A* and *B* exchange information. Eventually, the connection is terminated.

The reliable transmission of information between the two hosts requires many network operations. How are those operations organized? We will describe the OSI solution. Our description will be somewhat simplified, but it should illustrate the communications between layers and the decomposition of the functions.

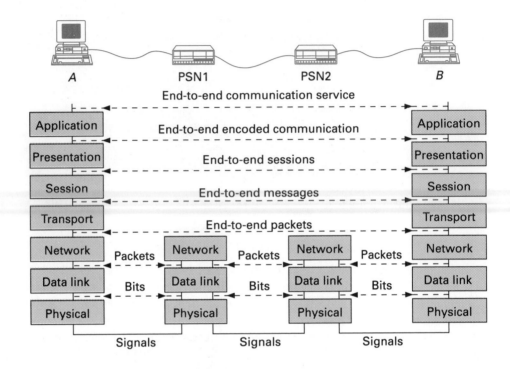

Figure 2.22 The OSI model.

The OSI model decomposes the network services into seven layers.
A layer implements a service which is used by the layer immediately
above it. For instance, the service implemented by the network layer
is the end-to-end transmission of packets. This service is used by the
transport layer to implement the end-to-end transmission of messages.
The physical layer uses the transmission of electrical or optical signals
provided by the transmission link hardware to implement a bit-transmission service. That is, the physical layer converts bits into signals
and conversely.

Application Layer

The user of the remote terminal is provided with a simple set of commands for exchanging messages with a remote computer. These commands are
provided by the *application layer*. Part of the application layer program runs in *A*,
and part runs in *B*. Thus, *A* and *B* execute a distributed script by exchanging
messages. The designer of the Application software assumes that the two parts of
the application layer are able to exchange messages reliably using the service
provided by the layer below. The actual implementation of the transport of the
messages is irrelevant for the design of the application layer.

Presentation Layer

The application layer program that runs in B should not need to be aware of the specific type of terminal which is used by A. Indeed, it would not be practical to have to design a different application layer program in B for every possible terminal type that might ever want to use B as a remote computer. As a consequence, the interpretation of the bit strings generated by A's keyboard and the correct display on A's terminal of information sent by B usually necessitate some format conversion. This conversion is needed to accommodate the different data representations and different terminal types that are typically used by A and B. Such conversion is performed by programs in the *presentation layer*. As in the case of the application layer, parts of the presentation layer program run in both A and B. The presentation layer in A is given the messages by the application layer in A, and it converts them into a "standard format" for transmission to the presentation layer in B, where they are converted into the format expected by the application layer in B. The presentation layer may perform some functions other than format conversion. For instance, it may encrypt the data at A and decrypt the data at B if the information transfer must be secure.

Session Layer

When the connection is first set up, computers A and B agree on some rules for the dialogue. For instance, they may agree that the communication will be full-duplex, meaning that both computers can transmit simultaneously. Such negotiation is performed by the *session layer*. The session layer may also supervise the communication by having the two computers periodically agree on *synchronization* points that are used to recover in the event of a failure: only the data sent since the last synchronization point need to be retransmitted.

Let us take a second look at the terminal example and the three layers that we have just described. The user sits at computer A and invokes the "Remote Terminal" application program. This program calls a specific application layer program which starts a user interface in A. The user interface is a program which presents the user with a set of possible commands. The user indicates to the interface the desire to call computer B, for instance by typing "rlogin klee" where "rlogin" is a special command and "klee" is the name of computer B. The service *rlogin* enables the user to access a computer from a remote location as if he or she were using the main terminal of that computer. The application layer program in A, which runs the interface, then passes the "rlogin klee" command to the presentation layer in A, which converts it into a standard format. The presentation layer in A asks the session layer in A to establish a connection with "klee." Eventually, that request reaches the session layer in B. The session layer programs in A and B execute some protocol to agree on some rules for the transmission. At the end of this phase, a connection is established between A and B and messages later sent by A will eventually reach B and vice versa. The presentation layer makes sure that the messages sent by the application layer in A are received by the application layer in B in the correct format, and similarly for the messages sent from B to A. For this to happen, the user may be asked to specify the terminal type that is being used. The application layers can then communicate; B can ask for the user password to determine whether to grant access, and computer A can then start being used as a remote terminal for computer B: The key strokes on A's keyboard reach B in the same format as if they had been typed on B's keyboard, and the symbols sent by B reach A's terminal as if they had been sent by A.

Transport Layer

The transport layer controls the delivery of the messages between the end nodes. This layer may divide the messages into smaller packets. When the application requires it, the transport layer uses acknowledgements to verify that the packets are well received by the destination. The transport layer also controls the rate at which packets are sent to the destination. In our examples, the messages sent by B are divided into numbered packets in B's transport layer; the packets are resequenced in A's transport layer. The numbering of packets is agreed upon at the start of the transmission and is designed to be robust in the case of failure of one of the two computers.

Notice that the application, presentation, session, and transport layers perform services between host computers. These layers are not present in the PSNs. These intermediate nodes act as switches that transport the individual packets independently of their role in a connection between the end nodes. Thus, the PSNs are oblivious to the sequence numbering or to the higher layer functions that will be performed on the packets.

Network Layer

The packets must find their way in the network. This is one of the tasks of the *network layer*. This layer keeps track of how congested various parts of the network are; it uses that information to select the paths followed by the packets.

Data Link Layer

Each packet is transmitted on a link as a sequence of bits. It is up to the *data link layer* to check that the packet was properly transmitted over the link. The data link layer supervises the retransmission of packets that arrive incorrectly.

Physical Layer

To transmit a packet, each bit is converted into an electrical (or optical) signal by the *physical layer*. The signals are sent over the physical link and are received at the other end, where they are converted back into bits. Successive bits are reassembled into a packet by the receiver. The packet is then passed to the data link layer of the receiver.

The above example illustrates the division of network functions into the seven layers of the OSI model. Figure 2.23 provides another illustration of the OSI model. It emphasizes the communication that takes place between the layers.

Figure 2.22 shows the virtual communication links that exist between peer layers in different nodes. For instance, the physical layer makes a *bit pipe* available to the data link layer. That is, the data link layer, which is distributed in two nodes, can exchange bits by means of the physical layer. Indeed, the physical layer in one node converts the bits into electrical or optical signals, and it transmits those signals; the signals are converted into bits by the physical layer in the receiving node. The data link layer does not need to know whether the signals are sent over a coaxial cable or an optical fiber. The *bit-transmission service* provided by the physical layer is used by the data link layer to construct a *packet-transmission service*. The packet-transmission service is reliable if the data link layer asks for the retransmission of packets that are not received correctly. In some networks, it is preferable to have an unreliable but faster data link layer. In such networks no error control is provided by the data link layer. Thus, the data link layer implements a packet-transmission service on a link between two nodes that are directly connected by a link. That packet transmission service is used by the network layer to carry the packets from the source host to the destination host. As was discussed in Section 2.4, this is done by transmitting the packets on the successive links along a path from the source to the destination. The paths are selected by the network layer. Some network layers use a datagram transport, whereas others use virtual-circuits. Thus, the network layer implements an *end-to-end packet-transmission service* between terminal nodes, or *hosts* of the network. That service is used by the transport layer to supervise the transmission of mes-

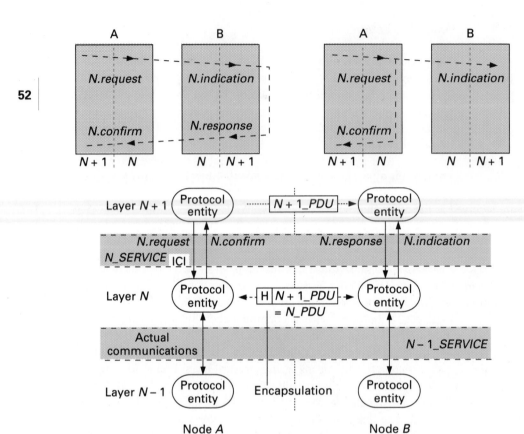

Figure 2.23 Communication in the OSI model.

A protocol entity of layer $N+1$ initiates an *N.SERVICE* by making an
N.request. Upon completion of the service, the protocol entity of layer N
sends an *N.confirm* to the entity of layer $N+1$. The protocol entity of
layer $N+1$ in the remote node receives an *N.indication* and replies with
an *N.response*.

sages by breaking them up into packets that are numbered. The transport layer
implements an *end-to-end message-transmission service* which is used by the
session layer to organize conversations, called *sessions*, between the hosts. The
sessions are used by the application layer to run user application programs; the
presentation layer is used for performing necessary format conversions and also
possibly for encryption and data compression.

The above decomposition of the OSI seven-layer model will help you understand the detailed discussions of network architectures and services. The subsequent chapters will look more closely at the functions performed by different layers. The details can be appreciated only by having a general view of the network operations.

Two important benefits result from the layer decomposition. As we mentioned previously, the different layers can be designed more or less independently, which greatly simplifies network design. Another advantage is the *compatibility* which is derived from the independence of the layers. For instance, the same applications can run on very different networks. And when different networks are interconnected, a computer on one network can access computers on all the networks, independently of the specific implementations of the different networks. Since connectivity is a primary objective of communication networks, compatibility is most valuable.

Figure 2.23 illustrates another aspect of the communication between layers: the *encapsulation*. When the information proceeds from the application layer to the physical layer, each layer adds some specific information. For instance, the presentation layer may indicate which *compression algorithm* is used for reducing the number of bits transmitted. The session layer adds a session identification number. The transport layer adds packet sequence numbers. The network layer may add a virtual-circuit number. The data link layer adds a link sequence number (to keep track of which packets were acknowledged by the next node, for instance). The physical layer adds error-control bits. Such specific pieces of *protocol-control information* added by the successive layers are removed by the successive layers at the destination when the information progresses from the physical layer to the application layer.

Using the terminology of Section 2.2, we will explain the communications between layers when layer $N + 1$ is the presentation layer and when the request is to establish a connection with computer B. The *N.request*, which is called a *SESSION_CONNECT.request*, specifies the address of the destination, the desired quality of service, some additional synchronization parameters, possibly a pointer to some data, and various options. The *N.indication*, here called a *SESSION_CONNECT.indication*, specifies the same parameters as the request. The *N.confirm*, called a *SESSION_CONNECT.confirm*, indicates whether the session was successfully set up and, if not, gives the reason why.

In the case of a connectionless communication, the *N.confirm* primitive is generated locally in host A, as indicated in the Figure 2.23.

Here is a summary of what you should remember from the discussion of the OSI model:

OSI Protocol Terminology

- The OSI model is a layered architecture with seven layers: physical, data link, network, transport, session, presentation, and application. These layers implement, respectively, a bit pipe, a packet link, an end-to-end packet transmission, an end-to-end message transmission, a session, an encoded communication service, and a communication service.

- Layer N makes $N\_SERVICES$ available to layer $N+1$; these services are used by the layer $N+1$ protocol entities to exchange the $N+1\_PDU$s.

- Layer $N+1$ uses the $N\_SERVICES$ via service primitives: $N.request$, $N.indication$, $N.response$, and $N.confirm$, which contain parameters and pointers to data.

2.8 Other Architectural Models: IEEE 802, DOD, TOP, and MAP

In this section, we will examine the architectures of a number of widely used computer networks. You will notice that these architectures differ slightly from that of the OSI model.

Our discussion begins with local area network (LAN) standards that were developed by the *Institute of Electrical and Electronics Engineers* (IEEE). We then introduce the protocols TOP and MAP used in office and manufacturing automation, respectively. The section concludes with the architecture of the Department of Defense networks.

The IEEE standards for LANs are known as IEEE 802.1 to IEEE 802.5. IEEE working groups IEEE 802.6–9 are developing additional standards. The IEEE standard activities for LANs are summarized in Figure 2.24. In addition, working group IEEE 802.10 is concerned with the security of networks.

Essentially, the OSI data link layer is replaced in the IEEE 802 standards by the *media-access-control* (MAC) layer together with the *logical-link-control* (LLC) layer. The IEEE 802.1 standard specifies the general architecture of LANs. The IEEE 802.2 standard specifies the LLC, while 802.3 through 802.6 describe the CSMA-CD Bus, the token bus, the token ring, and the metropolitan area network distributed queue dual bus (DQDB), respectively. In addition, the IEEE working groups 802.7 through 802.9 are developing standards for broadband networks, optical fiber networks, and integrated data and voice networks, respectively.

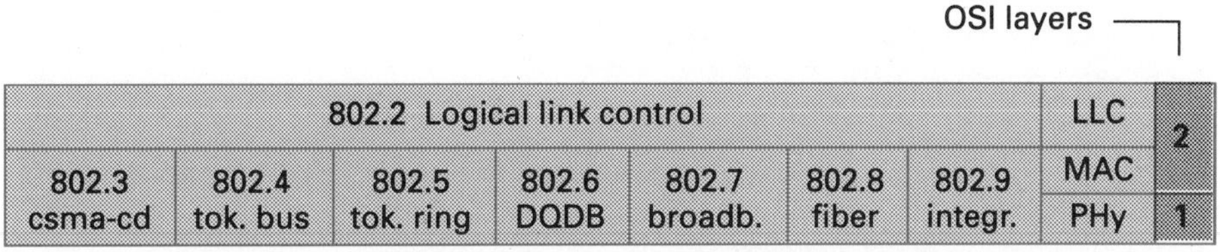

OSI layers

802.2 Logical link control							LLC	2
802.3 csma-cd	802.4 tok. bus	802.5 tok. ring	802.6 DQDB	802.7 broadb.	802.8 fiber	802.9 integr.	MAC	
							PHy	1

Figure 2.24 The IEEE 802 standards.

The standards developed by the IEEE 802 working groups are indicated in this figure. These standards specify the physical layer and the data link layer of LANs. The data link layer is decomposed into the media-access-control (MAC) layer and the logical-link-control (LLC) layer.

The details of some of the IEEE 802 standards will be covered in Chapter 5. In particular, we will discuss the Ethernet network, which is similar to IEEE 802.3, the Token Ring 802.5, and the Token Bus 802.4. We will also study the 802.6 DQDB network and the 802.2 LLC.

In an effort to standardize LANs all the way to the applications, protocol suites have been proposed. A protocol suite is a set of seven compatible layers. Examples of suites are the *technical and office protocols* (TOPs) and the *manufacturing automation protocols* (MAPs). The former is intended for general office applications, while the latter is designed for applications in automated factories. These two suites are illustrated in Figure 2.25. We will discuss these protocol suites in Chapter 8. For now, let us note that TOP is designed for Ethernet and token ring networks and MAP is for token bus networks. The main application layer programs in TOP are *file transfer and management* (FTAM); *message-handling system* (MHS), used for electronic mail; *virtual-terminal* (VT) for remote terminal applications; *directory service* (DS); and *job transfer and manipulation* (JTM), used for the remote execution of jobs. MAP provides a *manufacturing message service* (MMS) for communicating with control processors; it specifies primitives for reading and setting registers.

Figure 2.25 also shows the *Department of Defense* (DOD) protocols. The application protocols include the *file-transfer protocol* (FTP); the *simple mail-transfer protocol*, which is the electronic mail application; and *Telnet*, the remote terminal program. Those applications run on top of a transport protocol: either the connection-oriented *transport-control protocol* (TCP) or the connectionless *user datagram protocol* (UDP). These transport protocols rely on the *internet protocol* (IP), which is a datagram network layer. *Internet* is the name given to a collection of interconnected networks that use the TCP/IP protocols with its addressing scheme. Those networks include ARPANET, USENET, BITNET, NSFnet, and Cypress. There are tens of thousands of hosts in the United States, Europe, Japan, Australia, and Israel on the Internet.

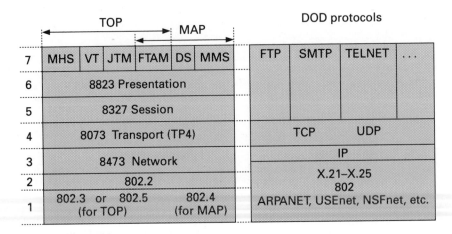

Figure 2.25 TOP, MAP, and DOD protocol suites.

TOP is a complete set of protocols for office applications. MAP is a set of protocols for manufacturing automation. The Department of Defense protocols are used by the Internet networks.

2.9 ISDN and BISDN

The OSI, IEEE, MAP, TOP, and DOD protocols that we discussed above apply to computer networks. What about networks for voice, audio, and video in addition to data? Standards are emerging for such networks. We will discuss proposals for the *integrated services digital networks* (ISDNs) and for the *broadband integrated services digital networks* (BISDNs). ISDN is a set of new communication services that will be provided by the telephone network. Implementing BISDN would require major modifications of the existing telephone network but would offer dramatically improved services. ISDN and the BISDN networks will radically transform the telecommunication infrastructure throughout the world and will have a significant impact on our lives. This section will introduce the architectures of these networks.

As we indicated in Chapter 1, ISDN provides a residential customer with two *B* channels at 64 kbps and one *D* channel at 16 kbps. These channels can be used for voice and also for data transmissions needed for facsimile transmissions, for electronic mail, for computer file transfers, for alarm monitoring, for the remote control of appliances and lights, for access to data bases, for information services, and for various other applications that could be provided by vendors.

Our discussion here applies to the *intelligent network* model of ISDN. The key components of the Intelligent Network model are shown in Figure 2.26.

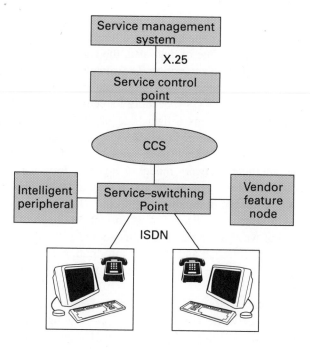

Figure 2.26 The intelligent network model.

The primary objective of the intelligent network is to separate the flow of control information from that of user information. This separation permits more flexible services and also a more efficient utilization of the network resources.

In the intelligent network model, customer premises are connected to *service-switching points* (SSPs) by the existing telephone lines, called *subscriber loops*. The SSPs are modern switches used for the ISDN channels. Nodes that provide phone company or vendor services are also attached to SSPs. In turn, the SSPs are connected to *service-control points* (SCPs) by the *common channel-signaling* (CCS) network. Finally, the SCPs are supervised by a *service management system* (SMS) with which it communicates via an X.25 network. The CCS and X.25 networks use store-and-forward packet-switching. You will recall from our brief discussion in Chapter 1 that CCS is used to transmit control information among switches. Similarly, the X.25 network will be used for exchanging control information.

We will come back to the operating principles of ISDN in Chapter 9, but we should look at a simple example to appreciate what can be gained by having a control network separate from the network used to transmit user information. We will use the 800 numbers service as our example. When you dial an 800 number, you are, in fact, connected to a different number which may depend on your location and on the time of day; also, the call is charged to the company that subscribes to the 800 number service. The advantage of using an 800 number is that customers must remember only one number and the company advertises a single phone number. The pre-CCS procedure for setting up an 800 call is to route the call to a switch that contains a data base of 800 numbers. This data base determines the ultimate destination to which the call is then routed by extending the circuit from the data base switch to the destination. In comparison, the solution based on the intelligent network model of Figure 2.26 is as follows. The SSP where the call originates recognizes that an 800 number is dialed and uses the CCS network to find out the destination of the call. That information is then used by the originating SSP to route the call to its correct destination. This method has the advantage of not wasting transmission links along paths that are needed only to exchange control information and not user information. Only the routing information, instead of the complete call, is transmitted from the originating SSP to the data base.

A common criticism of ISDN is that it offers relatively little more than the present telephone network. For instance, by connecting a personal computer via a fast modem to the existing telephone network, subscribers can already access a host of public data bases as well as their office or bank computers. Many services can already be offered over the telephone network, and it is not clear that many more will appear when ISDN becomes more widely available. Critics argue that ISDN offers too little too late. The same criticism does not apply to the *broadband integrated services digital network* (BISDN). As we saw in Chapter 1, BISDN would make four channels at 150 Mbps available to residential customers: one outgoing and three incoming. Such channels could be used for HDTV and digital audio broadcasting, for movies on demand, for videophones, and for accessing multimedia (i.e., video, audio, and data) information services.

The central design question for BISDN is how to meet economically the widely different requirements of the intended applications with a single network. The needed transmission rates range from a few kbps for voice and facsimile transmissions to about 150 Mbps for HDTV. The solution adopted by the BISDN designers is called *asynchronous transfer mode* (ATM). The basic idea of ATM is to divide time into slots called *cells*. A cell consists of 44 bytes of information and 9 bytes of control information. The control information specifies the virtual-circuit to which the cell belongs. The network is synchronized in the sense that the cells are sent at precise times as measured by a global clock used throughout the network. This synchronization makes time-division multiplexing possible by a straight interleaving of signals. It also simplifies the insertion and the extraction of signals from a given stream; these two operations are essential in the connection of customers. The transmission technology is based on single-

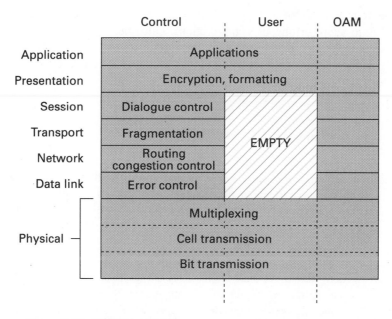

Figure 2.27 BISDN architecture.

The information is transported in cells. The network-control information is transmitted with routing and error control. User information is transmitted without error control and without routing.

mode optical fibers (see Chapter 3). The specific nature of the transport mechanism leads to the layered architecture shown in Figure 2.27.

The physical layer comprises three sublayers: the *physical 1 layer* performs the transmission and the reception of the bit stream on the optical fiber; the *physical 2 layer* provides access to the cells; and the *physical 3 layer* executes multiplexing and demultiplexing functions. The physical layer implements a bit-transmission service for the layers above, which are similar to the corresponding OSI layers.

Notice that the architecture distinguishes the *user plane*, the control plane, and the *operations and maintenance plane*. This distinction reflects the different requirements of the three types of information transmissions: user information, control information, and network management information. For the purpose of illustration, consider a videophone application. One user wants to establish a video connection with another user. To do this, the first user calls the network, which then transmits that request to switches and the connection is eventually established; at that time, the user information can start flowing along the virtual-circuit that has been set up. The control information is transmitted by a store-and-forward transport, with error control provided at the link level. An error in the transmission of the control information is corrected before it causes switches to adopt erroneous configurations. Once the virtual-circuits are set up, the user information does not require any further routing decision. No error control is performed for the user information, because infrequent errors are acceptable for video transmissions.

60

2.10 Network Management

As with most complex engineering systems, the management of communication networks involves both a crucial and difficult set of tasks. The first step is to define what is meant by management, i.e., to identify the objectives. The next step is to organize the strategy to meet those objectives. So far, the first step has been partially accomplished. The second is the subject of intense activity, but it is far from being completed.

What are the objectives of network management? The OSI has identified five tasks of network management. They are summarized in Table 2.1.

The main components of a management system are *monitoring*, *decision making*, and *implementation of decisions*. That is, the management system must be able to collect the relevant information about the status and the operations of the network; it must have efficient algorithms to decide on a suitable way to act; and it must be able to implement the actions. In particular, the monitoring requirement implies that network components are equipped with the necessary hardware and software. This basic feature is absent from many current network components.

How should the network management software and hardware be organized? As was the case for the data transmission hardware and software, two important design goals are *modularity* and *compatibility*. These goals justify current efforts toward network management standardization. Because this is an area

Task	Functions
Fault	Report faults, schedule diagnostic tests, correct faults
Configuration and name	Monitor system state, modifications
Performance	Monitor network performance
Accounting	Report costs, set limits
Security	Access control, encryption

Table 2.1 Network management tasks.

under study, we cannot be specific about the architecture of network management systems. We can, however, list a few of the ideas that are emerging from the research.

A network management system should have a software model of the physical network. This model should be an image of the physical network and should be updated by the monitoring information. The model should be organized in a modular and easily modifiable way. The network model can serve two functions: First a "network image" can be used to keep track of the network status: which components are up, which are down, which parts are overloaded, and which are underutilized. Second, a "dynamical model" can be used as a simulation tool to test repair or improvement strategies. Section 10.1 examines two emerging standards for network management.

Summary

- *Network architectures* define the organization of network *services* into simpler services.

- Information is transmitted in a network as *bit files* or *bit streams*.

- Communication services are *synchronous* or *asynchronous*. Asynchronous services can be *connection-oriented* or *connectionless*.

- Links in a meshlike network can be shared by *switching*. Two types of switching are *circuit-switching* and *packet-switching*. Packet-switching may use *datagrams* or *virtual-circuits*.

- In a packet-switched network, errors can be controlled by retransmitting packets that are not received correctly.

- A single link can be shared by *TDM*, *FDM*, *statistical multiplexing*, or *multiple access*; *ALOHA*, *Ethernet*, and *token bus* are examples of multiple-access protocols.

- In the *OSI model*, the network functions are decomposed into seven layers: from the physical layer to the application layer; protocol entities at one layer exchange *PDUs* by using service primitives of the layer below.

- The standards *IEEE 802*, *TOP*, and *MAP* are used by LANs. The *DOD* protocol suites are used by the Internet networks.

- The *intelligent network* is an architecture model for ISDN.

- The *BISDN* architecture distinguishes the user, control, and operations and maintenance planes; those networks will use the *ATM* transport.

■ Network management has five domains of concern: fault, configuration and name, performance, accounting, and security.

Problems

1. Why is digital transmission preferred to analog transmission for
   voice? (Indicate the correct answer(s).)
   a. Because it is faster.
   b. Because it is less noisy.
   c. Because optical fibers can be used.

2. When is packet-switching preferred to circuit-switching? (Indicate the
   correct answer(s).)
   a. Always.
   b. When delays have to be small.
   c. When the traffic is bursty.
   d. When the transmission rate is large.

3. What do virtual-circuits implement? (Indicate the correct answer(s).)
   a. Datagrams.
   b. Point-to-point connections.
   c. Connection-oriented communication services.
   d. Circuit-switched communications.

4. Why is the ISO's OSI model important? (Indicate the correct an-
   swer(s).)
   a. Because it leads to more efficient protocols.
   b. Because there is no other possible design.
   c. Because compatibility is desirable.
   d. Because it provides one unified way to discuss protocols.

5. Assume that writing a program of N lines of code costs N^2 units of
   cost. If the program is written in a modular form, assume that a module of n lines costs $a^2 + n^2$ to develop. The cost a^2 is caused by the
   need to follow the specifications of the modular construction. With
   these assumptions, what is the number k of modules of N/k lines that
   minimizes the cost of writing the program? For what values of N is it
   preferable to decompose a program of N lines into modules rather than
   to write it as a single program?

6. Assume that developing an application program with a specific user
   interface costs A. Thus, developing M different applications for N user

interfaces costs $M \times N \times A$. If we adopt the X Windows approach, we can write a client for each interface and a server for each application. Assume that it costs B to develop a client and C to develop a server. For what values of M and N is the client-server approach less expensive than the $M \times N$ programs?

7. We learned that voice can be transmitted as a bit stream at the rate of 64 kbps. How many minutes of voice signal can you store on a 20-MByte hard disk?

8. Take a letter-size sheet of paper (8.5 inches by 11 inches). Draw a fine grid with 300 lines per inch both vertically and horizontally. How many points are formed by the intersections of the grid lines? Assume that 3 bits are used to encode the level of gray of each of these points to represent a photograph printed on the page. How many bits do you need to encode the photograph? How many such photographs can you store in an 80-MByte hard disk? How long does it take to transmit the photograph by using a 2,400-bps modem?

9. Is it faster to transmit the contents of a full CD-ROM with a 2,400-bps modem or to mail the CD-ROM from San Francisco to Brussels?

10. We want to implement a packet-voice transmission. To do this, we build an electronic board that groups the bits arriving at 64 kbps into packets of 48 bytes. The packets are sent over a 230-km transmission line to a second board. The second board converts the packets into a 64-kbps bit stream. We assume that the packets are transmitted as soon as they are formed and that the second board converts each packet back into the bit stream as soon as it is fully received. The propagation time along the transmission line is 1 ms. What is the delay faced by the bit stream between the input of the first board and the output of the second board?

11. Consider a path in a store-and-forward network. The path goes through ten nodes. At each node, the packets are stored in a buffer before they are transmitted over the link to the next node. The packets contain 1,000 bits, and the transmission rates are equal to 56 kbps. The total propagation time over the links along the path is 15 ms. Assume that a packet is sent along that path and that it finds an average of five packets when it arrives at each buffer. How long does it take for the packet to go through the path if the nodes transmit from each buffer on a first come first served basis? How long is the packet travel time if it is transmitted as expedited data?

*12. We want to buy a *private branch exchange* (PBX), i.e., a telephone switch, to connect our office building to the telephone company's central office. The PBX will enable us to connect telephones inside the building without having to use the services of the telephone company. External telephone calls are connected by the PBX to the appropriate extension inside the building. How many telephone lines should there be between the PBX and the telephone company's central office? Our telecommunication engineer tells us that with N lines the blocking probability B is given by the formula

$$B = \frac{\dfrac{\rho^N}{N!}}{1 + \rho + \dfrac{\rho^2}{2!} + \dfrac{\rho^3}{3!} + \ldots + \dfrac{\rho^N}{N!}}$$

where $m!$ (*m factorial*) is defined as $1 \times 2 \times 3 \times \ldots \times (m-1) \times m$ for any integer m. (Thus, $2! = 2$, $3! = 6$, $4! = 24$.) Here, ρ is $n/30$ where n is the number of telephone sets in the building. Find how many telephones can be accommodated with one, two, three, and four lines if we want $B \leq 2\%$.

13. To transmit packets with virtual-circuit transport, we first set up a virtual-circuit and then we transmit the packets. The network is lightly loaded, and our packets do not face any queueing delay. The virtual-circuit setup time is 400 ms. The packets travel over a path that goes through ten nodes, and the links transmit at 56 kbps. Each packet has 400 bits of data, a header of 5 bytes to indicate the virtual-circuit number and the packet sequence number, and a trailer of 2 bytes that contains bits used for error detection. When we use datagram transport, no virtual-circuit is set up but each packet needs a header of 10 bytes instead of 5 to indicate the full destination address and source address, in addition to the packet sequence number. These packets also have the 2-byte trailer. Assume that datagrams also happen to follow the same path through ten nodes. How long does it take to transmit N packets when using virtual-circuit transport and when using datagram transport? For what values of N is it faster to use virtual-circuit transport?

14. Packets arrive at a node to be transmitted. The packets arrive at random times $T_1, T_2, \ldots$ and are transmitted in the order that they arrive. Packets that cannot be transmitted immediately are stored in a buffer until they can be. Assume that each packet is P bits long and the transmission rate is R bps. Draw a diagram showing how many bits are stored in the node buffer as a function of time. That number is zero before time T_1. At time T_1, that number is assumed to jump

instantaneously to P. Between T_1 and T_2, the number of bits stored decreases by R bits every second, and so on. Using your diagram, determine the delay faced by the first, second, and third packets as a function of (T_1, T_2, T_3). Note that the delay of a packet is the sum of the transmission time

$$\frac{P}{R}$$

and some *queueing time*. Give a simple condition on the arrival times (T_1, T_2, T_3) for the queueing time to be zero. Exhibit arrival times $\{T_n, n \geq 1\}$ that lead to a very large average queueing time per packet, even though the average arrival rate (in packets per second) is very small. (*Hint:* Consider infrequent arrivals of large batches of packets.)

15. Packets arrive in pairs every second at a transmitter equipped with a buffer. The transmission rate is 56 kbps, and each packet is 1,000 bits long. What is the average delay per packet through the buffer and transmitter? Assume now that packets arrive in pairs every 0.5 second and that the transmission rate is 112 kbps. What is the new average delay per packet? Think of the second model as being the statistical multiplexing of two packet streams sharing one 112-kbps transmitter, and of the first model as resulting from the division of the 112 kbps link into two 56-kbps channels (by FDM, say) used by one packet stream each. Conclude that statistical multiplexing achieves smaller delays than FDM or TDM. Discuss the limitations of this model and how the conclusions can be shown to be valid under more general assumptions.

16. Packets arrive in batches every second at a transmitter equipped with a buffer. The packets are 1,000 bits long, and the transmitter has rate 56 kbps. A batch is equally likely to contain one, two, three, ..., or ten packets. Calculate the average delay per packet.

17. Two stations S_1 and S_2 are attached on a common coaxial cable, as in Figure 2.20 (with $N = 2$). The stations wait until the channel is idle before transmitting a packet, and they stop when they detect a collision. Show that the maximum time wasted by a collision is twice the propagation time of a signal between the two stations.

*18. Consider the two stations described in the previous problem. Time is divided into time slots of 1 ms. During each time slot, both stations attempt to transmit a packet of 9,000 bits with the transmission rate of 10 Mbps. Each station flips a fair coin. If the coin toss yields "heads," the station transmits. If not, it waits until the next slot and repeats the experiment. The stations repeat the experiment when the packets collide. Assuming that the stations always have packets to transmit, find the rate at which packets are transmitted (in packets per second). Find the average delay faced by a packet from the time it is next in line to be transmitted until its transmission is completed.

19. Consider the N stations shown in Figure 2.21. The stations use the Token Bus protocol. That is, after transmitting its information packet, station S_1 transmits a token with label $S_{i(1)}$. Then station $i(1)$ transmits an information frame, then a token with label $S_{i(2)}$, and so on. The numbers $i(1)$, $i(2)$, ... are the numbers $\{1, 2, ... N\}$ in some order. Calculate the sum of the travel times of the tokens from station S_1 to station $S_{i(1)}$, then from $S_{i(1)}$ to $S_{i(2)}$, and so on until the token is retransmitted to S_1 and reaches that station. Find the positions of the stations on the cable and the order of token transmissions that maximize that sum of token travel times. How much larger than the propagation time of a signal on the cable can this sum be?

References

A clear discussion of the OSI model can be found in Ziemmerman (1980), Green (1982), and Falk (1983). Chapter 1 in Bertsekas (1987) is particularly lucid. The texts of Stallings (1988) and Tanenbaum (1988) give details about many networks. The directory LaQuey (1990) provides a listing of most academic and research networks.

Bertsekas (1987). Bertsekas, D. and Gallager, R., *Data Networks*. Prentice-Hall, 1987.

Falk (1983). Falk, G., "The structure and function of network protocols," in *Computer Communications, Vol. I.* (W. Chou, Ed.). Prentice-Hall, 1983.

Green (1982). Green, P., *Computer Network Architectures and Protocols*. Plenum, 1982.

LaQuey (1990). LaQuey, T. (Ed.), *The User's Directory of Computer Networks*. Digital Press, 1990.

Stallings (1988). Stallings, W., *Data and Computer Communications*, Second Edition. Macmillan, 1988.

Tanenbaum (1988). Tanenbaum, A., *Computer Networks*, Second Edition. Prentice-Hall, 1988.

Ziemmerman (1980). Ziemmerman, H., "OSI reference model—The OSI model of architecture for open systems interconnection," *IEEE Trans. Commun.*, COM-28, No. 4, 425–432, 1980.

Physical Layer

3

The communication services provided by networks, regardless of their configurations, allow users to exchange information. The most basic activity required for such information transmission is the conversion of bit streams or bit files into electrical or optical signals that can transfer the information from one part of the network—say, from one computer—to another over a transmission medium. This activity is performed by the physical layer described in Chapter 2's discussion of the OSI model.

Our focus in this chapter is on the steps required to transmit digital information. We represent these actions in Figure 3.1. The two nodes are connected by a physical medium. We break down the transmission of bits into the transmission of electromagnetic waves from one node to the next, the conversion of bits to electromagnetic waves at the first node and the conversion of the waves to bits at the second node, and error-control procedures that are incorporated into the transmission process. Specifically, Section 3.1 describes how signals propagate and how guided electromagnetic waves are capable of transmitting data. In Section 3.2 we turn to the problem of converting bits to optical waves that can be transmitted over optical fibers, and in Section 3.3 we observe how such transmission occurs over radio waves and transmission lines. We will see in Sections 3.2 and 3.3 that the signals are distorted during the transmission. We will explain how such distortions can be predicted and how the telecommunications engineer can

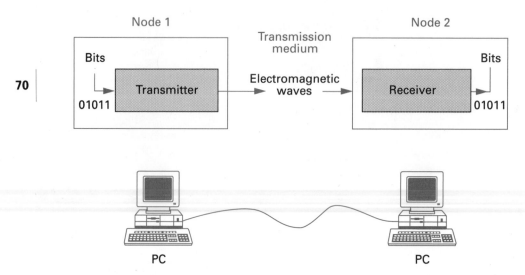

Figure 3.1 Transmission of information between two nodes.

Node 1 transmits bits to node 2. In node 1, a transmitter converts the bits into electromagnetic waves. The waves are transmitted over a transmission medium. A receiver in node 2 converts the electromagnetic waves into bits.

reduce the distortions or take them into account in designing the communication link. Section 3.4 explains how the receiver knows when it should measure the received signal to recover the bits. The problem is to keep the receiver synchronized with the received signal. We will see that the solution involves synchronization and framing techniques. In addition to the predictable signal distortions, some unpredictable corruptions also occur. Such unpredictable signal modifications, called noise, produce random errors. In Section 3.5 we examine techniques to minimize random transmission errors. We conclude the chapter by describing the conversion of information to bits in Section 3.6.

3.1 Signal Propagation

Electromagnetic Waves

Signals are transmitted as electromagnetic waves. Two qualities of electromagnetic waves make them suitable for information transfer in a network. First, they *propagate*, enabling them to move from one place to another, as from the transmitter to the receiver in Figure 3.1. Second, they contain energy that can be used to carry messages. We know, from quantum mechanics, that this energy should be viewed as being carried by *photons*. One can think of a photon as a minute burst of electromagnetic energy. An electromagnetic wave is a stream of photons. The energy of a single photon is so minuscule that an ordinary light bulb emits about 10^{20} photons every second. In this section we look at the propagation of electromagnetic waves to see how they can be guided between the nodes of a network. You will see that electromagnetic waves are guided by using their different propagation properties in different media. Waves are modified, distorted, and weakened during their propagation. The telecommunications engineer takes these modifications into account when designing the transmission equipment. We will see how the wave modifications limit the rate at which messages can be transmitted reliably. We will first discuss the propagation in optical media and then in wires or cables.

The propagation of electromagnetic waves is described by the equations postulated in 1863 by James Clark Maxwell, an ingenious Scottish physicist and mathematician. Maxwell understood that the phenomenon of propagation is caused by the interactions of an oscillating electrical field and an oscillating magnetic field "pushing" one another through empty space or some other medium. These ideas developed from Michael Faraday's work. Faraday had shown earlier that a changing magnetic field generates an electrical field; this effect is at work in a car alternator. Maxwell argued that in an electromagnetic wave a changing magnetic field induces a changing electrical field, which in turn generates a changing magnetic field, and so on, thus causing the wave to propagate. *Light* is a familiar example of propagating electromagnetic waves. *Radio waves* are electromagnetic waves, too, but they differ from light waves by their *frequency*, which is lower by a few orders of magnitude. The frequency is the number of oscillations of the electric and magnetic fields in one second. Frequency is measured in hertz; one hertz is written as 1 Hz, and it corresponds to one full oscillation per second. Thus, the electric and magnetic fields of an electromagnetic wave with a frequency of 10^8 Hz make 10^8 oscillations per second. In the case of visible light, different frequencies are perceived by the eyes and the brain as different colors. The *propagation speed* of an electromagnetic wave in a vacuum or in air is approximately equal to $c := 3 \times 10^8$ meters per second. Thus, light from the moon, which is about 400,000 km from Earth, reaches us in slightly more than one second.

To fix ideas, let us indicate that FM radio stations transmit electromagnetic waves with frequencies from 88 MHz (1 MHz = 10^6 Hz) to 110 MHz and TV stations from 30 MHz to 300 MHz. Satellites transmit microwaves (above 1,000 MHz). Visible light covers the frequencies from 4×10^{14} Hz (red light) to 7×10^{14} Hz (blue light). An electromagnetic wave can be described by its *wavelength* instead of by its frequency. The wavelength is defined as the speed of propagation in a vacuum (*c*) divided by the frequency. For instance, the wavelength of red light is the speed of light (*c*) divided by the frequency (4×10^{14} Hz)

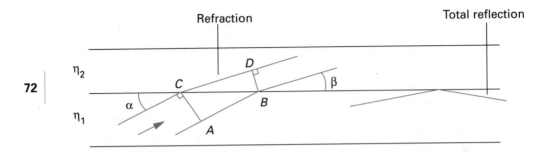

Figure 3.2 Refraction of light.

The beam of light indicated by the arrow reaches the second material, with refractive index η_2, at point C before point B. Since the propagation speed in that second material is larger than that in the first material, the direction of propagation changes. This effect is called *refraction*. The new propagation angle β is related to the former angle α by *Snell's Law* (3.1). If α is small enough, then the ray is *totally reflected* by the boundary between the two materials.

and is, therefore, equal to 0.75 μm. (1 μm = 1 micron = 10^{-6} m). Thus, the *wavelength* of visible light ranges from about 0.43 μm for blue light to 0.7 μm for red light. The wavelengths 0.8 μm, 1.3 μm, and 1.5 μm are in the *infrared range*, i.e., they correspond to frequencies less than that of red light; those are typical wavelengths in optical fiber communication systems.

Communication networks transmit information over electromagnetic waves that propagate in air, with radios, or in vacuums, with satellites. Communication networks also use transmission media that guide the propagation of electromagnetic waves, such as optical fibers and transmission lines and cables. Such transmission media are built with dielectric or nonconducting materials through which electromagnetic waves propagate. There are two differences between the propagation of electromagnetic waves in a vacuum and those in a dielectric. First, the propagation speed in a dielectric is less than in a vacuum. Second, when a wave propagates in a dielectric, some of its energy is absorbed by the material. We will see how these two effects, reduced speed and energy absorption, are taken into account in the design of guided transmission media for communication networks.

In a dielectric material, the propagation speed is less than c. In this case, the propagation speed depends on the frequency of the wave and is equal to c divided by the *refractive index* of the material, which typically depends on the frequency of the wave. We will see that the *refraction* of light is caused by the dependence of the propagation speed on the medium. To demonstrate this, consider a beam of parallel light rays that go from a material with a smaller refractive index η_1 to another with refractive index η_2 (Figure 3.2). Let α be the angle between the rays in the first material and the boundary between the two materials.

Let us calculate the angle β of the rays in the second material. The result will tell us how light is refracted. Ultimately, we will use that result to understand the propagation of light in optical fibers. In the time t that it takes for a ray to go from A to B, another ray goes from C to D. The length of AB is equal to t multiplied by the propagation speed c/η_1 in the first material, i.e., $AB = tc/\eta_1$. Similarly, $CD = tc/\eta_2$. Moreover, the figure shows that $AB = CB \times \cos\alpha$ while $CD = CB \times \cos\beta$. Rearranging these relations shows that $AB/CD = \eta_2/\eta_1 = \cos\alpha/\cos\beta$. Thus, α and β are related by the following identity:

$$\frac{\eta_2}{\eta_1} = \frac{\cos\alpha}{\cos\beta} \ . \tag{3.1}$$

Equation (3.1) is the basic law of refraction, known as *Snell's Law*. One consequence of this relationship that will be useful in our study of optical fibers is that if $\eta_2 < \eta_1$ and $\cos\alpha > \eta_2/\eta_1$, then there is no β that satisfies (3.1). Indeed, (3.1) shows that such an angle β would have to be such that $\cos\beta = (\eta_1 \cos\alpha)/\eta_2$; this is not possible since the right-hand side of the latter equality is larger than one. What happens is that light rays with $\cos\alpha > \eta_2/\eta_1$ are subject to *total reflection*: the boundary between the two materials acts as a perfect mirror for such rays. Thus, a light ray is totally reflected by a material with a lower refractive index if it is tangential enough.

Thus, the propagation speed of a wave in a dielectric material depends on the refractive index of the material. We used this dependency to explain the phenomena of refraction and total reflection. Note that, because the refractive index depends on the frequency, waves of different frequencies are refracted differently as they pass through boundaries between dielectric materials. The dependency explains rainbows and imposes limitations on transmission rate in optical fibers.

Electromagnetic Waves

- An electromagnetic wave is a stream of photons. Each photon carries some energy. This energy can be used to transport messages as the wave propagates through a transmission medium.

- As described by Maxwell's equations, electromagnetic waves propagate through space because of oscillating electrical and magnetic fields that "push" each other.

- The propagation speed is $c = 3 \times 10^8$ m/s in a vacuum. The speed is less in dielectric materials, and it depends on the frequency; the difference in speeds is the cause of refraction.

- Total reflection occurs for rays that hit material with a lower refractive index with a small angle.

Optical Fibers

So far we have looked at the transmission of electromagnetic waves in a vacuum or in a dielectric material, and we have discussed the phenomena of refraction and of total reflection. We now turn to the guided transmission of waves—the situation in pairs of electrical wires, coaxial cables, wave guides, and optical fibers. We start with the discussion of transmission through optical fibers. We will see how light waves are guided in such fibers and how the fibers influence the transmission.

The first type of optical fiber we will discuss is the *step-index* fiber. We will explain the propagation mechanism and the limitations on the transmission of messages in such fibers. A step-index optical fiber is a cylindrical *core* of glass or plastic with refractive index η_1 that is surrounded by a tube of glass or plastic, called *cladding*, with a smaller refractive index η_2. (See Figure 3.3.) Rays that hit the cladding tangentially (i.e., obliquely) enough are totally reflected into the core, as indicated in the figure; however, *not* all such rays can propagate effectively along the fiber. The reason is that the successive reflections of a ray interfere with each other and such interference may attenuate the energy carried by the wave. This phenomenon is somewhat similar to the phenomenon which makes a pipe organ vibrate only at specific frequencies. The analysis of the solutions of Maxwell's equations shows that there is only a finite set of angle values for the rays that can propagate along the fiber. The different angles of propagating rays are called *propagation modes*. Thus, a mode of propagation is a collection of light rays propagating through the optical fiber by a succession of total reflections and at a specific angle with the axis of the fiber. Notice that different propagation modes have different *axial speeds*, i.e., different speeds of propagation along the fiber.

Imagine then the following procedure for transmitting bits from one end of the fiber to the other. Short bursts of light are sent along the fiber to represent the 1 bits. The 0 bits are indicated by the absence of light. This can be accomplished by beaming a flashlight down the fiber. The flashlight is turned on for T seconds to indicate a 1, and turned off for T seconds to indicate a 0. Thus, the sequence 1011010 is transmitted by turning the flashlight on for T seconds, then off for T, on for $2 \times T$, off for T, on for T, and off for T. The light is monitored at the receiving end of the fiber in order to recover the bits. The presence of light will indicate 1, and the absence will indicate 0. The light burst that represents a 1 generally comprises rays that form different angles with the fiber axis and that propagate along different modes, at different speeds. As a consequence, the arrival times of the different rays that propagate on different modes are unequal. The staggered arrival times *spread* the burst as it propagates along the fiber. This spreading is called *modal dispersion*. The modal dispersion is illustrated in Figure 3.4(b), which shows the spreading of a burst of light as it

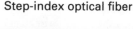

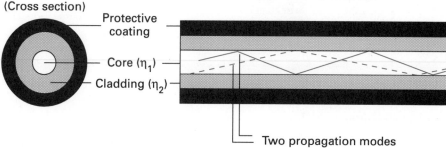

Figure 3.3 Step-index optical fiber.

A step-index optical fiber consists of a cylindrical core surrounded by a material with a smaller refractive index. The light propagates by total reflections. Different propagation modes correspond to different angles with the fiber axis. Such modes have different axial propagation speeds.

propagates along the fiber: The width of the burst increases as the light propagates. If the spreading is important enough, then the two light bursts which represent the first two 1's in the sequence 1011010 may overlap and fill the gap that represents the first 0. This overlap will make it impossible to recover the bits correctly at the end of the fiber. Thus, the effect of modal dispersion is to impose a minimum value of T, the time taken for transmitting each bit. As a consequence, modal dispersion limits the maximum bit-transmission rate. Also, since the spreading increases with the length of the fiber, it follows that the transmission rate cannot be as large for long fibers as for short ones. The analysis of the modal dispersion establishes the following limit for step-index fibers:

$$R \times L < \frac{c}{2(\eta_1 - \eta_2)} \text{ for step-index fibers.} \tag{3.2a}$$

In this expression, c is the speed of light, R is the bit rate, L is the length of the fiber, and η_1, η_2 are the refractive indices of the fiber. Typical values are $\eta_1 = 1.46$ and $\eta_2 = \eta_1(1 - 10^{-3})$. These values give $R \times L < 10$ Mbps $\times$ km.

The *rate $\times$ distance* product $R \times L$ of equation (3.2a) turns out to be a useful measure of performance of an optical communication link. Say that one wants to build a communication system that can transmit at rate R bps over a distance of L km. If the communication system is built with fibers that can transmit over l km at rate r bps, then one needs to use $R \times L / r \times l$ such fibers, as shown in Figure 3.5. In the figure, successive fiber lengths are connected through *repeaters* that regenerate the wave that carries the bit stream. This discussion shows that the *rate $\times$ distance* product is a measure we can use to compare different optical transmission links.

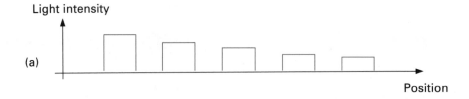

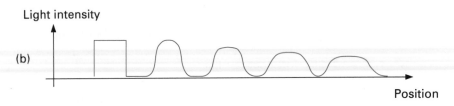

Figure 3.4 Modification of electromagnetic wave during propagation: attenuation (a) and dispersion (b).

Attenuation is the reduction of light power because of absorption and scattering. Dispersion has two causes: *modal dispersion* and *material dispersion*. Modal dispersion is due to the different propagation speeds of the various propagation modes. Material dispersion is caused by the different propagation speeds of different wavelengths.

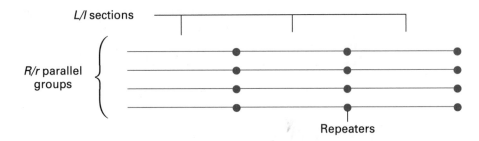

Figure 3.5 Interpretation of the *distance × rate* measure.

Transmitting at rate *R* bps over a distance of *L* km with links that can each transmit at rate *r* bps over *l* km requires $R \times L / r \times l$ such links. Thus, the number of links and associated repeaters (indicated by the colored circles) is inversely proportional to the *rate × distance* product of the links. This product is, therefore, a figure of merit which permits us to compare different links.

In addition to the step-index fibers, communication systems also use *graded-index* (GRIN) fibers. The refractive index of the core of a GRIN fiber decreases with the distance from the fiber axis. In such a fiber, the rays propagate along oscillatory paths as illustrated in Figure 3.6. The rays that travel longer

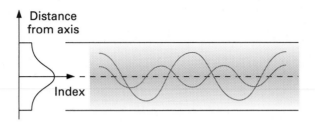

Figure 3.6 Propagation along a GRIN fiber.

The rays are continuously refracted by the changing refractive index. The longer paths, farther away from the fiber axis, travel faster than the shorter ones. This reduces the modal dispersion.

distances go through regions of the fiber where the refraction index is smaller and, therefore, where the propagation speed is larger. The propagation time of such rays is similar to that of rays which travel closer to the center of the fiber. As a consequence, the modal dispersion of GRIN fibers is substantially smaller than it is in step-index fibers. The analysis of GRIN fibers shows that (3.2a) becomes

$$R \times L < \frac{2c\eta_1}{(\eta_1 - \eta_2)^2} \text{ for GRIN fibers.} \tag{3.2b}$$

In this expression, η_1 is the refractive index at the center of the fiber and η_2 is the refractive index at the periphery of the fiber. Typical values give $R \times L < 4$ Gbps $\times$ km, i.e., 4×10^9 bps $\times$ km.

From these examples we can conclude that multiple modes limit the transmission rate in a fiber. The GRIN fibers reduce but do not eliminate the modal dispersion. Is it possible to construct a fiber having a single transmission mode? The answer is yes. If the radius of the core of a step-index fiber is small enough, then only one mode can propagate. Fibers with that property are called *single-mode fibers*. Because such fibers have no multimodal pulse spreading, they can be used with larger transmission rates.

Note, however, that all fibers—including single-mode fibers—are subject to *material dispersion*, i.e., to the spreading of a pulse because of the frequency-dependent refractive index. This spreading is due to the nonzero *spectral width* of the optical transmitters. That is, the light emitted by an optical transmitter is not of a single frequency. Instead, its energy covers some frequency band. The spectral width is defined as the size of the interval of frequencies where the power of light is at least equal to half its peak value. One can show that the material dispersion imposes a limit of the form

$$R \times L < \frac{1}{4D\sigma_\lambda} \qquad \text{(3.2c)}$$

where σ_λ is the spectral width and

$$D = \frac{d^2\eta(\lambda_0)}{d\lambda^2}$$

is the second derivative of the refractive index with respect to the wavelength, evaluated at λ_0. The value of D is 10^{-12}s/km $\times$ nm for a silica fiber at $\lambda_0 = 1.3$ μm. The value of σ_λ is about 1 nm for a GaAsP laser and about 3 nm for a laser diode. (GaAsP designates a specific semiconductor crystalline alloy.) Laser diodes and other transmitters will be discussed below. These values correspond to the limits $R \times L < 250$ Gbps $\times$ km and $R \times L < 80$ Gbps $\times$ km, respectively.

Another reason why the electromagnetic wave changes when it passes through a fiber is that it is *attenuated*. (See Figure 3.4a.) There are two main causes of attenuation: *absorption* and *scattering*. Absorption is the conversion of light into heat; it is caused by vibrations of the fiber material and of impurities, such as OH^- ions. *Scattering* is the refraction of light inside the core, due to a lack of homogeneity of the refractive index. All these effects combine into a frequency-dependent attenuation. The attenuation is measured in *decibels per kilometer* (dB/km). This attenuation specifies how the power of the wave is reduced by the propagation. The power is the energy by unit of time; it measures the rate of the photon stream. By definition, the attenuation of a fiber is equal to A dB/km if the power $P(m)$ of the light after m kilometers of fiber is related to the power $P(0)$ at the input of the fiber by the relation

$$P(m) = P(0) \times 10^{-\frac{Am}{10}}. \qquad \text{(3.3)}$$

The exponential form of (3.3) is explained by observing that if the power of the wave is multiplied by a factor $\alpha < 1$ after 1 km of propagation, then it must be multiplied by α^m after m km. Defining A by $\alpha = 10^{-A}$ yields (3.3). Equivalently,

$$10 \times \log_{10}\frac{P(0)}{P(m)} = Am. \qquad \text{(3.4)}$$

One says that the power has been reduced by Am decibels. Thus, the propagation reduces the power by A decibels per kilometer of fiber. Current fibers achieve attenuations from 0.2 dB/km to 1 dB/km. For instance, a 100-km-long fiber with an attenuation of 0.2 dB/km reduces the power by $100 \times 0.2 = 20$ decibels, which means that it divides the input power by a factor of 100 (see (3.3)).

Figure 3.4 illustrates the *attenuation* and the *dispersion* in an optical fiber. The attenuation in a low-loss all-glass fiber, as a function of the wavelength,

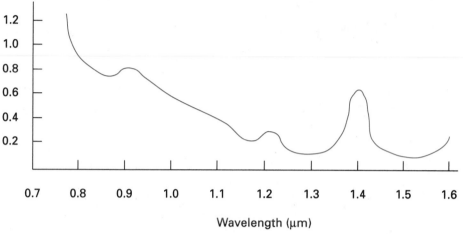

Attenuation (dB/km)

Wavelength (μm)

Figure 3.7 Attenuation in a low-loss all-glass fiber.

The attenuation caused by scattering is smaller at higher wavelengths. The absorption by SiO bonds is significant for wavelengths larger than 1.6 μm. The attenuation by OH ions is important at 0.95, 1.23, and 1.37 μm. The minimum attenuation is around 1.5 μm.

is illustrated in Figure 3.7. The attenuation due to scattering is proportional to λ^{-4}, where λ is the wavelength. It is about 0.1 dB/km at $\lambda = 1$ μm for a silica fiber. The vibrational attenuation in silica is due to oscillations of the SiO bonds. The resonant frequency of those bonds is in the infrared range. That source of attenuation becomes significant for wavelengths that exceed 1.6 μm. The vibrational loss due to OH^- ions is important at 1.37, 1.23, and 0.95 μm. The minimal attenuation in a silica fiber is about 0.15 dB/km, and it occurs at $\lambda = 1.55$ μm.

Transmission Lines

We now move from optical fibers to transmission lines, such as pairs of wires and coaxial cables. The propagation of electrical signals in wires or cables is caused by the interactions of electrical and magnetic fields in dielectric materials and in *conductors*; such propagation is again governed by Maxwell's equations. We will discuss the mechanism of propagation of the waves. Our discussion will indicate the possible distortions caused by *reflections* of the electromagnetic waves and how such distortions can be eliminated by properly *terminating* the transmission lines.

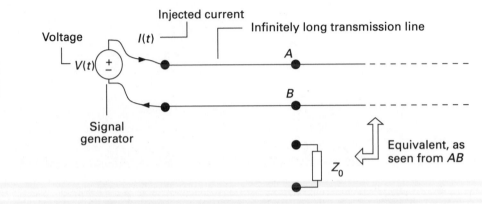

Figure 3.8 Infinite transmission line.

The voltage across an infinite transmission line is proportional to the injected current. As a consequence, such a line appears as an impedance Z_0 called the *characteristic impedance* of the line.

First, let us examine the propagation of an electrical signal in a pair of parallel wires. We assume, for simplicity, that the wires are infinitely long: they are connected to a signal generator at one end and extend forever from there on. We also assume that the conductors are perfect and that they are placed in a vacuum. (See Figure 3.8.) Maxwell's equations indicate that a changing electrical current in a short section of the wires generates a changing magnetic field orthogonal to the wires. In turn, this changing magnetic field generates a changing electrical field parallel to the wires; this field induces a current in the wires. This interaction of electrical and magnetic fields results in the propagation of the electromagnetic wave with a speed of about 3×10^8 m/s. It is a consequence of Maxwell's equations that, for our infinite line, the voltage $V(t)$ across the conductors at time t is proportional to the current $I(t)$ injected by the generator at time t into the conductors. That is, $V(t) = Z_0 I(t)$. The parameter Z_0 is called the *characteristic impedance* of the transmission line; its value depends on the geometry of the line, i.e., on the diameters of the conductors and their distances. As a consequence, a resistor with value Z_0 placed at the end of a transmission line preserves the relationship between the current and the voltage that would exist if the line were infinitely long. Thus, the resistor looks like an infinite continuation of the transmission line. It follows that if one *terminates* a transmission line with a resistor Z_0, then no energy transmitted on the line can be *reflected* by the terminating resistor. Indeed, if the line had been infinite, then the energy would have propagated forever down the line. This property has a practical application in avoiding signal distortions.

Similar observations also hold for a nonidealized transmission line, even though its conductors are not perfect and they are not surrounded by a

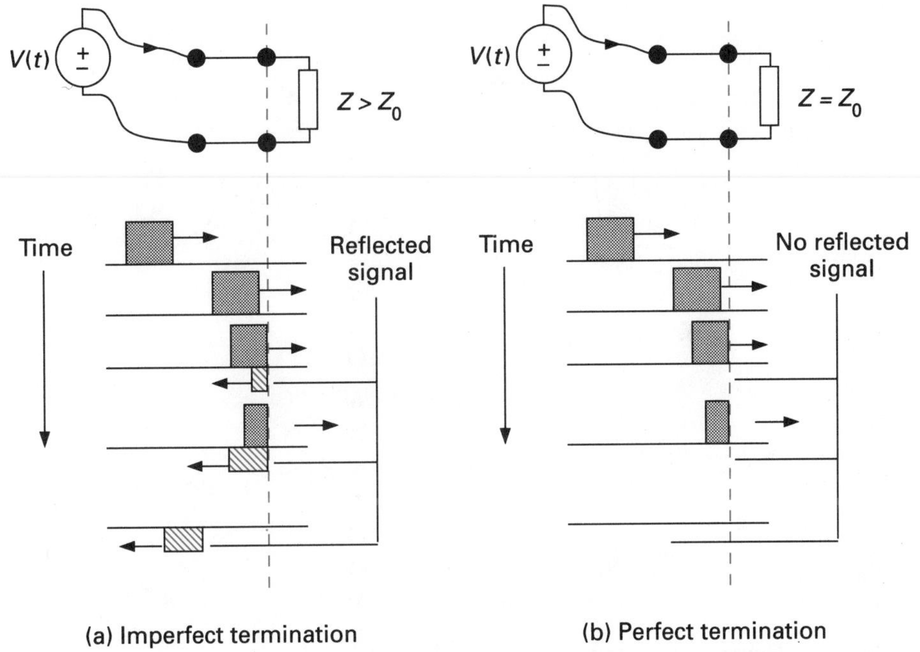

(a) Imperfect termination   (b) Perfect termination

Figure 3.9 Terminating a transmission line.

Signals are reflected by the imperfect termination of a transmission line, as shown in (a); they are completely absorbed by a perfect termination (b).

vacuum. Such a transmission line has a characteristic impedance Z_0, and reflections cannot occur if one terminates the line with a resistor Z_0. One then says that the line is *properly terminated*. If a transmission line is not properly terminated, then the electromagnetic waves that reach the end of the line are *reflected*, at least partially. Such reflections get superimposed on the original waves, leading to undesirable signal distortions. These effects are shown in Figure 3.9. The propagation speed in a nonideal transmission line depends slightly on the frequency of the wave. As in optical fibers, the dependence of the speed on the frequency leads to dispersion which spreads signals and reduces the maximum transmission rate.

A transmission line commonly used in communication networks is the *coaxial cable*. A coaxial cable (see Figure 3.10) consists of one conductor surrounded by a cylindrical conductor called the *shield*; the two conductors are separated by some dielectric material. The advantage of a coaxial cable over a pair of wires is that it generates very little electromagnetic field outside its shield. Similarly, almost no current is induced in a coaxial cable by an external electromagnetic field. This reduces the *interference* between the cable and the environment. Interference is created when the cable radiates an electromagnetic field which is

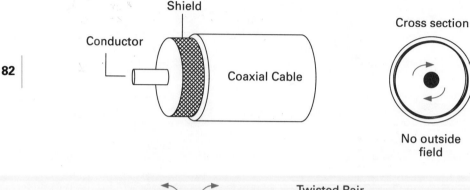

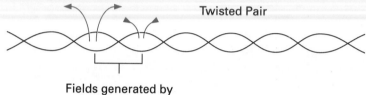

Figure 3.10 Coaxial cable and twisted pair.

Because of its axial symmetry, a coaxial cable generates a negligible external electromagnetic field. Conversely, an external field induces a negligible current in the cable. A twisted pair has similar properties because of the cancellations of fields generated in successive loops.

picked up by another electrical device, or when another device exerts an electromagnetic field on the cable. A pair of wires can be made less sensitive to interference by twisting. A *twisted pair* (Figure 3.10) has the property that the effects of an external electromagnetic field on consecutive loops almost cancel one another. Similarly, the electrical and magnetic fields generated by consecutive loops of a twisted pair almost cancel one another.

An electromagnetic wave is *attenuated* when it propagates in a pair of wires or in a coaxial cable. The attenuation depends on the frequency. The attenuation in two common cables and twisted pairs is illustrated in Figure 3.11. For comparison, we also indicated the attenuation of optical fibers in the same figure. You will notice that the attenuation is much smaller over a much wider range of frequencies in a fiber than in a coaxial cable. The characteristic impedance of a pair of wires is typically a few hundred ohms, whereas that of a coaxial cable ranges from 40 to 100 ohms.

Let us pause to summarize what we have learned about the propagation of guided electromagnetic waves.

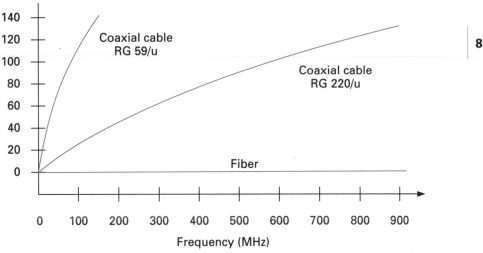

Figure 3.11 Attenuation in coaxial cables and fibers.

This figure shows the superiority of optical fibers at high frequencies: Their attenuation is much smaller than that of coaxial cables.

Guided Electromagnetic Waves

- Light propagates in a step-index optical fiber through total reflections.

- Only a finite set of modes can propagate along a fiber. If the radius of the fiber core is small enough, then only one mode can propagate: Such fibers are called *single-mode fibers*.

- Propagation in fibers is subject to *multimode pulse spreading, attenuation* because of *absorption* and *scattering*, and *dispersion*. These effects limit the transmission rate and the usable length of a fiber.

- Pairs of wires and coaxial cables are examples of *transmission lines*; they guide electromagnetic waves through interactions between electrical and magnetic fields in a dielectric and in conductors.

- Propagation in a transmission line is subject to attenuation and to delay. These effects depend on the wave frequency; they limit the transmission rate.

We are now somewhat familiar with the propagation of electromagnetic waves. Our next objective is to understand how electromagnetic waves can be used to transport *bits*. The key step is to encode the bits into waves. In the next section we will discuss the optical transmission of bits. Section 3.3 will then explore the transmission systems that use transmission lines and radio waves.

3.2 Optical Bit Transmission

In this section we look at the steps needed to translate a bit stream into a light wave that carries the bit stream along an optical fiber and to translate the light wave back into bits so that the receiving computer equipment can process the information. We have learned that light waves propagate and carry energy, but we must convert bits to waves and waves to bits to transmit information. In this section we build on our knowledge of wave propagation by adding the translation processes at the transmitter and at the receiver. Looking at Figure 3.12, which is a refinement of Figure 3.1, you can see that the following steps are required for the optical transmission of bits:

1. An *optical transmitter* converts the bit stream into light.
2. The light propagates along a fiber.
3. The light is converted into electrical signals by an *optical receiver*, and the signals are converted back into bits.

Our focus in this section is on steps 1 and 3. In addition, we describe how optical links can be designed to minimize the effects of corruptions of the transmitted signal when it arrives at the receiver. We have three main topics in this section: transmitters, receivers, and the power budget calculation. The power budget calculation determines the required transmitter power and receiver sensitivity for transmitting bits at a given rate over a given fiber. We start with the discussion of optical transmitters.

Optical Transmitters

A typical method for transmitting a sequence of bits over an optical fiber is to convert the 1s in the sequence of bits into short bursts of light wavelength and to indicate the 0s by the absence of light. An *optical transmitter* transforms an electrical signal into light. To transmit the bit sequence 1010011, one applies an electrical signal which is "on" for T seconds, then "off" for T seconds, "on" for T, "off" for $2 \times T$, and "on" for $2 \times T$. As we saw in Section 3.1, to produce a signal that crosses the optical fiber without excessive dispersion, the

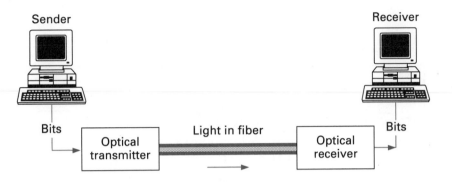

Figure 3.12 A fiber optic communication system.

An optical link transmits bits between two computers by converting them into optical signals that propagate over an optical fiber.

optical transmitter must generate electromagnetic waves with a similar wavelength. Also, the transmitter must turn on and off as soon as the applied electrical signal does. Thus, a transmitter is characterized by the range of emitted wavelengths and by the rapidity with which it turns on and off. As we saw in (3.2c), to convert an electrical signal to a light wave that can travel over a long fiber without substantial dispersion, it is desirable to select a transmitter with a small spectral width. *Laser diodes* (LDs) are such transmitters. When the application does not require high transmission rates or long distances, one can use less expensive optical transmitters which have a wider spectral width. *Light-emitting diodes* (LEDs) are used in such applications. Let us take a brief look at the way LEDs and LDs operate.

An LED is a *PN-semiconductor-junction*. (See Figure 3.13.) Such a junction consists of a piece of semiconductor crystal with two sections that have been *doped* positively and negatively, respectively. Let us explain the properties of those semiconductor sections: One way to understand the structure of that semiconductor is to view it as a crystal of atoms whose four outermost electrons, called valence electrons, bond to other atoms in the crystal. The semiconductor is doped negatively by introducing a number of atoms of a *doping material* with five valence electrons into the semiconductor crystal (see Figure 3.13). Four of the five valence electrons of an isolated atom of doping material in the semiconductor crystal are bound to electrons of four other atoms of the crystal. The fifth valence electron is then easily freed from its atom by thermal agitation or when the electron is "hit" by an energetic photon. One says that a negatively doped semiconductor has many free electrons. A semiconductor is doped positively by introducing atoms of a doping material with three valence electrons into the semiconductor crystal. The three valence electrons of a doping atom are bound to electrons of three of the four neighboring atoms in the semiconductor crystal. An

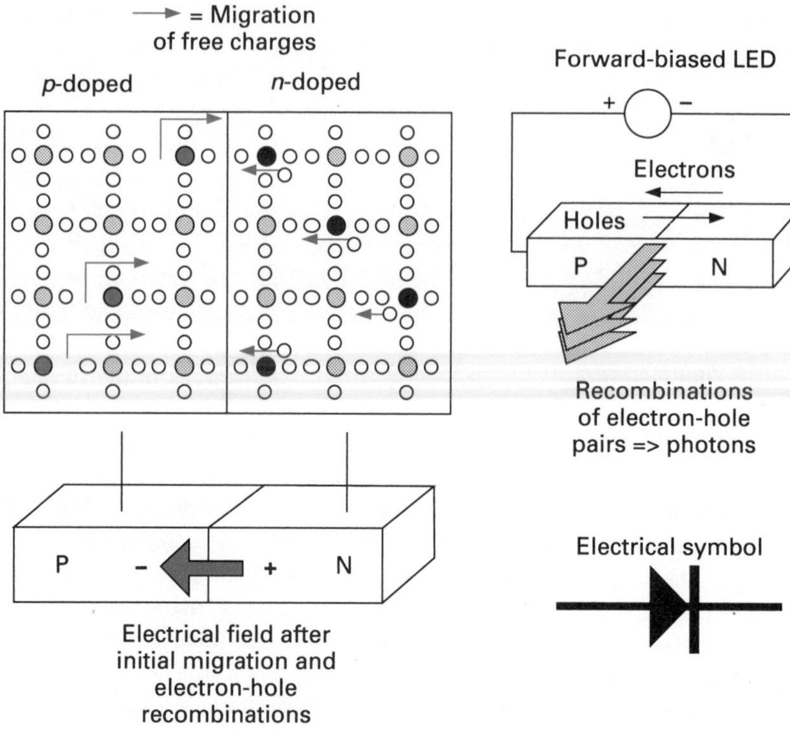

Figure 3.13 A light-emitting diode.

A light-emitting diode is a PN-junction, i.e., a semiconductor crystal with a *p*-doped section adjacent to an *n*-doped section. The *p*-doped section has a surplus of free holes due to the doping atoms that have one fewer valence electron than the semiconductor atoms. Conversely, the *n*-doped section has a surplus of free electrons. Those over-abundant free charges migrate to the other section, thereby creating a potential barrier at the junction. This potential barrier prevents further natural charge migrations. By applying a forward bias to the diode, the potential barrier is compensated and charges can move across the junction. The forced migration induces electron-hole recombinations that lower the energy of electrons. The lost energy is emitted as photons.

electron is missing to complete the four-way connections in the crystal; this missing electron is called a *hole*. An electron and a hole are said to *recombine* when the electron becomes bound to an unattached valence electron of a semiconductor atom, thereby filling up the hole. In a positively doped semiconductor, an electron that recombines with a hole leaves a new hole in the space that the electron occupied before recombining. Thus, one can consider that the hole moved in the positively doped semiconductor. To reflect such possible motion of holes, one says that a positively doped semiconductor has a number of free holes.

The PN-junction of Figure 3.13 is a semiconductor crystal with one positively doped region adjacent to a negatively doped region. There are many free electrons in the negatively doped region, and very few in the positively doped region. To compensate for this lack of equilibrium, the free electrons migrate to the *p*-region, where they recombine with holes; similarly, holes migrate from the *p*-region to the *n*-region, where they recombine with electrons. As this migration is taking place, an electrical field builds up at the junction: the *p*-region which was electrically neutral is collecting an excess of electrons and is building up a negative electrical charge; similarly, the *n*-region builds up a positive charge. Eventually, the electrical field that results from these charges in the two regions stops the migration process of electrons and holes. When this equilibrium is reached, the positively doped region is charged negatively and the negatively doped region is charged positively.

Further electron-hole recombinations can be induced in the junction by applying an external voltage so that the free electrons are driven from the *n*-region (the negatively doped region) to the *p*-region (the positively doped region), and the free holes are driven from the *p*-region to the *n*-region. Since the electrons are negatively charged, this will happen if one applies a positive voltage difference between the *p*-region and the *n*-region. The junction is said to be *forward-biased* when such an external potential difference is applied. An electron-hole recombination causes a drop in the energy of the recombining electron. This lost energy is emitted as a photon. The frequency of the photon is determined by this energy loss; it is characteristic of the junction materials. Thus, the recombination of an electron-hole pair, which occurs when the electron is brought in proximity to the hole, causes the emission of a photon. This emission is said to be *spontaneous* because it was not induced by another photon. Hence, the LED is a spontaneous emission device.

When an LED is connected to a *constant* current source (Figure 3.13), it produces a light beam with an intensity proportional to the current: a fixed fraction of the injected electrons induce electron-hole recombinations. Typical LEDs generate a few mW (1 mW = 10^{-3} watt) of optical power when about 50 mA (1 mA = 10^{-3} ampere) are injected. If the injected current changes rapidly, then the optical power emitted by the diode drops with the rate of change. Physically, the electron-hole pairs take some time to recombine and they cannot do so efficiently if the current changes too fast. This effect limits the frequency at which one can *modulate*, i.e., modify, the intensity of the light beam. This frequency limit is indicated by the *cutoff* frequency at which the power is reduced to 70%. Typical values of the cutoff frequency of LEDs range from 1 kHz to 100 MHz.

LEDs can be used for transmitting strings of bits or *analog* signals as light waves. An analog signal is one that takes a continuous set of possible values.

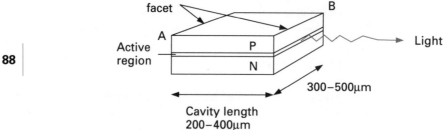

Figure 3.14 Laser diode.

A laser diode is a PN-junction in an optical cavity. Because of stimulated emissions and interference, the cavity favors light with a wavelength equal to multiples of twice the cavity length. As a result, the laser diode emits coherent light.

For instance, the signal that comes out of a microphone is analog. LEDs are used in consumer electronic devices ranging from remote controls to wireless headphones; in those applications, the LEDs emit infrared light. Infrared LEDs are also used in local area communication networks. LEDs that emit visible lights are also used as inexpensive and long lasting indicators.

Laser diodes combine the spontaneous emission of a forward-biased LED with the lasing effect. A simple LD is sketched in Figure 3.14. Essentially, an LD is a PN-junction in an optical cavity. That is, the junction is terminated by two parallel semi-reflecting faces A and B; the distance between the faces is some multiple of half a wavelength that can be generated by electron-hole recombinations. The junction is forward biased and emits photons. Some photons "hit" free electrons that then recombine and emit coherent photons, by *stimulated* emission. That is, when an incident photon leads an electron to lose an amount of energy equal to that of the photon, then a second photon is emitted with the same frequency and phase as the first photon. These stimulated emissions form a chain reaction. Some of the emitted light waves are attenuated by out-of-phase interference with reflections from the faces A and B. That is, the interference with the reflections acts as a filter which attenuates light waves unless they have a specific phase and wavelength. The chain reaction is self-sustaining if the gain due to stimulated emissions is larger than the loss due to the imperfect reflections (and to absorption). This self-sustaining reaction occurs when there are sufficiently many electron-hole pairs in the junction and, therefore, when the forward bias is sufficient.

Typical LD dimensions are indicated in Figure 3.14. The cutoff frequency of an LD is a few orders of magnitude larger than that of an LED. Some LDs can be modulated at up to 11 Gbps (1 Gbps = 10^9 bits per second). LDs are temperature sensitive. The optical power for a given value of the injected current depends significantly on the temperature because heat increases the generation of free electrons and free holes. This dependency can be controlled with sophisticated circuitry that monitors the LD temperature and adjusts the injected current correspondingly. LDs are used in compact disc players and in long distance optical communication systems.

Optical Transmitters

- An *optical transmitter* converts an electrical signal into an intensity-modulated optical beam.

- An LED is a spontaneous emission device. It generates photons when electron-hole pairs recombine in a forward-biased PN-junction.

- The power of the optical output of an LED is proportional to the injected current. For a given value of the injected current, the optical output power decreases with the modulation frequency.

- The maximum modulation frequency of LEDs ranges from 1 kHz to 100 MHz.

- An LD emits a narrow power spectrum when the injected current is sufficient. It is a PN-junction in an optical cavity which is made to *lase*.

- The maximum modulation frequency of some LDs exceeds 11 GHz.

Optical Receivers

Light emitted from the transmitter propagates along the optical fiber and reaches a *photodetector*. At this point, light must be converted back into bits. The photodetector performs this function by converting the photons of the light wave into an electrical signal that codes 0s and 1s. We now look at the way this conversion is done by three types of photodetectors: the PN-photodiode, the PIN-diode, and the avalanche photodiode (APD).

A *PN-photodiode* is a reverse-biased PN-junction, as shown in Figure 3.15. The reverse bias increases the electrical field in the junction and prevents charges from moving across it. When the junction is illuminated, the photons can be absorbed by electrons in the p-region close to the junction; these electrons can then become free, provided that the energy of the photons is adequate. The freed electrons are pushed across the junction by the large electrical field, and they

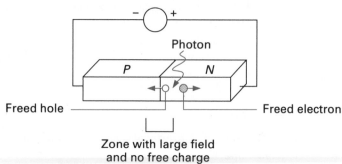

Reverse-biased PN-junction

Figure 3.15 PN-photodiode.

The potential barrier across a PN-junction is increased by applying a reverse bias. Electrons and holes that are freed by incident photons inside the junction are pushed across it by the large electrical field and contribute an external current proportional to the intensity of the received light.

have a good chance of making it through the device and, therefore, of contributing an external current. Thus, a PN-photodiode acts as a light-dependent current source.

The rate at which bits can be detected by the PN-photodiode is determined by how fast the photodiode can follow variations in the intensity of the light. The current produced by the photodiode does not change as soon as the light intensity is modified. It turns out that a PN-photodiode is rather slow at translating variations in light intensity into variations in current. The delay between these variations is called the *response time* of the photodetector. The physical reason for this slow response is that a good fraction of the photons are absorbed away from the immediate neighborhood of the junction; such photons free charges in a region where the electrical field is small; as a consequence, those freed charges move slowly and it takes them a rather long time to make it across the device. A typical response time is a few μs (1 μs = 1 microsecond = 10^{-6} second). The slow response limits the usefulness of PN-photodiodes to rather slow applications and precludes their utilization in high-speed digital transmission systems.

The second type of optical receiver is the *PIN-diode*, the most commonly used photodetector in communication networks. A simple PIN-diode is illustrated in Figure 3.16. The PIN-diode has three layers which are, respectively, p-doped, intrinsic (i.e., not doped), and n-doped, hence the name PIN. The intrinsic layer is large; since it is not doped, its resistivity is high. The operating principles of a PIN-diode are similar to those of a PN-photodiode: the diode is reverse-biased so that there is a large electrical field across the intrinsic region; when photons are absorbed in the intrinsic region, they free charges that race across the device. The key difference with the PN-photodiode is that most of the photons are absorbed in a region where the electrical field is large. As a consequence, the translation of a variation in the light intensity into a variation of the produced electrical signal is much faster for a PIN-diode than for a PN-photodiode. A typical response time of a PIN-diode is 1 ns (1 ns = one nanosecond = 10^{-9} second). Faster PIN-diodes are also available.

The third type of optical detector is the *avalanche photodiode* (APD). An APD is a PIN-diode with a very large junction electrical field. The idea is roughly that the reverse bias of the diode is so large that freed charges race through the diode so fast that they free additional charges through "impacts." This results in an avalanche effect that makes the APD much more sensitive than a PIN-diode: a single photon may, through the avalanche effect, free as many as 100 charges.

Before continuing our discussion of the communication system, let us review what we have learned about optical receivers.

Optical Receivers

- A *PN-photodiode* is a reverse-biased PN-junction. Electron-hole pairs that are freed by photons induce current across the diode. The response of a PN-photodiode is slow (μs) because many charges are freed in a region with a small electrical field.

- A *PIN-diode* has a large intrinsic region between a *p*-region and an *n*-region; it is reverse-biased. Most of the charges are freed in the *i*-region, where the electrical field is large. PINs have a fast response (ns).

- An *avalanche photodiode* (APD) is essentially a PIN-diode with a large reverse bias. Freed charges are so fast that they generate additional free charges.

Reviewing what we have learned so far in this section, we know how light waves propagate in an optical fiber, how a transmitter converts electrical signals into light, and how a photodetector converts light into electrical signals. We have seen that a propagating wave is subject to attenuation and to dispersion that alter the received signal. We now turn to the *power budget* calculations. The question is how much power must be transmitted so that enough reaches the photodetector. The answer to this question will be used to select the components of the optical communication link.

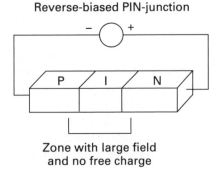

Reverse-biased PIN-junction

Zone with large field
and no free charge

Figure 3.16 PIN-diode.

The PIN-junction has a large section with an important electrical field. As
a consequence, the incident light frees many charges in a region where
the field is large enough to push the charges across the junction.

We will assume that a 1 is sent by turning the transmitter on for T
seconds and that a 0 is sent by turning the transmitter off for T seconds. This
method for transmitting bits is called *on-off keying* (OOK), and it is used by most
optical links. We will determine how much energy per bit must be received by the
photodetector to distinguish the 0s and the 1s. From this information we will
determine how much energy must be sent by the transmitter by calculating the
fraction of energy lost because of the attenuation during the propagation along the
fiber. The effect of dispersion will also be taken into account. We will use an
example to explain how this calculation can be performed.

Consider the communication link in Figure 3.17. The link uses an LD
and a PIN-diode. The characteristics of the LD and of the PIN-diode are indicated
in the figure. A bit 1 corresponds to a current of 100 mA being injected into the
LD. When 1s are not sent, the current through the LD is 75 mA. The latter value
is the current threshold of the LD. The characteristics show that a bit 1 corresponds to a beam intensity equal to 3 mW, while the intensity during 0s is about
0.5 mW. We will assume that the connector between the LD and the fiber introduces a loss of 1.5 dB at the transmitter end and that the connector between the
fiber and the PIN-diode introduces a loss of 1.5 dB at the receiver end. The fiber
has five sections of 10 km each. The fiber has a loss of 0.5 dB/km, and each of
the four splices between sections introduces an additional loss of 0.2 dB. Thus,
the total power loss between the LD and the PIN-diode is equal to

$$1.5 + (50 \times 0.5) + (4 \times 0.2) + 1.5 = 28.8 \text{ dB}.$$

We assume that the PIN-diode has a *dark current* equal to 2 nA $= 2 \times 10^{-9}$A. The
dark current is defined as the current through the reverse-biased diode when it is

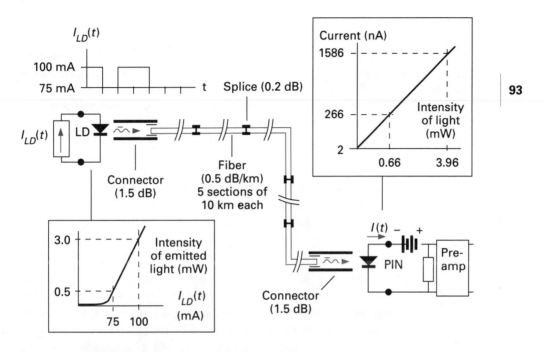

Figure 3.17 An optical communication link.

The bits are converted into a variable current $I_{LD}(t)$. The current drives a laser diode which emits light with a varying intensity. The light propagates along 50 km of fiber divided into five sections. A PIN-diode converts the light into a variable current which is amplified by a preamplifier.

not illuminated. Moreover, the *diode sensitivity* is equal to 0.4 A/W. This means that if the light that illuminates the PIN-diode has an intensity of x watts, then the current through the diode is equal to $0.4 \times x$ amperes (plus the dark current). Let us calculate the current through the PIN-diode when a 0 is sent. In that case, the light power at the transmitter is 0.5 mW. The power that reaches the PIN diode is 28.8 dB less than 0.5 mW. It is, therefore, equal to (see (3.3))

$$0.5 \times 10^{-3} \times \{(10^{-\frac{28.8}{10}})\} = 6.6 \times 10^{-7} \text{W}.$$

The current through the PIN-diode is then equal to

$$2 \times 10^{-9} + 0.4 \times 6.6 \times 10^{-7} \approx 2.66 \times 10^{-7} \text{A}.$$

Similarly, when a 1 is sent, the current through the diode is equal to

$$2 \times 10^{-9} + 0.4 \times 39.6 \times 10^{-7} \approx 15.86 \times 10^{-7} \text{A}.$$

Our results seem to show that the PIN-diode should have no problem in distinguishing 1s from the absence of 1s: the current through the PIN-diode is six times larger for a 1 than for a 0. However, there is one issue that we have neglected so far: the effect of *noise*. How likely is it that the useful signal will be swamped by noise? We address that question next.

There are two major sources of noise in optical communication systems: *thermal noise* from the agitation of electrons which induces a randomly varying current through resistors, and *shot noise* from the discrete electrons generating some ripple current in the receiver circuitry. The noise induces *bit errors* because the receiver mistakes noise power as coming from the signal. The *bit error rate* (BER) is defined as the probability that a bit is incorrectly detected by the receiver, i.e., that a transmitted 0 is detected as a 1, or a 1 is detected as a 0. Communication links are usually designed so that

$$\text{BER} \leq 10^{-9}, \tag{3.5}$$

i.e., so that fewer than one bit out of 10^9 is incorrectly detected, on average. The BER can be analyzed as follows. Let X_0 be the energy received by the photodetector during one bit-transmission interval when the light wave that represents a 0 is received, and let X_1 be the energy received by the photodetector when the signal that represents a 1 is received. The values X_0 and X_1 are random, because of the noise. Say that the power transmitted when a 1 is sent is larger than when a 0 is sent. One then expects X_1 to be larger than X_0. Figure 3.18 indicates the probability densities of the random variables X_0 and X_1. That is, the total area below the curve marked X_1 and to the left of some value x is equal to the probability that X_1 is less than x. The receiver detects 0s and 1s by comparing the amount of energy received to some *threshold* value A. The receiver decides that a 0 was received if the energy is less than A and that a 1 was received otherwise. As Figure 3.18 indicates, there is a positive probability that the received energy is less than A when a 1 is received and that it is larger than A when a 0 is received. Those two cases result in detection errors. For the BER to be less than 10^{-9}, it is necessary that the two curves for X_0 and X_1 be sufficiently far apart, i.e., that the mean values $\overline{X}_0$ and $\overline{X}_1$ be sufficiently different, which requires that the power of the received signal be large compared to the noise level.

In practice, an optical receiver is characterized by its *sensitivity*, which is defined as the optical power it requires at the given bit rate so that BER $\leq 10^{-9}$. The sensitivity is measured in *dBm* (decibels relative to one milliwatt). The receiver sensitivity depends on the bit rate. By definition, the sensitivity of a receiver is $-\sigma$ dBm if the BER is less than 10^{-9} whenever the received optical power P_R is such that

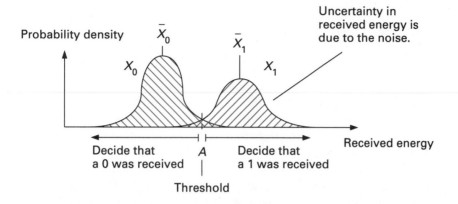

Figure 3.18 Distribution of measured values.

The quantity of energy received during a bit time is uncertain because the light diode generates photons at random times and also because of unpredictable effects during the propagation and reception of the signal. This uncertainty is summarized by a probability density that depends on whether a 0 or a 1 was transmitted.

$$10 \log_{10} \frac{P_R}{10^{-3} \text{ W}} \geq -\sigma. \tag{3.6}$$

The above inequality means that the received power is not more than σ dB below 1 milliwatt.

Power Budget

The receiver sensitivity is the basis for the calculation of the *power budget* of an optical communication link. Let us explain the procedure in one example. Consider the communication link in Figure 3.17. The average transmitted power is equal to

$$\frac{1}{2} \times 0.5 \text{ mW} + \frac{1}{2} \times 3 \text{ mW} = 1.75 \text{ mW}$$

where it is assumed that the 1s and the 0s are equally likely. This power corresponds to

$$10 \times \log \frac{1.75 \text{ mW}}{1 \text{ mW}} \approx 2.4 \text{ dBm}.$$

From our earlier calculation, we know that the transmission loss is equal to 28.8 dB. As a consequence, the received power is equal to

$$2.4 \text{ dBm} - 28.8 \text{ dB} = -26.4 \text{ dBm.}$$

Let us assume that the transmission rate is 100 Mbps and that the receiver sensitivity at that rate is equal to −40 dBm. The received power is 13.6 dB larger than required, so the BER should be less than 10^{-9}.

It should be noted that the received power should be larger than the receiver sensitivity to account for some additional receiver performance degradation due to *intersymbol interference* and to *jitter*. Intersymbol interference is the pulse-spreading phenomenon that we discussed previously. Its effect is to reduce the power separation between received 1s and 0s. Jitter is the timing fluctuations from an imperfect recovery of the clock at the receiver. Its effect is similar to that of symbol interference. The effect of intersymbol interference and jitter on the bit error rate is equivalent to a loss of received power of a few dB. In our example, the 13.6-dB excess power should be enough to compensate for the loss due to jitter and to intersymbol interference.

As we have seen, the power budget calculation can determine whether the selected transmitter, fiber, and receiver will result in a communication link with a BER less than 10^{-9}. If that is not the case, then the designer must choose a more powerful transmitter, a more sensitive receiver, or a fiber with a smaller attenuation, or he or she must reduce the length of the fiber by placing a *repeater* along the transmission link. A repeater is a combination of a receiver and a transmitter; the receiver converts the light wave into bits, which are then retransmitted by the transmitter.

Power Budget

- The received signal is *noisy*. There are two main sources of noise: thermal noise and shot noise.

- Because of the noise, enough power must be received by the photodetector to distinguish 1s and 0s.

- The *receiver sensitivity* specifies the received power required so that the bit error rate does not exceed 10^{-9}.

- The power budget is the calculation of the power received by the photodetector. The calculation subtracts the power loss during transmission expressed in dB from the transmitted power expressed in dBm. The difference is the received power in dBm, and it is compared with the receiver sensitivity.

- Intersymbol interference and jitter introduce an additional signal degradation equivalent to a loss in the received power of a few dB.

In addition to optical links, many communication networks use transmission lines or radio waves from transmitters to receivers. We discuss those transmission systems in the next section.

3.3 Transmitting Bits with Radio or Transmission Lines

Communications over transmission lines and using radio waves transmit electromagnetic waves at much lower frequencies than optical links. A light wave is an electromagnetic wave with a frequency around 10^{14} Hz. We saw that such a wave is emitted by injecting current into an LED or an LD. By modifying the intensity of the current injected in the optical transmitter, one controls the intensity, or power, of the emitted light wave. This power is proportional to the average rate of the photon stream produced by the transmitter. The power of the light wave is also proportional to the square of the amplitude of the electromagnetic field. Thus, an optical transmitter varies the amplitude of the light wave. In our discussion, we assumed that the transmitter used on-off keying (OOK), i.e., that it turned the wave on to represent 1s and off to represent 0s. The electromagnetic waves transmitted over transmission lines or through space range in frequencies from a few hundred hertz to a few billion hertz. The transmitter of such waves can modify not only their amplitude, as for light waves, but also their frequency and their phase. Such modifications are used to encode signals to be transmitted, and they are called *modulation schemes*. Thus, OOK is a modulation scheme, but many other modulation schemes are possible. We will discuss modulation schemes used for transmitting bits over transmission lines and radio waves. The modulation scheme must be selected so that the wave can be converted back into bits at the receiver, even after the wave has been distorted during its propagation. The selection of the modulation scheme depends on the specific distortion introduced by the transmission.

We first take a look at the distortion of the wave when it propagates over a transmission line. We do this by selecting a modulation scheme and by calculating the output of the transmission line. Consider the system shown in Figure 3.19. As a specific example we have illustrated a communication link that uses a twisted pair of wires. We want to understand how bits can be sent from the transmitter to the receiver over the wire pair. A simple strategy is to apply a voltage between points A and B (see figure) that depends on which bit (0 or 1) is to be transmitted. For instance, say that 5 v are applied when a 1 is transmitted and 0 v are applied when a 0 is transmitted. If the transmission rate is equal to R bps, then the voltage can be applied during R^{-1} second for each bit. This form of transmission is called *unipolar modulation*.

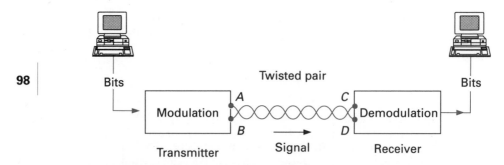

Figure 3.19 Communication link.

The bits are first converted into electrical signals by a transmitter. These signals propagate over a transmission line and are converted back into bits by a receiver.

Ideally, the received signal is identical to the transmitted signal. In that case, the receiver can easily recover the bits from the signal: the receiver knows that a 1 was transmitted when it measures 5 v and that a 0 was transmitted when it measures 0 v. This ideal case is observed when the transmission line is very short and when the transmission rate R is not too large. For long lines or fast transmissions, the received signal differs substantially from the transmitted signal. By using an oscilloscope between points C and D (see Figure 3.19), one finds that the received signal is as indicated in Figure 3.20. As the figure shows, the transmission *distorts* the signal. This distortion is a consequence of the *pulse-spreading* phenomenon that we discussed in Section 3.1. We would like to be able to predict the shape of the received signal. That information can be used to decide how long the line can be and at what rate one can transmit bits. Moreover, the knowledge of how the signals are distorted during transmission can be used to design modulation schemes that allow faster transmissions over longer lines.

The distortion of the pulses in Figure 3.19 is caused by the different propagation speeds of different frequencies. A pulse can be viewed as a sum of sine waves where each sine wave propagates at a slightly different speed. A systematic method for predicting the distortion of signals is *Fourier analysis*. Using Fourier analysis, the telecommunications engineer can predict how any transmitted signal will be received. We will apply Fourier analysis to unipolar transmission. It can be applied to any modulation scheme.

The basic elements of Fourier analysis are important to understand because of its significance in telecommunications. We will need some terminology. A *signal* is a function of time which specifies how a voltage (or a current) changes as time evolves. We will discuss specific signals known as sine waves and square waves. The terms *sine wave* and *square wave* refer to precise definitions of signals. The term *wave* in these definitions should not be confused with

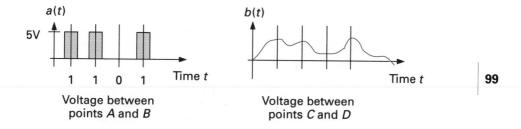

Figure 3.20 Transmitted and received signals.
The signal is distorted by the transmission line.

its use in electromagnetic wave. By definition, a *sine wave* is a signal $s(t)$ of the form (t denotes time)

$$s(t) = A \sin 2\pi ft + \theta, \quad -\infty < t < +\infty. \tag{3.7}$$

The value A is called the *amplitude* of the sine wave, θ is its *phase*, and f its *frequency*.

Fourier analysis is based on two observations: (1) essentially any signal can be written as a sum of sine waves; and (2) transmission lines do not distort sine waves; they only delay and attenuate them. The second observation, therefore, means that if the input voltage of a transmission line is the signal $s(t)$ in (3.7), then the output voltage is another signal of the form (3.7) but generally with different parameters A and θ. It is surprisingly easy to prove this remarkable result. The derivation is based on two properties of transmission lines: *linearity* and *time-invariance*. Linearity means that adding inputs yields the sum of the outputs. Time-invariance means that if one delays the input by τ seconds, then the output is simply delayed by the same amount of time. Physically, linearity means that the various inputs do not interact and time-invariance is a property of systems with characteristics that do not change in time. Let us assume for the time being that the input can be a complex-valued function of time. We will calculate the output $b(t)$ of the transmission line when the input is the function

$$a(t) = e^{st}$$

where s is an arbitrary complex number. The function $a(t)$ is called a *complex exponential*. Observe that

$$a(t - \tau) = e^{s(t-\tau)} = e^{st}e^{-s\tau} = a(t)e^{-s\tau}. \tag{3.8}$$

(We used the fact that the exponential of a sum is the product of the exponentials.)

Now, if the input is $a(t - \tau)$, then the output must be $b(t - \tau)$, by time-invariance. However, because of (3.8), we know that $a(t - \tau)$ is equal to a multiple of $a(t)$. As a consequence, by linearity, the output $b(t - \tau)$ must also be the same multiple of $b(t)$. Hence,

$$b(t - \tau) = b(t) \times e^{-s\tau}.$$

The parameter τ in the above equation is arbitrary. Let us choose $\tau = t$. This gives

$$b(0) = b(t) \times e^{-st},$$

so that

$$b(t) = b(0) \times e^{st}.$$

The value $b(0)$ is the output at time 0 when the input is the complex exponential e^{st}. In general, $b(0)$ is a complex number which depends on s. Let us write $b(0)$ as $H(s)$ to recall the dependence on s. We have shown that the output of the transmission line, when the input is the complex exponential e^{st}, is $H(s) \times e^{st}$. We will summarize this by writing

$$e^{st} \to H(s) \times e^{st}. \tag{3.9}$$

The function $H(s)$ is called the *transfer function* of the transmission line. Using

$$\sin(a) = \frac{e^{ia} - e^{-ia}}{2i}$$

and the linearity of the transmission line, one can conclude from (3.9) that

$$A \sin(2\pi ft + v) \to A \times G(f) \times \sin(2\pi ft + \theta + \varphi(f)). \tag{3.10}$$

We leave the verification of (3.10) as an exercise. Equation (3.10) shows that the effect of the transmission on a sine wave is: (1) to multiply its amplitude by $G(f)$; and (2) to delay it by some $\tau(f)$. Physically, $G(f)$ measures the attenuation and $\tau(f)$ the propagation time. We saw in Section 3.1 that the attenuation and the delay generally depend on the frequency f. The function $G(f)$ is called the *gain* and $\varphi(f)$ is the *phase shift* of the transmission line.

Going over the above derivation, we note that (3.9) holds because a function of time is a complex exponential if and only if delaying it is the same as multiplying it by a complex number. Hence, if the input has that property, the output must also have the same property (by linearity and time-invariance) and it must, therefore, be a complex exponential. To get (3.10), one takes the imaginary part of (3.9) for $s = i2\pi ft$, which is legitimate by linearity.

There is one point in the discussion above that may seem slightly mysterious: the use of complex numbers. What could be the meaning of a complex-valued input to a transmission line? Complex numbers are used for mathematical convenience; the derivation can be performed by considering only real-valued signals.

We have shown one of the two facts that underlie Fourier analysis: the preservation of sine waves. The other fact is the possibility of writing *essentially* any signal as a sum of sine waves. The adverb *essentially* alludes to some mathematical conditions that a signal must satisfy for that decomposition to be possible. The conditions are satisfied by all signals of interest in communication systems. The complete proof of the decomposition result can be found in mathematical analysis textbooks. We will limit our discussion to one example: the decomposition of a specific signal known as a *square wave*.

A square wave with period T is defined as the function $q(t)$ below:

$$q(t) = \begin{cases} 1, & \text{if } \dfrac{2n-1}{4}T \le t < \dfrac{2n+1}{4}T \text{ for some } n \in \{\ldots, -2, -1, 0, 1, 2, \ldots\} \\ 0, & \text{otherwise.} \end{cases} \tag{3.11}$$

This function is illustrated at the top of Figure 3.21. It can be shown that

$$q(t) = \frac{1}{2} + \frac{1}{\pi}\cos(\frac{2\pi}{T}t) - \frac{1}{3\pi}\cos(\frac{6\pi}{T}t) + \frac{1}{5\pi}\cos(\frac{10\pi}{T}t) - \ldots . \tag{3.12}$$

This decomposition is illustrated in Figure 3.21. One can view the partial sums as being increasingly precise approximations of the square wave. The first term is the average value of the square wave; the second term gives the *fundamental* frequency of the square wave (equal to $1/T$); the other terms are called *harmonics*, which means "multiples of the fundamental frequency."

A simple example will illustrate how to apply Fourier analysis to predict the output of a transmission line from its input. Consider a transmission line and assume that the input is the square wave $q(t)$ defined in (3.11). To calculate the output of the transmission line, we proceed as follows. First, one finds the gain $G(f)$ and the phase shift $\varphi(f)$ of the transmission line. Let us assume that those functions are provided by the manufacturer of the transmission line. Second, one looks up the decomposition (3.12). Third, one uses linearity to conclude that the response to $q(t)$ is the function $r(t)$ indicated below:

$$r(t) = \frac{1}{2} \times G(0) + \frac{1}{\pi}\cos(\frac{2\pi}{T}t + \varphi(\frac{1}{T})) \times G(\frac{1}{T}) - \frac{1}{3\pi}\cos(\frac{6\pi}{T}t + \varphi(\frac{3}{T})) \times G(\frac{3}{T})$$

$$+ \frac{1}{5\pi}\cos(\frac{10\pi}{T}t + \varphi(\frac{5}{T})) \times G(\frac{5}{T}) - \ldots .$$

The result is indicated in Figure 3.22.

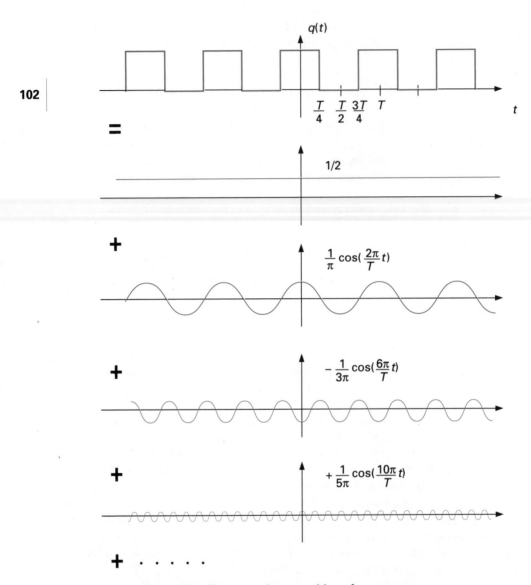

Figure 3.21 Sine wave decomposition of a square wave.

The square wave $q(t)$ can be decomposed into a sum of a constant term (1/2) and sine waves at the *fundamental frequency* $1/T$ and its odd multiples (called *odd harmonics*).

We can apply Fourier analysis to analyze systems other than transmission lines. A system is defined as a device that transforms inputs into outputs. Fourier analysis applies to any *system* that is linear and time-invariant. *Amplifiers*

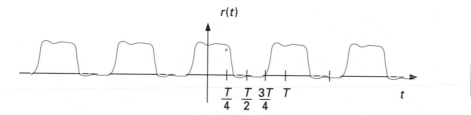

Figure 3.22 Output when the input is a square wave.

Figure 3.22 shows that the square wave is distorted. Only sine waves are guaranteed not to be distorted. Once again, recall that the cause of the distortion is the different attenuations and propagation speeds of different wavelengths. Those effects are what we called *dispersion* in Section 3.2.

and *filters* generally have those properties. We will see applications of filters shortly. Let us summarize what we know of Fourier analysis.

Fourier Analysis

- A system is *linear* if the outputs get added when one adds the inputs.

- A system is *time-invariant* if delaying the input only delays the output. This property means that the system characteristics do not change with time.

- A linear and time-invariant system does not distort sine waves. That is, the response to a sine wave is another sine wave; the original sine wave amplitude is multiplied by the system *gain*, and the phase is incremented by the system *phase shift*. The gain and the phase shift of the system are functions of the input frequency.

- Most signals can be expressed as sums of sine waves.

- To calculate the output of a linear and time-invariant system, one first decomposes the input into sine waves. One then calculates the response to each sine wave and adds up those responses.

- Linear and time-invariant systems include transmission lines, amplifiers, and filters.

We have learned to predict the distortion of signals by a transmission line. We saw that a signal which comprises square pulses is distorted by a transmission line. The intuitive explanation of the distortion is as follows. A square pulse contains fast transitions. These fast transitions contribute sine wave components at frequencies that may be much higher than the fundamental frequency of the signal. As a consequence, the range of frequencies in the input is very wide. Therefore, the output depends on the gain and the phase shift of the transmission line over a wide range of frequencies. These two functions typically vary substantially over such a wide range; hence, the distortion.

104

The distortion of arbitrary input signals caused by a transmission line can be reduced by using an *equalization filter*. Such a filter compensates for the different transmission speeds and the different attenuations at different frequencies by delaying the sine waves that travel faster along the line and by amplifying the frequencies that are more attenuated. In practice, the characteristics of the transmission line may not be known precisely and may vary in time. An *adaptive equalization filter* can then be used. An adaptive filter learns the characteristics of the line on the basis of test signals that are transmitted periodically.

To appreciate the need for equalization, let us look at a specific example. The attenuation of a typical coaxial cable at the frequency of f MHz is given by

$$A(f) \approx 11 \times f^{0.6} \text{ dB/km}.$$

For instance, if bits are transmitted using unipolar modulation at the rate of R bps, then the maximum frequency in the signal occurs when the bits 0 and 1 alternate. In that case, the signal is a square wave with period $T = 2/R$. Using the expansion (3.12), one then finds that the signal has most of its energy at the frequencies $1/T = R/2$, $3/T = 3R/2$, and $5/T = 5R/2$. One can then assume that the transmission of the bit stream is acceptable as long as the frequencies from $R/2$ to $5R/2$ are well transmitted. The attenuation of the coaxial cable may be very different at the frequencies $R/2$ and $5R/2$. For $R = 1$ MHz, one finds that

$$A(\tfrac{1}{2}) \approx 11 \text{ dB/km} \quad \text{and} \quad A(\tfrac{5}{2}) \approx 19 \text{ dB/km}.$$

If the coaxial cable has a length of 1 km, then the two attenuations differ by 8 dB. This range must be compensated for by an equalization filter.

The unipolar modulation scheme allows for the transmission of only one string of bits at a time. Also, it is not adequate if the gain and the phase of the channel are not essentially constant around the fundamental signal frequency $R/2$ Hz, or if the channel does not transmit low frequencies. The same considerations apply to such transmission systems as optical fibers and radio waves: these systems do not transmit low frequencies, so unipolar modulation is not suitable. We will discuss other modulation schemes that circumvent those difficulties.

When unipolar modulation is used to transmit a stream of bits, the input signal changes at the same rate as that of the bits. As a consequence, the power spectrum of the signal is centered on the frequency $R/2$ where R is the bit rate. Modulation schemes with that property are called *baseband transmissions*.

We will discuss three modulation methods that modify the power spectrum of the signal. That is, the power spectrum of the signal is no longer centered on $R/2$. Instead, it can be centered on another frequency which depends on the specific modulation scheme. Such methods are called *broadband modulation* schemes. These methods make *frequency-division multiplexing* possible, i.e., the simultaneous transmission of different signals on the same physical link by separating them in frequency; they also permit the network designer to adapt the signal to the transmission channel. Assume that one wants to transmit a bit stream at R bps. Define $a(t)$ to be the signal that would be transmitted if we used unipolar modulation. That is,

$$a(t) = \begin{cases} 1, & \text{for } \dfrac{n-1}{R} \le t < \dfrac{n}{R}, \text{ if the } n\text{th bit is a 1} \\[3mm] 0, & \text{for } \dfrac{n-1}{R} \le t < \dfrac{n}{R}, \text{ if the } n\text{th bit is a 0.} \end{cases}$$

The first broadband modulation scheme that we discuss is called *frequency shift keying* (FSK). Instead of transmitting the unipolar signal $a(t)$, the FSK modulation transmits the following signal:

$$s_{FSK}(t) = \begin{cases} A \sin(2\pi f_1 t), & \dfrac{n-1}{R} \le t < \dfrac{n}{R} \text{ if the } n\text{th bit is } 1 \\[3mm] A \sin(2\pi f_0 t), & \dfrac{n-1}{R} \le t < \dfrac{n}{R} \text{ if the } n\text{th bit is } 0. \end{cases}$$

In this definition, f_0 and f_1 are some given frequencies. Thus, the bits 0 and 1 are transmitted as bursts at different frequencies.

The *amplitude shift keying* (ASK) method transmits the signal $s_{ASK}(t)$ defined below:

$$s_{ASK}(t) = \begin{cases} A_1 \sin(2\pi f_c t), & \dfrac{n-1}{R} \le t < \dfrac{n}{R} \text{ if the } n\text{th bit is } 1 \\[3mm] A_0 \sin(2\pi f_c t), & \dfrac{n-1}{R} \le t < \dfrac{n}{R} \text{ if the } n\text{th bit is } 0. \end{cases}$$

Thus, the bits 0 and 1 are transmitted as sine waves at the same frequency f_c but with different amplitudes A_0 and A_1.

Phase shift keying (PSK) transmits the signal

$$s_{PSK}(t) = \begin{cases} A \sin(2\pi f_c t + \theta), & \dfrac{n-1}{R} \le t < \dfrac{n}{R} \text{ if the } n\text{th bit is } 1 \\[3mm] -A \sin(2\pi f_c t), & \dfrac{n-1}{R} \le t < \dfrac{n}{R} \text{ if the } n\text{th bit is } 0. \end{cases}$$

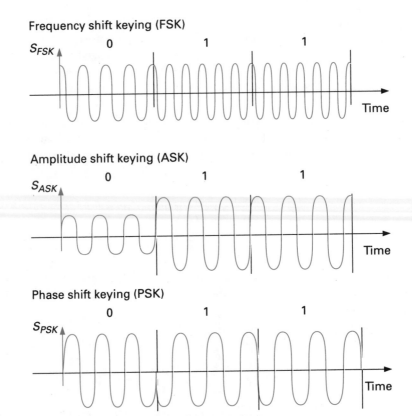

Figure 3.23 The signals s_{FSK}, s_{ASK}, and s_{PSK}.

The frequency of an FSK signal indicates whether a 0 or a 1 is transmitted. The transmitted value is indicated by the amplitude in the case of ASK and by the phase in the case of PSK.

The phase of the sine wave designates whether a 0 or a 1 is transmitted. The three signals are illustrated in Figure 3.23.

Why do these modulation methods enable frequency-division multiplexing? We will explain this possibility using FSK as an example. The same considerations can be adapted to ASK and PSK. Intuition suggests that the sine waves in the decomposition of $s(t)$ have frequencies around f_1 and around f_0. Let us justify our intuition by considering the case $a(t) = q(t)$. One has

$$s(t) = s_1(t) + s_0(t),$$

with

$$s_1(t) = q(t) \sin(2\pi f_1 t) \quad \text{and} \quad s_0(t) = (1 - q(t)) \sin(2\pi f_0 t).$$

Using the sine wave decomposition (3.12) of $q(t)$ we have

$$s_1(t) = \{\frac{1}{2} + \frac{1}{\pi}\cos(\frac{2\pi}{T}t) - \frac{1}{3\pi}\cos(\frac{6\pi}{T}t) + ...\} \times \sin(2\tau f_2 t). \qquad (3.13)$$

A general term in this sum is of the form (with $R = 2/T$)

$$u_n(t) := c_n \cos(2n\,\pi R t/2) \times \sin(2\pi f_1 t).$$

We will rewrite this term using the trigonometric identity

$$\sin a \cos b = \frac{1}{2}\sin(a + b) + \frac{1}{2}\sin(a - b).$$

We find

$$u_n(t) = \frac{c_n}{2}\sin(2\pi(f_1 + nR/2)t) + \frac{c_n}{2}\sin(2\pi(f_1 - nR/2)t).$$

This formula shows that $u_n(t)$ comprises sine waves at the frequencies $f_1 + nR/2$ and $f_1 - nR/2$ with n in $\{-5, -4,..., +4, +5\}$, say. Thus, the spectrum of $s_1(t)$ lies in $[f_1 - 5R/2, f_1 + 5R/2]$. The same analysis applies to s_0. As a result, we see that the signal $s(t)$ has its spectrum in the intervals $[f_1 - 5R/2, f_1 + 5R/2]$ and $[f_0 - 5R/2, f_0 + 5R/2]$. Assuming that $f_0 < f_1$, the above analysis indicates that the signal $s(t)$ requires a transmission channel that transmits the frequencies from $f_0 - 5R/2$ to $f_1 + 5R/2$. Consequently, the width of the frequency range transmitted by the channel is $f_1 - f_0 + 5R$. This width is called the *bandwidth*.

A finer analysis requires a better determination of the important terms in (3.13). In practice, the spectrum support is defined so that only a negligible amount of power can be found outside of that frequency range. The upshot of a detailed analysis is that one can reduce the bandwidth by transmitting rounded-off pulses instead of the square pulses. Such pulses contain less energy at high frequencies since they do not have fast transitions. By carefully choosing the rounded-off pulses, one can reduce the bandwidth to about $f_1 - f_0 + R$.

The idea behind frequency-division multiplexing (FDM) is that different signals can be transmitted over the same physical link as long as they use frequencies that are sufficiently far apart for the signal spectra not to overlap significantly.

One can recover the bits from a specific signal in an FDM transmission by using *synchronous demodulation*. Here is how this demodulation method works. Say that the received signal is

$$s(t) = s_1(t) + s_2(t) + ... + s_n(t)$$

where

$$s_i(t) = a_i(t) \sin\{2\pi v_i t\}.$$

108

In the definition of $s_i(t)$, the signal $a_i(t)$ is the unipolar signal that represents the i-th bit stream. We will assume that the bit rate of $a_i(t)$ is equal to R for each i, so that the spectrum of $a_i(t)$ lies in $[0, 5R/2]$. The frequencies v_i differ by at least $5R$. Say that the receiver wants to recover the signal $a_1(t)$ from $s(t)$. The first step is to multiply $s(t)$ by $\sin\{2\pi v_1 t\}$. The result is

$$s(t) \sin\{2\pi v_1 t\} = \sum_{i=1}^{n} a_i(t) \sin\{2\pi v_1 t\} \sin\{2\pi v_i t\}. \tag{3.14}$$

To evaluate this signal we will use the identity

$$\sin(a) \sin(b) = \frac{1}{2}\{\cos(a - b) - \cos(a + b)\}.$$

This identity shows that the signal (3.14) is a sum of terms of the form

$$\frac{1}{2} \times a_i(t) \cos\{2\pi(v_i - v_1)t\} + \frac{1}{2} \times a_i(t) \cos\{2\pi(v_i + v_1)t\}. \tag{3.15}$$

The spectrum of the first term in (3.15) is in $[v_i - v_1 - 5R/2, v_i - v_1 + 5R/2]$ and that of the second term is $[v_i + v_1 - 5R/2, v_i + v_1 + 5R/2]$. Since all the frequencies v_i differ by at least $5R$, we see that the spectra of these two terms lie above the frequency $5R/2$, except when $i = 1$. Indeed, for $i = 1$, the first term in (3.15) is

$$\frac{1}{2} \times a_1(t).$$

The above considerations show that if one *filters* the signal $s(t) \sin\{2\pi v_1 t\}$ so as to keep only the frequencies below $5R$, then the output of the filter is

$$\frac{1}{2} \times a_1(t),$$

i.e., the desired unipolar signal. Thus, synchronous demodulation to recover the signal $a_i(t)$ consists of two steps: (1) multiplying the received signal by $\sin\{2\pi v_i t\}$; and (2) filtering out all the high frequencies. The second step is called *low-pass filtering*. The first step requires that the local oscillator which produces $\sin\{2\pi v_i t\}$ be in phase with the sine wave in the received signal. This condition is achieved by using a *phase-locked loop* (PLL). The operations of the phase-locked loop are explained in Appendix C.

Quadrature amplitude modulation (QAM) is another widely used modulation method. (See Figure 3.24.) Instead of transmitting one bit at a time, QAM sends the bits four by four. (Some versions use larger bit groups.) QAM uses 16 different signals: one for each possible group of four bits. Each of the 16 signals is of the form $A \sin\{2\pi ft\} + B \cos\{2\pi ft\}$ where the pair (A, B) can take the 16 values indicated in the figure. The receiver uses synchronous demodulation to recover the values A and B. The pair (A, B) can then be decoded into a group of four bits. The discussion of the spectrum of FSK can be adapted for ASK, PSK, and QAM.

Why are so many different modulation schemes used? The reason is that each scheme has advantages that make it best suited for particular applications. For instance, FSK is relatively simple and permits FDM. QAM is very efficient in bandwidth. PSK is robust in the presence of noise.

We can summarize our discussion of broadband transmission.

Broadband Transmission

- *FSK, ASK, PSK*, and *QAM* modify the spectrum of the signal. These modulation methods are called *broadband transmissions*.

- Using Fourier analysis, one can derive the spectrum of broadband transmissions.

- Broadband transmissions permit *frequency-division multiplexing*.

- *Synchronous demodulation* consists of two steps: multiplying the received signal by a locally generated sine wave and low-pass filtering. The local sine wave is kept in phase by a PLL.

In addition to enabling FDM, broadband transmission also makes possible the amplification of signals, which permits longer cables. Let us show how a *broadband bus network* operates. By definition, a bus network is one in which all the stations are connected to the same communication link. (See Figure 3.25.) All the stations transmit on the cable at frequency f_1 and listen to frequency $f_2 \neq f_1$. A special device, the *head-end*, converts the incoming signals from the frequency f_1 to the frequency f_2 and sends them back on the cable. For instance, if a station transmits a signal (at frequency f_1), the signal goes all the way to the head-end, where it is converted to frequency f_2 and can then be heard by all the stations. Notice that the signal must travel longer distances than in baseband. The longer distances somewhat reduce the efficiency of the network.

The amplification of the signal is possible in broadband networks because of the separation in frequencies of the signals traveling in different directions. Figure 3.26 indicates the configuration of amplifiers on the cable.

110

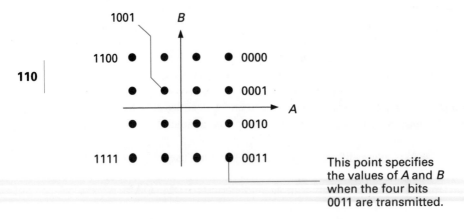

This point specifies
the values of *A* and *B*
when the four bits
0011 are transmitted.

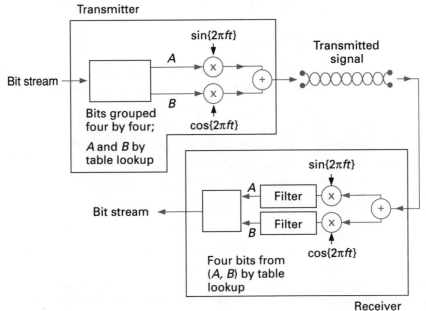

Figure 3.24 Quadrature amplitude modulation.

In QAM, bits are sent in groups. Each group is transmitted as a sum of
two signals (a sine wave and a cosine wave). The amplitudes of the sine
and of the cosine encode the specific bit group. These amplitudes are
selected so that different groups correspond to distinguishable signals.

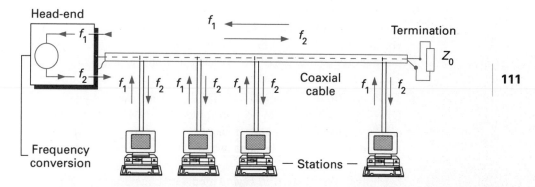

Figure 3.25 Broadband bus network.

The nodes transmit at frequency f_1 and they listen to frequency f_2. The *head-end* converts the signals from frequency f_1 to f_2.

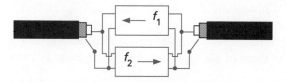

Figure 3.26 Amplifiers on a broadband network.

Two back-to-back amplifiers can be used provided they amplify different frequencies. This arrangement enables the amplification of the signals on a broadband bus network.

The amplifiers are tuned so as to amplify the signals around frequency f_2 from left to right and around frequency f_1 from right to left, and to block signals at other frequencies. This selectivity of the amplifiers prevents their saturation by feedback. If the amplifiers could amplify all signals by multiplying their amplitude, by some factor $K > 1$, then a signal with amplitude A appearing at the left of an amplifier would reappear with amplitude $K \times A$ at its right, then with amplitude $K^2 \times A$ at its left, and so on. This effect would lead to a saturation of the amplifiers (in fact, to oscillations) and to the destruction of the signals.

We will conclude this section by discussing some examples of *modems*. A modem (modulator-demodulator) transforms a bit stream into signals which fall in the frequency band transmitted by the phone network (i.e., in the "voice band"), and vice versa. The specific transformation of the bit stream into voice band signals depends on the modem type. The following types are commonly used:

- *300 bps [Bell 103]*: The originator of the transmission uses a positive sine wave at 1,070 Hz to send a 0 and a negative sine wave at 1,270 Hz to send a 1. The other modem (the answering modem) uses a positive voltage at 2,025 Hz to send a 0 and a negative voltage at 2,225 Hz to send a 1. This is an example of *frequency shift keying*.

- *1,200 bps [Bell 103 and 212A]*: The originator uses a signal at 1,200 Hz. It groups the bits to be transmitted two at a time and sends the corresponding value (among four possible ones) by selecting the corresponding *phase* of the sine wave. The answering modem uses a similar modulation of a sine wave at 2,400 Hz. This scheme is an example of the *phase shift keying* modulation method.

- *2,400 bps [V.22bis]*: This modem combines phase and amplitude modulation. It uses three different amplitudes and 12 different phases. The signal changes 600 times per second. Thus, 36 different signals can be sent, which could correspond to 6 bits. As a consequence, a bit rate of 3,600 bps would be possible. However, the modem restricts the pairs of possible adjacent signals. This restriction is used for error correction. This leads to a 2,400-bps modem with error characteristics similar to those of the 1,200-bps modem discussed before.

So far we have seen that modulation schemes are used to encode bits into signals which propagate along transmission lines as electromagnetic waves. Fourier analysis is used to predict the distortion of the received signals and to limit the distortion by a proper selection of the modulation scheme as well as by suitable equalization. Similar considerations apply equally to radio transmissions. The system composed of the transmitter antenna, the space where the waves propagate, and the receiver antenna can also be analyzed by Fourier analysis. One central fact which results from such analysis of radio transmission systems is that antennas are efficient at transmitting radio waves with a wavelength comparable to the physical lengths of the antennas. Thus, a 1-foot-long antenna is efficient at transmitting electromagnetic waves with a wavelength of about 1 foot, i.e., with a frequency of about $c/(1 \text{ ft}) = 3{\times}10^8 \text{ ms}^{-1}/0.3 \text{ m} = 1 \text{ GHz}$. As a consequence, modulation is used to adapt the spectrum of the signal to the antennas. The frequencies that are used by radio transmissions are regulated by the Federal Communications Commission (FCC) to prevent conflicting uses of frequencies. Some frequency bands are reserved for commercial radio, TV, pager, and satellite transmissions. Other frequency bands are reserved for public services. A few bands can be used freely, provided that the transmission power is small enough.

In our discussion of transmitters and receivers, we have implicitly assumed that the receiver knows at what time it should measure the received signal to convert it into a specific bit. For instance, when we explained unipolar modulation, we said that the receiver knows that a zero is transmitted when it measures 0 volt. The question that we address in the next section is when the receiver should make those measurements. The procedure used by the receiver to determine when it should measure the signal is known as *synchronization*. A related issue is the identification of special control bits in the transmitted bit sequence, called *framing*.

3.4 Synchronization and Framing

When does the receiver measure the signal to recover the bits? For simplicity, let us assume that unipolar modulation is used and that the signal is received without appreciable distortion. Thus, the received signal is as indicated in Figure 3.27. The receiver faces two problems: (1) keeping the correct pace when reading the bits; and (2) finding the start time T_1 and the end time T_2 of the signal corresponding to the bit sequences. We will explain how these two problems are solved; they constitute the *synchronization* and *framing* problems.

The first problem—keeping the correct pace when reading the bits—is solved by using some timing mechanism in the receiver. Such a mechanism, called a *clock*, attempts to "tick" in the middle of the bit epoch. A bit epoch is the interval of time during which a given bit is transmitted. In Figure 3.27 you see that a bit is sent by transmitting a constant signal for T seconds. The value of the signal in the middle of a bit epoch indicates whether the bit is a 0 or a 1. The idea is then to use a clock that ticks every T seconds and to start it at time $T_1 + T/2$. In practice, however, the receiver clock does not tick exactly every T seconds. As a consequence, the timing of the receiver may slowly drift relative to the received signal. At some point, one tick of the receiver clock may fall in the wrong bit epoch and the receiver reads the incorrect bit, either by skipping a bit or by reading the same bit twice.

Such a *loss of synchronization*, because of clock drift, can be avoided by specifying a short maximum length for the bit sequences. For instance, if one decides that every bit sequence comprises exactly 11 bits, including the extra 1 inserted at the beginning, then the receiver clock starts when the first 1 is received

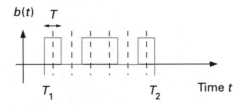

Figure 3.27 Received signal, assuming no distortion.

114

and it ticks 11 times, approximately in the middle of the 11 bit epochs. The clock then waits for the next 1—at the beginning of the next bit sequence—before restarting. Since the clock is resynchronized for every sequence of 11 bits, its accuracy need only be precise during 11 bits. Specifically, it is required that the eleventh clock tick fall in the eleventh bit time interval. Assuming that the synchronization at the start of the first bit is late at most by 10% of T, we find the period S of the receiver clock must be such that

$$(10 + \frac{1}{2}) \times S + 0.1 \times T < 11 \times T \text{ and } (10 + \frac{1}{2}) \times S > 10 \times T .$$

(The value 10% was chosen rather arbitrarily.) The first inequality specifies that the eleventh tick of the receiver clock occur before the end of the eleventh bit interval, even when the receiver clock starts $0.1 \times T$ after T_1. The second inequality specifies that the eleventh clock tick occur after the start of the eleventh bit time interval, even when the clock starts immediately at time T_1. These inequalities are satisfied if

$$|\frac{S-T}{T}| < 3.8\%.$$

As a consequence, the synchronization is good enough for sequences of 11 bits if the clocks of the transmitter and the receiver have rates that are within 1.5% of a specified value (for the clock rates can then differ by at most 3%).

The transmission of bits in short sequences of a fixed length is called *asynchronous transmission*. Note that asynchronous transmissions solve the second problem of the receiver—finding the last bit—since the number of bits is fixed. One typical example of asynchronous transmission is the use of the *ASCII code*. The ASCII code (American National Standard Code for Information Interchange) was adopted in 1963. The code specifies sequences of 7 bits that represent 128 letters, symbols, and control characters. For instance, the letter A is represented by the sequence 1000001 and the control character CR (carriage return) is represented by 0001101. An asynchronous transmission in ASCII sends sequences of 8 bits: each sequence comprises one start bit plus the 7 ASCII code bits. Some computer systems add one *parity bit* to each sequence. Such a bit might be chosen so that the total number of 1s in the sequence is even. In this instance, the letter A is sent as 1′1000001′1, where the first bit is the start bit, the following 7 bits are the ASCII code for A, and the last 1 is the parity bit added so that the sequence has an even number of 1s. Similarly, CR is sent as 1′0001101′0. When a parity bit is used, the receiver can check that the sequences that it receives have an even number of 1s. If a received sequence contains an odd number of 1s, then the receiver knows there has been a transmission error.

Computer devices that communicate using asynchronous transmissions contain an integrated circuit called *UART* (*universal asynchronous receiver and transmitter*). When transmitting, the UART frames the information bits between a start bit and a parity bit (if one is used) and it transmits the bits one after the other at the rate specified by a clock. The UART performs the reverse operations when the device receives bits.

The connection between a printer and a computer, or between a computer and a terminal, or between a computer and a modem often conforms to the Electronics Industries Association's (EIA) standard *RS-232-C* (*recommended standard 232-C*). A very similar version of this standard is recommended by the CCITT (see Chapter 1) under the name *V.24*. These standards specify the connectors, the assignment of connector contacts (pins) to the various signals, and the sequence of operations involved in a transmission. The transmission method is similar to unipolar modulation, except that the bits 0 and 1 are sent by using opposite polarities (one positive, the other negative).

The RS-232-C standard is intended for transmission at up to 38,400 bps over short distances (typically less than 15 meters). By convention, bit 0 is represented by a voltage value V in the range [+3 volts, +25 volts] and bit 1 by the voltage $-V$. This method is called *bipolar modulation* because of the two voltage signs (polarities), in contrast with unipolar modulation, which uses only one voltage sign. The receiver detects the bits by measuring the voltage between a ground line and the corresponding signal line. RS-232-C is suitable only for short connections since a current may flow between the two grounds of the two connected devices. Such a ground current induces a voltage drop which modifies the voltage differential between the signal and the ground wires. If the connection is too long, then the voltage drop may be so large that bits are received incorrectly. In addition, a large loop formed by the signal and the ground wires may be subjected to electromagnetic interference that might also introduce errors in the transmission.

The RS-232-C connectors have nine or 25 pins. A typical connection uses only four to nine connection wires. The pins are assigned to grounds, data signals (send and receive), and to control signals. The main control signals are *request to send, clear to send* and some *timing signals*. The pin allocations depend on the device type: either *DTE* (data terminal equipment, such as a terminal or a computer) or *DCE* (data circuit-terminating equipment, such as a modem or a printer).

A typical full-duplex transmission from a DTE (a computer, for example) to a DCE (a printer, for example) using RS-232-C proceeds as indicated in Figure 3.28. Here the connection between the DCE and the DTE is *full-duplex*, i.e., it can transmit information simultaneously in both directions. The communication proceeds as follows:

■ *DTE to DCE*: The DTE sends data on line 2; it can do so when line 6 (Data Set Ready) indicates a 0 (i.e., a positive value). Thus, the DCE can stop the transmission by the DTE by dropping the voltage value on the DSR line so as to indicate a 1. If line 5 (Clear to Send) is connected, the DTE can transmit only when it is positive (this is the case for many computers).

■ *DCE to DTE*: The DCE sends data on line 3; it can do so when line 20 indicates a 0. If line 4 is connected, the DCE can transmit only when it is positive.

Two additional lines are usually used when the DCE is a modem: CD (Carrier Detect) and RI (Ring Indication). CD signals that the carrier is present and RI that the modem is being called by a remote device.

One notices a form of *handshaking* between the two devices. Handshaking is the name given to a procedure for agreeing on the terms of an information exchange. In RS-232-C, the handshaking is a coordination between the DCE and the DTE to make sure that the transmission starts only when the destination is ready to receive the data.

Asynchronous Transmission

■ Even in the absence of distortion, the receiver must be *synchronized* to the received signal.

■ An *asynchronous transmission* transmits short sequences with a fixed length. Synchronization is then possible with clocks that have a reasonable tolerance.

■ *ASCII* is a 7-bit code for letters, symbols, and control characters.

■ *RS-232-C* uses bipolar modulation. The RS-232-C specifies standards for connections of up to 15 m at rates of up to 38,400 bps. The communicating devices—the DTE and DCE—execute *handshakes* to regulate the flow of data.

Although asynchronous transmissions make possible simple synchronization, their main disadvantage is that they require a gap between successive short sequences of bits. As a consequence, asynchronous transmissions are not very efficient. *Synchronous transmissions* are designed to improve efficiency by transmitting longer sequences of bits, called *packets*. The transmission of long packets requires an improved synchronization of the receiver. In addition, the transmission of long packets requires special *framing* structures to indicate to the receiver when the end of the packet is reached. Such framing structures are

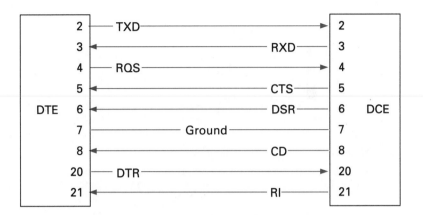

Abbreviations

DTE: Data Terminal Equipment (e.g., a computer)
DCE: Data Curcuit-Terminating Equipment
TXD: Transmit Data; RQS: Request to Send
DTR: Data Terminal Ready; RXD: Received Data
CTS: Clear to Send; DSR Data Set Ready
CD: Carrier Detect (used by modem when detects carrier)
RI: Remote Call Indication (used by modem)

Sample Protocol: To send from DTE to DCE

1. DSR and CTS are set to 0.
2. DATA is sent on TXD.
3. DCE can stop DTE by setting DSR or CTS to 1.

Electrical

0 = voltage between +3V
and +25V
1 = voltage between −25V
and −3V

Mechanical

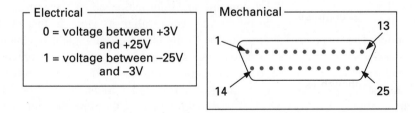

Figure 3.28 Typical transmission using RS-232-C.

The RS-232-C standard specifies the connectors and the allocations of
the pins to specific signals. The transmission from a DTE to a DCE takes
place as indicated.

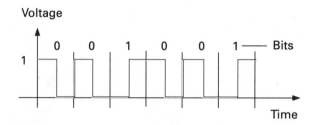

Figure 3.29 Manchester encoding.

There is a transition during every bit time. These transitions contain the timing information which is used by the receiver to detect the bits.

needed because packets of variable lengths are used. We first discuss the synchronization.

Synchronization can be achieved with precise quartz clocks if the packets are not excessively long. Transmissions of longer packets can be synchronized if the packet encoding contains clock information in addition to the bits being transmitted. Such codes are called *self-synchronizing codes*.

Manchester encoding is a widely used self-synchronizing code in computer networks. Other self-synchronizing codes include the *RZ* (return to zero), the bipolar *AMI* (alternate mark inversion) codes, and 4B/5B. All operate similarly to the Manchester code.

The Manchester encoding is illustrated in Figure 3.29. In the Manchester encoding, a bit 0 is indicated by a downward transition in the middle of the bit time interval, whereas a bit 1 corresponds to an upward transition in the middle of the bit time interval. Thus, a signal transition takes place R times per second during the transmission of a packet at a rate of R bits per second. Those transitions contribute a sine wave at R Hz in the sine wave decomposition of the signal. This sine wave at R Hz contains the information about the transmitter clock. That information is used by the receiver to align its clock to that of the transmitter. The receiver circuitry that performs the clock alignment is called a *phase-locked loop* (PLL). Its operations are explained in Appendix C. In practice, the receiver clock is locked onto the transmitter clock after a few bits are received. Each packet starts with a string of bits, called a *preamble*, used only for synchronization. The receiver clock is synchronized by the time the end of the preamble is received. A special character indicates the start of the information bits, i.e., the bits composing the message.

Messages are transmitted in one of two ways with a self-synchronizing code: *bit-oriented* transmissions and *character-oriented* transmissions. Bit-oriented transmissions allow the transmission of packets with an arbitrary number

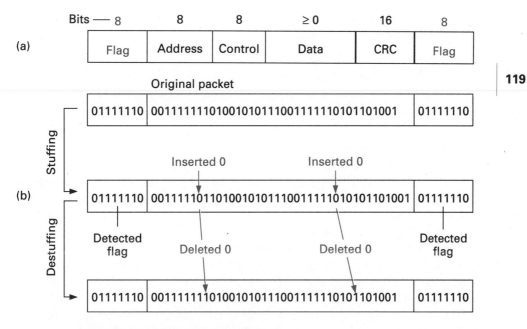

Figure 3.30 Bit-oriented transmission.

The packet is framed by two special bit patterns called flags. Bit stuffing is used to prevent a flag from occurring in the middle of a packet. The bit-stuffing procedure is illustrated in (b): a bit 0 is inserted after each pattern 011111 that appears in the packet. The reverse procedure (bit destuffing) is performed at the receiver to restore the original packet.

of bits. These two methods differ in the way they *frame* the bits, i.e., in the way they decompose the bits into control and information strings. We first explain the framing method used in bit-oriented and in character-oriented transmissions.

A typical bit-oriented transmission is indicated in Figure 3.30(a). As shown in the figure, the start and the end of the packet are indicated by a special bit pattern, called a *flag*. To make sure that the flag does not occur in the middle of a packet, which would lead the receiver to think incorrectly that it has reached the end of the packet when it has not, a special method, called *bit stuffing*, is used. To see how this method works, say that the flag is the pattern 01111110. (See Figure 3.30(b).) The bit-stuffing operation consists of adding an extra 0 after each group of 011111 that appears in the packet after the flag. The receiver performs the inverse operation (bit destuffing) by replacing every pattern 0111110 by 011111. The two flags appear before the destuffing, and the correct bit string is produced after destuffing. The start and end flags are not stuffed.

Bytes — 1   1   1   ≥ 0   1   1   2   1

| SYN | DLE | STX | Header | Data | DLE | ETX | CRC | SYN |

Figure 3.31 Character-oriented transmission.

The start of a packet is indicated by the sequence DLE-STX and the end by DLE-ETX. The occurrence of DLE-ETX in the packet is prevented by character stuffing.

The other synchronous transmission method, character-oriented transmission, assumes that the packets consist of an integral number of *bytes* (words of 8 bits). A typical frame for a character-oriented transmission is shown in Figure 3.31. The string of bits is preceded by one or more special *synchronization* characters (SYN) followed by a DLE (*data link escape*) and an STX (*start of text*) character. The end of the string is indicated by a DLE followed by an ETX (*end of text*). The correct reception is guaranteed by *character stuffing*, which consists of replacing every occurrence of the pattern DLE in the bit string between the two legitimate DLEs by DLE DLE. This procedure will make sure that the pattern DLE ETX (as opposed to DLE DLE ETX) does not appear where it should not. The character destuffing changes DLE DLE back to DLE.

Computer devices use a special integrated circuit that performs character-oriented synchronous transmission and reception. Such a circuit is called a *USART* (universal synchronous and asynchronous receiver and transmitter).

Synchronous Transmission

- Synchronous transmissions transmit long sequences of bits called *packets*. Long sequences increase the efficiency of transmissions.
- The receiver is synchronized by using either a very accurate clock or a *self-synchronizing code*.
- The *Manchester code* is a popular self-synchronizing code.
- A *phase-locked loop* (PLL) is used to align the receiver clock to the received signal. The PLL adjusts the receiver clock so that it tracks a specific sine wave component of the received signal.
- *Bit-oriented* and *character-oriented* transmissions are two forms of synchronous transmissions.

We have learned how bits are transmitted as electromagnetic waves. In addition to signal distortions, random errors can be introduced during the transmission. The next section explains how such random errors are controlled.

3.5 Error Control

Noise is the name given to the unpredictable corruption of signals. We mentioned two examples of noise in Section 3.2: thermal noise and shot noise. Interference is also a source of noise. Whatever its source, noise can introduce transmission *errors*, as we saw in the discussion in Section 3.2. In fact, you might expect such transmission errors to be unavoidable and reliable transmissions to be impossible.

In 1948, Claude Shannon proved that this conclusion is not correct. He showed that every transmission channel can transmit bits reliably provided that the transmission rate does not exceed a specific value called the *capacity* of the channel. More precisely, to each transmission channel corresponds some capacity C; a channel with capacity C can transmit at any rate $R < C$ with a bit error rate arbitrarily small. Moreover, it is not possible to transmit reliably at a rate larger than C. For instance, if the capacity of a channel is equal to 30 kbps, then it is possible to design a transmitter and a receiver that transmit 29,999 bits per second over the channel with an error rate smaller than 10^{-9}, i.e., with fewer than 1 bit out of 10^9 being incorrectly received. Shannon's result does not specify efficient ways of implementing the required transmitter and receiver. However, his result provides an important indication of what can be achieved with a given channel.

Shannon also found that the capacity of channels with dominant thermal noise is given by the following formula:

$$C = B \log_2\{1 + \frac{S}{N}\}. \tag{3.16}$$

In this expression, B is the bandwidth of the channel in Hz and S/N is the signal-to-noise ratio; i.e., the power S of the signal divided by the power N of the noise. The signal-to-noise ratio is equal to A dB if $S/N = 10^{A/10}$. (see Section 3.2). For instance, consider a telephone line which transmits the frequencies from 300 Hz to 3,400 Hz with a signal-to-noise ratio of 35 dB. The capacity of the line is given by

$$C = \{3,400 - 300\} \times \log_2\{1 + 10^{35/10}\} = 3,100 \times \log_2\{1 + 3,162\} = 36,044 \text{ bps}.$$

You will notice that (3.16) implies that a noiseless channel (with $N = 0$) has an infinite capacity. This should not be surprising: an infinite number of different signals can be received without ambiguity if the channel is noiseless. Since a sequence of n bits can be encoded into one of 2^n signals, it follows that n bits can be sent in the finite time T taken to propagate one of the signals. As a consequence, n bits can be sent reliably in T seconds for any arbitrarily large n. The derivation of (3.16) can be found in the references. You should expect the capacity to be proportional to the bandwidth B since you can use FDM. The fact that C is proportional to the logarithm of $1 + S/N$ depends on the Gaussian statistics of the thermal noise.

A good transmission channel is designed to have a small error probability. For instance, optical communication channels typically have bit error rates of the order of 10^{-9}. Transmission lines have larger bit error rates: 10^{-7} is typical. Consider then a synchronous transmission with packets of N bits on a transmission line with a bit error rate equal to BER. We will calculate the probability PER that the packet is received incorrectly. It is assumed that the bit errors are *independent* (see Appendix A). The probability that the N bits are not all received correctly is equal to

$$\text{PER} = 1 - (1 - \text{BER})^N.$$

You can verify that

$$\text{PER} \approx N \times \text{BER} \ \text{ if } \ N \times \text{BER} \ <<1.$$

For instance, if $N = 10^5$ and $\text{BER} = 10^{-7}$, then $\text{PER} \approx 10^{-2}$.

Two techniques control transmission errors: *error correction coding* and *error detection coding*. Error correction coding consists of adding enough redundant bits, called error correction bits, to the packets to be able to determine which bits are corrupted by noise. The incorrect bits can then be corrected. A simple error correction coding method is to send every packet three times. Three values are then received for each bit. The probability that a given bit is incorrectly received two or three times is equal to

$$\varepsilon = 3 \times \text{BER}^2(1 - \text{BER}) + \text{BER}^3.$$

Therefore, the probability that at least one of the N bits of the packet is received incorrectly two or three times is equal to

$$\text{PER}_c = 1 - (1 - \varepsilon)^N \approx N\varepsilon \approx 3N \times \text{BER}^2.$$

For $N = 10^5$ and $\text{BER} = 10^{-7}$, one finds

$$\text{PER}_c \approx 3 \times 10^{-9}.$$

The calculation shows that by repeating every packet three times the packet error rate is reduced from 10^{-2} to 3×10^{-9}. The price paid is that the useful transmission rate has effectively been reduced by a factor of 3. There exist much more efficient error correction coding techniques than simply repeating the packet. Such techniques are based on the following idea. The encoder calculates M bits on the basis of the N packet bits. The resulting $N + M$ bits are called a *codeword*. There are 2^N possible codewords $C(1), C(2), \ldots, C(2^N)$: one for each packet of N

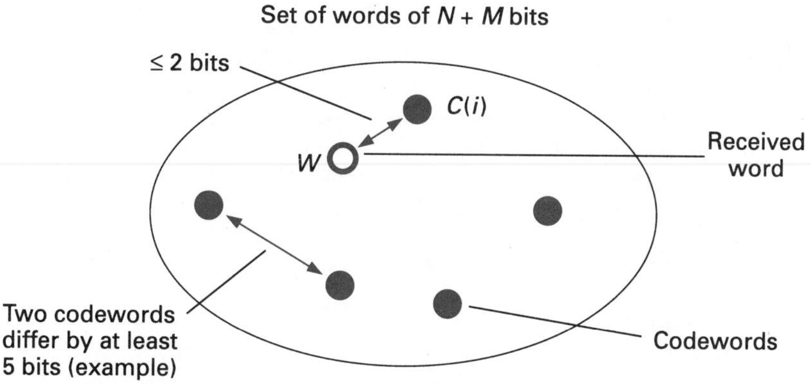

Set of words of $N + M$ bits

≤ 2 bits

$C(i)$

W

Received word

Two codewords differ by at least 5 bits (example)

Codewords

Figure 3.32 Error correction.

Assume that the transmitted codewords differ by at least 5 bits. If a transmission modifies at most 2 bits, then the transmitted codeword must be the one that differs from the received word by the smaller number of bits.

bits. Define the *distance* between two codewords as the number of bits which differ in those codewords. The M bits are calculated so that the 2^N codewords are as far apart as possible. Specifically, the M bits are chosen so as to maximize the distance between the two closest codewords. Assume that two codewords differ by at least 5 bits. When the receiver gets the string W of $N + M$ bits (see Figure 3.32), it finds the codeword $C(i)$ which is the closest to W. You can check that if at most 2 bits are incorrectly received, then the codeword $C(i)$ is precisely the codeword which was sent. One says that the code can correct 2 bit errors.

The *Bose-Chaudhuri-Hocquenghem* (BCH) codes are commonly used error-correction codes. Let p be a prime number and q an arbitrary power of p. For any $m, t \geq 1$ there exists a BCH code which can correct t bit errors for packets with $N + M = q^m - 1$ and $M < 2mt$. Such a BCH code is designated by *BCH* $(N + M, N, t)$. Examples of BCH codes are *BCH*(1023, 1003, 2), *BCH*(1023, 1003, 2), and *BCH*(1023, 923, 10). The BCH codes with $m = 1$ are called the *Reed-Solomon* (RS) codes. RS codes are used in compact discs.

Instead of adding enough redundancy to be able to *correct* transmission errors, one can add just enough redundancy to be able to *detect* transmission errors. This method is called *error detection coding*. The advantage of error detection over error correction is that it requires fewer additional bits. For instance, a single parity bit can detect that a bit is not correct in a packet but cannot identify which one. The disadvantage is that the packets which are received incorrectly must be retransmitted. Retransmission may not always be possible, as in a compact disc. Also, retransmission may be too time-consuming, as in video and audio applications and also in data transmissions from deep space probes. Error detection is the error-control method used by all computer net-

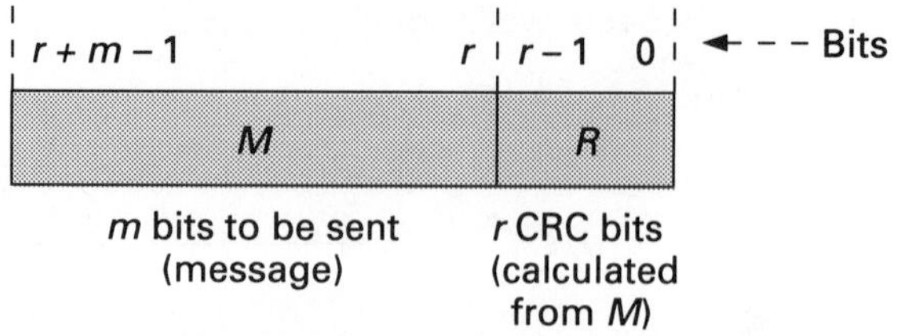

Figure 3.33 Message with CRC bits.

The group *R* of *r* error-control bits is added to the message *M* of *m* bits to be transmitted.

works. Future high-speed networks may use error correction. The packet with its error detection bits is a codeword. If two codewords differ by at least *d* bits, then the code can detect all errors that corrupt up to $d - 1$ bits. Indeed, a codeword that is transmitted cannot be converted into another codeword by corrupting fewer than *d* bits. Notice that such a code could only correct errors that corrupt fewer than $d/2$ bits, as we saw in the discussion of error-correcting codes.

The error detection code used by almost all communication networks is the *cyclic redundancy code* (CRC). Such codes detect the occurrence of transmission errors by adding a few bits, called *CRC bits* or *checksum bits*, to each packet. The CRC is a specific method for calculating the bits that are added to a packet. We will explain how the calculations are performed, and we will then discuss the error detection properties of the code.

Let *M* be a string of *m* bits. (Typically, *m* is a few hundreds or thousands.) The string *M* is the *message* to be transmitted. Another string *R* of *r* bits will be added to *M*. (Typically, $r = 16$ or $r = 24$.) The bits *R* are the *CRC bits*. (See Figure 3.33.) One may consider the strings *M*, *R*, and $T := MR$ as being binary words, with the leftmost bit being the most significant. For instance, the string 10001011 corresponds to the value $2^7 + 2^3 + 2^1 + 2^0 = 139$. With this interpretation, one sees that the string $T = MR$ corresponds to the value

$$T \equiv M.2^r + R.$$

This string is called *T* to remind us that it is *transmitted*.

The procedure for choosing *R* is as follows:

a. A string *G* of $r + 1$ bits is first agreed upon (the *generator*).

b. *R* is then chosen so that $T \equiv A \times G$ for some *A*.

Thus, *R* is chosen so that *T* is an exact multiple of the generator *G*. The idea is that if the received string $\hat{T}$ is found not to be a multiple of *G*, then the receiver knows that a transmission error must have occurred.

In order to explain the calculations, let us adopt the convention that all the operations on strings of 1s and 0s are done modulo 2 without carry. With this convention, one has $1 + 1 = 0 + 0 = 0$ and $1 + 0 = 0 + 1 = 1$. An addition modulo 2 is the same as an *exclusive or*. Since the operations are performed digit by digit without carry, one has

$$10001011 + 10100010 = 00101001$$

and

$$10001011 + 10001011 = 00000000.$$

Note that these rules are not the same as those of additions in base 2. In base 2, $10 + 11 = 101$, whereas in operations modulo 2 without carry, one has $10 + 11 = 01$.

Thus, to indicate that the received string $\hat{T}$ differs from the transmitted string T in the two leftmost bits and in the rightmost bit, one can write that $\hat{T} = T + E$ with $E = 1100\ldots001$. The string E will then be called the *error pattern* since its 1s indicate which bits of T were flipped by noise. Now,

$$\hat{T} = T + E = A{\times}G + E,$$

so that the received message $\hat{T}$ will be a multiple of the generator G if and only if the error pattern E is a multiple of G. Indeed, the rules of operations are such that $E = \hat{T} + A \times G$, so that $\hat{T} = B \times G$ if and only if $E = (A + B) \times G$.

The generator G should be chosen so as to minimize the likelihood that the error pattern E is a multiple of G. It turns out that if $G = 1'0001'0000\,'0010'0001$, then E cannot be a multiple of G if E has fewer than 32,768 bits and if it has one, two, or three 1s. Thus, this choice of G allows us to detect all the single, double, and triple bit errors in messages M of up to 32,752 bits. (In addition, this G detects all the errors that involve an odd number of bits and most errors that affect up to 18 consecutive bits.) The code obtained by using this particular G is called *CRC-CCITT*.

The calculation of R so that $T = M.2^r + R = A{\times}G$ is based on the observation that this equation is equivalent to

$$M.2^r = A{\times}G + R,$$

so that R is the remainder of the division of $M.2^r$ by G (using addition modulo 2 without carry). This remainder can be determined by long division. As a numerical example, Figure 3.34 details the calculation that shows that if $r = 3$, $G = 1001$, and $M = 110101$, then $R = 011$ so that the transmitted string is $T = 110101011$.

In communication devices, these calculations are performed by dedicated integrated circuits. The circuit that corresponds to $G = 1001$ is illustrated in

126

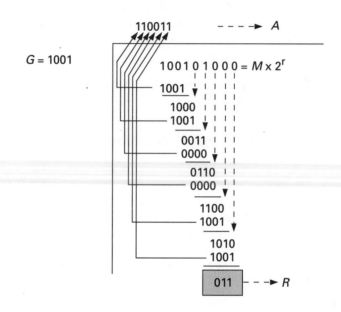

Figure 3.34 starts here:

$$r = 3,\ G = 1001,\ M = 110101$$

$G = 1001$

110011 — — — → A

$1\ 0\ 0\ 1\ 0\ 1\ 0\ 0\ 0 = M \times 2^r$

1001

1000
1001

0011
0000

0110
0000

1100
1001

1010
1001

011 — — → R

Figure 3.34 Calculation of CRC bits.

The CRC bits are the remainder ($R = 011$) of the long division of $M \times 2^r = 110101000$ by $G = 1001$. The operations are modulo 2 without carry.

Figure 3.35. In this circuit, the memory cells are organized as a *shift-register* which is activated by a clock. That is, at every clock tick, a new bit enters from the left and all the bits in the cells are shifted to the right by one position. The circle with a plus indicates a circuit that performs an addition modulo 2 (an exclusive or). We will explain how the circuit calculates the long division. As an example, say that $M = M_1 M_2 \ldots M_n$ and that $G = 1001$. Let us first take a look at the long division itself.

The long division is a sequence of simple steps. A generic step in the long division is a calculation of the form

$$(S_m, S_{m+1}, S_{m+2}, M_{m+3}) - G.$$

The result of this subtraction is

$$\begin{cases} (S_{m+1}, S_{m+2}, M_{m+3}), & \text{if } S_m = 0; \\ (S_{m+1}, S_{m+2}, M_{m+3}+1), & \text{if } S_m = 1. \end{cases}$$

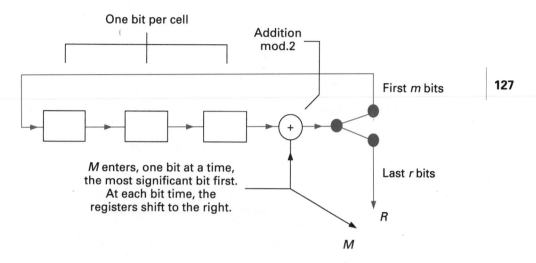

One bit per cell

Addition
mod.2

First m bits

M enters, one bit at a time,
the most significant bit first.
At each bit time, the
registers shift to the right.

Last r bits

R

M

Figure 3.35 Circuit for checksum calculations.

The circuit has three cells which contain the three bits representing the
word still to be subtracted in the long division. The cells initially contain
the bits 000. When the last bit (the least significant) of M has entered the
circuit, the cells contain the error detection bits.

Therefore, the result can be written as

$$(S_{m+1}, S_{m+2}, S_m + M_{m+3}).$$

This shows, by induction on m, that this result is

$$(\Sigma_{m+1}, \Sigma_{m+2}, \Sigma_{m+3})$$

where

$$\Sigma_m := 0, \text{ for } m = -2, -1, 0, 1, 2;$$
$$\Sigma_{m+3} := \Sigma_m + M_{m+3}, \text{ for } m \geq 0 .$$

We will now show that the circuit performs the same calculations as
the long division. Assume, as an induction hypothesis, that when the digit M_{m+3}
enters the circuit, the registers hold the values

$$(\Sigma_m, \Sigma_{m+1}, \Sigma_{m+2}) \qquad (3.17)$$

which are stored from right to left. That is, the rightmost cell holds Σ_m, the middle
cell holds Σ_{m+1}, and the leftmost cell holds Σ_{m+2}. As the bit M_{m+3} enters, the cells

are shifted to the right and the content of the leftmost cell is replaced by the sum of M_{m+3} and the rightmost cell. Thus, the new cell contents are

$$(\Sigma_{m+1}, \Sigma_{m+2}, \Sigma_m + M_{m+3} = \Sigma_{m+3}).$$

128

This derivation shows that the induction hypothesis (3.17) holds for $m + 4$ if it is satisfied for $m + 3$. Since it is trivially satisfied for $m = -2$, it follows that (3.17) is indeed the contents of the registers when bit M_{m+3} enters. This proves that the circuit calculates successively the steps of the long division.

Error Control

- Noise introduces transmission errors. Such errors limit the rate at which bits can be sent reliably over a given channel. The maximum rate of reliable transmissions is called the *channel capacity*.

- The capacity of a channel with a thermal-type noise is given by Shannon's formula (3.16).

- *Error detection* is performed by adding enough error-control bits for the receiver to detect the occurrence of transmission errors. Incorrectly received packets can be retransmitted. The *CRC* is a commonly used error detection code.

- *Error correction* is performed by adding more error control bits so that the receiver can correct the corrupted packet. Error correction is preferable to error detection when the bit error probability is large or when retransmissions are not possible or practical.

This chapter has explained how bits are transmitted. The importance of bit transmissions results from the fact that most information can be converted into bits. In a communication network, the conversion of information into bits is done by the user's equipment. In the OSI terminology, the conversion takes place before the information reaches the application layer. That conversion is certainly not part of the physical layer. However, since it is the fundamental justification for the transmission of bits performed by the physical layer, it is appropriate to discuss this conversion in this chapter. That is the subject of the next section.

3.6 Digitizing Information

We explained in Section 2.3 that information is transmitted as bits to reduce the effects of transmission errors. In this section we will discuss the principles that underlie the digitization of information, i.e., its conversion into bits. We will explain these principles in the cases of voice signals and video signals. You will see that there are two steps in the digitization of voice and video, and, more generally, of a time-varying analog signal $v(t)$: *sampling* and *quantization*. Sampling is the periodic measurement of the signal every T seconds. These periodic measurements are called *samples*. Quantization is the approximation of the possible values of the samples by a finite set of values. The advantage of quantization is that we can number the finitely many approximate values with binary numbers. Each sample is then replaced by the binary number that designates its approximating value. As a result, the succession of periodic samples is replaced by a succession of binary numbers, i.e., by a bit stream. Thus, the signal has been digitized. We will explain these steps in more detail below.

Let us first consider the digitization of a voice signal. A microphone produces an analog signal $v(t)$ which represents the pressure of the air to which it is exposed at time t. As time goes by, the air pressure and $v(t)$ change. The variations in the pressure are perceived by the ears and the brain as sounds. If the microphone picks up the sound of voice, then most of the energy of the signal is in the frequency range from 300 Hz to 4,000 Hz. Assume that the signal does not contain any energy at frequencies higher than 4,000 Hz. *Nyquist's sampling theorem* (see Appendix C) establishes that $v(t)$ can be recovered *exactly* from the samples $\{v(nT), \ n = 0, \pm 1, \pm 2, \ldots\}$ provided that $T \leq 1/8{,}000$ s, i.e., provided that the signal is sampled at least 8,000 times per second. In other words, there is only one signal $v(t)$ with maximum frequency 4,000 Hz which takes the value $v(nT)$ at time nT for all n. In general, Nyquist's theorem states that a signal with maximum frequency f_{max} can be recovered exactly from samples that are measured more frequently than $2 \times f_{max}$ every second. That is, the *sampling* frequency must be at least twice the maximum frequency in the signal. That theorem confirms the intuitive idea that the faster a signal changes, the faster bits must be sent to communicate the changes.

Sampling is the first step in the digitization of a voice signal. The second step is to *quantize* the samples. That is, the samples which can take a continuous range of values are approximated by values in a finite set. For instance, if a sample $v(nT)$ can take arbitrary values but is very likely to be between -1 and 1, then that sample can be approximated by the closest multiple of $2^{-(N-1)}$ which is in the interval $(-1, +1)$. (See Figure 3.36.) There are $2^N - 1$ such multiples, and they can be identified with N bits. We write the approximation of $v(nT)$ as $v_s(nT)$. The *sampling error* $e(nT) := |v(nT) - v_s(nT)|$ is less than 2^{-N} whenever $|v(nT)| < 1 - 2^{-N}$. One can view the sampling error as adding a *sampling noise* to the signal. The power of that noise is the average value of $e^2(nT)$. Assuming that $v(nT)$ is equally likely to take any value in $(-1, +1)$, one can calculate that the average value of $e^2(nT)$ is approximately equal to

$$N_s = \frac{1}{3} \times 2^{-2N}.$$

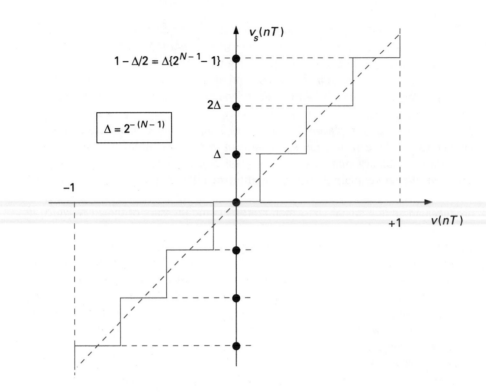

Figure 3.36 Quantization.

Quantization consists in replacing a value v by the closest value in a specified finite set. In the figure, the finite set contains the multiples of $\Delta = 2^{-(N-1)}$ between $-1 + \Delta/2$ and $1 - \Delta/2$. The quantized value can then be identified by N bits. The resulting *quantization error* can be viewed as some noise.

Under the same assumptions, the average power of the signal is the average value of $|v(t)|^2$, which is equal to

$$S = \frac{1}{3}.$$

It follows that the *signal-to-noise ratio* S/N_s is equal to

$$\frac{S}{N_s} = 2^{2N}.$$

This signal-to-noise ratio can be expressed in decibels:

$$10 \times \log_{10} \frac{S}{N_s} = 10 \times \log_{10}\{2^{2N}\} \approx 6 \times N \text{ dB}.$$

(We used the fact that $\log_{10} x = \log_{10} 2 \times \log_2 x \approx 0.3 \times \log_2 x$.)

Let us look at two examples of sampling and quantization. The first example is the digital transmission of voice in the telephone network. The sampling rate is 8,000 Hz, and 8 bits are used per sample. The sampling rate corresponds to a maximum frequency of 4,000 Hz. The voice signal is filtered so that its spectrum is in [300 Hz, 3,400 Hz]. The 8 bits per sample introduce a quantization noise with a signal-to-noise ratio equal to $6 \times 8 = 48$ dB. The second example is a compact disc. The sampling rate is about 41 kHz, which corresponds to a maximum frequency of 20 kHz. Each sample is encoded into 16 bits. The signal-to-noise ratio is, therefore, about equal to 96 dB. Thus, to send a voice signal as a bit stream, one must send 8 bits 8,000 times per second. This corresponds to a bit rate of 64 kbps. The bit rate in a compact disc is about $41 \times 10^3 \times 16$ for each of the two channels (left and right), i.e., the total rate is 1.3 Mbps. Reed-Solomon error correction bits are added to that bit stream.

The digitization of a video signal follows similar rules. For instance, the maximum frequency in the NTSC video signal is about 5 MHz. Using 8 bits per sample and a sampling frequency of 11 MHz leads to a bit rate equal to 88 Mbps. Alternatively, if the camera uses a grid of photosensors, one can quantize each sensor value. Say that the camera uses $300 \times 400 = 12 \times 10^4$ sensors for each of the three fundamental colors red, green, and blue. Using 8 bits per sample requires $8 \times 3 \times 12 \times 10^4 \approx 2.88 \times 10^6$ bits per image. If 30 images are sent every second, the needed bit rate is equal to 86.4 Mbps.

The number of bits needed to transmit a given piece of information can be reduced by a technique called *information compression*. This technique will be explained in Chapter 7 when we discuss the presentation layer.

Digitizing Information

- Two methods are used to convert information into bits: *sampling* and *quantization*.

- Sampling consists of measuring periodically the values of a signal. No information about the signal is lost if the sampling frequency is at least twice the maximum frequency of the signal.

- Quantization is the approximation of a variable by one of finitely many values. This approximation introduces a quantization error which can be considered as noise.

Summary

The objective of this chapter was to explain the digital transmission of information.

■ Information is transmitted as electromagnetic waves whose propagation is described by Maxwell's equations. Guided propagation is subject to dispersion, attenuation, and noise, which limit the rate × distance characteristic of a transmission line.

■ Optical transmitters include LEDs and LDs; receivers include PN-photodiodes, PIN-diodes, and APDs.

■ Fourier analysis is the main technique for analyzing linear and time-invariant systems, such as transmission lines, filters, and amplifiers.

■ Asynchronous transmissions send short bit sequences of a fixed lengths. That method simplifies the receiver synchronization.

■ Synchronous transmissions improve the efficiency of asynchronous transmissions by sending long packets. The receiver can be synchronized by using a self-synchronizing code and a PLL.

■ RS-232-C is a commonly used connection for low bit rates and short distances.

■ Frequency-division multiplexing is made possible by broadband transmission methods, such as FSK, PSK, ASK, and QAM. The signals are recovered by synchronous demodulation.

■ Shannon's theorem specifies the capacity of a channel. The capacity is the maximum rate at which bits can be transmitted reliably over the channel. Errors can be controlled by error correction codes, such as BCH and Reed-Solomon. They can be detected by using a CRC.

■ Nyquist's sampling theorem establishes that a signal can be recovered exactly from samples if the sampling frequency is at least twice the maximum frequency of the signal. The quantization of the signal samples introduces a *quantization noise*.

Problems

1. Why do optical fibers have more capacity than coaxial cables? (Indicate the correct answer(s).)

132

a. Because light travels faster than electricity.

b. Because photons require less energy than electrons.

c. Because fibers are better isolators.

d. Because of another reason (explain).

2. The CRC is a method for: (indicate the correct answer(s) and explain)

a. Correcting some errors.

b. Correcting all errors.

c. Detecting some errors.

d. Detecting all errors.

e. Reducing the bit error rate.

3. What is the capacity of a channel with thermal-type noise that transmits only the frequencies between 7MHz and 11MHz?

4. Consider Figure 3.2 and define the angle θ such that $\cos \theta = \eta_2/\eta_1$. Calculate θ when $\eta_1 = 1.46$ and $\eta_2 = \eta_1 \times 0.999$.

5. For the step-index fiber of Figure 3.3, draw the propagation mode with the slowest propagation speed along the fiber. The slowest rays make an angle θ with the axis of the fiber, where θ was calculated in the previous problem. Calculate the propagation time of those rays over a fiber with length L. Calculate the propagation time over the same length of fiber for rays parallel to the fiber. Calculate the difference in travel times of the two modes above. Use your result to justify (3.2a).

6. An electromagnetic wave travels through a fiber with an attenuation of 0.5 dB/km. Find the distance after which the power of the wave is reduced by 50%.

7. Bits are transmitted from Berkeley (California) to Boston (Massachusetts) over an optical fiber at 1.8 Gbps (1 Gbps = 10^9 bps). The bits go through a number of repeaters. The propagation speed is 2×10^5 km/s. The total length of the fiber is 3,200 miles (1 mile = 1.6 km). Find how many bits have been transmitted and are propagating over the fiber when the first bit reaches Boston.

8. We want to build an optical transmission link. Our LED transmits an average power of 4 dBm. The receiver sensitivity is –32 dBm. The fiber comes in lengths of 10 km. The connectors between the LED and the fiber and between the fiber and the PIN at the receiver introduces a loss of 1.2 dB. The fiber attenuation is 0.5 dB/km. Each splice between fiber sections introduces a loss of 1.5 dB. Find the maximum length of our transmission link.

*9. Consider a linear time-invariant system and assume that the input is $x(t) = \sin(2\pi f_0 t)$ for $-\infty < t < +\infty$. Show, without using complex numbers, that the output is of the form $y(t) = A\,\sin(2\pi f_0 t + \varphi)$. (*Hint:* Calculate the output to $x(t + a)$ by using the relation $\sin(\alpha + \beta) = \sin\alpha\cos\beta + \sin\beta\cos\alpha$, then write the expressions when $a = -t$ and $a = \{1/(4f_0)\} - t$. You now have two equations that you can solve for $y(t)$.)

*10. The *mean square power* $<x^2>$ of a signal $x = \{x(t), t \geq 0\}$ is defined as the average over time of the square of $x(t)$. That is,

$$<x^2> := \frac{1}{T}\int_0^T \{x(t)\}^2 dt, \text{ for very large } T.$$

a. Using the trigonometric identity $\{\cos\alpha\}^2 = [1 + \cos(2\alpha)]/2$, show that if $x(t) = \cos(2\pi f_0 t)$, then $<x^2> = 1/2$.

b. The house voltage in the United States has the form $V(t) = A\cos(120\pi t + \varphi)$. The amplitude A is such that $<V^2> = (110)^2$. Find the value of A.

c. Let $x(t) = A\cos(\alpha t) + B\cos(\beta t)$. Show that $<x^2> = (A^{2/2}) + (B^{2/2})$ whenever $\alpha \neq \beta$. Thus, the mean square power of a sum of sine waves is the sum of the mean square powers of the individual sine waves.

11. Let us assume that the FSK modulation of a bit stream with rate R results in a signal with bandwidth $5R$. We want to transmit many such bit streams over a single coaxial cable that has a bandwidth of 200 MHz. The bit streams are produced by digital encoding of audio programs. Each bit stream has a rate equal to 1.5 Mbps. How many audio programs can be carried simultaneously by the coaxial cable?

12. Review the analysis of the receiver synchronization with OOK modulation. What is the required crystal accuracy when the packets are up to 1,000 bits long?

13. Consider the following method for encoding bits. The sequence of bits $b_1 b_2 b_3 \ldots$ is represented by the voltage $V = b_1 \times 2^{-1} + b_2 \times 2^{-2} + b_3 \times 2^{-3} + \ldots$. The voltage V is applied at one end of a transmission line. After some time T, the voltage, attenuated by a known factor because of power dissipation in the line, appears at the other end of the line. There, a circuit measures the voltage, calculates V by compensating for the attenuation, and reconstructs the bit sequence. This method enables us to transmit an arbitrary large number of bits in a fixed time T. Thus, the *capacity* of this transmission line is infinite.

Discuss the validity of the previous argument and of the resulting conclusion. Does this conclusion contradict Shannon's result (3.16)?

*14. We are given a bit transmission facility that transmits each bit correctly with probability $1 - \text{BER}$ and incorrectly with probability BER, where $\text{BER} = 10^{-6}$. The bit errors are independent. We send bits in groups of 7, and we add a parity bit so that the groups of 8 bits that we send always contain an even number of 1s. What is the probability that a group of 8 bits arrives with transmission errors not detected by the parity bit?

15. Explain why an error-detection scheme that adds n error-detection bits to a packet has at least the probability BER^n of not detecting a transmission error, under the assumptions of the previous problem.

16. A transmission link with $\text{BER} = 10^{-10}$ is used to transmit the contents of a full CD-ROM. Estimate the probability that no transmission error occurs.

17. Calculate the CRC error-detection bits when $G = 1001$ and $M = 10010010011$. Is $G = 1001$ a good choice for calculating a CRC?

18. A digital audio tape (DAT) recorder samples the left and right audio signals 44,000 times per second. Each sample is quantized with 16 bits. How many pages of text can you store on a two-hour DAT if each page amounts to 2 kbytes?

19. You want to build a communication network to provide access to a library data base of text and photographs. The design goal is to be able to access and view a requested photograph within five seconds. Assume that the photographs are stored in a large CD-ROM collection that is searched by a multiple-CD player. The collection should contain about 10,000 photographs. Discuss the required specifications for the CD player and for the communication network.

References

There are many good texts and tutorials on the physical layer. The tutorial by Henry (1985) is an excellent introduction to optical communications. The text by Palais (1988) is a very readable presentation of the same subject. Lin (1989) is a collection of articles about the different components of optical communication links. Couch (1983), Cooper (1986), and Lee (1988) are recommended texts on communication theory. Lin (1983) is a readable text on error-control codes.

Cooper (1986). Cooper, G. R., and McGillem, C. D., *Modern Communications and Spread Spectrum.* McGraw-Hill, 1986.

Couch (1983). Couch, Leon W., *Digital and Analog Communication Systems.* Macmillan, 1983.

Henry (1985). Henry, P., "Lightwave primer," *IEEE Journal of Quantum Electronics,* QE-21, No. 12, 1862–1879, 1985.

Lee (1988). Lee, E. A., and Messerschmitt, *Digital Communication.* Kluwer, 1988.

Lin (1989). Lin, C. (Ed.), *Optoelectronic Technology and Lightwave Communications Systems.* Van Nostrand Reinhold, 1989.

Lin (1983). Lin, S., and Costello, D. J., *Error Control Coding.* Prentice-Hall, 1983.

Palais (1988). Palais, J. C., *Fiber Optic Communications.* (2nd Ed.). Prentice-Hall, 1988.

Data Link Layer | 4

Moving bits from one node to another—the task performed by the physical layer—is the most basic step in establishing network communication and in offering network users communication services. The transmission of bits is an elementary service performed by the physical layer. More complex services are built on top of this elementary service. The transmission of *packets* between nodes attached to the same transmission link is one such service. This chapter explains how packet transmissions are built from the bit-transmission service provided by the physical layer.

Many applications require the reliable transmission of information. However, we learned in Chapter 3 that the transmission of bits is never perfectly reliable. Random errors occur even with the most carefully designed transmission link. The physical layer provides an unreliable bit-transmission facility commonly called an *unreliable bit pipe*. We will learn in this chapter that special procedures can be followed by the network nodes to transmit packets *reliably* over unreliable bit pipes. This situation is not unlike that discussed in Section 2.2 where two secretaries could provide reliable communications between two executives even though they were using unreliable facsimile transmissions. The procedures followed by the network nodes specify how transmission errors can be detected and corrected by retransmissions. These procedures are a distributed script called a *data link protocol*.

Our discussion of the data link protocols is divided into four major themes. First, we discuss the general objectives of data link protocols in Section 4.1. Second, in Sections 4.2–4.4, we explain the data link protocols used by most computer networks. These are the *alternating bit protocol* (ABP), the *selective repeat protocol* (SRP), and the *GO BACK N* protocol. We will see that some protocols transmit packets faster than others. The faster protocols are more complex. The increased complexity is justified when the application demands fast packet transmissions. We will learn that the packet transmission rate of a data link protocol depends on some parameters of the protocol and that the network designer must adapt these protocol parameters to the transmission link. As we explained in Chapter 2, protocols—that is, distributed algorithms that supervise information transfers—are found at all layers of the OSI model. The new communication networks necessitate complex protocols whose development requires efficient specification and verification techniques. In Section 4.5 we describe techniques that network designers use to verify that a protocol is working properly and the methods used to specify the steps of a protocol. These techniques apply not only to data link protocols but also to protocols of the other layers. Finally, in Section 4.6, we see how the data link protocols are implemented in popular networks. The network designer who implements a data link protocol must choose the protocol and its parameters as well as the structure of the packets. The objective of Section 4.6 is to indicate the choices that are made in popular networks.

4.1 Data Link Protocols

In Chapter 2 we described how a store-and-forward packet-switching network transmits a bit stream or a bit file from one network user to another. The bit stream or bit file is first divided into packets. Each packet is then transmitted from one node to the next along a path from the sending user to the receiving user. The network layer selects the paths taken by the packets. Consider two network nodes connected by a communication link. (See Figure 4.1.) Assume that the network layer decides that a given packet must travel along the link between these two nodes. The network layer requests the data link layer of that link to transmit the packet. The data link layer uses the physical layer of the link to transmit the bits of the packet. Thus, the data link layer converts the unreliable bit pipe provided by the physical layer into a *packet link*, i.e., a facility for transmitting packets.

A packet may arrive at the data link layer in the receiving node with an indication that a transmission error occurred. How should the data link layer handle transmission errors? The answer depends on the communication service provided to the network users. For connectionless services implemented by data-

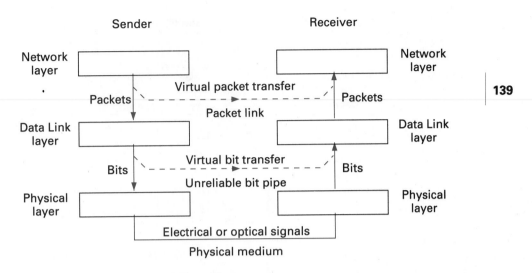

Figure 4.1 Two nodes communicating over a direct link.

The network layer in the sending node requests the data link layer to transmit a packet. The data link layer in the sending node requests the physical layer to transmit the bits of the packet. The physical layer in the receiving node delivers the bits to the data link layer. The data link layer in the receiving node then delivers the packet to the network layer.

gram packet-switching, the data link layer simply drops the incorrect packets. (See Figure 4.2(a).) The network layer requests the data link layer to transmit a packet by making a data link request (*D.req*). If the transmission is successful, the network layer in the receiving node gets a data link indication (*D.ind*) that a packet has been received. For connection-oriented services implemented by virtual-circuit packet-switching, the data link layer requests retransmissions of copies of each packet until a correct version is received. In addition, the data link layer in a connection-oriented service delivers the packets in the correct order and it confirms the successful delivery of the packets. (See Figure 4.2(b).) Thus, the network layer makes a data link request (*D.req*) for the transmission of a packet. Eventually, the network layer in the receiving nodes gets a *D.ind*, which it acknowledges by a data link response (*D.resp*). When the data link layer in the sender is informed of the *D.resp*, it gives a data link confirmation (*D.conf*) to the network layer in the sender that the packet was delivered to the network layer in the receiver.

We devote this chapter to the second class of data link layers. For simplicity, we consider the problem of transmitting packets from one packet-switching node (PSN) called the *sender* to another called the *receiver*. In actuality, traffic may exist in both directions. The two PSNs are connected by a communication link that can transmit signals in both directions. The physical layer

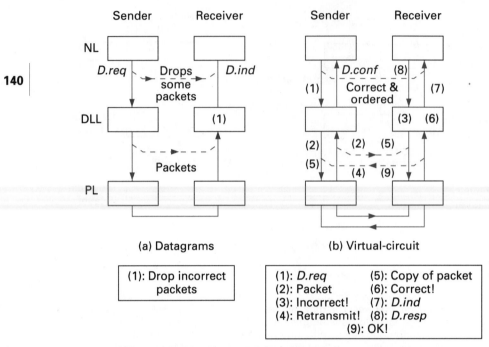

(a) Datagrams   (b) Virtual-circuit

(1): Drop incorrect packets

(1): *D.req*	(5): Copy of packet
(2): Packet	(6): Correct!
(3): Incorrect!	(7): *D.ind*
(4): Retransmit!	(8): *D.resp*
	(9): OK!

Figure 4.2 Objectives of data link layer.

The data link layer converts the bit pipe provided by the physical layer into a packet link. For datagram transmissions, the packet link drops the incorrect packets (a). For virtual-circuit transmissions, the packet link delivers the packets correctly and in the correct order (b). The numbers indicate the sequence of events.

implements an unreliable bit pipe in each direction over the link. The problem solved by the data link layer protocols is the conversion of the unreliable bit pipes into a reliable packet link.

Figure 4.2(b) indicates a possible sequence of events in the transmission of packets. The figure assumes that there is a transmission error. We need to specify how the data link layer compensates for such transmission errors. Most data link protocols use the following procedure to transmit packets reliably from sender to receiver. (See Figure 4.3.) The sender keeps a copy of a packet until it learns that the packet has been received correctly by the receiver. Each packet contains an error detection code (see Section 3.5). When a packet arrives correctly at the receiver, the receiver transmits an *acknowledgement* (ACK) to the sender. ACKs are packets that also contain an error detection code so the sender can verify their accuracy. When there is no transmission error, the packet is received correctly by the receiver and the ACK of that packet is then received correctly by the sender. If either the packet or its ACK is corrupted by a transmis-

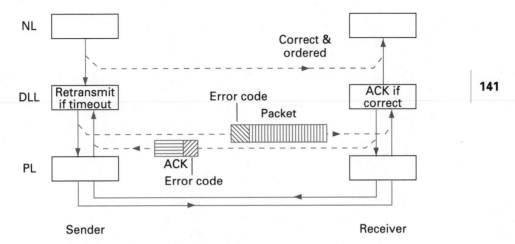

Figure 4.3 Packets and ACKs used by the data link layer.

The data link layer transmits a packet reliably by retransmitting copies of the incorrectly transmitted packets until a successful copy is received. The data link layer detects transmission errors by using a timer and acknowledgements. The data link layer suspects that an error occurred when a packet is not acknowledged before a timeout expires.

sion error, then the sender does not receive a correct ACK. The sender uses a *timer* to establish whether there was a transmission error. The timer functions as follows: The sender starts a timer whenever it transmits a packet. If the sender does not receive the acknowledgement within a specified amount of time, called *timeout*, the sender suspects that a transmission error corrupted either the packet or its ACK. The sender then retransmits a copy of the packet. The length of the timeout is usually chosen so that there is sufficient time for the transmission of both the packet and its acknowledgment. The link between the sender and the receiver must be able to transmit in both directions: it is used to transmit packets from the sender to the receiver and ACKs from the receiver to the sender. We will see that some protocols are faster when the link between the nodes is full-duplex, i.e., when it can transmit in both directions at the same time.

Figure 4.4 illustrates the sequence of events in the transmission of a packet and of its ACK. The figure shows a packet flowing from the network layer to the data link layer in the sender (1), then to the physical layer (2), then being transmitted (3) and propagating through the physical medium (4), and so on. The line (4) is oblique to represent the time taken to go through the physical medium. Event (1) designates the request made by the network layer to the data link layer to transmit a packet. It is a *D.req*. Eventually, the network layer in the receiver gets an indication designated by (7) that the packet has been received. Thus, (7) is a *D.ind*. Step (8) is a *D.resp* and (11) is the *D.conf* once the ACK has been received.

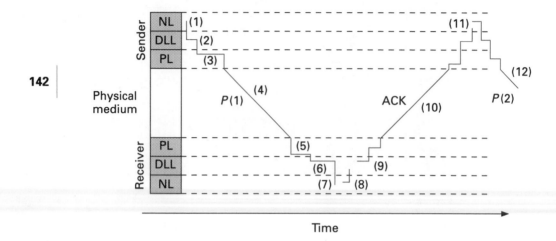

Figure 4.4 Sequence of events in transmission of packet and ACK.

Time flows from left to right. The events, as numbered in the figure, are the following: (1) *D.req*—the network layer requests the transmission of packet *P*(1); (2) *P.req*—the data link layer requests the transmission of the bits of *P*(1); (3) the physical layer transmits the bits as signals that propagate in the medium (4); (5) the physical layer gives the bits to the data link layer (*P.ind*) in the receiver; (6) the data link layer puts the bits together into packet *P*(1) and verifies its correctness by checking the error detection code; (7) the packet is given to the network layer (*D.ind*); (8) the network layer acknowledges the reception to the data link layer (*D.resp*); (9) the data link layer prepares an ACK, which eventually propagates as signals (10); (11) the ACK eventually reaches the data link layer, and a confirmation (*D.conf*) is sent to the network layer; another packet can then be sent (12).

Figure 4.5 provides another representation of the events in Figure 4.4. The figure shows the bottom three layers of the sender and the receiver. The physical paths of the messages are indicated by solid lines. In step (2), the data link layer in the sender asks the physical layer to send the bits of packet *P*(1). Eventually, these bits appear at the data link layer in the receiver (5). Thus, the data link layer in the sender uses the bit transmission by the physical layer to transmit *P*(1). This bit transmission from the data link layer in the sender to the data link layer in the receiver is represented in the figure by a dashed line labeled *bits of P*(1). The data link layer need not know how the bits are transmitted physically; it needs to know only that the physical layer transmits the bits. Similarly, the data link layer in the receiver uses the physical layer to transmit the bits of ACK to the sender. This transmission is indicated by the dashed line labeled *bits of ACK*. The sender and the receiver execute a data link protocol when they exchange bits of packets and bits of ACKs. The data link protocol implements the

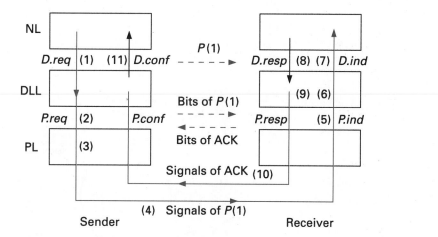

Figure 4.5 Another representation of transmissions of packet and ACK.

The network layer in the sender requests the data link layer to transmit a packet with a *D.req* (1). The data link layer requests the physical layer to transmit the bits of the packet with a *P.req* (2). The physical layer transmits the bits as signals (3); these signals propagate through the transmission medium (4). The physical layer indicates to the data link layer in the receiver when it has received the bits with a *P.ind* (5). In the receiver, the data link layer verifies the correctness of the packet (6) and, if it is correct, sends an indication *D.ind* to the network layer (7). The network layer replies that it received the packet with a *D.repl* (8), and the data link layer sends an ACK by replying to the physical layer with a *P.repl* that the packet was received and should be acknowledged. The ACK signals propagate (10) and eventually generate a *P.conf* and a *D.conf* (11).

transfer of packets from the sender to the receiver. That is, the data link layer implements a packet link.

The packet link implemented by the data link layer can be used by the network layer as illustrated in Figure 4.6. In the figure, the network layer selects the path $A \rightarrow B \rightarrow C$ instead of $A \rightarrow D \rightarrow C$. The selection is usually based on some information about network delays and congestion. For example, the network layer may know that computer D has a large backlog of packets to transmit so that packets would take a long time to reach C if they were sent through node D. The network layer then requests the transmission of the packet from A to B, then from B to C. These transmissions use the packet links implemented by the data link layer. Note that the representation in Figure 4.6 hides the data link protocols. The figure provides a simplified representation of complex distributed algorithms.

In the network in Figure 4.7, there is a unique path from computer A to computer C. Consequently, the network layer in node B need not participate in the transmission.

144

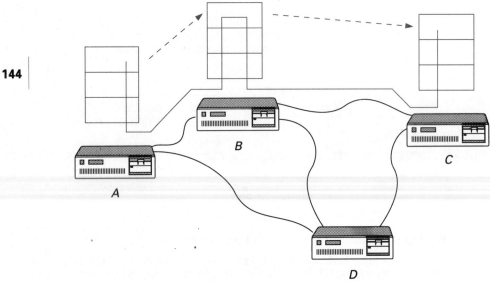

Figure 4.6 Store-and-forward transmission of packets.

Four computers are connected by coaxial cables. The figure shows the transmission of packets from computer *A* to computer *C*. The stacks of three rectangles symbolize the first three OSI layers in the corresponding nodes. The packets are first transmitted from *A* to *B*, then from *B* to *C*. The network layer in *A* asks the data link layer of link $A \rightarrow B$ to send the packet to the network layer in *B*. That network layer then asks the data link layer of link $B \rightarrow C$ to transmit the packet to the network layer in *C*. The result is the transmission of the packet along the dashed lines in the figure. The physical path of the information is indicated by the solid line.

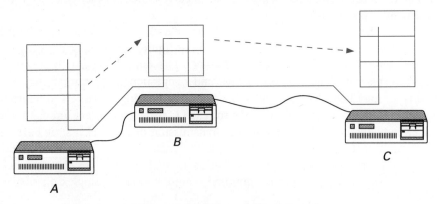

Figure 4.7 Network with unique path from *A* to *C*.

The transmission of packets from computer *A* to computer *C* via node *B* does not require any routing decision in node *B*. Once the data link layer in node *B* receives the packet, it can transmit it along link $B \rightarrow C$ without invoking the network layer.

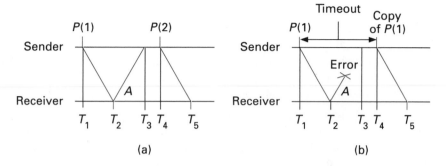

Figure 4.8 Transmission of unnumbered packets.

If the packets are not numbered, then the receiver is not able to determine whether the packet it receives at time T_5 is a new packet, as in (a), or a copy of a previously received packet, as in (b).

Network engineers call node B in Figure 4.6 a *router*, to indicate its role in the routing of packets; in Figure 4.7, they call it a *bridge*.

Since a data link protocol may request the transmission of multiple copies of a packet, some care must be taken to distinguish copies from new packets. Some care is also required to keep track of the packets that must be acknowledged. The various data link protocols differ by the methods the data link layer in the sender uses to determine which packets have not been acknowledged and the methods the data link layer in the receiver uses to distinguish retransmitted copies of packets from new packets. Two simple examples will demonstrate that the packets and their ACKs must be numbered to avoid possible confusion of the sender and receiver. The first example, illustrated in Figure 4.8, shows that the packets from sender to receiver must be numbered.

Figure 4.8(a) is a *timing diagram* which represents a sequence of transmissions. Time is represented by the horizontal axis; it flows from left to right. The transmissions of packets and of ACKs are represented by oblique lines. The leftmost oblique line represents the transmission of packet $P(1)$. The sender starts transmitting the packet $P(1)$ at time T_1, and the receiver gets the packet at time T_2. The figure assumes that the receiver transmits an ACK as soon as it receives the packet. The transmission of the ACK is represented by the oblique line that leaves the receiver at time T_2 and reaches the sender at time T_3. The sender starts transmitting a new packet $P(2)$ at time T_4. The receiver gets that packet at time T_5. Figure 4.8(b) represents another sequence of events. The sender starts transmitting packet $P(1)$ at time T_1. The receiver gets that packet at time T_2 and sends the ACK. The line that represents the transmission of the ACK is marked with a cross to indicate a transmission error. The ACK is considered lost.

In practice, the sender may not be able to identify the corrupted packet as an ACK. The sender retransmits a copy of packet $P(1)$ after a timeout, at time T_4. That copy arrives at the receiver at time T_5. Note that the two situations at time T_5 in Figures 4.8(a) and 4.8(b) appear identical to the receiver. As a consequence, the receiver cannot distinguish whether the packet that it receives at time T_5 is a new packet or a copy of a previously received packet. You might argue that the receiver could compare the packet received at time T_5 with the packets that it received previously. However, such a comparison is not feasible because it would take a long time and would require that the receiver keep a copy of previously received packets. Also, successive packets may happen to be identical. In a practical protocol, the sender and the receiver only remember and compare packet *numbers* and ACK numbers, not the complete sets of bits that constitute the packet. A packet number is a string of bits inserted at a specific location into the packet. Note that the number is not reliable if the packet contains transmission errors.

We can conclude from this example that the sender must number the packets in some way for the receiver to distinguish between copies and new packets.

The second example will show that ACKs must also be numbered. Let us assume that the sender numbers the packets with the successive numbers 1, 2, 3, and so on. That is, packet $P(1)$ is numbered 1, packet $P(2)$ is numbered 2, and so on. All the retransmitted copies of packet $P(n)$ are also numbered n. In Figure 4.9, the number of a packet is indicated next to the oblique line that represents the transmission of that packet. This numbering will prevent all confusion for the receiver: a copy of $P(1)$ is numbered 1, and it cannot be mistaken for $P(2)$. However, we will show that there remains a possibility of confusion for the sender if the ACKs are not numbered. Figure 4.9 describes the following sequence of events. At time T_1, the packet $P(1)$ is sent by the sender to the receiver. Packet $P(1)$ is received correctly at time T_2. For some reason, the receiver is busy and it cannot send the ACK of $P(1)$ before time T_3. The ACK is received at time T_5. The figure is drawn under the assumption that $T_5 > T_4 := T_1 +$ *timeout*. At time T_4, the sender transmits a copy of $P(1)$ since the timeout has expired. The copy of $P(1)$ is received correctly at time T_6, and its ACK is received by the sender at time T_7. When the first ACK of the original $P(1)$ is received at time T_5, the sender sends the packet $P(2)$, which is corrupted by transmission errors. At time T_7, the sender gets the ACK and cannot tell whether the ACK is for $P(2)$ or for the copy of $P(1)$. The sender would not be confused if each ACK had the same number as the packet that it acknowledges.

From these two examples we can conclude that both packets and ACKs must be numbered to avoid possible confusion.

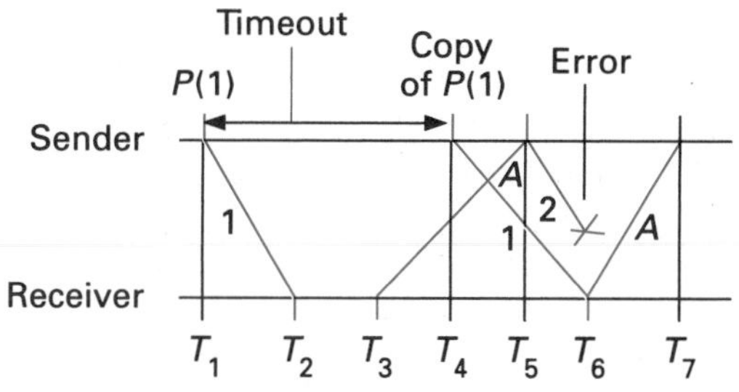

Figure 4.9 Transmission with unnumbered ACKs.

The sequence of transmissions is such that the sender cannot tell whether the ACK it receives at time T_7 is for the copy of $P(1)$ or for $P(2)$.

Here is a summary of our discussion:

Data Link Protocols

■ The objective of the data link layer is to convert the bit pipe provided by the physical layer into a packet link. This is achieved by the nodes' following a set of procedures called a data link protocol.

■ The subject of this chapter is data link protocols, which implement reliable and ordered packet links.

■ Packets that are not received correctly are retransmitted. The sender is informed of transmission errors by timers and acknowledgements.

■ Packets and ACKs must be numbered to avoid misidentified packets or acknowledgements.

Using the previous observations, we propose the following data link protocol. The sender numbers the packets successively 1, 2, 3, and so on. The receiver acknowledges every packet that it receives correctly and numbers the ACK with the number of the packet that it acknowledges. The sender retransmits a copy of a packet that is not acknowledged before a timeout. The data link layer in the receiver places the packets that it receives in a buffer and delivers them to the network layer in the correct order. You can convince yourself that such a data link protocol would deliver each packet correctly to the network layer in the correct order. However, this protocol cannot be used in communication networks, because it requires that the receiver be able to buffer an arbitrarily large number of packets. We demonstrate this requirement in Figure 4.10. The figure shows a

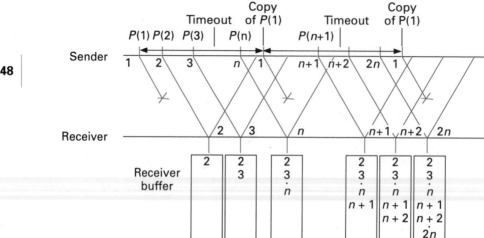

Figure 4.10 The need for buffering an arbitrarily large number of packets.

Packet $P(1)$ is lost, then packets $P(2)$, ..., $P(n)$ are received correctly. The first copy of $P(1)$ is lost. Packets $P(n + 1)$, ..., $P(2n)$ are received correctly. The second copy of $P(1)$ is also lost, and so on. To deliver the packets in the correct order to the network layer, the data link layer in the receiver must store the packets $P(2)$, ..., $P(2n)$, and so on, until it receives $P(1)$.

sequence of events that requires the receiver to store the packets $\{P(2), ..., P(2n), ...\}$ while it waits to receive the first correct copy of $P(1)$. Our next task is to discuss data link protocols that necessitate the storage of only a limited number of packets.

In Sections 4.2 through 4.4, we describe three commonly used protocols. Each solves the problem of misidentified packets or ACKs by adopting a specific numbering scheme. In addition to describing how packets are sent, received, and acknowledged between two nodes in the data link layer, we measure the efficiency of each protocol and compare their advantages and disadvantages.

4.2 Alternating Bit Protocol (ABP)

The *alternating bit protocol* (ABP) is the simplest of the three data link protocols that we will discuss. We will explain how ABP numbers the packets and the ACKs. We will also analyze the *efficiency* of ABP. The efficiency of a data link protocol is the average fraction of time that the protocol transmits new packets. During the rest of the time, the protocol waits for ACKs or for timeouts, or it retransmits copies of packets. For example, consider a data link protocol that transmits 1,000-bit-long packets with a transmitter that sends 56,000 bits per second. If the protocol efficiency is 100%, then the protocol is always transmitting new packets and transmits 56,000/1,000 = 56 packets per second. If the protocol efficiency is 10%, then the protocol transmits new packets only 10% of the time, i.e., 5.6 new packets per second, on the average. We will learn that ABP is inefficient when the *propagation time* of the signals is long compared to the *packet transmission time*. Recall that the propagation time is equal to the distance traveled by the signals divided by the propagation speed. For example, the propagation time of signals through 5 km of coaxial cable is equal to 5 km divided by 2.3×10^5 km/s—the propagation speed in coaxial cables—i.e., to 8.7 μs. The packet transmission time, in seconds, is equal to the number of bits in the packet divided by the transmission rate in bits per second. Thus, the transmission time of a 1,000-bit packet by a 56-kbps transmitter is equal to (1,000 bits)/(56,000 bps) = 17.9 ms. You see that the propagation time (8.7 μs) is much smaller than the packet transmission time (17.9 ms) in this example. The first bit of the packet is transmitted after (1 bit)/(56,000 bps) = 17.9 μs, and the signals start arriving at the receiver after 8.7 μs, even before the first bit is completely transmitted, i.e., before the signals that represent that first bit have completely left the sender. The signals that represent the last bit of the packet leave the sender at time 17.9 ms, and they arrive at the receiver 8.7 μs later. Consider now a 100-Mbps transmitter attached to an 80-km-long optical fiber. The transmission time of a 1,000-bit packet is now equal to (1,000 bits)/(10^8 bps) = 10 μs, and the propagation time is (80 km)/(2×10^5 km/s) = 400 μs. The transmission speed in a typical fiber is 2×10^5 km/s. Thus, if the transmission starts at time $t = 0$, then the last signals leave the sender at $t = 10$ μs, the signals start arriving at the receiver at $t = 400$ μs, and the last signals arrive at $t = 410$ μs. The transmission time is much smaller than the propagation time in this second example.

The alternating bit protocol can be described as follows. The *sender* transmits a first packet numbered 0 after storing a copy of that packet. The sender then waits for an acknowledgement numbered 0, ACK0, of that packet. If the acknowledgement ACK0 does not arrive before a timeout, the sender makes another copy of the first packet, also numbered 0, and transmits it. If ACK0 arrives before a timeout, the sender discards the copy of the first packet and is ready to transmit the next packet, which it numbers 1. The sender repeats the previous steps, with the numbers 0 and 1 interchanged. The *receiver* initially waits for a packet numbered 0 and ignores the incorrect packets that it receives. When the receiver receives a correct packet numbered 1, it acknowledges the packet by sending an acknowledgement numbered 1 to the sender and it *discards* the packet. When the receiver receives a correct packet numbered 0, it sends an acknowledgement numbered 0 to the sender. In addition, the receiver *delivers* the packet—without its number—to the network layer in the receiver if the receiver is a router or a destination node. The receiver delivers the packet to another data

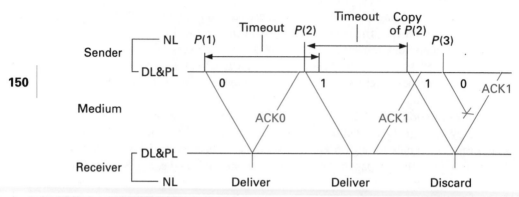

Figure 4.11 Example of events with the alternating bit protocol.

The packets and their acknowledgements are numbered 0, 1, 0, 1, ... A packet is retransmitted if it is not acknowledged before a timeout. The numbers of the packets and acknowledgements are indicated next to the oblique lines that represent their propagation.

link layer entity if the node is a bridge, like node B in Figure 4.7. The receiver then repeats the previous steps with the numbers 0 and 1 interchanged.

Figure 4.11 illustrates a sequence of events when ABP is used. The figure assumes that the node is a router or a destination node. The first packet, $P(1)$, is numbered 0 and arrives correctly. The acknowledgement of $P(1)$, also numbered 0, arrives at the sender before the timeout. Packet $P(1)$ is delivered by the data link layer to the network layer in the receiver. The sender numbers the second packet $P(2)$ with the number 1 and transmits the packet, which arrives correctly. For some reason—the receiver being very busy, for instance—packet $P(2)$ is acknowledged too late with ACK1, which arrives at the sender after the timeout. At the expiration time of the timeout, the sender assumes that packet $P(2)$ did not get to the receiver and it sends a copy, again numbered 1. This copy arrives correctly at the receiver. Since the last received packet was not numbered 0, the receiver discards the packet but acknowledges the reception by another ACK1. The next packet, $P(3)$, is numbered 0 and does not arrive correctly. Just after the transmission of $P(3)$, ACK1 arrives. Since it is not an ACK0, the sender does not confuse it with an acknowledgement of $P(3)$.

The advantages of ABP are its simplicity and its small buffer requirements: the sender needs to keep only a copy of the packet that it last transmitted, and the receiver does not need to buffer packets at the data link layer. The main disadvantage of ABP is that it does not use the communication link very efficiently. Indeed, if we assume that the packets and acknowledgements are always correctly transmitted, we can represent the channel usage with the timing diagram shown in Figure 4.12.

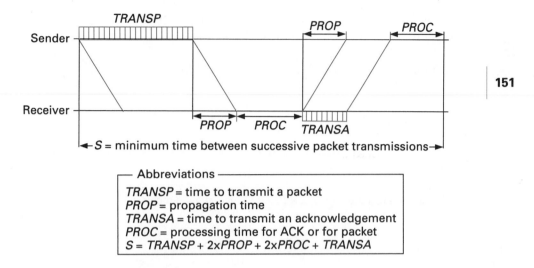

Figure 4.12 Timing of error-free ABP.

The ABP is not very efficient, because the sender must wait for each packet to be acknowledged before it can send the next packet.

In Figure 4.12, *TRANSP* denotes the transmission time of a typical packet, i.e., the number of bits in a packet divided by the transmission rate in bits per second. *TRANSA* is the transmission time of an ACK, i.e., the number of bits in an acknowledgement divided by the bit-transmission rate. *PROP* is the propagation time of a packet or an ACK, i.e., the length of the channel divided by the signal propagation speed. Also, *PROC* is the time needed to process a packet or an ACK, i.e., to check the error-detection bits and get ready for the next transmission. This processing time depends on the node hardware. Typically, *PROC* is a fraction of 1 ms.

Figure 4.12 shows that the total time taken for transmitting a packet and for preparing to transmit the next one is equal to

$$S := TRANSP + 2 \times PROP + 2 \times PROC + TRANSA. \tag{4.1}$$

The *efficiency* of a data link protocol is defined as the fraction of time that new packets are being sent, assuming that the sender always has packets to transmit. In the absence of errors, the sender transmits one new packet every S seconds. The sender transmits a new packet during *TRANSP* seconds out of these S seconds. Consequently, the efficiency $\eta(ABP, 0)$ of ABP in the absence of errors is equal to

$$\eta(ABP, 0) = \frac{TRANSP}{S}. \tag{4.2}$$

For instance, with a transmission line of 500 km at 56 kbps, if the packet and the acknowledgement have 700 bits, one finds that

$$TRANSA = TRANSP = \frac{700 \text{ bits}}{56{,}000 \text{ bps}} = 0.0125 \text{ s}, \ PROP = \frac{500{,}000 \text{ m}}{2.3 \times 10^8 \text{ m/s}} \approx 0.00217 \text{ s}.$$

Consequently,

$$S \approx 0.0125 \text{ s} + 2 \times (0.00217 \text{ s}) + 2 \times PROC + 0.0125 \text{ s}$$
$$= 0.02934 \text{ s} + 2 \times PROC.$$

We can neglect the term $2 \times PROC$ since it is typically of the order of 1 ms. Using (4.2) we conclude that

$$\eta(ABP, 0) \approx \frac{0.0125 \text{ s}}{0.02934 \text{ s}} \approx 43\%.$$

In this example, the loss in efficiency arises mostly from the transmission time of the ACKs.

Consider now an optical fiber of 500 km at 100 Mbps and assume that the packets and acknowledgements have 10,000 bits. One finds that

$$TRANSP = TRANSA = \frac{10{,}000 \text{ bits}}{10^8 \text{ bps}} = 10^{-4} \text{ s},$$

$$PROP = \frac{5 \times 10^5 \text{ m}}{2 \times 10^8 \text{ m/s}} = 2.5 \times 10^{-3} \text{ s}.$$

If we assume that $PROC = 1$ ms, we get from (4.1)

$$S = 10^{-4} + 2 \times 2.5 \times 10^{-3} + 2 \times 10^{-3} + 10^{-4} = 7.2 \times 10^{-3} \text{ s}.$$

We can then conclude from (4.2) that

$$\eta(ABP, 0) = \frac{10^{-4} \text{ s}}{7.2 \times 10^{-3} \text{ s}} \approx 1.4\%.$$

In this example, the loss of efficiency arises from the propagation and processing times.

Since data link protocols are designed to compensate for transmission errors, it is desirable to investigate their efficiency in the presence of such errors. We will see that, not surprisingly, transmission errors reduce the efficiency of ABP. In the case of an error, either during the transmission of a packet or of its ACK, the sender restarts the transmission after a time equal to *timeout*. We summarize the possible sequences of events in Figure 4.13.

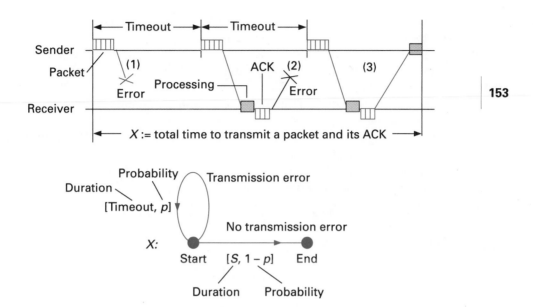

Figure 4.13 Events in packet transmission.

The top part of the figure shows a typical sequence of events. It shows a random number of incorrect transmissions before the first successful one: (1) A packet is corrupted. (2) An ACK is corrupted. (3) Successful transmission of packet and ACK. The total time taken by the successful transmission of a packet and of its ACK is a random variable X. The bottom part of the figure summarizes the random events in the transmission. It is a symbolic representation of the random duration X of a successful transmission. The arrow from START to END represents the successful transmission of a packet and of its ACK: it takes S seconds and occurs with probability $1 - p$. The arrow from START to START represents an unsuccessful transmission of either the packet or its ACK; it occurs with probability p, and it wastes *timeout* seconds.

The top part of Figure 4.13 shows a possible sequence of events: a corrupted packet, a corrupted acknowledgement, then a successful transmission of a packet and of its ACK. Note that a transmission error wastes *timeout* seconds and occurs with probability p, where we denote by p the probability that a packet or its ACK is corrupted by transmission errors. Also, a successful transmission of a packet and its ACK takes S seconds and occurs with probability $1 - p$. The bottom part of Figure 4.13 summarizes all the possible sequences of events. The figure shows two *states*: START and END. The states represent stages in the execution of the data link protocol. START designates the beginning of the transmission of a given packet; END signifies that the sender is ready to transmit the next packet. The horizontal arrow from START to END is marked with the time S

taken by a successful transmission of a packet and its ACK and with the probability $1 - p$ of such a transmission. That arrow signifies that with probability $1 - p$, it takes S seconds to go from START to END. Indeed, with probability $1 - p$, the packet and its ACK are correctly received and the sender is ready to transmit the next packet after S seconds. The circular arrow from START to itself is marked with *timeout* and with p. That arrow signifies that with probability p, the sender restarts the transmission of the same packet after *timeout*.

Figure 4.13 is the key to a straightforward analysis of $E\{X\}$, the average value of the random time X taken by the protocol to reach END from START, i.e., for the sender to be ready for the next packet. Using the *regenerative method* of Appendix A, one can write (see Figure 4.13)

$$E\{X\} = (1 - p) \times S + p \times (timeout + E\{X\}). \tag{4.3}$$

Solving for $E\{X\}$ gives

$$E\{X\} = S + \frac{p \times timeout}{1 - p}.$$

The *efficiency* of ABP, defined as the fraction of time during which new packets are transmitted, is equal to

$$\eta(\text{ABP}, p) := \frac{TRANSP}{E\{X\}} = \frac{(1 - p) \times TRANSP}{(1 - p) \times S + p \times timeout}. \tag{4.4}$$

Indeed, $E\{X\}$ is the average time between successive transmissions of new packets. It is, therefore, the average total time spent per packet. The actual transmission time per packet is *TRANSP*. Consequently, the fraction of time during which the sender transmits packets is given by (4.4). The efficiency is maximized by choosing the smallest possible value for the timeout. If the channel is full-duplex, i.e., if it can transmit in both directions simultaneously, then one can choose *timeout = TRANSP*, which corresponds to transmitting copies of packets back-to-back. If the channel is half-duplex, i.e., if it can transmit in only one direction at a time, then the minimum value of *timeout* is S. This leads to the following values of the efficiency of the full-duplex and half-duplex ABP, respectively:

$$\begin{cases} \eta_{FD}(\text{ABP}, p) = \dfrac{(1 - p) \times TRANSP}{(1 - p) \times S + p \times TRANSP} \\ \eta_{HD}(\text{ABP}, p) = \dfrac{(1 - p) \times TRANSP}{S}. \end{cases} \tag{4.5}$$

Let us summarize what we learned about ABP.

Alternating Bit Protocol (ABP)

- The packets transmitted using ABP are numbered alternatively 0, 1, 0, 1, ...

- The receiver acknowledges the correct packets with an ACK that has the same number as the packet.

- The sender retransmits a copy of the packets not acknowledged before a fixed *timeout*.

- The *efficiency* of a protocol is defined as the fraction of time spent transmitting new packets.

- The efficiency of ABP for half-duplex and for full-duplex lines is given by

$$\begin{cases} \eta_{FD}(\text{ABP},p) = \dfrac{(1-p) \times TRANSP}{(1-p) \times S + p \times TRANSP} \\ \eta_{HD}(\text{ABP},p) = \dfrac{(1-p) \times TRANSP}{S} . \end{cases} \quad (4.5)$$

From our discussion of ABP, you can see that we could make better use of the network resources with a protocol that can transmit a packet without having to wait for the preceding one to be acknowledged. The selective repeat protocol solves this problem; it is discussed in the next section.

4.3 Selective Repeat Protocol

The *selective repeat protocol* (SRP) improves on the efficiency of ABP by permitting more than a single unacknowledged packet. As its name implies, this protocol repeats only selective transmissions—those that are not acknowledged before a timeout. Using SRP, the data link layer in the receiver delivers exactly one copy of every packet in the correct order. The data link layer in the receiver may get the packets in the wrong order from the physical layer, however. This occurs, for instance, when transmission errors corrupt the first packet and not the second one: the second packet arrives correctly at the receiver before the first. The data link layer in the receiver uses a buffer to store the packets that arrive out of order. Once the data link layer in the receiver has a consecutive group of packets in its buffer, it can deliver them to the network layer, or to another data link layer entity if the receiver is a bridge. (Recall Figures 4.6 and 4.7.) The sender also uses a buffer, to store copies of the unacknowledged packets. You will see that the buffers at the sender and at the receiver

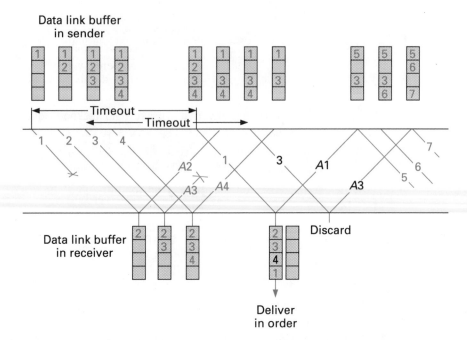

Figure 4.14 Sequence of events in selective repeat protocol.

The sender transmits packets 1, 2, 3, and 4. Packet 1 is corrupted. The receiver sends ACK2, ACK3, and ACK4, and ACK3 is corrupted. The sender retransmits packet 1 and packet 3 after a timeout and the sender receives ACK1 and ACK3. The sender then transmits packets 5, 6, and 7. The figure indicates the contents of the buffers.

must be able to hold only a finite number of packets. That finite number is a design parameter of SRP. SRP requires a full-duplex link: the receiver transmits acknowledgements to the sender while the sender transmits packets to the receiver.

We first describe a version of SRP that uses a simplified numbering scheme for the packets. We assume that the sender and receiver buffers can hold four packets each. The sequence of events is represented in Figure 4.14. The sender numbers the packets successively 1, 2, 3, 4, 5, and so on. The sender first transmits four packets numbered 1, 2, 3, 4 and keeps copies of these packets in its buffer. The sender then waits for the acknowledgement ACK1 of packet 1. If ACK1 arrives before a timeout, the sender transmits the next packet, numbered 5, and replaces the copy of packet 1 with a copy of packet 5 in its buffer. If ACK1 does not arrive at the sender before a timeout, the sender retransmits a copy of packet 1. The sender continues the transmissions while making sure that the numbers of the unacknowledged packets differ by less than four. For example, the sender cannot transmit packet 5 while packet 1 is still unacknowledged, even after the sender receives the acknowledgements of packets 2 and 4, so that its buffer has space for holding two more packets. The receiver acknowledges all the packets that it receives correctly with acknowledgements numbered with the same numbers as the packets. The receiver stores the packets it receives out of order in a buffer. You can see that, since the numbers of unacknowledged packets differ by less than four, the receiver buffer will never hold more than four packets. For example, the receiver must receive a correct copy of packet 1 before it sends an ACK1 to the sender and, therefore, before the sender can transmit packet 5. Consequently, when packet 1 is unacknowledged, only packets 2, 3, and 4 can also be unacknowledged, and only those packets can be received out of order. The receiver may have to store these three packets, and the receiver buffer can then store the copy of packet 1 when it receives it correctly. The receiver then empties its buffer when it delivers the four packets 1, 2, 3, and 4.

Summarizing, the sequence of steps in SRP obeys the following rules:

1. The packets are numbered consecutively 1, 2, 3, and so on.
2. The numbers of the unacknowledged packets differ by less than four.
3. The sender stores copies of the unacknowledged packets and retransmits them after a timeout.
4. The receiver stores copies of the packets it receives out of order and acknowledges all the correct packets; it delivers the packets in the correct order.

An example will show you that the receiver may have to store an arbitrarily large number of packets if the sender does not follow rule 2. Consider the sequence of events in Figure 4.15.

Assume that transmission errors corrupt only packet 1 and its copies. Then the receiver must store all the packets that it receives correctly. Note that the sender keeps transmitting packets since it receives acknowledgements that free space in its buffer.

The SRP that we described numbers the packets 1, 2, 3, and so on. This numbering scheme is not practical, because it uses arbitrarily large numbers. The SRP implemented in communication networks numbers packets with finitely many different numbers. The numbers are $\{0, 1, ..., 7\}$ when the buffers in the sender and receiver can hold four packets each. These eight different numbers can be represented by three bits as $\{000, 001, ..., 111\}$. In this new numbering, the nth packet is numbered with the remainder of the division of $(n - 1)$ by 8. Thus, the packets are numbered successively 0, 1, 2, ..., 7, 0, 1, 2, ..., 7, 0, 1, 2, ... As before, an ACK has the same number as the packet it acknowledges. We will call this new numbering *numbering modulo 8*.

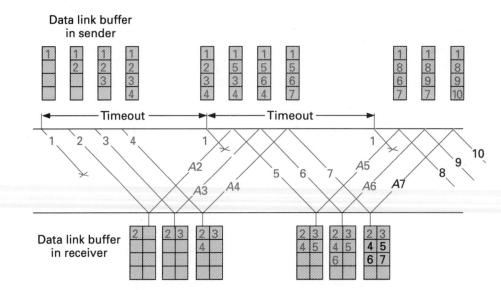

Figure 4.15 Sequence of events when the sender does not follow rule 2.

If the sender transmits whenever it can store copies of the unacknowledged packets in its buffer, the receiver may have to store an arbitrarily large number of packets. This example shows that, if transmission errors corrupt only packet 1 and its copies, then the receiver must store all the packets that it receives correctly.

Before we explain why numbering modulo 8 does not confuse the sender nor the receiver, let us show you that numbering modulo 7 can confuse them. When using numbering modulo 7, the sender numbers the nth packet with the remainder of the division of $(n-1)$ by 7. That is, the sender numbers the packets successively $0, 1, ..., 6, 0, 1, 2, ..., 6, 0, 1, 2, ...$. We use the example illustrated in Figure 4.16.

In Figure 4.16(a), there is no transmission error and the second packet numbered 0 that arrives at the receiver is the eighth packet. In Figure 4.16(b), transmission errors corrupt the first ACK0. The second packet 0 received by the receiver is a retransmitted copy of the first packet. The receiver cannot distinguish between these two cases. Consequently, the receiver does not know whether to store or to discard the second packet numbered 0. We can conclude from this example that the numbering modulo 7 is not suitable. The receiver is confused because it may receive different packets with the same number.

You will see that, when numbering modulo 8 is used, the different packets that the receiver can get at any given time have different numbers and the ACKs that the sender can get at any one time also have different numbers. Consider once again SRP when the nth packet is numbered n. (See Figure 4.17.)

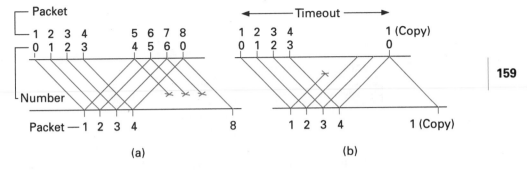

Figure 4.16 SRP with numbering modulo 7.

This example shows that numbering modulo 7 confuses the receiver when the buffers can hold 4 packets. When the receiver gets the second packet numbered 0, it cannot determine whether it is the eighth packet (a) or a copy of the first packet (b).

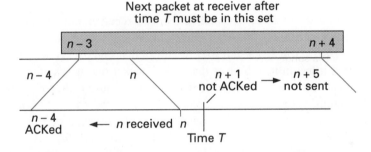

Figure 4.17 The last packet delivered by the receiver is packet n.

The figure considers SRP when the data link in the receiver has delivered packet n to the network layer but has not yet delivered packet $n + 1$. The number of the next packet to be received by the receiver must be in the set $\{n - 3, n - 2, ..., n + 4\}$.

Denote by n the number of the last packet delivered by the data link layer to the network layer in the receiver. Packet $n + 1$ has not yet arrived correctly at the receiver, for it would have been delivered to the network layer. Consequently, the receiver has not sent ACK($n + 1$) and the sender has not received that acknowledgement. Therefore, the last packet transmitted by the sender is at most packet $(n + 4)$, since the numbers of unacknowledged packets differ by less than four. Moreover, the sender must have received all the acknowledgements up to ACK($n - 4$), since it transmitted packet n. We conclude that the number of the next packet the receiver can get is in the set $NEXT(n) := \{n - 3, n - 2, ..., n + 4\}$. Also, if the receiver gets a packet whose number is in the set $OLD(n) := \{n - 3, n - 2, n - 1, n\}$, it knows that the packet is a copy of a packet

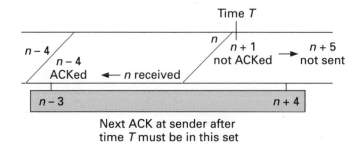

Next ACK at sender after
time *T* must be in this set

Figure 4.18 The last ACK received is ACK*n*.

Let ACK*n* be the last ACK received by the sender. Packet *n* – 4 must have
been acknowledged, and the last packet transmitted by the sender is at
most packet (*n* + 4). As a consequence, the only ACKs that the sender can
receive have a number in {*n* – 3, *n* – 2, ..., *n* + 4}. These numbers are different when the sender numbers the packets modulo 8.

that it has already received and delivered. The receiver must acknowledge and
discard such a packet. If the receiver gets a packet whose number is in the set
$NEW(n) := \{n + 1, n + 2, n + 3, n + 4\}$, it knows that this packet is either a copy of
a packet that it has in its buffer or that it is a packet that it has not received. The
receiver must store such a packet if it is not in its buffer already. Now, assume
that SRP numbers the packets modulo 8. Consider the case when $n = 135$. The
135th packet is numbered with the remainder of the division of $135 - 1 = 134$ by
8, i.e., 6. When $n = 135$, the sets $OLD(n)$ and $NEW(n)$ are $OLD(135) =
\{132, 133, 134, 135\}$ and $NEW(135) = \{136, 137, 138, 139\}$. These packets are
numbered with the elements in $OLD = \{3, 4, 5, 6\}$ and $NEW = \{7, 0, 1, 2\}$,
respectively. Consequently, when the receiver has delivered a packet numbered 6,
it knows that a packet numbered with an element in the set OLD is a copy of a
previously delivered packet and that a packet numbered with an element in the set
NEW should be stored if it is not in the receiver buffer. Thus, the receiver cannot
be confused when the packets are numbered modulo 8. We now show that the
sender cannot be confused when SRP numbers the packets modulo 8. (See Figure
4.18.) Consider once again SRP when the *n*th packet is numbered *n*. Assume that
the largest number of the acknowledgements received by the sender is *n*. The
sender has received ACK($n - 4$) since it transmitted packet *n*. Also, the largest
number of a packet transmitted by the sender is at most $n + 4$. Consequently, the
number of the next ACK that the sender will receive must belong to the set
$\{n - 3, n - 2, ..., n + 4\}$. The numbers of these packets are also different when the
sender numbers the packets modulo 8. You can conclude that the sender cannot be
confused by this numbering.

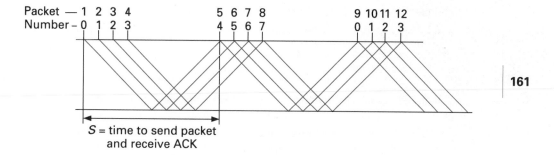

S = time to send packet
and receive ACK

Figure 4.19 Timing diagram of error-free SRP.

When no transmission error occurs, SRP transmits a group of four packets every S seconds.

Let us summarize our discussion of the packet numbering in SRP. When the sender and receiver follow rules 1–4 and when the number of the last packet delivered by the receiver is n, the number of the next packet that the receiver will get must be in the set $NEXT(n) = \{n - 3, n - 2, \ldots, n + 4\}$. Moreover, the receiver must acknowledge and discard the next packet if its number is in the set $OLD(n) = \{n - 3, n - 2, n - 1, n\}$; otherwise, the receiver must store that packet if it is not already in its buffer. When the sender and receiver follow rules 2–4 and number the packets and ACKs modulo 8, the receiver can distinguish the numbers of the packets in $OLD(n)$ and $NEW(n)$ since it knows the number of packet n. Consequently, SRP can use numbering modulo 8 without confusing the receiver. Similarly, one shows that the sender cannot be confused by this numbering.

You can verify that one may replace the values 8 and 4 with $2W$ and W, respectively, in the definition of SRP, for any $W \geq 1$. That is, when the sender and receiver buffers can hold W packets each, SRP can number the packets modulo $2W$. For the remainder of this section we will assume that SRP uses the numbering modulo $2W$. The value W is called the *window size* of SRP. Note that ABP is identical to SRP with a window size $W = 1$.

The SRP protocol can be expected to be significantly more efficient than ABP if the timeout and the window size are well chosen. We will calculate the efficiency first in the absence of errors. The sequence of events in SRP in the absence of errors is illustrated in Figure 4.19.

Figure 4.19 has a window size of 4, as in Figure 4.14. The evolution proceeds in cycles of duration S during which W packets are transmitted. The time S is defined as

$$S := TRANSP + 2 \times PROP + 2 \times PROC + TRANSA. \tag{4.6}$$

The time S, identical to that defined in (4.1), is equal to the time between the start of the transmission of a packet and the reception of the acknowledgement of that packet. Figure 4.19 assumes that

$$W \times TRANSP < S, \tag{4.7}$$

162

i.e., that the acknowledgement of the packet numbered 0 is received after the packets numbered $0, ..., W-1$ have been transmitted. If the reverse inequality holds, then the sender transmits continuously and the efficiency (defined as for ABP) is 100%. Under (4.7), the efficiency is equal to $W \times TRANSP/S$: new packets are transmitted during $W \times TRANSP$ out of S seconds. Thus, in the general case,

$$\eta(SRP, 0) = \min \{\frac{W \times TRANSP}{S}, 1\}, \tag{4.8}$$

where $\min\{a, b\}$ denotes the minimum of two numbers a and b. The 0 in $\eta(SRP, 0)$ indicates that this is the efficiency of SRP without errors.

To apply this expression, consider the case of packets with 10,000 bits, ACKs with 100 bits, a 100-km-long link, a propagation speed of 2.3×10^8 m/s, a transmission rate of 100 Mbps, and $PROC = 0.2$ ms. Using (4.6) and (4.8), you can check that the efficiency is equal to

$$\eta(SRP, 0) = \min \{\frac{W}{13.7}, 1\}.$$

For example, the efficiency is about 7.3% when $W = 1$ (i.e., for ABP), while it is about 29% for $W = 4$ and 100% for $W = 14$.

We have seen that SRP with $W \geq 2$ is more efficient than ABP when there is no transmission error. Now let us examine the effect of noise on the efficiency of SRP. We will first consider the case $W = \infty$ where the sender and the receiver both have buffers that can hold an arbitrarily large number of packets. Choose *timeout* $> S$ so that the sender never retransmits copies of packets when there is no transmission error. Denote by p the probability that a transmission error corrupts either a packet or its acknowledgement. Under these assumptions, you can verify that each packet will be transmitted an average number of times equal to $1/(1 - p)$. For instance, each packet is transmitted once when $p = 0$, i.e., when there is no transmission error. Also, the sender transmits each packet twice, on the average, if $p = 50\%$. Since $W = \infty$, the sender never has to wait; it keeps sending all time. For a given packet, the useful transmission time is $TRANSP$ and the total time is $TRANSP/(1 - p)$. As a consequence, the efficiency is equal to

$$\eta_\infty(SRP, p) = 1 - p. \tag{4.9}$$

The subscript of η_∞ recalls the assumption $W = \infty$. Note that this model implicitly assumes that the sender can process ACKs while it is transmitting packets. These two operations are usually performed concurrently by different pieces of hardware.

Formula (4.9) provides an upper bound on the efficiency of SRP implementable with buffers that can hold only finitely many packets. Indeed, the sender has to stop transmitting when its buffer is full, and such stoppage reduces the protocol efficiency. An exact analysis of SRP with finite buffers is complicated. We will analyze SRP under the *round-trip assumptions*:

$$S = timeout = W \times TRANSP. \tag{4.10}$$

These two assumptions mean that the sender detects a transmission error just when it is about to have to wait for an ACK. In addition, we will also assume that errors are rare. Specifically, we assume that

$$pW \le 10\%. \tag{4.11}$$

Under assumption (4.11), the transmission errors are rare enough so that one can neglect the probability that more than one packet or its ACK is lost out of W successive transmissions. This is so because that probability is equal to $1 - (1 - p)^W - Wp(1 - p)^{W-1}$, which can be seen to be very small when (4.11) is satisfied. In Figure 4.20, drawn for $W = 4$, transmission errors corrupt the second packet. As a consequence, the sender retransmits packet 2 after a timeout. Figure 4.20 indicates that, instead of transmitting four packets in time S, the sender transmits $N_2 := 5$ packets in $T_2 := S + TRANSP + timeout$. The cases when other packets or ACKs are lost are treated similarly. One finds that if packet 1 or its ACK is lost, then the sender transmits $N_1 := 4$ packets in $T_1 := S + timeout$. When packet 3 or its ACK is lost, $N_3 := 6$ packets are transmitted in $T_3 := S + 2 \times TRANSP + timeout$. When packet 4 or its ACK is lost, $N_4 := 7$ packets are transmitted in $T_4 := S + 3 \times TRANSP + timeout$. These four cases occur with probability $p(1 - p)^3$ each: the probability that one specific packet or its ACK is lost and the others are not. This probability is approximately equal to p. With probability close to $1 - 4p$, the first four packets and their ACKs are correctly received and the $N_0 := 4$ packets are transmitted in $T_0 = S$. It can be observed from Figure 4.20 that the sequence of events starts afresh after the retransmitted copy has been acknowledged. For instance, in Figure 4.20, the sequence of events starts afresh when packet 6 is transmitted (up to the shifted numbering of the packets). As a consequence, we can view the evolution of SRP as a succession of cycles that are statistically equivalent. For $n \ge 1$, cycle number n has a random duration τ_n and it transmits a random number X_n of packets.

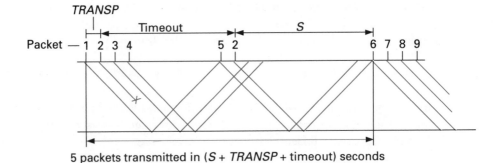

5 packets transmitted in (S + $TRANSP$ + timeout) seconds

Figure 4.20 Evolution of SRP with errors.

A transmission error wastes transmission time and reduces the efficiency of the protocol. In the case illustrated in the figure, five packets are transmitted in S + $TRANSP$ + timeout.

One finds that

$$(\tau_n, X_n) \approx \begin{cases} (T_0, N_0), & \text{with prob.} \quad 1 - Wp \\ (T_i, N_i), & \text{with prob.} \quad p \text{ for } 1 \le i \le W \end{cases} \tag{4.12}$$

with

$$T_0 = W \times TRANSP, N_0 = W \tag{4.13}$$
$$T_i = (2W + i - 1) \times TRANSP, \text{ for } 1 \le i \le W$$
$$N_i = W + i - 1, \text{ for } 1 \le i \le W.$$

The number of packets transmitted in the first n cycles is equal to $X_1 + \ldots + X_n$, and the duration of those n cycles is $\tau_1 + \ldots + \tau_n$. It follows that the efficiency of SRP can be obtained as

$$\frac{TRANSP \times (X_1 + \ldots + X_n)}{\tau_1 + \ldots + \tau_n}. \tag{4.14}$$

This ratio expresses the time during which the sender is transmitting new packets divided by the total duration of the first n cycles. The key to the evaluation of (4.14) is the *Strong Law of Large Numbers*, which establishes that the arithmetic mean of a large number of statistically equivalent and independent random variables is almost equal to their expected value. To use this result, one first rewrites (4.14) as

$$TRANSP \times \frac{(X_1 + \ldots + X_n)/n}{(\tau_1 + \ldots + \tau_n)/n}. \tag{4.15}$$

One then observes that the numerator in (4.15) is the arithmetic mean of n independent and statistically equivalent random variables. Therefore, by the Strong Law of Large Numbers, this arithmetic mean is approximately equal to the expected value $E\{X_n\}$ of the random variable X_n. Similarly, the denominator of (4.15) is approximately equal to $E\{\tau_n\}$. This shows that the efficiency of SRP is given by

$$\frac{TRANSP \times E\{X_n\}}{E\{\tau_n\}}.$$

The two expected values are obtained from (4.12)–(4.13). One finds that

$$E\{X_n\} = (1 - Wp) \times N_0 + p \times \{N_1 + \ldots + N_W\}$$
$$= W + \frac{pW(W-1)}{2}.$$

Similarly,

$$E\{\tau_n\} \approx (1 - Wp) \times T_0 + p \times \{T_1 + \ldots + T_W\}$$
$$= W \times TRANSP \times \{1 + \frac{p}{2}(3W - 1)\}$$

The above formulas show that the approximate efficiency of SRP in the case of rare errors is given by

$$\eta_{RT}(SRP, p) \approx \frac{2 + p(W - 1)}{2 + p(3W - 1)} \quad \text{with} \quad W = \frac{S}{TRANSP} \quad \text{and} \quad pW \leq 10\%. \tag{4.16}$$

The subscript in η_{RT} reminds us that we have made the *round-trip* assumptions (4.10). The efficiency (4.16) can be improved by choosing a window larger than $S/TRANSP$.

For a numerical illustration of (4.9) and (4.16), assume that $S = 10 \times TRANSP$. Then,

$$\eta_\infty(SRP, 1\%) = 99\% \quad \text{and} \quad \eta_{RT}(SRP, 1\%) \approx 91\%.$$

These numbers show that an efficiency between 91% and 99% is achievable.

Let us summarize what we have learned about SRP:

Selective Repeat Protocol (SRP)

- SRP is more efficient than ABP because the sender does not have to wait for a packet to be acknowledged before sending the next one.
- The packets are numbered consecutively 0, 1, 2, ..., 2W − 1, 0, 1, 2, ..., 2W − 1, ...
- The $(n + W)$th packet cannot be transmitted while the nth packet is still unacknowledged.
- The sender retransmits a copy of a packet that has not been acknowledged before a timeout.
- The receiver acknowledges the reception of a correct packet with an ACK that has the same number as the packet.
- The receiver stores the packet it receives out of order, and it delivers the packets in order.
- The efficiency of SRP in the absence of errors is given by

$$\eta(SRP, 0) = \min\{\frac{W \times TRANSP}{S}, 1\}. \qquad (4.8)$$

- For very large W, the efficiency in the presence of errors is given by

$$\eta_\infty(SRP, p) = 1 - p. \qquad (4.9)$$

- The efficiency of SRP under rare errors and with the round-trip assumptions

$$S = timeout = W \times TRANSP \qquad (4.10)$$

is given by

$$\eta_{RT}(SRP, p) \approx \frac{2 + p(W - 1)}{2 + p(3W - 1)}. \qquad (4.16)$$

SRP is a very efficient protocol, but it requires buffering packets at both the sender and the receiver. The protocol that we discuss in the next section is simpler than SRP. However, it is somewhat less efficient.

4.4 GO BACK N

The *GO BACK N* protocol allows the sender to have multiple unacknowledged packets without the receiver having to store packets. This is done by not allowing the receiver to accept packets that are out of order and by retransmit-

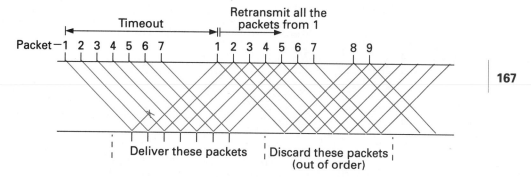

Figure 4.21 Sequence of events with the GO BACK N protocol.

When a packet is not acknowledged before a timeout, the sender retransmits that packet and all the subsequent packets.

ting the packets not acknowledged before a timeout and all the subsequent packets. The GO BACK N protocol improves on the efficiency of ABP, but is less efficient than SRP.

We first describe the GO BACK N protocol with *window size W* with simplified packet numbering. The sender numbers the packets consecutively 1, 2, 3, and so on. The receiver acknowledges every correct packet it receives by transmitting to the sender an acknowledgement with the same number as the packet. Also, the receiver discards the packets received out of order, whereas it delivers the packets received in order to the network layer or to another data link layer entity. The sender can have up to W unacknowledged packets, and it keeps copies of the unacknowledged packets in a buffer. The sender transmits packets 1, 2, ..., W and waits for the acknowledgement ACK1 of packet 1 before transmitting packet $W + 1$. If the sender does not receive the acknowledgement of packet n before a *timeout*, it retransmits copies of packet n and *of all the packets it transmitted after packet n*. These retransmissions are needed because the receiver does not store packets received out of order: when the sender fails to receive ACKn before a timeout, it suspects that the receiver did not get packet n and that the receiver discarded all the subsequent packets, even though it may have acknowledged them. A possible sequence of events with the GO BACK N protocol is shown in Figure 4.21 when $W = 7$.

The sender transmits the packets $\{1, ..., 7\}$. These seven packets can be unacknowledged. The receiver accepts the packets $\{1, ..., 7\}$ since they arrive in order, and it acknowledges them with ACK(1),..., ACK(7). Transmission errors corrupt ACK1. After a timeout, the sender restarts the transmissions with packet 1. The receiver then discards the retransmitted copies of $\{1, ..., 7\}$ since they are out of order. The next packet which can be accepted and delivered by the receiver is packet 8.

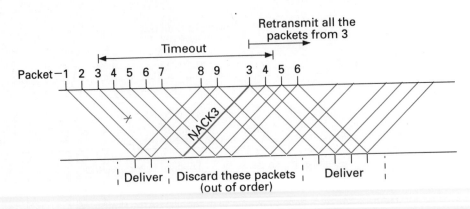

168

Figure 4.22 GO BACK N with negative acknowledgements.

A negative acknowledgement initiates the retransmission of a packet before the timeout. This improves the efficiency of GO BACK N.

Negative acknowledgements (NACKs) can be used to speed up the GO BACK N protocol. This speed-up is demonstrated in Figure 4.22. A negative acknowledgement (NACK) is sent as soon as the receiver realizes that it received an incorrect packet. This occurs when the receiver notices a gap in the numbering of the correct packets it receives. The sender can then retransmit a copy of the corrupted packet immediately without having to wait for the timeout, as would be the case without NACKs.

GO BACK N is less efficient than SRP in the presence of errors. Decreased efficiency is the price paid for not having to store packets at the receiver. Specifically, GO BACK N with window size W is less efficient than SRP with window size W. We will analyze the efficiency of GO BACK N under the *round-trip assumptions* (4.10), recalled below for convenience:

$$timeout = S = W \times TRANSP. \qquad (4.17)$$

Figure 4.23 shows a sequence of events with GO BACK N under these assumptions. As the figure indicates, an error in packet 1 or in its ACK eventually leads the sender to waste an amount of time equal to *timeout* before restarting the transmissions. If there is no error during the transmission of packet 1 or of its ACK, then the sender takes a time equal to *TRANSP* before transmitting the next packet. As a consequence, the evolution of GO BACK N can be represented as in Figure 4.24. The black circle marked n is *state n*; it designates a stage in the execution of the GO BACK N protocol. Specifically, state n represents the start of the transmission of a sequence of n packets. Similarly, state $n-1$ represents the start of the transmission of a sequence of $n-1$ packets. We denote by p the

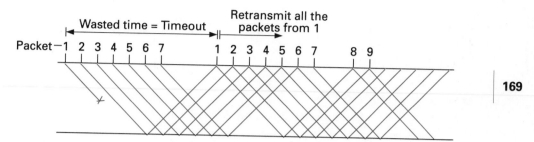

Figure 4.23 Errors in GO BACK N.

A transmission error in packet 1 wastes an amount of time equal to a timeout.

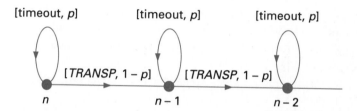

Figure 4.24 The random evolution of GO BACK N.

The black circles indicate the number of packets remaining to be transmitted. The random evolution of that number is summarized by the diagram.

probability that transmission errors corrupt a packet or its ACK. Thus, both the packet and its ACK arrive correctly with probability $1 - p$. The horizontal arrow from state n to state $n - 1$ signifies that with probability $1 - p$ the first of the n packets and its ACK are correctly transmitted, and the sender starts transmitting the first of the remaining $n - 1$ packets after a time equal to *TRANSP*. The circular arrow from state n to itself signifies that with probability p the first of the n packets or its ACK is not correctly transmitted; the sender restarts the transmission of those n packets after having wasted an amount of time equal to *timeout* $= W \times TRANSP = S$. By analogy with the analysis of Figure 4.13(b), one finds that the average time per packet, i.e., to move from state m to state $m - 1$ for an arbitrary value of m, is equal to

$$TRANSP + \frac{p \times timeout}{1 - p}$$

and the useful time is *TRANSP*. It follows that the efficiency of GO BACK N is given by

$$\eta_{RT}(GBN, p) = \frac{1}{1 + \dfrac{p}{1-p} \times W} \quad \text{with} \quad W = \frac{S}{TRANSP}. \tag{4.18}$$

170

It is interesting to note that

$$\eta_{RT}(SRP, p) \approx \eta_{RT}(GBN, p) \approx 1 - pW$$

$$\text{when} \quad pW := \frac{p \times S}{TRANSP} \leq 10\%. \tag{4.19}$$

You can verify that the efficiencies of GO BACK N and SRP deteriorate rather quickly when the window size W becomes smaller than $W \leq S/TRANSP$.

In our discussion of SRP, we explained the necessity of numbering packets with a finite set of different numbers. The packet numbers can then be encoded with a finite string of bits. The same observation applies to GO BACK N. You should verify that the packets can be numbered modulo W when GO BACK N uses the window size W.

Let us summarize what we have learned about GO BACK N:

GO BACK N

- The efficiency of the GO BACK N protocol falls between ABP and SRP. No buffering is required at the receiver.
- The packets are numbered consecutively 0, 1, 2, ..., $W - 1$, 0, 1, 2, ..., $W - 1$, and so on.
- The receiver acknowledges a correct packet with an ACK that has the same number as the packet. The receiver delivers packets in order, and it discards packets received out of order.
- The sender can have up to W unacknowledged packets.
- When the sender does not receive the acknowledgement of a packet before a timeout, it retransmits copies of that packet and of all the subsequent packets.
- The efficiency of GO BACK N for full-duplex lines under the *round-trip assumptions*

$$timeout = S = W \times TRANSP \tag{4.17}$$

is given by

$$\eta_{RT}(GBN, p) = \frac{1}{1 + \dfrac{p}{1-p} \times W}. \tag{4.18}$$

We now have three protocols: ABP, SRP, and GO BACK N. When two communication nodes attached to a duplex communication link use one of these protocols, they transmit packets reliably and in the correct order. In the OSI terminology, these protocols are data link protocols that implement a reliable packet link on top of the unreliable bit pipe provided by the physical layer. We explained that such a reliable packet link is used when connection-oriented communication services are implemented by virtual-circuit packet switching. We also explained that these protocols use the communication link more or less efficiently: GO BACK N is more efficient than ABP but less efficient than SRP. For instance, on a given communication link, SRP can transmit more packets in one minute than ABP or GO BACK N. Moreover, you learned that GO BACK N and SRP are more efficient with larger window sizes. More precisely, the window size should be at least large enough for the sender to keep transmitting when there is no transmission error. That is, the window size should be at least equal to $S/TRANSP$. Therefore, the network designer must adapt the window size to the communication link and to the packet and acknowledgement sizes. These three data link protocols are used in the most popular communication networks. We will discuss specific implementation details in Section 4.6.

As we learned in Chapter 2, protocols are distributed algorithms that supervise information transfers. Protocols are used in all the layers of the OSI model. Network designers have to invent new protocols for new applications of communication networks. Before proposing a new protocol, the network designer must establish that the network will operate satisfactorily with that protocol. In the next section, we explain automatic protocol verification procedures and we apply them to the data link protocols that we have discussed.

4.5 Correctness of Protocols

This section addresses the *correctness* of protocols. Loosely speaking, a protocol is correct if it performs as the network designer expects it to. The three data link protocols ABP, SRP, and GO BACK N are correct and do not require further verification before being implemented. However, network designers must occasionally invent new protocols of various layers. Before implementing a new protocol, the network designers must verify it. An error in a protocol can lead to severe disruptions in the operations of a communication network which may have serious consequences for its users, such as a loss of connections or of data. In 1990, a protocol error brought down a number of major telephone exchanges in the United States. This error caused a substantial loss of revenues for the telephone company and inconvenienced many customers who were unable to make telephone calls.

A protocol error is an error in a computer program. The error may be a coding error, i.e., a faulty translation of the program into computer code. The error may also be a design error in the protocol. We discuss only design errors in this section. Most protocols are complex, and their verification is complicated. Automatic protocol verification methods are needed for all but the simplest protocols. To use such a method, a network designer first provides a computer with a description of the protocol and a specification of how the protocol is expected to operate. The computer then executes the automatic procedure and determines whether the protocol is correct. To declare that a protocol is correct, the automatic method must explore the possible sequences of steps of the protocol and verify that these sequences are all acceptable. A complex protocol has a vast number of acceptable sequences of steps. When applied to such a complex protocol, an automatic procedure spends excessive time exploring many acceptable sequences before detecting an unacceptable one. This exploration time limits the complexity of protocols that can be verified automatically by existing methods.

There are two reasons why you may want to learn about protocol verification methods, even if you never have to develop a new protocol. First, these methods employ precise descriptions of protocols that are also used for specifying protocols. You need to know how to interpret these descriptions if you want to know precisely how a protocol is defined. Second, the protocol verification methods require precise definitions of correctness. By learning how a protocol is defined to be correct, you will improve your understanding of the protocol.

A data link layer protocol is said to be *correct* if the data link layer implements the required packet communication service when it executes that protocol. Note that this definition assumes that the physical layer is working properly. More precisely, a data link layer is built to operate with a physical layer that has specific properties. For instance, a data link protocol may assume that the physical layer does not duplicate packets. In that case, the verification method should not look for errors that the data link layer makes when the physical layer duplicates packets. Notice that correctness is a *logical* property: it only concerns the *order* in which events take place; the *timing* of those events is not a factor in the definition of correctness. Thus, the *performance measures* of a protocol, such as its efficiency, are, in a sense, independent of the correctness. For instance, ABP is a correct protocol even though it may not be efficient in a given communication network.

You will learn verification procedures based on the representation of the execution of protocols by *finite state machines* (FSMs) and by *Petri nets* (PNs). These representations lend themselves to algorithmic methods. That is, a computer can explore systematically the possible sequences of steps of an FSM or a PN. At the same time, these representations are easily specified and understood by network engineers. Thus, FSMs and PNs are good for specifying protocols:

172

these representations are easily understood by network engineers, and they translate easily into computer programs for verification.

Finite State Machines

We will first learn the general definition of an FSM. We will then see how an FSM can be used to represent a simple data link protocol and to show that this protocol is not correct. Then we will verify the correctness of ABP using its FSM representation.

An FSM is a model of the evolution of a device (machine) that is subject to external inputs. The machine can be in finitely many different *states*. For instance, the device could be a door that can be in one of two states: open or closed. The device could be a buffer that can hold four packets, and the state would be 0, 1, 2, 3, or 4 to represent the number of packets in the buffer. The set of possible states of the FSM, the *state space*, is denoted by X. The FSM is subject to external inputs: the door can be opened or closed, packets can be added to or removed from the buffer. The inputs occur one at a time and take values in a finite set U. In the buffer example, the set of input values is $U = \{a, r\}$ where a represents "adding a packet" and r "removing a packet." Inputs modify the state of the FSM. In the buffer example, if the input is a when the state is 2, then the state becomes 3. The new state depends on the previous state and on the input. Generally, if an input with value $u \in U$ occurs while the machine is in state $x \in X$, then the machine jumps to a new state $g(x, u)$ where $g : X \times U \to X$ is a given function, called the *state transition function*. Thus, in the buffer example, one has $g(2, a) = 3$. In order to determine the sequence of states that results from a given sequence of inputs, it suffices to know the function g and the *initial state* x_0. For instance, if the buffer initially contains two packets and if the sequence of inputs is *aararrar*, then the sequence of states of the buffer, starting with the initial state, is 2343432121. If the input sequence of the FSM is $\{u_n, n \geq 0\}$, then the sequence of successive states is $\{x_n, n \geq 0\}$ where

$$x_{n+1} = g(x_n, u_n), n \geq 0.$$

The *state transition diagram* summarizes the definition of an FSM. It represents all the states of the FSM together with arrows between states that represent the possible transitions. Figure 4.25 shows the state transition diagram for the buffer that can hold four packets.

Let us see how one can model the evolution of a protocol with FSMs. We first consider a protocol with unnumbered packets and ACKs. This is the protocol that was introduced at the beginning of Section 4.1 to explain why some

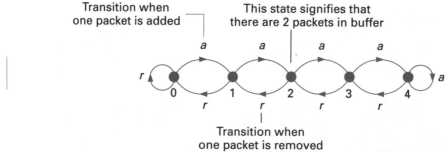

Transition when
one packet is added

This state signifies that
there are 2 packets in buffer

Transition when
one packet is removed

Figure 4.25 State transition diagram for four-packet buffer.

Consider a buffer that can hold four packets. The state indicates how
many packets are in the buffer. The state space is $X = \{0, 1, 2, 3, 4\}$. There
are two possible inputs: a, which represents "adding a packet to the
buffer," and r, which represents "removing a packet from the buffer."
The possible states and the possible transitions between states are indicated by arrows. For instance, the arrow from 3 to 4 represents the addition of one packet to the buffer when it contains three packets. Each
arrow is labeled with the input that produces the transition.

numbering scheme is required. We will model this protocol by an FSM, and we
will show that it cannot deliver the packets in the correct order and without error.

The first step is to identify the device and its states. The device consists of a sender, a receiver, a communication link from the sender to the receiver,
and a communication link from the receiver to the sender. We will identify states
that suffice for representing steps in the execution of the protocols. For instance,
we will not differentiate between the sender's having transmitted a packet 3 ms
ago and 5 ms ago. In fact, we will consider the states of the device only at the end
of the propagation of packets and of acknowledgements. For simplicity, the communication link is assumed to be half-duplex. Denote by AE (acknowledgment
expected) the state of the sender when it is expecting an ACK and by NAE (no
acknowledgement expected) when it is not expecting an ACK. Similarly, denote
by MA (must acknowledge) the state of the receiver when it must acknowledge a
packet that it received and by NA (no acknowledgement) when it has no ACK to
send. The receiver may get a packet while it is in state MA. This case happens
when the receiver waits for a long time before sending an acknowledgement. A
possible state will be denoted by $x = (s, r)$ where $s \in \{AE, NAE\}$ is the state of the
sender and $r \in \{MA, NA\}$ is the state of the receiver.

The second step is to determine the state transitions. To do this, we
must identify all the possible transitions out of any given state. The transitions are
caused by certain inputs. For instance, say that $x = x_0 := (NAE, NA)$: the sender
does not expect an ACK and the receiver has no packet to acknowledge. This is
the state before the first packet transmission, when the system is first turned on.

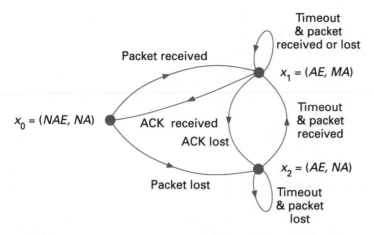

Figure 4.26 State transition diagram for unnumbered packets.
The state describes the sender and the receiver just after the propagation of packets and acknowledgements. A state is of the form $x = (s, r)$. The state of the sender s is *AE* if it expects an *ACK* and *NAE* otherwise. The state of the receiver r is *MA* if it must acknowledge a packet and *NA* otherwise. The diagram shows the transitions between states, and the events that correspond to those transitions are indicated next to the arrows.

The state changes when the sender transmits a packet. Two evolutions are possible: either the packet arrives correctly at the receiver, or it is lost because of transmission errors. In the first case, the next state at the end of the propagation of the packet is $x_1 := (AE, MA)$. This state represents that the sender is expecting an ACK for the packet that it transmitted and that the receiver must acknowledge the packet that it just received. In the second case, the next state is $x_2 := (AE, NA)$ since the receiver does not have to acknowledge incorrect packets. By exploring all the possible transitions out of states x_1 and x_2, one derives the transition diagram in Figure 4.26, where we have indicated the events that each arrow represents. When there is no transmission error, the sequence of events is

$$x_0, x_1, x_0, x_1, \ldots .$$

We claim that the following sequence represents an unacceptable execution of the protocol:

$$x_0, x_1, x_2, x_1.$$

This is the sequence of states when the first packet arrives correctly at the receiver ($x_0 \rightarrow x_1$), its acknowledgement is corrupted ($x_1 \rightarrow x_2$), the sender retransmits a copy of the first packet after a timeout, and that copy arrives correctly at the receiver $(x_2 \rightarrow x_1)$. The sequence is unacceptable because the receiver gets two correct packets—the second one is a copy of the first—without the sender getting an ACK. The receiver has no way of knowing that the second packet is a copy, and it will confuse it with a new packet.

176

In this example, the FSM representation was useful for finding all the sequences of events possible when the protocol is executed. An automatic verification is not required for such a simple example.

We are now ready to apply the FSM approach to the verification of ABP. Recall that packets and ACKs are numbered 0 and 1. We assume that the link is half-duplex, and we consider the state of the device at the end of the propagation of packets and ACKs, as in the previous example. The state of the sender is either 0, 1, or −. The state 0 represents that the sender is waiting for an ACK0. It is 1 when the sender is waiting for an ACK1, and it is − when the sender is not waiting for an ACK, i.e., when there is no unacknowledged packet. The state of the receiver is 0 if it is waiting for a packet numbered 0. It is 1 if it is waiting for a packet numbered 1. The state of the protocol is $x = (s, r)$, where s is the state of the sender and r is the state of the receiver. The protocol is assumed to be in state $x_0 := (-, 0)$ initially. The state transition diagram is shown in Figure 4.27.

When there is no transmission error, the sequence of states of the protocol is

$$(-, 0) \rightarrow (0, 1) \rightarrow (-, 1) \rightarrow (1, 0) \rightarrow (-, 0) \rightarrow (0, 1) \rightarrow \dots .$$

These transitions represent the arrival of a packet numbered 0, the arrival of an ACK0, the arrival of a packet numbered 1, the arrival of an ACK1, and so on. Once Figure 4.27 has been verified, the correctness of ABP is proved. Indeed, that figure proves that, even with arbitrary transmission errors, the receiver gets a packet numbered 0, then the sender gets an ACK0, then the receiver gets a packet numbered 1, and so on.

A computer cannot "look" at Figure 4.27 as we just did. It needs an automatic method for doing the verification. Let us explain one such method. Denote by y a variable initially set to 0. The computer generates sequences of events that are allowed by the transition diagram. If $y = 0$ and the sequence makes a transition that corresponds to the sender getting an ACK0, then the computer sets $y = 1$. If $y = 0$ and the transition represents the receiver getting a packet numbered 1, the computer sets $y = \theta$. Similarly, if $y = 1$ and the transition represents the sender getting an ACK1, then the computer sets $y = 0$. If $y = 1$ and the transition represents the receiver getting a packet numbered 0, then the computer sets $y = \theta$. These operations are summarized in Figure 4.28. Note that y reaches θ if and only if the sequence of states in ABP corresponds to the reception of a packet numbered 0 followed by the reception of a packet numbered 1 with no

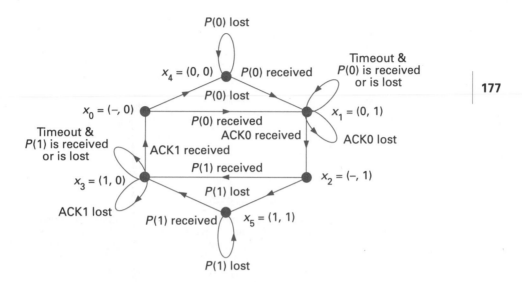

Figure 4.27 State transition diagram of ABP.

State (0, 0) means that the sender is waiting for an ACK0 and the receiver is waiting for a packet numbered 0. This state is observed at the end of a propagation of a packet or an ACK. The communication links are assumed to be idle at that time. When the protocol is in that state, the sender cannot get the ACK0 before a timeout. After the timeout, the sender retransmits a copy of the last transmitted packet numbered 0. If that packet arrives correctly at the receiver, the next state is (0, 1). Otherwise, the next state is again (0, 0). You can verify that the other transitions are as indicated in the figure.

intermediate reception of an ACK0, or to the reception of a packet numbered 1 followed by the reception of a packet numbered 0 with no intermediate reception of an ACK1. To verify the protocol, one could ask the computer to generate sequences at random. If the computer generates sequences of values x and y for a long time without y ever reaching θ, the odds are very small that there is an unacceptable sequence. Such an approach is a rudimentary *probabilistic verification method*. The variable y is called a *monitor* of the FSM x because it watches the sequence of states visited by x to determine whether it is acceptable.

If the state space is not large, then one can propose a more systematic method. This method uses the fact that $z := (x, y)$ is an FSM, and it determines whether it is possible for z to reach a value such as (x_i, θ), i.e., for y to reach θ. If the algorithm determines that this is not possible, then we conclude that the protocol is correct. We will first explain why $z = (x, y)$ is an FSM. Then we will describe the algorithm used to identify the states that can be reached by an FSM. Finally, we will apply that algorithm to the ABP protocol.

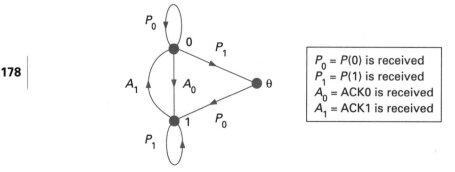

$P_0 = P(0)$ is received
$P_1 = P(1)$ is received
$A_0 = $ ACK0 is received
$A_1 = $ ACK1 is received

Figure 4.28 The transitions of the variable y.

While generating sequences of states of ABP, the computer updates a variable y. The arrows P_0 are transitions that take place when the ABP makes a transition that represents the arrival of a packet numbered 0 at the receiver. The arrow A_0 is a transition of y when ABP makes a transition that represents the sender getting an ACK0. The sequence of ABP is unacceptable when y reaches θ.

Let $x = x_0$ and $y = 0$. Assume that the input to the FSM x induces the transition $x_0 \rightarrow x_1$. Then Figure 4.27 shows that x makes a transition P_0 which represents that a packet numbered 0 arrives at the receiver. Consequently, Figure 4.28 shows that y makes a transition $0 \rightarrow 0$. Therefore, the pair (x, y) makes a transition from $(x_0, 0)$ to $(x_1, 0)$. Thus, the inputs of ABP which cause the transitions in Figure 4.27 are seen to cause specific transitions of (x, y). We conclude that $z = (x, y)$ is an FSM with state space $X \times \{0, 1, \theta\}$ and with the same inputs as the FSM x. The transition functions of z are obtained by combining the transitions of x with the resulting transitions of y.

Let us explain a procedure that determines the set R of all the states that can be visited by an FSM. The initial state x_0 is certainly visited and, therefore, $x_0 \in R$. Also, if a state x can be visited, then all the states $g(x, u)$ for $u \in U$ can also be visited. These observations can be used to build the set R of reachable states by the procedure shown in Figure 4.29. In this figure, it is assumed for simplicity that $U = \{0, 1\}$. At each step, a state is discarded if it has already been generated. The set R of reachable states is determined once no new state is generated by the procedure.

The procedure illustrated in Figure 4.29 can easily be converted into the algorithm described below, called the *reachability algorithm*. In that description, the notation

$$A \cup B$$

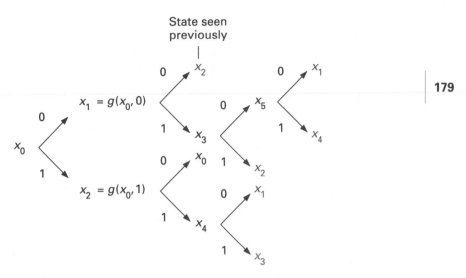

Figure 4.29 Reachability analysis.

The reachability algorithm builds up the set of reachable states by exploring the states that can be reached from the known reachable states. The algorithm starts with the initial state. It then adds the states that can be reached from the initial state to the set of reachable states. The states that are reachable from those states are then added, and so on. The algorithm keeps track of the states that have not been explored. The algorithm terminates when no new state is discovered.

represents the *union* of two sets A and B, i.e., the set of elements that belong to A or to B or to both A and B. For instance,

$$\{2, 3, 5\} \cup \{3, 6\} = \{2, 3, 5, 6\}.$$

Also, the notation $A - B$ represents the *set difference* of A and B, i.e., the set of elements that belong to A but not to B. For instance, $\{2, 3, 5\} - \{3, 6\} = \{2, 5\}$.

Reachability Algorithm:

Step 0: Let $n := 0$ and $V(n) = R(n) := \{x_0\}$.

Step $n + 1$: Let $V(n + 1) := \{g(x,u), x \in V(n), u \in U\} - R(n)$.
　　　If $V(n + 1) = \emptyset$, then let $R := R(n)$ and STOP else, let
　　　$R(n + 1) := R(n) \cup V(n + 1)$, $n := n + 1$ and repeat the last step.

The execution of the reachability algorithm parallels that of the procedure shown in Figure 4.29. The set $R(n)$ accumulates the reachable states as they are discovered, while the set $V(n)$ keeps track of the states whose successors have not been explored. The algorithm stops when $V(n) = \emptyset$.

As an illustration of the algorithm, consider the following FSM: $X = \{1, 2, 3\}$, $U = \{a, b\}$, $x_0 = 2$, and

$$[g(x, u), x = 1, 2, 3 \text{ and } u = a, b] = \begin{bmatrix} 3 & 2 \\ 3 & 2 \\ 2 & 3 \end{bmatrix}.$$

The matrix entries are the values of $g(x, u)$ with the convention that the first column indicates the values of $g(x, a)$ for $x = 1, 2, 3$ successively, and similarly for the second column. For instance, $g(1, b) = 2$ and $g(3, a) = 2$. You can check that the successive steps of the algorithm are as follows:

Step 0: $R(0) = V(0) = \{2\}$.

Step 1: $V(1) = \{g(2, a), g(2, b)\} - \{2\} = \{3\}$.
$\qquad R(1) = R(0) \cup V(1) = \{2, 3\}$.

Step 2: $V(2) = \{g(3, a), g(3, b)\} - \{2, 3\} = \emptyset$.
$\qquad R = R(1) = \{2, 3\}$, STOP.

We will use the reachability algorithm to determine the correctness of ABP. Here are the steps of the reachability algorithm applied to the FSM $z = (x, y)$:

Step 0: $R(0) = V(0) = \{(x_0, 0)\}$.

Step 1: $V(1) = \{(x_1, 0), (x_4, 0)\}$,
$\qquad$ and $R(1) = \{(x_0, 0), (x_1, 0), (x_4, 0)\}$.

Step 2: $V(2) = \{(x_2, 1)\}$,
$\qquad$ and $R(2) = \{(x_0, 0), (x_1, 0), (x_2, 1), (x_4, 0)\}$.

Step 3: $V(3) = \{(x_3, 1), (x_5, 1)\}$,
$\qquad$ and $R(3) = \{(x_0, 0), (x_1, 0), (x_2, 1), (x_3, 1), (x_4, 0), (x_5, 1)\}$.

Step 4: $V(4) = \emptyset$, $R = R(3)$, STOP.

This algorithm shows that no state of the form (x_i, θ) is reachable. Hence, ABP is correct.

The practical limitations of this approach are not difficult to appreciate. The FSM that represents a complex protocol has a large number of states. Consequently, the reachability algorithm takes a very long time. As a numerical illustration, imagine ten protocol entities that jointly execute a protocol. Assume that the execution of the protocol is represented by 100 possible states for each entity. The FSM x that describes the state of the ten entities can have up to $(100)^{10} = 10^{20}$ states. If the monitor y of that FSM also has 100 states, then the joint FSM (x, y) can have up to $10^{20} \times 100 = 10^{22}$ states. If 0.01% of these states are reachable, then the reachability algorithm must execute at least $0.0001 \times 10^{22} = 10^{18}$ instructions. Assuming that we run the reachability algorithm on a 100-Mips computer, i.e., a computer that can execute 100 million instructions per second, we find that the algorithm takes at least $(10^{18})/(10^8) = 10^{10}$ seconds, or more than 300 years. This numerical example makes many arbitrary assumptions, but it illustrates the limitations of the FSM approach to verification. The Petri net approach that we will discuss next does not, unfortunately, remove these limitations. Researchers are exploring different verification methods that would enable them to verify protocols more complex than those they can verify with FSMs or PNs.

Petri Nets

Another approach to the automatic verification of protocols is based on the *Petri net* (PN) model. The class of PNs is larger than that of FSMs. That is, the evolution of any FSM can be modeled by a PN, but the converse is not true. Moreover, many protocols lend themselves to a relatively simple PN representation. Unfortunately, many important questions about the evolution of PNs are hard to answer. The practical usefulness of PNs is, therefore, limited. However, the method is used and you should know about it.

A Petri net is illustrated in Figure 4.30. As Figure 4.30 shows, there are four types of components in a PN: circles, which are called *places*; bars, called *transitions*; dots, called *tokens*; and *arrows* from a place to a transition or from a transition to a place. The places with one or more arrows to a given transition are called the *input places* of that transition. Similarly, arrows go from a transition to its *output places*. The tokens move around the PN according to the following rules. A transition can *fire* when each of its input places contains at least as many tokens as there are arrows from that place to the transition. When the transition fires, one token is removed from each input place for each arrow that goes from the place to the transition, and one token is added to each output place for each arrow that goes from the transition to the place. The configuration of tokens in the places is called the *marking* of the PN. Figure 4.31 shows a possible evolution of the marking of the PN of Figure 4.30.

A PN is said to be *live* if every transition can fire infinitely often; it is *bounded* if the total number of tokens in the net is always smaller than some finite value K. Say that the PN is *simple* if there is at most one arrow between a place and a transition and between a transition and a place. It is straightforward to

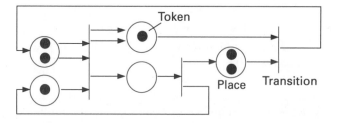

Figure 4.30 Petri net.

A Petri net is a directed graph with two types of vertices: places (represented by circles) and transitions (vertical bars). The places contain tokens.

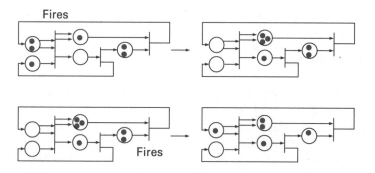

Figure 4.31 Evolution of the marking of the PN in Figure 4.30.

The first figure indicates the initial configuration of the tokens, i.e., the initial marking. A transition can fire when each of its input places contains at least as many tokens as there are arrows from that place to the transition. When the transition fires, one token is removed for each input arrow and one is added at the end of each output arrow.

verify whether a simple PN is live: a simple PN is live if and only if every *cycle* contains at least one token. A cycle is a closed path in the PN. To see why this criterion is true, notice that the number of tokens in a cycle does not change when a transition fires; also, if no transition can fire, then one can find an empty cycle that goes through the empty input places of the transitions. For instance, PN(1) in Figure 4.32 is live because each of its three cycles $(1, a, 3, c, 1)$, $(1, a, 4, b, 5, c, 1)$, and $(2, a, 4, b, 2)$ contains at least one token. By contrast, PN(2) in Figure 4.32 is not live because its cycle $(1, a, 4, b, 5, c, 1)$ is empty.

Let us see how PNs can be used to model protocols and to verify their correctness. Consider a protocol with packets numbered alternately 0 and 1 but with unnumbered ACKs. The PN model of this protocol is illustrated in Figure 4.33. The left-hand side of the PN corresponds to the sender. The sender transmits

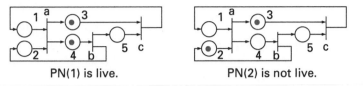

PN(1) is live.   PN(2) is not live.

This PN has three cycles: (1, *a*, 3, *c*, 1), (1, *a*, 4, *b*, *c*, 1), and (2, *a*, 4, *b*, 2).

Figure 4.32 Two simple Petri nets.

PN(1) is live because each cycle contains at least one token. PN(2) is not live since its cycle (1, a, 4, b, 5, c, 1) is empty.

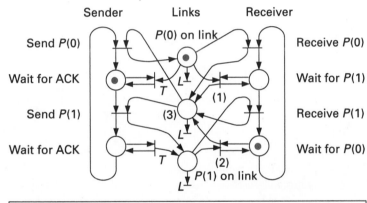

(1): Packet $P(0)$ is received while the receiver waits for $P(1)$
(2): Packet $P(1)$ is received while the receiver waits for $P(0)$
(3): A token in this place indicates that there is an ACK on link
T: Transition fires at expiration time of timeout
L: Loss of a packet or of an ACK

Figure 4.33 Petri net model of ABP with unnumbered ACKs.

a packet numbered 0, then waits for an ACK. If the ACK is received before a timeout, the sender transmits a packet numbered 1; otherwise, the sender transmits a copy of the packet numbered 0. The middle part of the PN describes the state of the links. A token in the upper place of the middle section indicates that there is a packet numbered 0 on the link from the sender to the receiver. A token in the middle place in the center of the PN indicates that an ACK is on the link from the receiver to the sender. The rest of the PN is similar.

The normal evolution of the PN is as follows: Packet 0 is sent; that packet is received, and an ACK is sent; the ACK is received; packet 1 is sent; and so on. One evolution that leads to an error of the protocol is as follows: Packet 0 is sent; after a timeout, the sender sends out another copy of packet 0 before the ACK is received; packet 1 is sent and is lost; the copy of packet 0 is received, and an ACK is sent; another packet 0 is sent. The first packet 1 is never received.

184

As you can see from this example, it is relatively easy to draw the Petri net model of the protocol. The analysis of its correctness is, however, not systematic. To make this verification automatic, note that a bounded PN is an FSM. The states of the FSM are the markings of the PN, and the inputs of the FSM are the transition firings. Consequently, we can use the monitor idea that was explained for finite state machines to verify protocols described by bounded PNs. Therefore, a network designer can use a PN to represent the protocol and apply to this PN the techniques developed for FSMs. The advantage of this approach is that some protocols are easier to model first by a PN than directly by an FSM.

Protocol Verification

- To *verify* a protocol is to determine that it has the intended behavior.

- Two methodologies for the automatic verification of protocols are *finite state machines* and *Petri nets*.

- A finite state machine (FSM) describes how *inputs* make a *state* evolve. When a protocol is defined, one can derive the FSM model of the communication link. Unacceptable sequences of states of the FSM can be detected by a *monitor*. Reachability analysis can be then used to determine the correctness of the protocol.

- A Petri net specifies the evolution of tokens in places connected to transitions by arrows. The set of reachable markings can also be analyzed.

The FSM and PN models can be used to describe a protocol. For instance, the PN model of the protocol in Figure 4.33 defines the actions taken by the sender and receiver in response to the arrivals of packets and acknowledgements. Many protocols are specified by such FSM or PN models. When a protocol is complex, the FSM or PN description may be cumbersome. In that case, another description is preferred. Some protocols are described in English, but the descriptions can be ambiguous and tedious to translate into a precise script. Network designers utilize a number of protocol specification languages that are more precise and compact than natural languages. Compilers have been developed that translate these protocol specifications into the language of the processors that run the protocols.

4.6 Examples of the Data Link Layer

We conclude this chapter by discussing the data link layers of some widespread communication networks. We learned that the data link layer converts the bit pipe provided by the physical layer into a packet link. We have focused on the *data link protocol*, which regulates the transfer of packets and supervises the retransmissions of copies of corrupted packets. We saw that packets must be numbered and that the receiver sends numbered acknowledgements to the sender. Implicit in that discussion is the need for specifying the *structure* of the packets. That is, the network designer must specify the number of bits in the packet, the position of the bits that encode the packet number, and how acknowledgements are distinguished from data. We will indicate the structure of the packets in some networks.

Data Link of SNA

SNA is IBM's *Systems Network Architecture*. The first version was released in 1974. SNA, a store-and-forward network, provides communication between IBM computers and peripherals. An SNA network consists of a collection of interconnected *nodes* (terminals, device controllers, communication processors, and computers). Each node contains one or more *network addressable units* (NAUs). The NAUs are grouped into *domains*. Each domain contains one special NAU called a *system services control point* (SSCP) that supervises it.

A user process, i.e., an active program, that wishes to use the network must connect itself to an NAU, which can then be thought of as being a "socket" or plug into the network. Different NAUs have different addresses.

SNA was designed before ISO's OSI model, and as a result, its architecture differs from that of the OSI model. An approximate correspondence of the functions of SNA to OSI appears in Figure 4.34.

The *data link control* of SNA converts a stream of bits into packets and takes care of error recovery. It produces a reliable sequence of packets from an unreliable bit stream. Thus, the functions of the data link control are similar to those of OSI's data link layer. SNA's data link control protocol is *SDLC* (synchronous data link control). It is GO BACK N with positive and negative acknowledgements. The SDLC packet structure is indicated in Figure 4.35. It is a bit-oriented synchronous packet (see Section 3.4).

The *control field* is used for the sequence number and for acknowledgements and for specifying the type of the packet. The *CRC* (cyclic redundancy code, see Section 3.5) field contains error detection bits. Neighboring nodes in SNA are usually connected by multiple channels (called a transmission group) for

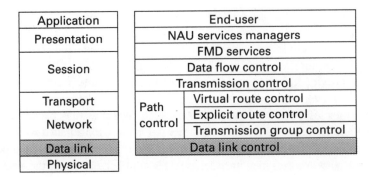

Figure 4.34 Correspondence between OSI and SNA layers.

IBM's SNA architecture is slightly different from that of OSI.

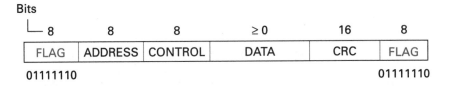

Figure 4.35 SDLC packet.

The SDLC packet is bit-oriented. It is framed by two FLAGs. A FLAG is the pattern 01111110. A FLAG cannot occur in the packet by bit stuffing.

reliability and increased bandwidth. The data link control selects one available link for each packet. Packets are resequenced at each node.

Data Link Layer of Public Data Networks (X.25)

By *X.25* one denotes the CCITT standards for layers 1, 2, and 3 of *public data networks*. These are networks that are accessible to the general public, in contrast to private networks. *Telenet* and *Tymnet* are examples of U.S. public data networks. The X.25 recommendations, first published in 1974 and periodically revised since, specify the interface required between the computer and the network and the protocols to be used at layers 2 and 3. The recommended physical layer is X.21, which is similar to RS-232-C. The physical layer RS-232-C is also supported by X.25.

This section will review the data link layer of X.25. It is known under the name *LAPB* (link access protocol B), and it is similar to SNA's data link protocol. The data link layer of X.25 uses the GO BACK N protocol with both positive and negative acknowledgements. The window size is 8 or 128. The win-

Bits

FLAG	ADDRESS	CONTROL	DATA	CRC	FLAG
01111110					01111110

Figure 4.36 Packet structure of X.25.

The X.25 packet is similar to that of SDLC. The control field is explained in Figure 4.37.

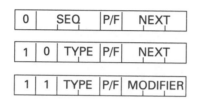

Figure 4.37 Possible CONTROL fields of X.25.

These are the three control fields in X.25.

dow size 128 is used for satellite links and for slow radio channels. The packets in X.25 have the structure shown in Figure 4.36.

X.25 uses synchronous bit-oriented transmissions (see Section 3.4). The FLAG is the pattern 01111110, which is also repeated when the link is idle. This pattern is avoided in the packet by *bit stuffing* (see Section 3.4).

The ADDRESS field is essential when many devices are connected in parallel. The CONTROL field admits the possible values indicated in Figure 4.37. In the first case in Figure 4.37, *SEQ* indicates the sequence number of the packet; P/F (poll/final) takes the value 1 (representing F) if it is the final packet of the message and takes the value 0 (= P) otherwise; NEXT contains the acknowledgement number. In the second case, TYPE has the value 0 if the packet is an ACK, the value 1 if it is a NACK (negative acknowledgment), and the value 2 if the receiver is not ready. In the third case, the MODIFIER may indicate that the machine is going down, that it is coming back up, or that some error condition has occurred.

Data Link Layer in ARPANET

ARPANET is a store-and-forward network developed in the late 1960s by the Advanced Research Project Agency. It has been progressively transformed into a vast collection of interconnected networks known as the *Internet*. The

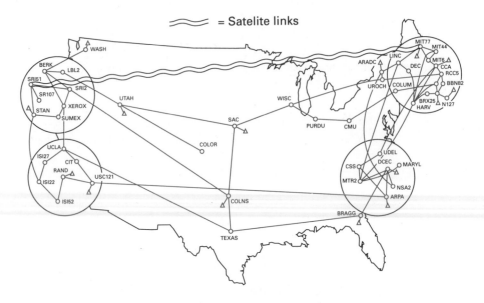

Figure 4.38 The ARPANET network, January 1988.

It is estimated that more than 60,000 computers are part of Internet.

Internet consists of many thousands of nodes, mostly universities and research institutions, throughout the world. Most of the connections are 56-kbps links. There are also a few satellite channels. (See Figure 4.38.)

We will describe the data link layer in ARPANET. Each nonsatellite ARPANET link (at 56 kbps) is divided into eight full-duplex logical channels. The ABP is used on each channel. The packets are sent on any available channel. The channel becomes idle when the acknowledgement comes back. The result of this complicated procedure is somewhat similar to that of SRP: up to eight packets can be unacknowledged at any given time. Satellite links are divided into 16 logical channels and are otherwise treated similarly to nonsatellite links.

The packet structure of ARPANET is indicated in Figure 4.39. This packet is that of a character-oriented synchronous transmission (see Section 3.4). Each packet contains, in the PSN-PSN header, the pattern shown in Figure 4.40.

The first bit S is the sequence number of the packet, the field CHA contains the logical channel number to which the packet belongs, and the pattern RECEIVED indicates, for each of the eight logical channels, the number of the last packet received.

Notice that, as is common on most networks, the acknowledgements are *piggy-backed* onto data packets. That is, a packet containing data being sent from station A to station B also contains the acknowledgement information about the traffic from B to A.

Bits

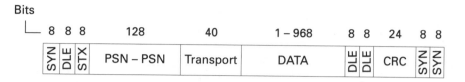

Figure 4.39 Packet structure of ARPANET.

The start of a packet is indicated by the DLE-STX characters and the end
by DLE-ETX. Character stuffing is used to prevent DLE-ETX from occurring in the packet. SYN are synchronization bits. DLE means data link
escape; STX, start of text; and ETX end of text.

Bits

Figure 4.40 Data link layer information.

S is the sequence number in the alternating bit protocol. CHA indicates
the logical channel to which the packet belongs. RECEIVED indicates
acknowledgements for the eight logical channels.

XMODEM

XMODEM is a popular data link protocol for communications via
modems between two personal computers or between a personal computer and a
mainframe.

XMODEM is similar to ABP. It is rather primitive in that it does not
permit variable packet lengths and does not make use of the full-duplex link.
However, we discuss it because its relative universality and ease of implementation make its use widespread. The packet structure is indicated in Figure 4.41.
The SOH (start of header) is the character 00000001. The NUM field contains the
packet number (modulo 256). The packets are numbered successively, starting
with 1. The field CNUM contains 2's complement of NUM, i.e., the character
obtained by flipping every bit in NUM. The DATA take up the next 128 bytes.
The last byte, CKS (checksum), is equal to the sum (modulo 2 without carry) of
the 128 data bytes.

The receiver sends a NACK (character 00010101) every 15 seconds
when it is not receiving data. If the sender has data to transmit, it waits for the
next NACK, then starts transmitting. After receiving each packet, the receiver
checks the CKS and sends an ACK (character 00000110) if it was correct or a
NACK if it was not.

Bytes

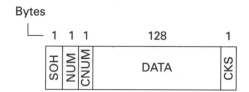

Figure 4.41 XMODEM packet structure.

XMODEM transmits packets of 128 bytes. The packets are numbered modulo 256 by NUM. CNUM is 2's complement of NUM; it is used for error-control purposes. Each packet is acknowledged positively or negatively.

If the packet was not correctly received (indicated by a NACK), then the sender retransmits the same data. At the end of the file transmission, the sender transmits EOT (character 00000100) and waits for it to be acknowledged (retransmitting it if it is not).

A number of variations have been developed. The first one is *XMODEM-CRC*, which uses a 16-bit CRC instead of CKS. The receiver indicates that the CRC option is to be used by sending the ASCII character *C* instead of NACK to initiate the transmission.

Another variation is *YMODEM*, which permits the transmission of blocks of 1,024 bytes of data in addition to blocks of 128 bytes. It also makes it possible to abort a transfer by sending two consecutive 110001000 characters. Batch file transfers are also made possible by YMODEM.

Kermit

Kermit is a protocol designed to provide error-free file transfers between mainframe computers, workstations, and personal computers attached by a point-to-point link, usually with modems. It uses variable length packets with a maximum length of 94 characters. The protocol is similar to ABP, but a version of SRP can be supported.

Kermit converts the 256 possible 8-bit bytes into *printable* 7-bit ASCII characters. The *ASCII* characters correspond to the decimal values 0 through 127 (using only 7 bits). Of these 128 characters, only those from 32 to 126 are printable (uppercase and lowercase letters, numbers, punctuation marks, and other common symbols, such as "space," @, +, *, and &). The characters corresponding to the numbers 0 through 31 and to 127 are called *control characters* and have special meanings, such as line feed and carriage return.

The packet structure in Kermit is illustrated in Figure 4.42. The fields of that packet are as follows:

Characters

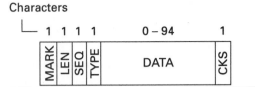

Figure 4.42 Kermit packet structure.

Kermit converts data into ASCII characters. The packet length is variable. The packets are acknowledged positively or negatively.

- MARK is the start of the packet; it is usually the ASCII character "Control A" sent as is (not converted).

- LEN indicates the length of the packet in ASCII characters (values 0–94 encoded as explained above).

- SEQ is the packet sequence number (modulo 64) starting at 0 (encoded as before).

- TYPE indicates the packet type. Here are the most common types: D = data, Y = acknowledge (ACK), N = negative acknowledge (NACK), S = send initiate, R = receive initiate, B = break transmission, F = file header, Z = end of file, E = error, G = generic command (the data field then contains the specifics: L for log out, F for finish but don't log out, D for directory query, U for disk query, E for erase file, T for type, Q for query server status), C = host command, X = text display (indicates text to be displayed on screen), I = initialize (exchange parameters but do not start a file transfer), and A = file attributes.

- DATA is the data (if any).

- CKS is the checksum.

The Kermit protocol is the following:

Step 1—Initialization

In order to start a transaction, the sender sends an initiation packet which contains the following parameters:

- *MAXL*: maximum length packet that can be sent
- *TIME*: timeout for other device
- *NPAD*: number of padding characters before each packet

- *PADC*: control character required for padding
- *EOL*: character to terminate packets (if any)
- *QTCL*: character to precede control character (usually #)

  (Some other optional information may also be contained in this packet indicating that CKS is replaced by a CRC or how repeated characters are indicated. A special *CAPAS* field is used to indicate special capabilities, such as long packets and selective repeat.) The receiver then acknowledges with an ACK packet which contains the same parameters indicating the values that it supports.

192

Step 2—Data Transfer

Each packet is acknowledged with an ACK (correctly received) or a NACK (incorrectly received). Retransmissions use the original packet number. Received copies are acknowledged but discarded.

When the connection is full-duplex, Kermit can use a selective repeat protocol. This protocol is requested in the initialization phase by marking the corresponding bit in the *CAPAS* field. The window size is also negotiated during the initialization. The protocol used is then SRP.

Summary

- Data link protocols convert an unreliable bit pipe into a reliable packet link by means of retransmissions controlled by timers and acknowledgements.
- ABP, GO BACK N, and SRP are three commonly used protocols, in order of increasing efficiency and complexity.
- Finite state machines and Petri nets can be used to specify and to verify protocols.
- The data link protocol of IBM's SNA is SDLC; it uses bit-oriented transmissions with GO BACK N with positive and negative acknowledgements.
- The data link layer of *X*.25 public data networks is LAPB. It uses bit-oriented transmissions with the GO BACK N protocol with positive and negative acknowledgements.
- ARPANET uses character-oriented transmissions on eight or 16 parallel logical channels with ABP.

■ XMODEM and Kermit are widely used communication protocols for workstations and personal computers. Each transmitted packet in XMODEM is ACKed or NACKed. Kermit uses a protocol similar to that of XMODEM, but it also supports a version of SRP.

Problems

1. Why is SRP more efficient than ABP? (Indicate the correct answer(s).)
   a. Because it retransmits fewer packets.
   b. Because it retransmits only incorrect packets.
   c. Because it is used with faster links.
   d. Because it uses a full-duplex link.
   e. For another reason. (Explain.)

2. How is the reachability analysis for FSMs used in verifying a protocol? (Indicate the correct answer(s) and explain.)
   a. To determine the possible states of the protocol.
   b. To determine the impossibility of certain sequences of states.

3. Using GO BACK N with negative acknowledgements, which packets does the sender retransmit after it gets a NACK? (Indicate the correct answer(s) and explain.)
   a. Only the negatively acknowledged packet.
   b. All the packets that were not acknowledged.
   c. All the packets after and including the negatively acknowledged packet.

4. Why is SRP more efficient than GO BACK N when they use the same window size?

*5. Two nodes A and B use the ABP. The time to send a packet from A to B or an ACK from B to A is equal to T. Acknowledgements are sent as soon as correct packets are received. The processing time is negligible. The transmission time of a packet is *TRANSP*, and the transmission time of an ACK is *TRANSA*. A fraction α of the packets and a fraction β of the ACKs are corrupted by transmission errors. Find the average time needed to send a correct packet from A to B.

6. Packets are transmitted using the ABP over a full-duplex 5-km coaxial cable with a 10-Mbps transmission rate. The packets and ACKs are 100 bits long. The transmitter and receiver use a CRC chip and their processing time is negligible. How many packets are transmitted every second when there is no transmission error?

*7. Ten transmission lines identical to the one discussed in the previous problem are connected in series. A buffer is used at each connection between the links to store packets as required. How many packets will go through the ten lines every second when there is no transmission error? Now assume that a packet or its acknowledgement is corrupted on any given link with probability p. What is the new packet transmission rate through the ten links? Compare this rate with the transmission rate when a single 50-km link is used and when there is no transmission error. What transmission error probability should be assumed for the 50-km link to be consistent with the probability p for each link? What does the transmission rate become with this error probability?

8. Consider two transmission links in series. The first link is a 10-km full-duplex 10-kbps coaxial cable. The packets are 1,000 bits long. The link uses the ABP with 100-bit ACKs and the error probability is $p = 1\%$. The second link is a 5 km full-duplex 5 kbps coaxial cable. The packets are also 1,000 bits long and the link uses ABP with 100-bit ACKs. The error probability is $p = 0.1\%$. What is the transmission rate achievable through the two links?

*9. Consider a transmitter equipped with a buffer. The transmitter uses the ABP, and it transmits a packet in 10 ms with probability $1 - p$. With probability p, the transmission fails and the transmitter tries again in the next 10 ms. Calculate the average time to transmit a packet. Now, assume that one packet arrives in the buffer exactly every 15 ms. For what values of p is the transmitter able to keep up with the arriving packets? Let p be very small. Estimate the probability that an arriving packet finds two other packets in the buffer.

10. You have to design a satellite transmission link. The transmission rate is 64 kbps. The propagation time between the earth's stations through the satellite is the time needed by the electromagnetic waves to make the 60,000-mile round-trip. The packets and ACKs have 1,000 bits. The processing times are 5 ms. The link is full-duplex between the earth's stations. You propose to use the SRP. What is the minimum window size you recommend? Assume a transmission error probability of $p = 0.1\%$. What is the average packet transmission rate with that window size? Compare this rate with the transmission rate using GO BACK N.

*11. We are given the specifications of a finite state machine. That is, we are given the state space X, the set of possible input values U, the state transition function g, and the initial state x_0. We want to find the set of states that can be visited infinitely often by the FSM. Explain how this set can be discovered from the state transition diagram. Propose an algorithm that constructs this set.

*12. Construct an FSM to represent the sequence of events in the GO BACK N protocol.

13. You have learned that a monitor y can be added to an FSM x to trap its unacceptable sequences of states. Design a monitor for the FSM that represents the SRP.

14. Explain how a bounded Petri net can be represented by an FSM.

15. Are the Petri nets in Figures 4.30 and 4.32 bounded?

16. An algorithm to verify whether a Petri net is bounded can be based on the following observation: If the net can reach a marking $(y_1, y_2, ..., y_N)$ from the marking $(x_1, x_2, ..., x_N)$ with $y_i \geq x_i$ for all i and $y_i > x_i$ for some i, then the Petri net is unbounded. Explain this observation.

*17. Consider the state transition diagram of an FSM. Attach positive numbers that add up to one to the arrows that leave every given state. The interpretation is that the arrow from state x to state y is marked with the number α to indicate that the probability that the FSM jumps from x to y is α. The random evolution of the state that results from your construction is called a Markov chain. The graph in Figure 4.13 was an example of a Markov chain. Can you suggest a method for calculating the average number $\alpha(x)$ of transitions that your Markov chain must make to go from state x to a fixed state w? (*Hint:* If the arrows out of x go to the states y and z with respective probabilities a and b, then argue that $\alpha(x) = 1 + a \times \alpha(y) + b \times \alpha(z)$.)

*18. Can you extend your construction in the previous problem to include transition times on the arrows? Give a method for calculating the average time to go from one state to another. (*Hint:* Review the discussion of Figure 4.13.)

References

Data link protocols have been the object of an abundance of literature. We have limited our discussion to the most widely used protocols. An accessible presentation of more advanced results on protocol efficiency can be found in Chapter 15 in Lin (1983). Chapter 2 in Bertsekas (1987) contains an original discussion of the overhead imposed by the framing. A standard reference on Petri nets is Peterson (1981). Cohen's paper (1989) discusses analytical methods for Petri nets. Har 'El (1990) explains a software system (COSPAN) for protocol verification. Figure 4.33 is from Tanenbaum (1988), which describes a number of examples of the data link layer. SNA is discussed in Meijers (1983).

Bertsekas (1987). Bertsekas, D., and Gallager, R., *Data Networks.* Prentice-Hall, 1987.

Cohen (1989). Cohen, G., Gaubert, S., Nikoukhah, R., and Quadrat, J. P., "Convex analysis and spectral analysis of timed event graphs," *Proceedings of the 28th Conference on Decision and Control,* 1515–1520, 1989.

Har'El (1990). Har'El and Kurshan, R. P. "Software for analytical development of communications protocol," *AT&T Tech. J.,* 45–59, Jan/Feb., 1990.

Lin (1983). Lin, S., and Costello, D. J., *Error Control Coding.* Prentice-Hall, 1983.

Meijer (1983). Meijer, A. and Peeters, P., *Computer Network Architectures,* Computer Science Press, 1983.

Peterson (1981). Peterson, J. L., *Petri Net Theory and the Modeling of Systems.* Prentice-Hall, 1981.

Tanenbaum (1988). Tanenbaum, A., *Computer Networks* (2nd Ed.). Prentice-Hall, 1988.

Local Area Networks | 5

In this chapter, we will study the physical layer and the data link layer of some popular *local area networks* (LANs). The LANs are a popular group of networks because they provide inexpensive and fast interconnections of minicomputers, personal computers, and workstations that proliferate among business users and educational and research institutions. LANs enable microcomputer users to share such resources as expensive printers, plotters, and file servers. Attaching a microcomputer to a LAN requires some hardware and software. The cost ranges from less than $100 to a few thousand, depending on the network. The transmission rate between computers attached to a LAN ranges from a few hundred kbps (1 kbps = 1,000 bits per second) to a few hundred Mbps (1 Mbps = 1 million bits per second).

The most widely used LANs are *Ethernet*, *token ring*, *token bus*, and *AppleTalk*. In a LAN, computer devices share a common transmission medium instead of being connected by point-to-point links. Because they differ in transmission rates and by how they share access to the common links, different LANs are best suited for different applications. For instance, Ethernet is adequate for low-load conditions when the delivery of packets is not subject to a hard time constraint. The token ring and token bus networks are preferable for high-load applications and also for hard time constraints. The current trend is toward faster LANs that can also cover larger geographical regions. The need for such LANs

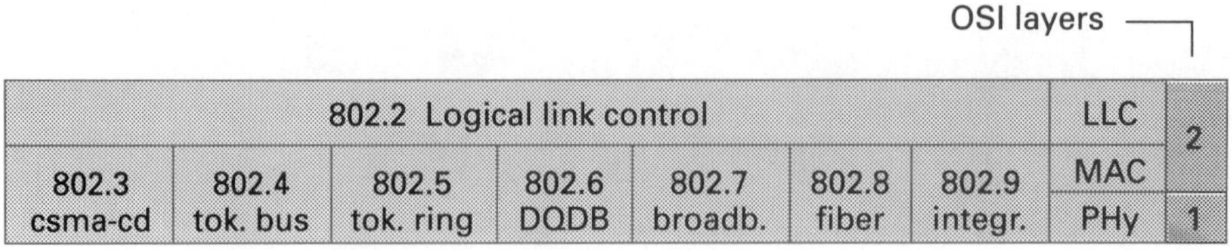

OSI layers ⎤

802.2 Logical link control							LLC	2
802.3 csma-cd	802.4 tok. bus	802.5 tok. ring	802.6 DQDB	802.7 broadb.	802.8 fiber	802.9 integr.	MAC PHy	1

198

Figure 5.1 Correspondence between MAC and LLC and the data link layer.

Computer devices on a LAN must share a common link. The access to the link is regulated by the MAC layer. The LLC layer uses the transmissions regulated by the MAC to implement reliable packet transmissions between devices on a LAN.

arises from the increased speed of workstations and from applications that use graphics or video. Such applications require transfers of very large files with small delays. The *fiber distributed data interface* (FDDI) and *distributed queue dual bus* (DQDB) networks are examples of high-speed LANs.

We learned in Chapter 2 that computers are interconnected either by point-to-point links in a mesh network or by shared links in a local area network. In a mesh network, the packets are transmitted from one node to the next, in a store-and-forward manner, from the source to the destination. We saw in Chapter 3 how a point-to-point link carries electromagnetic waves that encode bits. We then learned in Chapter 4 how a data link protocol converts this bit transmission into a reliable packet link on the point-to-point link. In a local network, there is no point-to-point link dedicated to the transfer of packets between two computer devices, i.e., between two network nodes. Instead, a common link is shared by many nodes. Consequently, regulating the access to the shared link is an important task in the transmission of packets on a LAN that is absent in other networks. As a result, the organization of the protocols for LANs is different from those in other networks. We will see that the OSI layer 2, i.e., the data link layer, is divided in LANs into two sublayers: the *media access control* (MAC) and the *logical link control* (LLC), as shown in Figure 5.1. The *MAC protocol* regulates the access to the channel by giving each node a chance to transmit its packets. The LLC implements packet transmission services between the nodes. The IEEE 802.2 standards specify the LLC, and the IEEE 802.3–9 are working groups defining standards for the physical layer and the MAC sublayer of LANs. The LANs specified by the IEEE 802 standards are compatible above the LLC. The IEEE 802 LANs differ in the physical layer and the MAC sublayer, both in the characteristics of the transmission equipment and the MAC protocol.

In this chapter, we will discuss the following LANs: *ALOHA, Ethernet, token ring, token bus, FDDI,* and *DQDB*. We will explain the principles of operation and the performance characteristics of these networks. The main performance measures of a LAN are the *throughput* and the *delay*. The throughput is the maximum bit transmission rate when the LAN is heavily loaded by many nodes. The throughput is a fraction of the rate of the transmitters. This fraction is called the *efficiency* of the MAC protocol. For instance, a network that uses a MAC protocol with an efficiency of 75% and 10-Mbps transmitters has a throughput of 7.5 Mbps. The delay is usually measured as the typical time taken to transmit a packet between two nodes on the network. The delay has three components: the *queueing time*, the *transmission time*, and the *propagation time*. The queueing time is the time that a packet waits before the start of its transmission. That queueing time comprises the time to transmit other packets and the time needed to access the transmission medium. In this chapter, we will focus on the efficiency and the throughput of LANs. We will discuss queueing times in Chapters 6 and 10. The transmission time, in seconds, is equal to the number of bits in the packet divided by the transmission rate in bits per second. The propagation time is the time taken by the signals to propagate along the transmission medium. This propagation time is the length of the signal path divided by the signal propagation speed. The propagation speed is about 2.3×10^8 m/s in a coaxial cable and 2×10^8 m/s in an optical fiber with a refractive index of 1.46, a typical value.

MAC and LLC

- The data link layer of LANs is decomposed into the media-access control (MAC) and the logical-link-control (LLC) sublayers.
- The MAC sublayer regulates the access to the channel shared by nodes on a LAN.
- The LLC sublayer supervises the packet links between nodes.
- The *efficiency* of a MAC protocol is the maximum fraction of time that the nodes can transmit packets successfully when they use the protocol and when the network is heavily loaded by many nodes.
- The *throughput* of a LAN is the maximum rate of successful bit transmissions on the LAN when it is heavily loaded by many nodes. The throughput is the product of the transmission rate and the efficiency of the MAC protocol.
- The propagation speed of signals is about 2.3×10^8 m/s in a coaxial cable and 2×10^8 m/s in a typical optical fiber.

5.1 ALOHA Protocol

ALOHA is a packet-switched radio communication network that was built at the University of Hawaii in the early 1970s, as discussed in Section 1.4. Figure 5.2 depicts the main components of that network. A central node listens to packets transmitted by the other nodes at the radio frequency $f_0 = 407$ MHz and retransmits these packets at the radio frequency $f_1 = 413$ MHz. The nodes in the ALOHA network transmitted the packets at the rate of 9,600 bps.

The protocol used by ALOHA, called the *ALHOA protocol*, is a media-access control protocol. The ALOHA protocol was the first *multiple-access protocol*. A multiple-access protocol is a method for sharing a transmission channel by enabling the transmitters to access the channel at random times. This method contrasts with the time-division multiplexing method, which allocates specific time periods to the different transmitters. The ALOHA protocol can be used with radio transmitters, as in the original ALOHA network, or with a coaxial cable, a twisted wire pair, or optical fibers. The ALOHA protocol and some variants are used in satellite networks. ALOHA inspired Ethernet, which is based on a minor variation of the ALOHA protocol and which is the most widely used LAN.

The ALOHA protocol is used by nodes that transmit on a common channel and that listen to the same channel. The nodes transmit packets of a fixed length. When two transmissions occur simultaneously, they garble each other. In such an instance, packets are described as *colliding*. In the original ALOHA network, the central node acknowledges the correct packets it receives. When a node does not get an acknowledgment within a specific timeout, it assumes that its packet collided. When a packet collides, the transmitting node schedules a retransmission after a random delay.

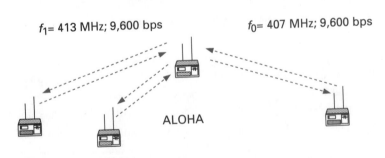

Figure 5.2 The ALOHA network.

The nodes transmit their packets around the radio frequency $f_0 = 407$ MHz at the rate of 9,600 bps. A central node listens to the transmissions and repeats them at the frequency $f_1 = 413$ MHz. The central node acknowledges the correct packets it receives. A node that does not get an acknowledgement assumes that its packets collided with another packet.

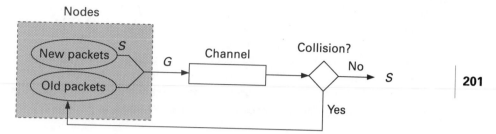

Figure 5.3 Packet transmissions using the ALOHA protocol.

A number of nodes use the slotted ALOHA protocol. When a node gets a new packet to transmit, it starts transmitting at the beginning of the next time slot. If the packet collides with another packet, the packet becomes an *old* packet that is transmitted after a random delay. Here G is the average number of transmission attempts during a transmission time, and S is the average number of successful transmissions during the same time.

There are two versions of the ALOHA protocol: *slotted* and *pure*. In the slotted ALOHA protocol, the time axis is divided into time slots with durations equal to the time required to transmit a packet on the channel. Nodes must start their transmissions at the beginning of a time slot. In the pure ALOHA protocol, the nodes can start transmitting at any time.

How well do the ALOHA protocols perform? The analysis we use to answer this question will determine the *efficiency* of the protocols, i.e., the maximum fraction of time during which packets are transmitted successfully when the ALOHA protocols are used. We first analyze the slotted ALOHA protocol.

Figure 5.3 represents the flow of packets transmitted by a large number of nodes that use the slotted ALOHA protocol. When a node gets a *new* packet to transmit, it starts transmitting it at the beginning of the next time slot. If the packet is the only one transmitted during that time slot, the transmission is successful. Otherwise, the packet suffers a collision, and the node schedules a retransmission after a random delay. We view the packets that collide as joining a pool of *old* packets.

We want to calculate the *efficiency* $\eta_{S.ALOHA}$ of the slotted ALOHA protocol, i.e., the maximum fraction of time during which the nodes can transmit packets successfully. That is, we want to calculate the maximum possible value of S in Figure 5.3. The protocol wastes some fraction of the time slots because of collisions and some other fraction when all the nodes are postponing their transmissions because of the random delays in scheduling retransmissions. During the remaining fraction of the time slots, the nodes transmit one packet at a time. The transmissions in these time slots are said to be successful. We will find out that successful transmissions occur in at most $\eta_{S.ALOHA} = 36\%$ of the time slots when the slotted ALOHA protocol is used. Thus, if the transmission rate is 100 kbps and if the packets are 1,000 bits long, then the slotted ALOHA protocol can transmit successfully at most 36% of the time, with a successful transmission rate of 36 kbps, i.e., of 36 packets per second.

202

To carry out the analysis of the efficiency of the slotted ALOHA protocol, we define G as the *total* rate of transmission attempts, in packets per time slot, and S as the rate of successful transmissions, also in packets per time slot. Then,

$$S = G \times p \tag{5.1}$$

where p is the likelihood that the transmission of an arbitrary packet is successful. We can expect p to decrease when G becomes larger since collisions are more likely when the nodes attempt to transmit more packets. To derive an expression for p as a function of G, we assume that the probability that n packets, either new or old, become ready to be transmitted in an arbitrary time period of duration T (measured in time slots) is given by

$$Prob\{n \text{ packets in } T \text{ time slots}\} = \frac{(GT)^n}{n!} e^{-GT} \tag{5.2}$$

for $n \geq 0$. This assumption is justified when there is a large number of nodes that attempt to transmit, each with a small probability. In that situation, the packets are transmitted independently of one another by many nodes and some analysis shows that (5.2) holds. By using this assumption, we can show that

$$p = e^{-G}. \tag{5.3}$$

To see this, consider one arbitrary packet P that becomes ready for transmission at some time t during the time slot $[k, k+1]$. That packet P will be transmitted successfully if no other packet becomes available for transmission during the same time slot. Thus, the transmission of P is successful if no packet becomes ready for transmission in the time interval $[k, t)$ or in the time interval $(t, k+1]$. The notation $[k, t)$ represents the set of times that are larger than or equal to k and that are strictly smaller than t. Similarly, the notation $(t, k+1]$ represents the set of times that are strictly larger than t and smaller than or equal to $k+1$. According to (5.2), the probability that no packet arrives during $[k, t)$ or $(t, k+1]$, an epoch with total duration $T = 1$, is given by $p = e^{-G}$, as announced. (Recall that $G^0 = 1$ and that $0! = 1$.) Combining (5.1) and (5.3), we find

$$S = Ge^{-G}. \tag{5.4}$$

This formula is plotted in Figure 5.4, which shows that the maximum value of the right-hand side of (5.4) is $e^{-1} \approx 36\%$. The maximum fraction of time during which

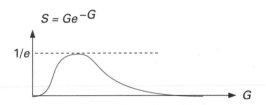

$$S = Ge^{-G}$$

$1/e$

G

Figure 5.4 Throughput of the slotted ALOHA protocol.

G is the total transmission rate of new packets and retransmitted packets. S is the rate of new packets. The figure shows that the maximum transmission rate of new packets is equal to $1/e \approx 0.36$ packet per transmission time. This maximum value is, by definition, the *efficiency* of the protocol.

the slotted ALOHA protocol can transmit packets successfully is the efficiency $\eta_{S.ALOHA}$ of the slotted ALOHA protocol. Therefore, $\eta_{S.ALOHA} \leq 36\%$. It can be shown that if the nodes randomize their retransmissions suitably, then the efficiency of the slotted ALOHA protocol approaches this upper bound of 36%. Hence,

$$\eta_{S.ALOHA} = 36\% . \tag{5.5}$$

The efficiency and throughput values that we have computed require some interpretation. When a single node tries to transmit on the channel, all its transmissions are successful and the efficiency is 100%. This is not the situation captured by the model that we analyzed. Only when many nodes generate the aggregate traffic can one assume that (5.2) holds. Thus, the efficiency $\eta_{S.ALOHA} = 36\%$ corresponds to the case of many nodes having comparable transmission rates and sharing a common channel by using the slotted ALOHA protocol.

The analysis of the efficiency of the pure ALOHA protocol is very similar to that of the slotted ALOHA protocol. The only difference is that the nodes can start transmitting at arbitrary times instead of only at the beginning of time slots. A given packet P that is transmitted at time t will be successful if no other packet's transmission begins in the time interval $(t-1, t+1)$, as illustrated in Figure 5.5. Thus, the probability that the transmission of packet P is successful, when the pure ALOHA protocol is used, is the probability that no packet's transmission begins during $(t-1, t)$ or $(t, t+1)$, an epoch with total duration 2. According to (5.2), with $n = 0$ and $T = 2$, this probability is equal to e^{-2G}. Therefore, when the nodes use the pure ALOHA protocol,

$$S = Ge^{-2G}$$

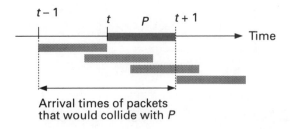

Arrival times of packets
that would collide with P

Figure 5.5 Packets colliding with P with the pure ALOHA protocol.

A packet P whose transmission begins at time t collides with packets
whose transmission starts between $t-1$ and $t+1$.

In particular, $S \leq 1/(2e) = 18\%$. As for the slotted ALOHA protocol, this upper bound of 18% can be achieved if the nodes randomize their retransmissions suitably. Thus, the efficiency of the pure ALOHA protocol is

$$\eta_{P.ALOHA} = 18\% \ . \tag{5.6}$$

The slotted ALOHA protocol is more difficult to implement than the pure ALOHA protocol because it requires that the nodes have access to a common time reference, i.e., a common clock, to identify the beginning of the time slots. The efficiency of the two ALOHA protocols is rather poor. It is desirable to improve the efficiency of these protocols if they share an expensive transmission channel, such as a satellite channel. A simple method for improving the efficiency of the ALOHA protocols is to use *reservations*. Two protocols based on ALOHA that use reservations are SPADE and the R.ALOHA protocol.

SPADE is the reservation protocol used by the Intelsat telecommunications satellites. In SPADE, there are 397 bidirectional 64-kbps channels for voice transmissions and one 128-kbps channel used for reservations. The reservation channel is divided into frames of 50 small slots, where 50 is an upper bound on the number of nodes allowed to use the satellite. Slot k is allocated to node k, which can use it to reserve one (chosen at random) of the 397 bidirectional channels. Each communication channel is then used for voice transmission by the nodes in the order in which it was reserved. After the completion of its voice transmission, the node indicates in its slot on the reservation channel that it no longer needs the communication channel. Note that, under heavy usage, the voice channels are used with perfect efficiency since they are reserved by the time they become free again. As a result, the 397 bidirectional channels are used with 100% efficiency and the 128-kbps reservation channel is wasted in that it cannot be used for voice transmission. Since the reservation channel has the same transmission rate as one of the 397 bidirectional channels, we conclude that the efficiency of SPADE is 397/398.

The R.ALOHA (reservation.ALOHA) protocol is for nodes that use the same channel for the reservations and for the transmissions of packets. The protocol begins with a *reservation phase*. During the reservation phase, the nodes use the slotted ALOHA protocol to attempt to access the channel. A node which succeeds in accessing the channel broadcasts a reservation by transmitting a packet that contains the node identification number. At the end of the reservation phase, the nodes which made reservations transmit in the order of the reservations. At the end of the transmission phase, a new reservation phase starts, which, in turn, is followed by a new transmission phase, and so on. The R.ALOHA protocol uses the reservation phases with an efficiency of about 36% and the transmission phases with perfect efficiency. Thus, a reservation takes an average of 1/0.36 reservation slots, since each time slot has the probability 0.36 of being used successfully. Thus, if a reservation slot has duration *TRES* and if a packet transmission lasts *TRANSP*, the efficiency $\eta_{R.ALOHA}$ of the R.ALOHA protocol is

$$\eta_{R.ALOHA} = \frac{TRANSP}{TRES/0.36 + TRANSP} \approx \frac{1}{1 + 2.8 \times \dfrac{TRES}{TRANSP}}. \qquad (5.7)$$

To apply (5.7), assume that the duration of a reservation slot is 5% of that of a packet transmission. We find that the efficiency of the R.ALOHA protocol is $\eta_{R.ALOHA} = 1/(1 + 2.8 \times 0.05) \approx 88\%$.

The throughput of the pure, slotted, and R.ALOHA protocols is the efficiency of the protocol times the transmission rate. The transmission rate of radio transmitters is limited by the bandwidth of the radio channel available to the transmitters. The frequencies used for radio transmissions are strictly controlled by the *Federal Communications Commission* (FCC) in order to avoid interference and to maintain an orderly utilization of that valuable resource. The restrictions on the available frequencies limit the transmission rate, and, therefore, the number of nodes that can use radio transmitters simultaneously. When a large number of users must be accommodated, as in the case of the *mobile telephones* used in automobiles in urban areas, a solution is to divide the geographical area into cells, as illustrated in Figure 5.6. The users must transmit on frequencies determined by their locations. Figure 5.6 indicates possible allocations of frequencies in the cells. The figure assumes that the power of the transmitters is small enough for cells that use the same frequencies not to interfere. Each cell has a base node, and the mobile users communicate with the base node. Every mobile transmitter identifies the cell it belongs to by comparing the powers of the signals it receives from the different base nodes. The mobile transmitter receives the greatest power from the base node of the cell it belongs to.

Analog cellular telephones use frequency modulation, with a bandwidth of 30 kHz per channel, and cells with a radius from 20 km to 40 km.

Digital cellular telephones support a larger number of users because they use time-division multiplexing to utilize the bandwidth more efficiently, and they have better connections. The allocation of frequencies to cells can be applied to small cells that cover only a few rooms in a building or a fraction of a city block. Such a division of a region into *microcells* permits even higher transmission rates over the same total range of frequencies. Such a system can be used for portable computer terminals with connections that have bit rates high enough for applications that require small response times and that use graphics or video.

ALOHA Protocol

- The ALOHA protocol enables nodes to share a common transmission channel provided that they can learn when packet transmissions collide.

- There are two versions of the ALOHA protocol: pure and slotted.

- With the slotted ALOHA protocol, the nodes start transmitting at the beginning of time slots. A node retransmits after a random delay if the packet collides with another packet. The efficiency of this protocol is

$$\eta_{S.ALOHA} = 36\% \, . \tag{5.5}$$

- With the pure ALOHA protocol, the nodes can transmit at arbitrary times. A node retransmits packets that collide after a random delay. The efficiency of this protocol is

$$\eta_{P.ALOHA} = 18\% \, . \tag{5.6}$$

- Reservations can improve the efficiency of the ALOHA protocol. The efficiency of SPADE is 397/398. The efficiency of the R.ALOHA protocol is

$$\eta_{R.ALOHA} \approx \frac{1}{1 + 2.8 \times \dfrac{TRES}{TRANSP}} \, . \tag{5.7}$$

- Cellular allocations of frequencies permit a higher total transmission rate over the same bandwidth.

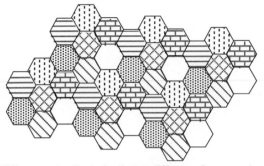

Different shadings indicate different frequencies.

Figure 5.6 Cellular frequency allocations.

In a cellular communication system, the region is divided into cells. The mobile transmitters operate on a frequency f which depends on the cells that they are in. This division of the region into cells permits users to transmit simultaneously on the same frequency in distant cells. As a result, a smaller set of frequencies is required for a given number of simultaneous connections.

5.2 Ethernet and IEEE 802.3

Networks based on the IEEE 802.3 standards compose the most widely used LANs. These are bus networks that use a media-access control protocol called *carrier sense multiple access with collision detection* (CSMA-CD). You will see that the CSMA-CD protocol is very similar to the ALOHA protocol. In this section we discuss Ethernet and some other networks based on the IEEE 802.3 standards. Recall that the IEEE 802.3 standards specify the physical layer and the media access control of the local area networks. In particular, these standards specify the protocol that the nodes use to access the common channel.

There are five versions of IEEE 802.3: *10BASE5*, *10BASE2*, *1BASE5*, *10BASE-T*, and *10BROAD36*. The characteristics of these five versions are summarized in Figure 5.7. These networks are built from segments of coaxial cable, twisted wire pairs, or optical fibers that are attached together by *repeaters*. A repeater is a device that receives the signals on one segment, reconstructs the bits represented by the signals, and retransmits these bits as signals on another segment. In these five designations, the first number (1 or 10) indicates the transmission rate in megabits per second. *BASE* indicates that the nodes transmit the information in baseband by using the Manchester encoding. *BROAD* identifies a

208

	10BASE5 Ethernet	10BASE2 CheaperNet	StarLAN1BASE5 StarLAN	10BROAD36 Broadband	10 BASE – T
Medium	Coaxial cable 50 ohms-10 mm	Coaxial cable 50 ohms-5 mm	Twisted pair unshielded	Coaxial cable 75 ohms	2 simplex twisted pair unshielded
Signals	10 Mbps-Manch	10 Mbps-Manch	1 Mbps-Manch	10 Mbps-DPSK	10 Mbps-Manch
Maximum segment	500 m	185 m	500 m	1,800 m	100 m
Maximum distance	2.5 km	0.925 km	2.5 km	3.6 km	1 km
Nodes per segment	100	30			2
Collision detection	Excess current		2 active hub inputs	Transmission ≠ reception	Activity on receiver and transmitter
Notes	Slot time = 512 bits; gap time = 96 bits; jam = 32 to 48 bits				

Figure 5.7   IEEE 802.3 networks.

The IEEE 802.3 networks use twisted pairs or coaxial cables. Some use optical fibers. The baseband networks use Manchester encoding. The broadband network uses differential phase shift keying (DPSK). The figure shows the maximum segment length, the maximum distance between nodes, and the maximum number of nodes per segment. The figure also indicates the methods used for collision detection. The slot time is used to schedule retransmissions, and the gap time is the minimum time between two successive packets.

broadband network that encodes the bits using DPSK (differential phase shift keying), a modulation method that transmits the difference between successive bits using the PSK modulation explained in Chapter 3. The number at the end of the designation (5, 2, or 36) is the maximum length of a segment of the network as a multiple of 100 m. *10BASE-T* designates a 10-Mbps baseband network that uses twisted pairs as the transmission medium. Thus, 10BASE5 is a 10-Mbps baseband network with segments of at most 500 m. *Ethernet*, which was developed before the IEEE 802.3 standards, is almost identical to 10BASE5, except for minor differences in the frame structure. The network 10BASE2 is known as *Cheapernet* because it uses a *thin* coaxial cable of 5 mm in diameter which is less expensive than the *thick* 10mm-cable used in Ethernet. *StarLAN* is another name for 1BASE5. The name of this network is derived from its star topology, which is also used by *10BASE-T*. In *10BASE-T*, each computer or peripheral is attached to a *medium access unit* (MAU) by two simplex twisted pairs. Each MAU is connected to a central *repeater unit* by two unidirectional point-to-point links. The repeater unit repeats a signal that it receives on one link onto all the other links. The links between an MAU and the repeater unit are usually standard telephone unshielded 0.5 mm twisted pairs of up to 100 m. Some *10BASE-T* networks attach the MAUs to the repeater units with optical fibers that can be up to 500 m long.

The MAC protocol specified by these five standards is the CSMA-CD protocol, which will be discussed below. Essentially, the CSMA-CD protocol specifies that a station must wait for the channel to be idle before it can transmit (carrier sense) and that it must stop transmitting as soon as it detects a collision (collision detection). The five standards specify different methods for detecting collisions, as shown in Figure 5.7. The nodes on a *10BASE5* or *10BASE2* network detect a collision when they measure a large current on the cable. Collisions on *1BASE5* or *10BASE-T* are detected by the MAU when it detects activity both on the transmitter and the receiver lines. The repeater unit then transmits a special signal that informs the nodes of the collision. The nodes on the *10BROAD36* network detect collisions by comparing what they transmit on one frequency with what is repeated by a head-end station on another frequency.

In this section, we will describe the operation of Ethernet. The other networks use the same MAC protocol. A typical layout of an Ethernet network is illustrated in Figure 5.8. Each network node contains a special *network interface board* attached to the bus inside the node. The interface board is connected by a *transceiver cable* to a *transceiver* attached to a network segment. The transceiver cable is a bundle of twisted wire pairs up to 50 m long.

To receive packets, the transceiver converts the electrical signals on the cable into binary values for the interface board. This conversion is performed by a receiver circuit in the transceiver that measures the voltage on the cable. The circuit outputs a signal representing the binary value 1 when that voltage exceeds

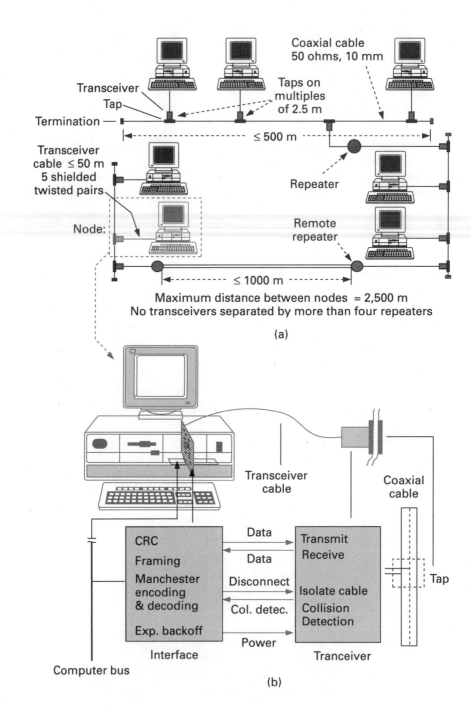

Coaxial cable
50 ohms, 10 mm

Transceiver

Tap

Taps on
multiples
of 2.5 m

Termination

≤ 500 m

Transceiver
cable ≤ 50 m
5 shielded
twisted pairs

Repeater

Node:

Remote
repeater

≤ 1000 m

Maximum distance between nodes = 2,500 m
No transceivers separated by more than four repeaters

(a)

Transceiver
cable

Coaxial
cable

Tap

CRC

Framing

Manchester
encoding
& decoding

Exp. backoff

Interface

Data

Data

Disconnect

Col. detec.

Power

Transmit
Receive

Isolate cable

Collision
Detection

Tranceiver

Computer bus

(b)

Figure 5.8 (opposite) Ethernet layout.

Part (a) of the figure shows that the network consists of *segments* connected by repeaters. An *interface board* is installed in each node (b). A *transceiver cable*, also called *drop cable*, connects the interface board to a *transceiver* attached to a segment by a *tap*. When the node wants to transmit a packet, the CPU (central processing unit) of the node arranges for the packet to be delivered through the bus from the main node memory to a buffer in the interface. The interface waits for the transceiver to signal that the cable is idle. When it gets that signal, the interface board communicates the bits of the packet to the transceiver which transmits them on the segment. If the transceiver detects a collision while it is transmitting, it informs the interface board, which then schedules a retransmission after a random delay. Received packets follow the reverse path from the segment to the transceiver to the interface board to the node memory. The interface board calculates the CRC (cyclic redundancy code) bits to detect transmission errors.

a fixed threshold and a signal representing the value 0 otherwise. As a result, the interface board receives the Manchester-encoded bits transmitted on the cable. The interface board decodes the bits, stores them in its buffer, and informs the node when a full packet has been received. To decode the bits, the interface board is synchronized by a phase-locked loop, as we explained in Section 3.4.

To transmit a packet, the node copies it into a buffer on the interface board which waits for the transceiver to indicate when the coaxial cable is idle, i.e., when its receiver circuit does not detect any activity. The interface board then delivers the Manchester-encoded bits of the packet to the transceiver. The transceiver contains a current source that is switched on and off by the binary values of the Manchester code and that injects currents with an average value between 18 mA and 24 mA into the coaxial cable. While a transceiver is transmitting, it monitors the current flowing through the coaxial cable by measuring the average voltage across the cable. If that average value shows that the current is larger than 24 mA, then the transceiver knows that another transceiver is also injecting some current and it informs the interface board that a *collision* is occurring. When the interface board learns of the collision, it stops transmitting the packet and transmits a sequence of 32 to 48 randomly chosen bits, called the *jam signal*. The objective of the jam signal is to guarantee that all the nodes become aware of the collision. The interface board then schedules a retransmission of the packet after a random time. The interface board contains an integrated circuit that calculates the cyclic redundancy code bits (see Section 3.5) to detect transmission errors.

In summary, the Ethernet MAC protocol (CSMA-CD) specifies that a node with a packet to transmit must proceed as follows:

1. Wait until the channel is idle.

2. When the channel is idle, transmit and listen while transmitting.

3. In case of a collision, stop the packet transmission, transmit a jam signal, and then wait for a random delay and GO TO (1).

The protocol gives up the transmission attempt after 16 successive collisions. The size of the random delay after a collision is selected according to the following rule, called the *binary exponential backoff algorithm*: if a packet has collided n successive times, where $n < 16$, then the node chooses a random number K with equal probabilities from the set $\{0, 1, 2, 3, ..., 2^m - 1\}$ where $m := \min\{10, n\}$; the node then waits for $K \times 512$ bit times. (At 10 Mbps, one bit time = 10^{-7} second.) Thus, after the first collision, the nodes choose the random delay 0 or 512 bit times, with equal probabilities. After two successive collisions, the delay is equally likely to be 0, 512, 1,024, or 1,536 bit times. After three successive collisions, it is equally likely to be 0, 512, 1,024, 1,536, 2,048, ..., or 3,584 bit times. The rationale for using this method for selecting the value of the delays is that it reduces quickly the chances of repeated collisions by spreading out the range of waiting times. For instance, if the transmissions of two nodes have collided three successive times, the likelihood that they choose the same delay for the fourth transmission attempt is one out of eight, since both nodes independently select among eight equally likely delay values. Also, if two nodes choose to wait for different multiples of 512 bit times, then the node that chooses the smallest delay transmits successfully. Indeed, the propagation time between any two nodes is shorter than 512 bit times, and the signal from the node with the smallest delay reaches the other node before it starts transmitting. According to the protocol, that second node waits before transmitting.

Note the similarity between the CSMA-CD protocol and the ALOHA protocol. In both protocols, nodes retransmit after a random delay when the packets collide. The two protocols differ in how they avoid collisions. Nodes that use the ALOHA protocol start transmitting as soon as they get a packet to transmit. Moreover, they transmit the complete packets even if they collide. With the CSMA-CD protocol, a node waits until the channel is idle before starting a transmission and it stops transmitting as soon as it detects a collision. Thus, the CSMA-CD protocol is a polite version of the ALOHA protocol. You will see that this politeness makes the CSMA-CD protocol more efficient than the ALOHA protocol. Note, however, that the ALOHA protocol is designed for networks with long propagation times that render carrier sensing ineffective and delay the collision detection until after the packet has been transmitted. Our analysis of the efficiency of the CSMA-CD protocol will confirm that it is lower when the propagation delays are larger.

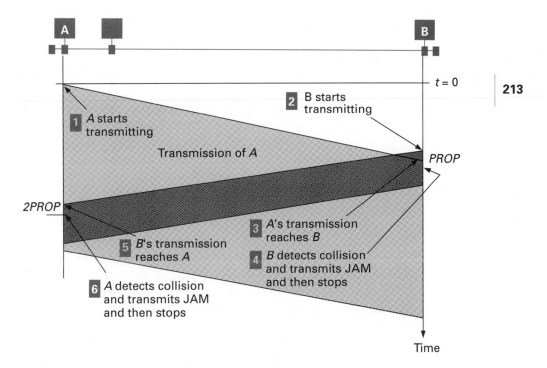

Figure 5.9 Maximum collision detection time.

The longest collision detection time occurs when node *A* at one end of the cable starts transmitting and node *B* at the other end of the cable starts its transmission just before the signal from node *A* has reached it. Node *A* detects the collision when the signal from node *B* reaches it, i.e., about one round-trip propagation time after node *A* started transmitting. Notice that if node *B* did not transmit a jam signal, then it could stop transmitting so quickly that the energy of the signal that *A* receives from *B* might not suffice to indicate a collision.

We saw that a node detects a collision while transmitting when its transceiver measures an excessive current on the cable. The nodes that are not transmitting detect a collision when they observe a packet shorter than 500 bits, which is shorter than the minimum length of a valid frame (544 bits). A packet with fewer than 500 bits appears on the cable when a collision occurs because the transmission time of a packet that collides cannot exceed the maximum collision detection time plus the longest jam pattern. The maximum collision detection time is shown in Figure 5.9 to be twice the maximum end-to-end propagation time. The propagation time is determined by the cable length and the delays in the repeaters. The specifications of Ethernet result in a maximum collision detection time of 450 bit times. Consequently, the length of a packet that collides is at most 450 bits plus the maximum length of a jam signal (48 bits).

214

The packets are sent in the form of *frames*, i.e., strings of bits, that have the structure shown in Figure 5.10 (pages 216–217). The frame is divided into *fields*, which are groups of bits with a precise location inside the frame and a specific signification. The *logical link control* (LLC) field indicates the *destination service access point* (DSAP) and the *source service access point* (SSAP). Service access points are numbers that enable nodes to distinguish among communication streams. For instance, a computer may be running different applications that exchange packets with other nodes on the network. The computer reads the DSAP of the packets it receives to direct them to the appropriate application. The *preamble* (PRE) synchronizes the receiver, as explained in Section 3.4. The *starting frame delimiter* (SFD) indicates the start of the frame. In addition to the *source address* (SA) and *destination address* (DA), the frame contains an indication of its *length* (LEN), the *cyclic redundancy code* (CRC) bits, and a *padding* (PAD) field that guarantees that valid frames contain at least 544 bits. The *control* (CONT) field specifies whether the transmission is connection-oriented, unacknowledged connectionless, or acknowledged connectionless (see Section 5.7). The control field also indicates the frame or acknowledgement number.

How do we measure the *efficiency* $\eta_{CSMA.CD}$ of the CSMA-CD protocol? As for ALOHA, the efficiency is defined as the maximum fraction of time that the nodes using the protocol can send new packets under a heavy load imposed by all the nodes. The CSMA-CD protocol that we will analyze is similar to the IEEE 802.3 MAC protocol, except that we assume that the backoff time after a collision is a random multiple of the round-trip propagation time. In IEEE 802.3, the backoff time is a random multiple of 512-bit times, so that the interface board does not have to be programmed by indicating the length of the network it is installed in. Since the IEEE 802.3 backoff delays are longer than necessary, we can expect that the efficiency that we will calculate is higher than that of an actual IEEE 802.3 network. However, our analysis provides a better evaluation of the efficiency that can be achieved with the CSMA-CD protocol. We will use that efficiency to compare the CSMA-CD protocol with other MAC protocols.

You will see that

$$\eta_{CSMA.CD} \approx \frac{1}{1 + 5a} \text{ with } a := \frac{PROP}{TRANSP} \qquad (5.8)$$

where *PROP* denotes the one-way propagation time of a signal from one end of the cable to the other end and *TRANSP* designates the transmission time of a packet. The analysis leading to (5.8) goes as follows: Say that N ($N \geq 2$) nodes compete for a time-slotted channel by transmitting packets with probability $p \in (0, 1)$, independently of one another, in any given time slot. Denote by $\alpha(p)$

the probability that exactly one node transmits in a given time slot. The claim is that

$$\alpha(p) = Np(1 - p)^{N-1} .$$ (5.9)

To see this, notice that there are N ways that exactly one node can transmit in a given time slot, according to which of the N nodes transmits. Also, each of those N ways requires that the successful node transmits and that the other $N - 1$ nodes do not. Now, one node transmits with probability p and does not transmit with probability $1 - p$. The probability that a collection of independent events all occur is the product of the probabilities of the individual events. Therefore, the probability that one given node transmits and that the other $N - 1$ nodes do not is $p \times (1 - p) \times ... \times (1 - p) = p(1 - p)^{N-1}$. This is the probability of a specific way in which a packet transmits successfully. Now, the probability that one of a collection of mutually exclusive events occurs is the sum of the probabilities of the individual events. (Events are mutually exclusive if at most one can occur.) The N ways in which a packet transmits successfully are mutually exclusive since they differ by which node is successful. Therefore, we conclude that the right-hand side of (5.9) is the probability that one of these N events occurs, i.e., that a packet is transmitted successfully. (See Appendix A for the needed probability theory.)

If the nodes knew the number N of competing nodes, then they could determine the value of p that maximizes $\alpha(p)$ and the efficiency of the protocol. The value of p that maximizes $\alpha(p)$ is $p = 1/N$. Indeed, this value is obtained by setting to zero the derivative of (5.9) with respect to p. One finds

$$\frac{d}{dp}\alpha(p) = N(1 - p)^{N-1} - N(N - 1)p(1 - p)^{N-2} ,$$

so that the value of p that makes this derivative equal to zero is $p = 1/N$, as claimed.

The corresponding maximum value of $\alpha(p)$ is

$$\alpha(\frac{1}{N}) = (1 - \frac{1}{N})^{N-1} \approx 40\% .$$ (5.10)

To see the approximation, you can verify that

$$\alpha(1/4) = 42\%, \ \alpha(1/10) = 39\%, \ \alpha(1/20) = 38\% .$$

In the CSMA-CD protocol, a node does not know the number N of nodes that have packets to transmit and are competing for the channel. Consequently, the nodes cannot use the value $p = 1/N$. For the purpose of the analysis, we assume that the CSMA-CD protocol with the exponential backoff algorithm is almost optimal, i.e., that it leads the nodes to randomize their transmission attempts as well as they would if they knew the number of competing nodes. That

216

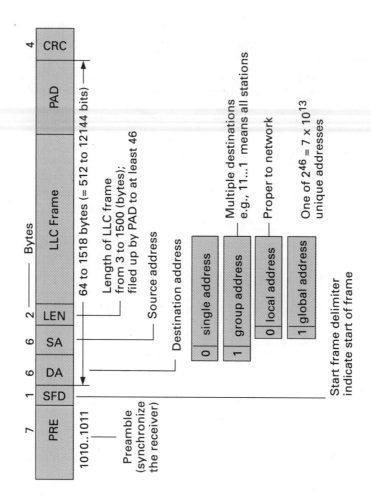

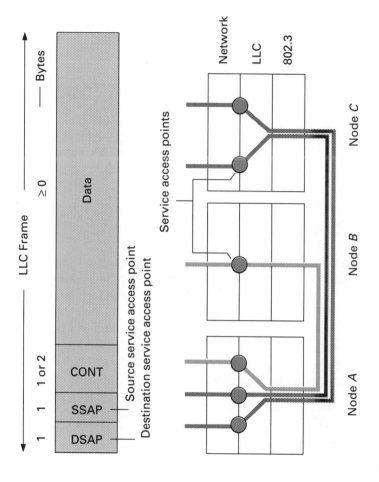

Figure 5.10 IEEE 802.3 frame structure.

The figure shows the frame structure for IEEE 802.3 networks. The destination address is either a single or a group address, and it is either local or global. The padding field guarantees that the minimum valid frame contains 68 bytes after the SFD.

is, we assume that the CSMA-CD protocol is such that each time slot is used for a successful transmission with probability $\alpha = 0.4$. A time slot has a duration $2 \times PROP$, the maximum collision detection time.

218

The average number of time slots A wasted by CSMA-CD before a successful packet transmission can be calculated is as follows: With probability $\alpha = 0.4$, the first time slot is successful, so that no time slot is wasted. With probability $1 - \alpha$, the first slot is wasted. After the first wasted slot, we are essentially back to the initial situation, so that an average number A of slots will again be wasted before the first successful transmission. Hence,

$$A = \alpha \times 0 + (1 - \alpha)(1 + A) \,.$$

Solving for A, we find $A = \alpha^{-1} - 1$. With $\alpha = 0.4$, this gives $A = 1.5$.

As a consequence, every successful transmission (with duration $TRANSP$) is accompanied by a waste of time equal to 1.5 time slots, i.e., to $1.5 \times 2 \times PROP = 3 \times PROP$, on the average. (See Figure 5.11.) It follows that the efficiency $\eta_{CSMA.CD}$, i.e., the fraction of time when the CSMA-CD protocol transmits successfully, is given by

$$\eta_{CSMA.CD} \approx \frac{TRANSP}{TRANSP + 3 \times PROP} = \frac{1}{1 + 3a} \,.$$

In actuality, the CSMA-CD protocol is not really optimal, and it wastes a larger amount of time than $3 \times PROP$ per packet transmission. Simulations show that the amount of time wasted is closer to $5 \times PROP$. Hence, the approximate efficiency of the CSMA-CD protocol is given by (5.8).

To develop a concrete feel for the efficiency of the CSMA-CD protocol, let us calculate $\eta_{CSMA.CD}$ when the coaxial cable is 2.5 km long, the transmission rate is 10 Mbps, and the packets have 620 bits. We find that $PROP$, the one-way propagation time of a signal from one end of the cable to the other, is given by

$$PROP = \frac{2500 \text{ m}}{2.3 \times 10^8 \text{ m/s}} \approx 1.09 \times 10^{-5} \text{ s} \,.$$

The transmission time $TRANSP$ of a packet is

$$TRANSP = \frac{620 \text{ bits}}{10 \times 10^6 \text{ bps}} = 6.2 \times 10^{-5} \text{ s.}$$

From these two values we conclude that $a = PROP/TRANSP \approx 0.176$ and, therefore,

$$\eta = \frac{1}{1 + 5a} = \frac{1}{1 + 5 \times 0.176} \approx 53\% \,.$$

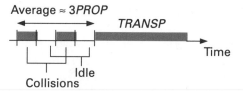

Figure 5.11 Time slots wasted per transmission.

The transmission of a packet lasts *TRANSP* plus the time required to access the channel. This channel access time is a random number of time slots defined by the MAC protocol. The average channel access time is about 3 × *PROP*.

Consequently, the effective transmission rate of this 10 Mbps network is only 53% of 10 Mbps, i.e., 5.3 Mbps, when the network is heavily loaded by many nodes. If the network transmits the frames shown in Figure 5.10, we see that about 30 bytes, i.e., 240 bits, of the 620 frame bits are not user data. Thus, only a fraction $(620 - 240)/620 \approx 61\%$ of the frame bits are user data bits. Therefore, the maximum rate at which the network can transmit user data is $61\% \times$ 5.3 Mbps = 3.2 Mbps. Note that it is possible that the nodes are not able to supply frames to utilize the 5.3-Mbps transmission rate of the network.

We can compare the efficiency of the CSMA-CD protocol with the efficiency of the ALOHA protocol (18% or 36%). Using (5.8), we find that the CSMA-CD protocol is more efficient than the pure ALOHA protocol whenever a is smaller than 89% and more efficient than the slotted ALOHA protocol when a is smaller than 34%.

IEEE 802.3 and Ethernet

■ The IEEE 802.3 standards specify the physical layer and the MAC sublayer of five versions of bus LANs.

■ Ethernet is a widely used LAN. To connect a computer on an Ethernet, one inserts an interface board in the computer. The board is connected to a transceiver attached to a coaxial cable segment of Ethernet.

■ The MAC protocol of the IEEE 802.3 LANs is *carrier sense multiple access with collision detection* (CSMA-CD). This protocol is a polite version of the ALOHA protocol. Its approximate efficiency is given by

$$\eta_{CSMA.CD} \approx \frac{1}{1 + 5a} \text{ with } a := \frac{PROP}{TRANSP}. \qquad (5.8)$$

5.3 Token Ring Networks

Token ring networks are another widely used family of LANs. The token ring networks were developed by IBM in the early 1980s. We will first explain the operations of some token ring MAC protocols, and we will calculate their efficiency. We will then discuss the IEEE 802.5 standard, which specifies the physical layer and the MAC protocol of a token ring network.

Figure 5.12 is a schematic diagram of a token ring network. The transmission medium is typically a twisted pair or a coaxial cable, although some versions use optical fibers. The MAC protocol of the token ring is as follows: A specific bit pattern, called the *token*, circulates on the ring. When a node wants to transmit, it waits until the token comes by. It then replaces the token with another pattern (SFD) which indicates the *start of frame*, and it appends its packet. The node converts the token into an SFD by monitoring the signal it receives from the ring and by modifying the token while it is stored in the interface buffer (see Figure 5.12) before retransmitting it. For instance, if the token and the SFD are bit patterns that differ by only the value of the last bit, it is enough for the interface buffer to delay the ring signal by one bit. Once the packet has been transmitted, the node transmits the token, which then becomes available to another node. We will see two versions of this protocol: *release after transmission* (RAT) and *release after reception* (RAR). These versions differ by when the node releases the token.

A node that is not transmitting repeats the packets that it receives. To do this, the node recovers the bits from the signal it receives on the input cable

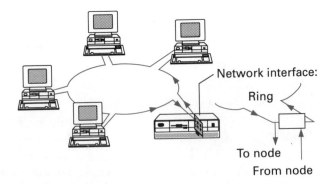

Figure 5.12 Token ring.

The nodes are attached to a unidirectional ring by a network interface. The network interface delays the signal on the ring by a few bits, and it sends the signal to the node. The node either retransmits the delayed signal unmodified on the ring or it modifies it.

and it retransmits these bits on the output cable. The rate of the bit transmission is controlled by a quartz oscillator in the transmitter. This transmission rate differs from the bit reception rate, which is the transmission rate of the upstream node, because no two quartz oscillators have exactly the same rate. This difference in rates means that each node must have a buffer. This node, called the *elasticity buffer*, stores the bits that accumulate when the input rate is higher than the transmission rate. A transmission rate higher than the input rate is handled as follows: the node starts transmitting when the buffer contains a specified number B of received bits; it stops when the complete incoming packet is repeated. The network designer selects a large enough number B for the buffer to prevent the buffer's becoming empty during the packet retransmission.

The steps of the *release after transmission* (RAT) *protocol* are shown in Figure 5.13. With this protocol, the node releases the token as soon as it has completely transmitted the packet.

We will calculate the *efficiency* η_{RAT} of the RAT protocol, defined as the fraction of time that the nodes transmit packets when they use that protocol and when all the nodes have packets to transmit. From the analysis, you will see that

$$\eta_{RAT} \approx \frac{1}{1 + \dfrac{a}{N}} \text{ with } a = \frac{PROP}{TRANSP + TRANST} , \qquad (5.11)$$

where N is the number of nodes, $TRANSP$ is the time to transmit a packet, and $PROP$ is the propagation time of a signal around the ring. Consider the timing diagram in Figure 5.14. Node 1 starts transmitting a packet and the transmission lasts $TRANSP$. The transmission of a token lasts $TRANST$. After $TRANSP + TRANST$, the last bit of the token has just been transmitted by node 1. That bit arrives at node 2 at time $TRANSP +, TRANST + PROP(1 \rightarrow 2)$, where $PROP(1 \rightarrow 2)$ designates the propagation time of a signal from node 1 to node 2. The first bit of the packet sent by node 2 leaves that node at time $TRANSP + TRANST + PROP(1 \rightarrow 2) + 1$ where the last 1 refers to the one-bit delay in node 2. That is, we assume that the nodes delay the signal by one bit to be able to replace the token with an SFD. The result of the analysis would not change if the node delay were a small number of bits different from one. Such a small delay is negligible compared with the packet transmission time. Each station takes an equivalent amount of time to transmit a packet and the token. Figure 5.14 shows that the N nodes transmit one packet each in a time

$$TOTAL = N \times (TRANSP + TRANST) + PROP(1 \rightarrow 2) + \ldots + PROP(N \rightarrow 1) + N$$
$$\approx N \times (TRANSP + TRANST) + PROP .$$

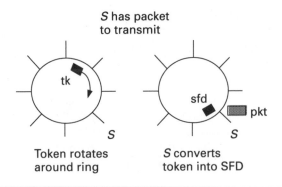

S has packet
to transmit

Token rotates around ring	S converts token into SFD

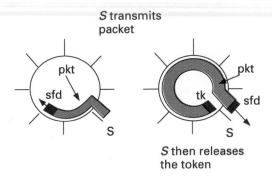

S transmits
packet

S then releases
the token

Figure 5.13 Release after transmission (RAT) protocol.

When using the RAT protocol, a node that has a packet to transmit waits
for the token. It then converts the token into a start frame delimiter (SFD)
and appends its packet. The node transmits a token (releases the token)
as soon as it has finished transmitting its packet.

Of this *TOTAL* time, only $N \times TRANSP$ time units are occupied by the actual
transmission of packets. Thus, the fraction of time η_{RAT} when the nodes transmit
packets is equal to

$$\eta_{RAT} = \frac{N \times TRANSP}{TOTAL} \approx \frac{1}{1 + \dfrac{a}{N}},$$

as we stated in (5.11). To derive the approximation, we assume that TRANST ≈
TRANSP.

The efficiency η_{RAT} of this protocol can be further improved by
enabling a node to hold the token and to transmit packets for up to some time,
called the maximum *token holding time (THT)*. By adapting our derivation to this
variation, we find that the efficiency becomes $\eta_{RAT}(THT)$ given by

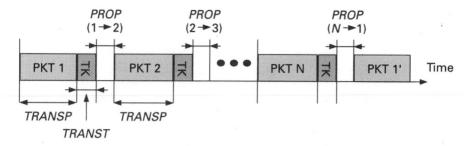

Figure 5.14 Timing diagram of release after transmission.

Time flows from left to right. Node 1 transmits packet 1 (PKT 1) and then the token (TK). The token propagates from node 1 to node 2 during the time epoch marked *PROP* (1 → 2) on the figure. The other nodes follow the same procedure. Eventually, node 1 gets the token again and transmits another packet designated PKT 1′.

$$\eta_{RAT}(THT) \approx \frac{1}{1 + \dfrac{PROP}{N \times THT}} . \tag{5.12}$$

The timing diagram of Figure 5.14 can be used to calculate the *maximum media access time* (MMAT) for the nodes using the RAT protocol. The MMAT is defined as the maximum time that a node has to wait before it can transmit. The value of MMAT may be an important design element for networks that are used in control equipment. The value of MMAT for nodes on an Ethernet network is infinite since a station can be unlucky and keep on colliding and randomly generating backoff times that are longer than those of the other stations. However, the MMAT for nodes using the RAT protocol is finite. This maximum access time occurs when all the other nodes have a packet to transmit. That situation is shown in Figure 5.15. The figure shows the sequence of transmissions. Assume that an urgent packet arrives at node 1 and must be transmitted as soon as possible. In the worst case how long does the packet have to wait? The worst case is shown in the figure. It occurs for a packet that arrives at node 1 just after that node has started to transmit another packet and when node 1 cannot transmit another packet without exceeding the admissible token holding time, THT. The packet must then wait for the N nodes to transmit and for the token to travel around the ring. If the $N-1$ nodes other than node 1 transmit for the maximum acceptable duration (THT), then the figure shows that the packet must wait for a time $MMAT_{RAT}$ given by

$$MMAT_{RAT} = PROP + N \times TRANST + TRANSP + (N-1) \times THT . \tag{5.13}$$

223

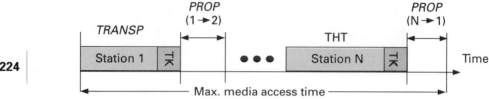

Figure 5.15 Maximum media access time for RAT protocol.

This figure shows the timing diagram of transmissions on a token ring using the RAT protocol. Node 1 must wait until the token comes back to it before it can transmit another packet. In the worst case, node 1 must wait for all the stations to transmit and for the token to travel around the ring before it can transmit another packet. This worst case waiting time is the maximum media access time.

The IEEE 802.5 standard specifies the *release after reception* (RAR) MAC protocol. RAR differs from RAT in that the transmitting node releases the token only after the complete frame has come back. As you will see from our analysis, RAT is significantly more efficient than RAR when the propagation time around the ring is not much smaller than the packet transmission time. However, RAR has the advantage of simplifying acknowledgements: a destination node can signal the correct reception of a packet by appending an acknowledgement at the end of the frame. That acknowledgement is then received by the transmitting node. The steps in the RAR protocol are shown in Figure 5.16.

Let us calculate the efficiency of the RAR protocol. The timing diagram of transmissions on a token ring when the nodes use the RAR protocol is given in Figure 5.17. As in Figure 5.14, this diagram assumes that all the nodes always have packets to transmit. The figure also assumes that the delays introduced by the nodes are negligible. The figure shows that the time between successive transmissions by node 1 is now equal to $TOTAL = N \times (TRANSP + TRANST + PROP) + PROP$. This identity implies that the efficiency is given by

$$\eta_{RAR} = N \times \frac{TRANSP}{TOTAL} \approx \frac{1}{1+a} \text{ with } a := \frac{PROP}{TRANSP}. \tag{5.14}$$

The efficiency of the RAR protocol increases when the nodes can hold the token for up to a specified maximum token holding time *THT*. The efficiency $\eta_{RAR}(THT)$ of the protocol with this modification is given by (5.14), where *TRANSP* is replaced by *THT*, i.e., by

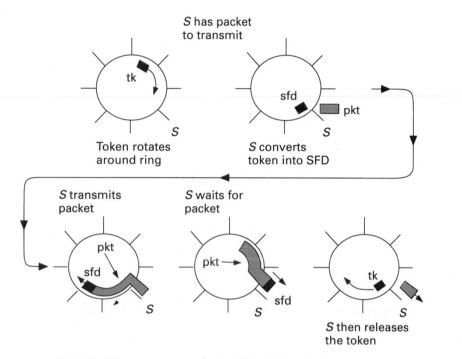

Figure 5.16 Release after reception (RAR) protocol.

A node that has a packet to transmit waits for the token (TK), converts it into a start of frame delimiter (SFD), and appends its packet. The node waits for the complete packet to come back completely before it releases the token.

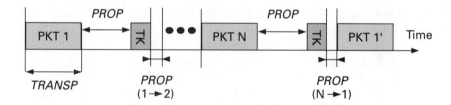

Figure 5.17 Timing diagram for release after reception.

Node 1 transmits a packet PKT 1, then waits for *PROP* for the packet to come back. Node 1 then transmits a token TK which takes *PROP* (1 → 2) to propagate to node 2. These steps are then repeated by the other nodes.

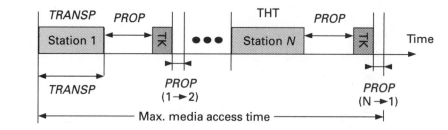

226

Figure 5.18 Maximum media access time for the RAR protocol.
The timing diagram shows the worst case waiting time for node 1 until it can transmit another packet.

$$\eta_{RAR}(THT) \approx \frac{1}{1 + \dfrac{PROP}{THT}} . \tag{5.15}$$

The maximum media access time $MMAT_{RAR}$ of the RAR protocol can be derived from the timing diagram shown in Figure 5.18, as we did for the RAT protocol. One finds

$$MMAT_{RAR} = (N + 1) \times PROP + N \times TRANST + TRANSP + (N - 1) \times THT. \tag{5.16}$$

Note that the protocols RAT and RAR are substantially more efficient than the CSMA-CD protocol. In some versions of the token ring protocol, the token is released by the receiving node. That is, once the node has received the packet, it transmits a token. This protocol is more efficient than RAR, as you can verify by drawing the timing diagram of the transmissions when nodes use that protocol.

We conclude the discussion of the token ring with some details specific to the IEEE 802.5 standard. These networks transmit at 1 or 4 Mbps over shielded twisted pairs and at 16 Mbps over shielded twisted pairs or optical fibers. Products are also available for transmitting over unshielded twisted pairs. The MAC protocol is release after reception (RAR). Every station can hold the token for up to 10 ms. In addition, the IEEE 802.5 standard provides for multiple packet *priorities*. The node with the packet that has the highest priority gets to transmit before the other nodes. This feature of the IEEE 802.5 is rarely implemented in actual networks. It can be used to speed up the delivery of urgent packets, such as control packets, by giving them priority over less pressing pack-

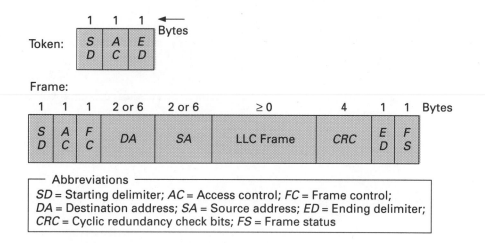

Figure 5.19 IEEE 802.5 frame structure.

The figure shows the structure of a token and of a regular frame. *SD* is the start frame delimiter, and *AC* is the access control field that indicates whether the bits are a token or a frame. In addition, the *AC* field specifies the priority and reservation levels. *FC* is the frame control field used for monitoring the operations of the ring. The destination address *DA* and source address *SA* are as in IEEE 802.3. *ED* is the end delimiter. *FS* is the frame status field. It indicates whether the destination is down or up and whether it accepted or rejected the frame.

ets, such as those carrying electronic mail messages. The frame structure is shown in Figure 5.19.

Tokens are identified by a special access control (*AC*) field that specifies the priority and reservation levels. To transmit a packet at some priority level, a node needs to wait for a token with a lower level and to place a reservation. If a reservation is already indicated on the token, a node can make another reservation at a higher level. After transmitting at a given level, the node lowers the token priority level to its previous value. The frame control (*FC*) field is used to monitor the ring. One of the nodes is the ring monitor. That node verifies that there is a token and that there is no cycling frame. The possible values of the field *FC* include *monitor_present*, which is issued periodically by the monitor, *reinitialize* to restart the ring, and *I_want_to_be_monitor* issued by a node when it realizes that the monitor is down. The frame status (*FS*) field is set by the destination to signal that it is up and whether it accepted the frame or not.

Token Rings

- Token rings are LANs with nodes that are connected in a ring topology and that use a token passing MAC protocol.

- In the RAT protocol, a node releases the token when it completes the transmission of a packet. The efficiency of this protocol is given by

$$\eta_{RAT}(THT) \approx \frac{1}{1 + \dfrac{PROP}{N \times THT}}. \tag{5.12}$$

- The maximum media access time of the RAT protocol is given by

$$MMAT_{RAT} = PROP + N{\times}TRANST + TRANSP + (N-1){\times}THT. \tag{5.13}$$

- In the RAR protocol, a node waits until the frame it transmitted comes back before releasing the token. The efficiency is given by

$$\eta_{RAR}(THT) \approx \frac{1}{1 + \dfrac{PROP}{THT}}. \tag{5.15}$$

- The maximum media access time of the RAR protocol is

$$MMAT_{RAR} = (N+1){\times}PROP + N{\times}TRANST + TRANSP$$
$$+ (N-1){\times}THT. \tag{5.16}$$

- The IEEE 802.5 MAC protocol is the RAR protocol. The destination can indicate whether it accepted the frame in the *FS* field.

5.4 Token Bus Networks

As the name indicates, the token bus network is a bus network that uses a token-passing MAC protocol. IEEE 802.4 specifies a standard for the physical layer and the MAC sublayer of token bus networks. The MAP (manufacturing automation protocol) of General Motors uses the token bus network. MAP is used to interconnect sensors, tools, and processors with bounded communication delays (see Chapter 8).

A typical layout of a token bus network is shown in Figure 5.20. The figure shows four nodes attached to a common coaxial cable. The nodes use a token-passing mechanism to regulate the access to the cable and to avoid collisions. The figure illustrates one example of the sequence of events. Initially, node

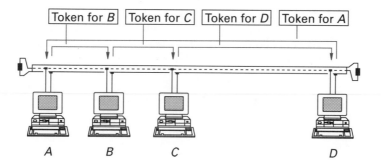

Figure 5.20 Token bus network.

The nodes are attached to a common coaxial cable, as in an IEEE 802.3 network. The access to the cable is regulated by a token-passing mechanism in which the token is passed from one node to the next in some cyclic order. A node cannot transmit a frame unless it holds the token.

A holds the token and transmits a frame of data. The destination of that frame is any other node on the network. After having transmitted its data frame, node A transmits a token with destination address B. A token is a small frame identified as a token by the value of its access control field, as in an IEEE 802.5 token ring. All the nodes on the network see the token and recognize that it is for node B. Node B transmits its data frame and then the token with destination address C. Node C then transmits its data frame and the token with destination address D. Node D then transmits its data frame followed by the token with destination address A. The transmissions continue in this cyclic order. This token-passing protocol is the *token bus MAC protocol*.

We analyze the efficiency of the token bus MAC protocol with the help of the timing diagram of Figure 5.21. The figure shows the transmissions on the network of Figure 5.20. The figure assumes that all the nodes always have packets to transmit. This figure shows that the four nodes transmit four packets in a time $TOTAL = 4 \times TRANSP + 4 \times TRANST + PROP$ where $PROP$ is the sum of the propagation times of a signal from A to B, then from B to C, then from C to D, and finally from D to A. Note that $PROP$ depends on the ordering of the nodes. In the case of the figure, $PROP$ is twice the one-way propagation time of a signal from one end of the bus to the other. If the nodes transmit in the order A, D, B, C, A, D, B, C, and so on, then $PROP$ is larger.

The timing diagram (Figure 5.21) shows that the efficiency η_{TB} of the token bus MAC protocol with N nodes is given by

$$\eta_{TB} = \frac{N \times TRANSP}{TOTAL} \approx \frac{1}{1 + \frac{a}{N}} \text{ with } a := \frac{PROP}{TRANSP}. \qquad (5.17)$$

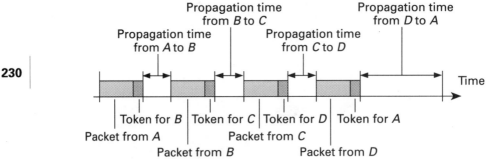

Figure 5.21 Timing diagram of the token bus protocol.

The figure assumes that the four nodes A to D transmit in that order.
Node A first transmits a packet and then a token. Node B starts transmitting a packet as soon as it gets the token. The other nodes eventually
transmit their packets and tokens.

The expression for η_{TB} is the same as that for η_{RAT} given in (5.11). However,
keep in mind the different value of the term *PROP*.

How does the network manager add or remove a node on a token bus
network? This question does not arise on an Ethernet since there is no fixed order
for the stations to transmit and the manager can plug a node in or take it out
without having to inform the other nodes. The problem is also different on a
token ring network since the connections are active and the ring stops operating
when a node is disconnected. The nodes in a token bus network are either active
or passive. A passive node is not participating in the communications and can be
viewed as disconnected from the bus. Each active node knows its predecessor in
the cyclic ordering. In the example shown in Figure 5.20, the successor of node A
is B and the predecessor of node A is D. A node needs to know its successor to be
able to send it the token. By inserting or removing a node, the manager modifies
the successor of a node. We will explain an automatic procedure for informing the
nodes of such modifications.

Consider the network in Figure 5.20 and assume that node E wants to
become active, as shown in Figure 5.22. Periodically, and only when it has the
token, each node sends a special packet called SAS (for *solicit a successor*). Any
node that wishes to become active can reply just after the SAS has been transmitted. If no node replies, then the nodes resume the normal operation of the token
bus MAC protocol. If one node replies to the SAS, then the other nodes modify
their predecessor and their successor as needed to insert that new node. For
instance, say that node C sends the SAS and that node E replies *I want to join*.

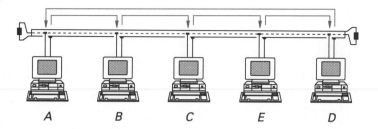

Figure 5.22 Adding a node to the token bus.

The figure shows how the order of transmissions can be modified to add node E to the token bus.

The SAS sent by C indicates that C is its sender and that the successor of C is D. The reply from E indicates the address of E. When it sees the SAS from C, node E notes that its predecessor is now C and that the successor of E is D. When it gets the reply from E, node C replaces its successor D with E. If more than one node replies to the SAS, then the transmissions of these nodes collide. The collision is resolved as in CSMA-CD: the nodes whose transmissions collide repeat their transmission, with random delays, until one node is successful and is then inserted in the network.

When a node wants to be removed from the token bus, it waits until it gets the token. It then transmits a special message saying *I want out*. The other nodes then update their successor and predecessor information. For instance, if node B on the network of Figure 5.22 sends the *I want out* message, that message includes the predecessor A and the successor C of B. When node A sees that message, it learns that its successor is no longer B but is instead C (B's successor). When C sees that its predecessor left the ring, it knows that its new predecessor is now B's old predecessor A.

When the network is started, or when the token is lost, the nodes detect the absence of activity. One of the nodes then sends an *I claim the token* packet. That node then sends the token to its successor if the lack of activity was due to a lost token. The node sends an SAS if this is the first transmission after starting the network. Collisions are handled as explained before.

The network deals with the failure of a node as follows: If node A sends the token to node B and node B does not respond, node A transmits a special message *Who follows B*. The nodes use the answer to that message to drop node B by updating their predecessor and successor.

The structures of the frames for the IEEE 802.4 token bus standard are similar to those of the IEEE 802.5 frames.

Token Bus

232

■ A token bus network has a bus topology and uses a token passing MAC protocol. IEEE 802.4 is a standard for token bus networks. These networks have passive connections to the bus and bounded media access times.

■ The efficiency of the token bus protocol is

$$\eta_{TB} \approx \frac{1}{1 + \dfrac{a}{N}} \text{ with } a := \frac{PROP}{TRANSP} \cdot \qquad (5.17)$$

■ Nodes can be removed or added by using *solicit a successor* and *I want out* messages. Lost tokens are handled with *I claim the token* messages. Failing nodes can be bypassed with *who follows X* messages.

5.5 FDDI

The *fiber distributed data interface* (FDDI) network is a dual-ring network (see Figure 5.23) with a transmission rate of 100 Mbps on optical fibers. This network was proposed in 1986, and the first sets of integrated circuits appeared in 1987. The specifications of FDDI are the subject of an ANSI (American National Standard Institute) standard. FDDI will replace Ethernet for connecting fast workstations and for interconnecting LANs. FDDI connects up to 500 nodes, and the maximum length of the fibers is 200 km. The distance between successive nodes cannot exceed 2 km. In 1990 there were about 40 vendors of FDDI interface boards.

The ANSI FDDI standard specifies the layers shown in Figure 5.24. The *physical medium dependent* (PMD) sublayer of FDDI specifies the fiber, the optical transmitters and receivers, the connectors, and the optical bypass switches. The transmission is over step-index fibers with a core diameter of 62.5 µm and a cladding diameter of 125 µm. The attenuation of the fibers is at most 2.5 dB/km. Other fibers may be used. Some vendors have announced fibers that enable a separation of 4 km between nodes. Specifications for single-mode fibers are being developed by ANSI. The optical transmitters are LEDs with a wavelength of 1.3 µm. The receivers are PIN-diodes. The bit error rate of a link must not exceed 0.04×10^{-9}. Some vendors provide equipment for FDDI networks that transmit over unshielded twisted pairs.

The *physical sublayer* (PHY) specifies the encoding and modulation methods and also the isolation of a malfunctioning station that we will explain

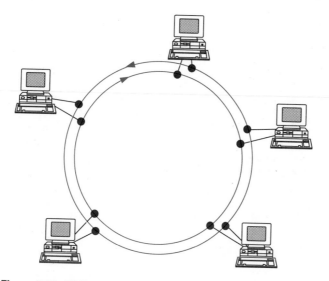

Figure 5.23 FDDI is a dual-ring network.

The nodes in FDDI can be attached to two rings that transmit in opposite directions.

Data link	LLC		
	MAC		SMT
Physical	PHY		
	PMD		

Figure 5.24 The layers specified by the FDDI standard.

The FDDI standard specifies the physical layer, the MAC layer, and the station management (SMT) protocol. The physical layer comprises the physical medium dependent (PMD) sublayer and the physical sublayer (PHY).

below. FDDI uses the *4B/5B* encoding, in which a group of 4 bits is encoded into a group of 5 bits. The groups of 5 bits are selected to contain at most two successive 0s. The groups of 5 bits are transmitted using the *nonreturn to zero with inversion* (NRZI) modulation. This modulation method represents the bits by a signal that has two values. The signal makes a transition in the epoch that represents a 1, and it makes no transition in the epoch that represents a 0. Thus, the 4B/5B + NRZI signal makes one transition at least every three bit epochs. A phase-locked loop uses that feature of the signal to synchronize the 125-Mbps

234

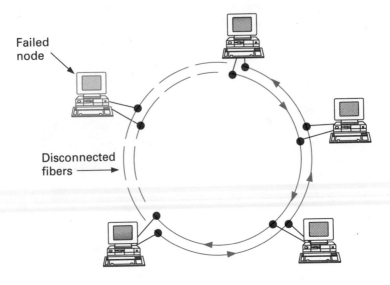

Failed
node

Disconnected
fibers

Figure 5.25 Reconfigured dual-ring network.

The dual ring is reconfigured as a single ring after the nodes have
detected a malfunction.

clock of the receiver with a 16-bit preamble. Each node uses a 10-bit elasticity
buffer. Note that the transition rate of the 4B/5B + NRZI signal is at most 125
MHz, whereas the Manchester encoding would make transitions at 200 MHz. The
detection of faults and the reconfiguration of the ring is performed by the *station
management protocol*. The isolation of a malfunctioning node is performed as
follows: When all the components of the FDDI network are operational, the two
rings operate as independent token rings. That is, when a node wishes to transmit,
it can choose to transmit on either ring. If a node malfunctions, either because of
a failure of the interface or of the node itself, both rings are disabled (see Figure
5.25). The nodes on the ring detect that failure and reconfigure the network as a
single ring as shown in Figure 5.25. This design is useful in applications that
require reliability and short down times.

   We will see shortly that FDDI uses a token-passing MAC protocol.
Figure 5.26 shows the structure of a token and an information frame for FDDI.
These frames are similar to those of IEEE 802.5. A symbol is a group of 4 bits
that is encoded into a group of 5 bits by the 4B/5B code. Some symbols are
control words. FDDI uses eight 5-bit control words. These eight control words are
among the sixteen 5-bit words not used to encode the groups of 4 bits. These
control words are used as delimiters and as signaling words.

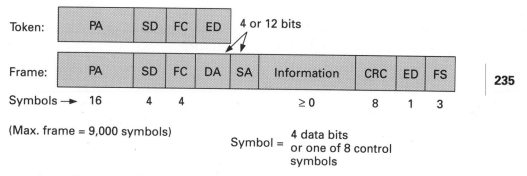

Figure 5.26 FDDI token and frame.

The structure of the FDDI token and information frames is similar to those of IEEE 802.5.

The *MAC protocol* of FDDI is a timed token mechanism. It is similar to the RAT token ring MAC protocol, except that there is a bound on the time between two successive visits to a node by the token. The nodes start by negotiating the value of a parameter called the *target token rotation time* (TTRT). The MAC protocol makes sure that the time between two successive visits to any node by the token never exceeds $2 \times TTRT$. Thus,

$$MMAT_{FDDI} \leq 2 \times TTRT.$$

With the MAC protocol, the traffic is classified into *synchronous* and *asynchronous* traffic. Synchronous traffic, like audio or video information, must be transmitted within a fixed time. Asynchronous traffic, such as data traffic, tolerates variable delays. Each node is allocated a fraction of TTRT for its synchronous traffic. The sum of the fractions of TTRT allocated to the nodes is less than 100%. If node A releases the token at time t, then the next time that node A gets the token, it cannot start transmitting a frame of asynchronous traffic after time $t + TTRT$.

Let us show that the token intervisit time at any node is less than $TTRT + TRANSP$ when there is no synchronous traffic. Here, $TRANSP$ denotes the maximum frame transmission time. Consider some node A on the ring and assume that it gets the token at time T_A, then transmits during U_A, and sends the token that reaches the next node B along the ring after a propagation time T_{AB}, i.e., at time $T_B = T_A + U_A + T_{AB}$. Assume that node A gets the token for the next time at time S_A, transmits during V_A, and releases the token that arrives at B after T_{AB}, i.e., at time $S_B = S_A + V_A + T_{AB}$. We claim that it is not possible for B to be the first station to experience an intervisit time larger than $TTRT + TRANSP$. In other words, we claim that if $S_A - T_A \leq TTRT + TRANSP$, then $S_B - T_B \leq TTRT +$

TRANSP. To prove this claim, we will consider two cases. In the first case, $TTRT < S_A - T_A \leq TTRT + TRANSP$. According to the protocol, node A cannot transmit data in that case, so that $V_A = 0$. Therefore,

$$S_B - T_B = S_A - T_A + V_A - U_A = S_A - T_A - U_A \leq TTRT + TRANSP,$$

as was to be shown. In the second case, $S_A - T_A < TTRT$. Node A is then allowed to transmit data. However, node A cannot start transmitting a new frame when more than *TTRT* has expired since it last released the token. Consequently, $(S_A + V_A) - (T_A + U_A) \leq TTRT + TRANSP$ and this bound is achieved when node A starts transmitting a frame just when its timer is about to reach the value *TTRT*. It follows that

$$S_B - T_B = S_A - T_A + U_A - V_A \leq TTRT + TRANSP.$$

Say that a node gets the token *in time* if the last intervisit time of the token is less than *TTRT* + *TRANSP*. We have shown that if node A gets the token in time, then node B also gets it in time. Consider the operations of the ring as starting when no node has a packet to send. In that case, if *TTRT* is larger than the token rotation time along the ring, all the stations get the token in time. It follows from our argument that all the nodes will always get the token in time thereafter.

This argument can be modified when there is synchronous traffic to show that each node always gets the token within less than $2 \times TTRT$ after it last released it.

A node is responsible for removing the frames it transmits from the ring. This frame removal is similar to what happens in the IEEE 802.5 MAC protocol, except that many frames may be on the ring since the MAC protocol is RAT instead of RAR. Thus, a transmitting node cannot remove everything that is on the ring. Instead, the node must check the source address field *SA* of the frame to see whether it transmitted it. When the node observes one of its frames, it replaces the symbols after the *SA* field with idle symbols, i.e., the symbols of the preamble. The fragments *SD-FC-DA* that have not been stripped are removed by a node that starts transmitting after receiving a token. These operations are shown in Figure 5.27.

The efficiency of the FDDI MAC protocol can be evaluated by using the same procedure as the one we used for the RAT protocol. The token takes approximately *TTRT* to rotate once around the ring. As in Figure 5.14, some of that time is the transmission time of frames and the rest of the time is the propagation of the token around the ring, the transmission times of tokens, or the delays inserted by the nodes to be able to modify the token into a start of frame. The inserted delays add up to $N \times D$ if each of the N nodes inserts a delay of D seconds. The token propagation time around the ring is denoted by *PROP*. We then find that the efficiency of the FDDI protocol η_{FDDI} is given by

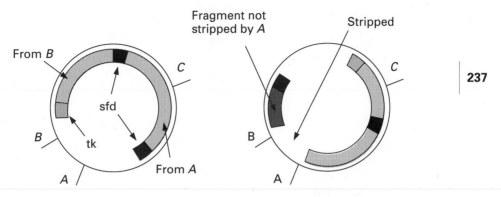

A and B transmit

A strips its frame but leaves
a fragment on ring

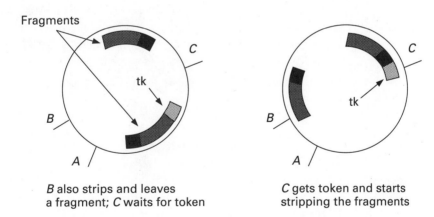

B also strips and leaves
a fragment; C waits for token

C gets token and starts
stripping the fragments

Figure 5.27 Removing frames from an FDDI network.

The transmitting station removes its frame after checking the *source address* field *SA*. The sequence of operations is shown in the figure.

$$\eta_{FDDI} = \frac{TTRT - N \times (D + TRANST) - PROP}{TTRT} \qquad (5.18)$$

where *TRANST* is the token transmission time. As a numerical illustration, consider an 80-km ring at 100 Mbps, with 300 nodes, a 16-bit delay per node, and a token of 100 bits. We will assume that the fiber has a refractive index of 1.46. For this network,

$$PROP = \frac{80 \text{ km}}{c/1.46} = \frac{1.46 \times 80 \text{ km}}{3 \times 10^5 \text{ km/s}} = 3.9 \times 10^{-4} \text{ s}.$$

Substituting in (5.18), we find

238

$$\eta_{FDDI} = \frac{TTRT - 300 \times (16 + 100) \times 10^{-8} - 3.9 \times 10^{-4}}{TTRT} = 1 - \frac{7.38 \times 10^{-4}}{TTRT}.$$

With $TTRT = 10 \ ms$, one finds $\eta_{FDDI} \approx 92.6\%$. This value of $TTRT$ is adequate for voice and video transmissions. We can see from this example that FDDI is able to support a large number of stations with small delays.

Fiber Distributed Data Interface

- FDDI connects up to 500 nodes with up to 200 km of 100-Mbps fibers arranged as a dual ring. The transmitters use the 4B/5B + NRZI modulation. FDDI will be used to connect fast workstations and LANs.

- When a node fails, the dual ring is reconfigured as a single ring.

- The MAC protocol of FDDI is a timed token-passing mechanism. It guarantees that the media access time is bounded by $2 \times TTRT$, where $TTRT$ is a parameter that the nodes agree upon.

- The bounded token intervisit time is used for synchronous transmissions that require bounded delays.

- The efficiency of FDDI is given by

$$\eta_{FDDI} = \frac{TTRT - N \times (D + TRANST) - PROP}{TTRT}. \qquad (5.18)$$

5.6 DQDB

DQDB (distributed queue dual bus) has been selected by the working group IEEE 802.6 as the standard for metropolitan area networks. The layout of a DQDB network is illustrated in Figure 5.28. DQDB will be used to connect LANs and for providing high-speed and low-delay transmissions for video and graphics applications.

The DQDB standard specifies the MAC sublayer. The frames that propagate on the busses have the structure indicated in Figure 5.29.

This 53-byte frame structure is the same as those of the frames of the *asynchronous transfer mode* (ATM) networks that we will discuss in Chapter 9.

The MAC protocol of DQDB attempts to have the nodes transmit the packets in the order in which they arrive at the MAC layer, i.e., in the order in

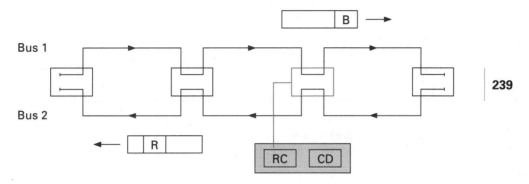

Bus 1

Bus 2

Figure 5.28 The DQDB layout.

The DQDB network uses a dual-bus topology. Each node is attached to two unidirectional fibers. The MAC protocol attempts to have the nodes transmit their packets in the order in which the packets become ready to be transmitted. That is, the packets are transmitted almost as if there were a central controller aware of all the packet generation times that would enforce first come, first served transmissions. The two counters CD and REQ are used to implement the protocol.

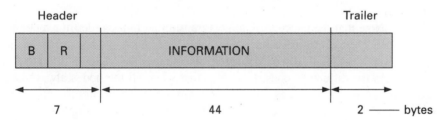

Header   Trailer

| B | R | INFORMATION |

7   44   2 —— bytes

Figure 5.29 Frame of DQDB.

The DQDB frames have 44 bytes of user information and 9 bytes of header and trailer. The two fields B (*busy*) and R (*reservation*) are used for the access control. The header is used by the higher layer protocols to reassemble the frames into larger messages. The trailer contains the error detection CRC bits and the indication of the length of user information when the information field is not full.

which the packets become ready for transmission. You will see that the MAC protocol almost achieves this objective.

The MAC protocol operates as follows: Each node is attached to two unidirectional fibers that we call bus 1 and bus 2. Note that the terminology *bus* is not quite proper since the nodes are attached by point-to-point links. We will explain how the nodes are able to transmit on bus 1. The procedure is identical for transmitting on bus 2. The operations of the two busses are symmetric. The leftmost station on bus 1 generates frames of 53 bytes. The frames contain two special bits: the *busy* bit (B) and the *request* bit (R). The busy bit B is 1 when the frame is busy, i.e., when it carries user data. The bit B is 0 when the frame is idle.

240

Each node has two counters CD (*count down*) and RC (*request counter*). When a node has a packet ready for transmission on bus 1, it issues a request by setting to 1 the request bit R in a frame of bus 2 that arrived at the node with R = 0. Each node keeps track, in its counter *RC*, of how many requests were made by nodes to its right and are still pending. To keep track of that number of requests, the node increases RC by one when it sees a request bit R equal to 1 on bus 2 and it decreases RC by one whenever it sees an empty frame on bus 1. The empty frame on bus 1 will be used by some node to the right to fulfill a pending request. In addition, each node keeps track in its counter CD of the number of requests made by nodes that are to its right *before* it got a packet to transmit and that are still pending. To do this, the node sets CD = RC when it gets a packet to transmit and it decreases CD by one whenever it sees an empty frame on bus 1. When CD reaches the value 0, the node assumes that all the pending requests that were made before it got its packet to transmit have been fulfilled and it then waits for the next empty frame on bus 1. The node transmits its information in that frame after marking it busy by setting its busy bit B to 1. As we stated before, the operations for bus 2 are similar. To transmit on bus 2, a node places a request on a request bit of a frame on bus 1. Each node has two counters CD and RC for bus 2, and so on.

Note that the packets are almost transmitted in the order in which they become available for transmission, so that the MAC protocol essentially implements a first come, first served queueing discipline, even though the queue is distributed in the different nodes. Note also that when all the nodes always have packets to transmit, the frames are all eventually busy. Therefore, the efficiency of this MAC protocol is close to 100%. Priorities are easily implemented by having distinct *B* and *R* bits and distinct counters for the different priorities.

The MAC protocol of DQDB is slightly unfair because of the network topology. For example, if each node has the same amount of traffic to transmit to each of the other nodes, then the nodes in the middle of the busses get to transmit more often than the nodes at the extremities of the busses. Indeed, a node in the middle of the network gets to transmit half of its packets on each bus and it competes with only half of the other nodes for each bus. The nodes at the extremities of the bus compete with all the other nodes and can transmit on only one bus. To correct this unfairness, one can modify the protocol as follows: The network manager selects a parameter *F* for each node. The MAC protocol of each node prevents it from transmitting in *F* successive frames. That is, when the node gets the *F*th successive empty frame, it lets that frame go by without using it. The node needs an additional counter to keep track of the number of its successive transmissions. The node resets that counter to zero when it does not use a frame. A larger value of *F* improves the access of the node on the bus. Thus, the network manager can correct the observed unfairness of the DQDB network by suitably choosing the values of *F* for the different nodes.

Distributed Queue Dual Bus

- DQDB is the network selected by IEEE 802.6 as the standard for metropolitan area networks. The nodes in a DQDB network are attached to two unidirectional busses. IEEE 802.6 only specifies the MAC protocol.

- Each node has two counters RC and CD for each bus. The node increases the RC counter of one bus when it sees a request on the other bus, and it decreases the RC and CD counters of one bus when it sees an empty frame on that bus. When it gets a packet to transmit on one bus, the node sets $CD = RC$ for that bus. The node can transmit when $CD = 0$.

- To correct the unfairness of DQDB, the network manager limits the number of successive frames that each node can transmit.

- DQDB is a very efficient protocol which can accommodate different priorities of traffic.

5.7 Logical Link Control

The MAC layer of LANs provides an unreliable packet transmission service over a shared communication medium. The *logical-link-control* (LLC) layer converts this unreliable transmission service into packet links between *access points*. The basic functions of LLC are error control, frame multiplexing, and flow control (if required).

The LLC frame structure and the access points were shown in Figure 5.10 and are redrawn in Figure 5.30 for convenience.

The LLC frame control field specifies that the message is either *DATA*, an *XID* (exchange identification), or a *TEST*. No reply to a data packet is expected. An XID is used to find all the members of a given group—which are then expected to reply with an XID—or to broadcast the presence of a node. A TEST packet is used to test a connection to another node. The LLC frame also specifies a service class in the form of a priority that can be used by IEEE 802.4–802.6 networks.

The IEEE 802.2 standard for LLC provides for three types of services: *acknowledged connectionless*, *connectionless*, and *connection-oriented*. An acknowledged connectionless service is used only for point-to-point connections, and it assumes that a frame cannot be sent before the previous one is acknowledged. The connectionless service is a datagram transmission: there is no guarantee the packet will be delivered or that it will arrive without errors. The exchange

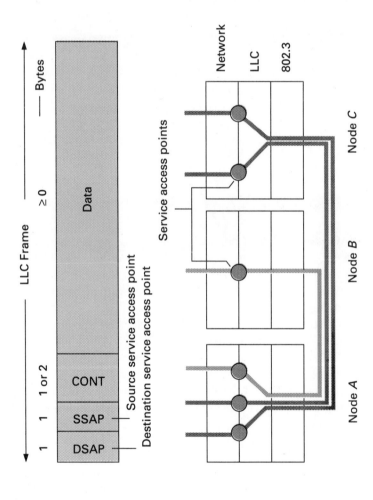

Figure 5.30 LLC frame and access points.

The LLC frame contains the fields *destination service access point* (DSAP), *source service access point* (SSAP), and *control* (CONT). The nodes use the service access points to distinguish different information streams. The control field indicates the type of packet.

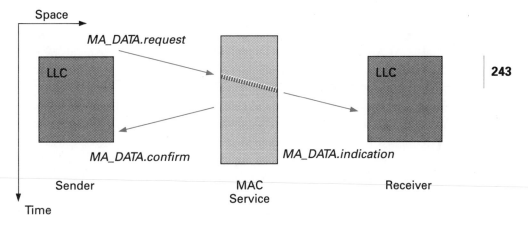

Figure 5.31 Connectionless transmission.

The LLC requests the MAC to transmit a packet with an *MA_DATA.req*. Eventually, the MAC confirms that it transmitted the packet with an *MA_DATA.confirm* and indicates the reception of a packet in the destination by an *MA_DATA.indication*.

of messages between LLC and MAC at the source and destination in connectionless transmissions is indicated in Figure 5.31.

The connection-oriented service is called *HDLC-ABM*, i.e, high-level data link control, asynchronous balanced mode. This is the data link layer protocol of X.25 (see Chapter 4). The normal sequence of operations in a connection-oriented transmission is a *connection setup*, then *data transmission*, and then a *connection release*. HDLC-ABM uses 7-bit sequence numbers.

Some MAC protocols have a built-in *flow control mechanism*. This is the case for the token-passing schemes. Some, such as the CSMA protocols, do not. In the latter case, it may be necessary to control the transmission rate of a node.

Logical Link Control

■ LLC is specified by IEEE 802.2. The LLC sublayer uses the MAC sublayer to implement packet links between nodes.

■ Three types of packet transmission services are implemented by LLC: acknowledged connectionless, connectionless, and connection-oriented.

■ The connection-oriented service of LLC is HDLC-ABM.

Summary

- Nodes on a LAN share a common channel. The data link layer of a LAN is decomposed into the MAC sublayer, which regulates the access to that common channel, and the LLC sublayer, which implements packet transmission services.

- The ALOHA protocols, slotted and pure, are multiple-access protocols in which nodes transmit and, after a random delay, retransmit the packets that collide. The efficiencies of these protocols are 36% and 18%, respectively.

- The IEEE 802.3 standards cover the physical layer and the MAC sublayer for five bus networks that use the CSMA-CD protocol. The efficiency of that protocol is $1/(1 + 5a)$ where a is the ratio of the one-way propagation time of a signal on the medium to the transmission time of a packet. Ethernet is a network of this class; it is suitable for fast delivery of packets when the load is not too heavy and when the nodes do not require bounded delays.

- Nodes in a token ring network use a token-passing protocol. The efficiency of the RAT version is $1/(1 + a/N)$ where a is the ratio of the propagation time around the ring to the time necessary to transmit a packet, and N is the number of nodes. The efficiency of the RAR protocol is $1/(1 + a)$. These versions have different maximum media access times. The IEEE 802.5 uses the RAR version, which enables acknowledgements.

- Token bus networks have a bus topology and use a token-passing MAC protocol. The efficiency of this protocol is $1/(1 + a/N)$ where a is the ratio of the sum of propagation times of the token from node to node in a cycle to the time necessary to transmit a packet. The IEEE 802.4 is a standard for token bus networks. Nodes can be added and removed and failures can be handled by special messages.

- FDDI is the ANSI standard for 100-Mbps networks. The nodes are attached in a dual-ring configuration. The encoding is 4B/5B + NRZI. The media access time is bounded by $2 \times TTRT$, where $TTRT$ is a parameter that the nodes agree upon. The efficiency of FDDI is given by (5.18).

- DQDB is the IEEE 802.6 MAC protocol for metropolitan area networks. The nodes in DQDB are attached to two unidirectional busses. To transmit on one bus, a node waits until all the requests by downstream nodes that were pending for that bus when it got its packet are fulfilled. DQDB is an efficient protocol that can be made fair by a suitable selection of parameters.

■ The IEEE 802.2 standards for LLC provide for three types of packet transmission services: acknowledged connectionless for point-to-point connections, unacknowledged connectionless, and the HDLC-ABM connection-oriented services.

Problems

1. Under a high load, which of the following MAC protocols has the smallest media access time: slotted ALOHA, pure ALOHA, token ring, or Ethernet?

2. One thousand nodes are connected to a 2000-meter-long bus. Each node needs to send 30 packets of 1,000 bits every second. The transmission rate is 100 Mbps. Which of the following MAC protocols can be used: Ethernet, pure ALOHA, slotted ALOHA, or token bus? Justify your answer.

3. Is the token bus more sensitive than the token ring to node failures? Explain.

4. Consider the slotted ALOHA protocol. Assume that 20% of the time slots are idle. Calculate the throughput of the network by making the same assumptions that we made to analyze the efficiency of that protocol.

*5. Consider four nodes that are all attached to two different bus cables. The nodes exchange packets of a fixed length ($TRANSP = 1$ s). Time is divided into slots of 1 s. When a node has a packet to transmit, it is equally likely to choose either bus. It then transmits in the next time slot with probability p. Find the value of p that maximizes the rate at which packets are successfully transmitted.

6. Consider a token ring with the RAT protocol. Assume that the packet lengths are variable. Calculate the efficiency of the protocol.

7. You build a 100-Mbps CSMA-CD network over a 3-km coaxial cable. The packets have 1,000 bits, including 100 bits of overhead in header and trailer. What is the throughput of the network in information bits per second?

8. The 200 computers in a research laboratory are attached to an Ethernet with a coaxial cable of 1,500 m in three segments of 500 m. The packets have 800 bits. On the average, how many packets can each computer send every second?

9. Consider a token ring that uses the RAR protocol with $THT = 10$ ms over a coaxial cable of 3 km. The transmission rate is 16 Mbps. There are 60 nodes on the ring. Estimate the MMAT and the efficiency of this network.

*10. We know that the MMAT of CSMA-CD is infinite. Should this deter us from using CSMA-CD in time-critical applications? We explore this question in this problem. There are 50 nodes on a CSMA-CD network. The coaxial cable is 2 km long. Assume that two transmissions collide. What is the probability that these two nodes would collide during their five subsequent attempts? How large can the delay be in that case? Can you repeat these calculations to include the possibility that another node would transmit in a time slot with duration $2 \times PROP$ with probability 0.01%?

11. Consider an FDDI network with 500 nodes over a dual ring. The nodes are separated by 0.2 km of fiber. What is the efficiency of the network if $TTRT = 15$ ms. On the average, how many packets of 5,000 bits can each node transmit?

12. This problem explores the fairness of FDDI. We assume that a single ring is operational and that there is no synchronous traffic. All the packets take $TRANSP$ to transmit. Consider the case where $TTRT = PROP + N{\times}D + 1.2{\times}TRANSP$. Assume that the N nodes always have packets to transmit. Initially, node 1 has the token, transmits a packet, then releases the token. Which node transmits next? Describe the sequence of operations. What is the average time between two successive transmissions by a node? How does the sequence of events change when $TTRT = PROP + N{\times}D + 2.2{\times} TRANSP$?

13. You want to design an optical CSMA-CD network. The transmitters are LEDs with an average power of 3 dBm. The fibers are multimode with an attenuation of 0.4 dB/km. The receivers have a sensitivity of -20 dBm. Each node has an LED attached with a 2 dB loss connector to a 100-m fiber that connects to a special connector, also with a 2-dB loss. The connector divides each input into N outputs with equal powers. Each output is attached, with a 2-dB loss to another 100-m fiber connected with a 2-dB loss to the receiver of a node. What is the maximum value of N for this design?

*14. Consider a DQDB network with three nodes. Assume that the propagation times are negligible. The leftmost node gets a packet to transmit on bus 1 with a small probability $2p$ in every frame time. At the same time, the center node gets a packet to transmit on bus 1 with probability p and a packet to transmit on bus 2 also with probability p.

In every frame time, the rightmost node gets a packet to transmit on bus 2 with probability $2p$. Estimate the rate of packet transmissions by the three nodes. Comment on the fairness of DQDB.

*15. Prove the result on the MMAT of FDDI when there is synchronous traffic.

*16. Consider a large number of nodes that use the slotted ALOHA protocol with the following retransmission algorithm. A new packet arrives and is transmitted in a time slot with probability ε. Every old packet is transmitted with probability p. All these transmissions are independent of one another. Show that if a random sequence of events leads the number of old packets to reach a large value N, then the average number of old packets after the next time slot is larger than N.

References

Local area networks are the subject of frequent articles in *Byte*, *PC Magazine*, *Mac User*, and similar trade magazines. A discussion at that level can be found in Schatt (1987) and Stallings (1990). The performance analysis of LANs is explained in Hammond (1986). Massey (1980) analyzes multiple-access protocols. Stallings (1987) gives details on the IEEE 802 standards. The IEEE publishes the IEEE 802 standards. This is the ultimate source for these standards, but it is not user friendly.

Hammond (1986). Hammond, J. L., and O'Reilly, P. J. P., *Performance Analysis of Local Computer Networks*. Addison-Wesley, 1986.

Massey (1980). Massey, J. L., "Collision-resolution algorithms and random-access communications," *Technical Report UCLA-ENG-8016*. UCLA, School of Engineering and Applied Science, April 1980.

Schatt (1987). Schatt, S., *Understanding Local Area Networks*. Howard W. Sams & Company, 1987.

Stallings (1987). Stallings, W., *Local Networks, Second Edition*. Macmillan, 1987.

Stallings (1990). Stallings, W., *The Business Guide to Local Area Networks*. Howard W. Sams & Company, 1990.

Network Layer

Our goal in this chapter is to explain how a *packet-switched* communication network guides and regulates the flow of packets. We will show you how regulating the flow reduces the travel times of packets through the network and increases the amount of traffic the network can carry. We will also show you how engineers design or improve a network by selecting the location of communication nodes and the transmission rates of the links between the nodes.

A communication network enables users to exchange information. The users interact with terminal nodes, also called *hosts*. In a typical network, there is more than one path between any two hosts, as shown in Figure 6.1.

The multiple data paths improve the reliability of the network by preserving the connectivity between hosts in the event of equipment failure. Whenever there is more than one path to a destination, the network or its users must select the paths to be followed by the packets. Some applications let the user or the network manager select the paths to be followed by packets. In other applications, the network performs the path selection. We will demonstrate how a network selects the paths to balance the traffic among the different network links and to reduce the packet travel times. In particular, we will show you how a network learns that certain paths are congested or disabled and how it uses that information to improve the path selection. The selection of paths is called *routing*. The network must know the location of a destination before selecting a path leading to

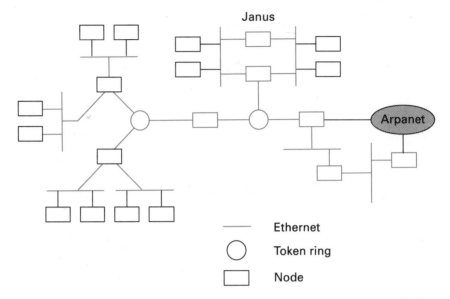

Figure 6.1 A network example.

The figure shows a small subset of the network at the University of California at Berkeley. The network consists of computers and peripherals interconnected by Ethernets and by token ring networks.

it. A user normally specifies a destination by name, rather than by giving the location of that destination on the network. For instance, the name of my computer is janus.berkeley.edu. This name does not tell you precisely where my computer is. Accordingly, the network must translate the destination name into a network location. We will explain how networks perform this translation.

In addition to routing, the network can regulate the traffic by controlling when packets are transmitted from one node to the next. When exercising this control, called *congestion control*, the network prevents some nodes from becoming excessively congested by asking less congested nodes to postpone their transmissions.

In the OSI model, the routing and congestion control functions are discharged by the *network layer*. This layer lies above the data link layer, as shown in Figure 6.2. The data link layer provides packet links between nodes connected by a communication link. The network layer routes packets from their sources to their destinations, along paths made of successive packet links, in the store-and-forward manner explained in Chapter 2. By doing this, the network can implement the transport of packets between any two hosts on the network. Thus, packets arrive at the network layer in one host and they eventually are delivered by the network layer in the destination host. Figure 6.3 shows the path followed by packets in a network.

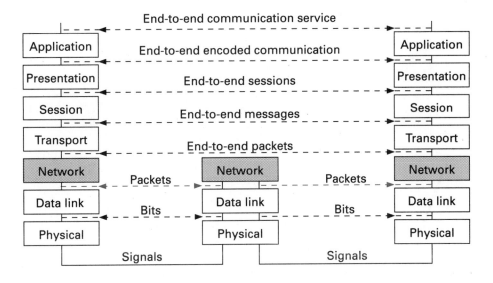

Figure 6.2 The network layer in the OSI model.

The network layer lies on top of the data link layer. It implements the transmission of packets between hosts by using the packet transmissions on individual links implemented by the data link layer.

The terms *bridge* and *router* in Figure 6.3 were introduced in Chapter 4. A bridge converts the format of the packets between two LANs. Some difficulties arise when packets transit through a bridge. For example, the priority level bits become meaningless for a packet that goes from an IEEE 802.5 network to an IEEE 802.3 network. Delays through a bridge may also cause timeouts. In addition, the 802.2 standard does not provide for fragmentation of long packets into smaller ones nor for the reverse reassembly operation. Thus, special software is required if long IEEE 802.5 frames must be sent on an IEEE 802.3 network. A router performs the bridge operations and makes some routing decisions. We will discuss the routing below. If node A, connected to one network running some protocols, wishes to talk with node B on a second network running different protocols, the connection would have to be made through an intermediate computer G, called a *gateway*. The connection between A and G uses one set of protocols and that between G and B uses another set. The difficulties mentioned for bridges exist for gateways, in addition to problems raised at the higher layers, as we will explain when discussing these higher layers. In addition, the gateway may perform routing functions. Be aware that the terms *bridge, router*, and *gateway* are sometimes used with different meanings by network engineers.

In Section 6.1 we explain how packets find their way to their destinations. This section also clarifies the problems raised by interconnecting networks.

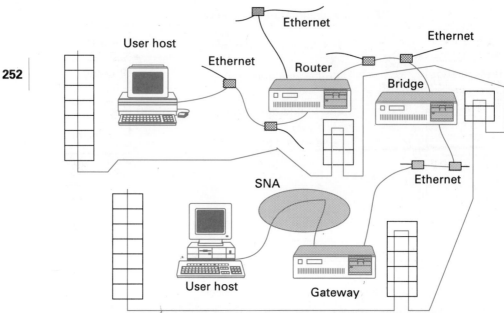

Figure 6.3 Packet path in a network.

Packets follow a trajectory between hosts. Typically, the network consists of interconnected LANs and WANs. The packets go through *bridges* between similar LANs, through *routers* when routing decisions must be taken, and *gateways* when protocol conversions are required. The stacks of rectangles represent the OSI layers involved in the packet transmission.

Section 6.2 is devoted to routing. We will discuss how the network selects paths for datagrams and for virtual-circuits. We explain congestion control in Section 6.3. The traffic engineering of networks is explained in Section 6.4, including techniques used by network engineers when they design a new network or when they modify an existing network to improve its performance. Section 6.5 concludes the chapter with examples of the network layer in widely used networks.

6.1 Names and Addresses

How do packets find their way in a communication network? Figure 6.1 shows a collection of computers interconnected by a number of LANs. Information is sent as packets to *nodes* in the networks. For example, information is sent to computers and peripherals. Also, information is sent to communication nodes that relay that information along paths in the network. Information is not destined to an amplifier on a broadband network nor to an Ethernet repeater (see Chapter 5). Thus, information is sent from a terminal node to another, possibly through a set of intermediate communication nodes. To receive information, a node must have a *name* that identifies it. For example, the name of my computer is janus.berkeley.edu (see Figure 6.1). A node can have more than one name, but any given name must identify a unique node.

To deliver information to a node, the network needs to know the location of that node. More precisely, the network needs to know the location of at least one connection of the node to the network. A *network address* designates each connection of a node to a network. Janus is attached to two Ethernets, and the addresses of the two connections are 128.32.134.46 and 128.32.156.99. These are 32-bit Internet addresses written with the decimal value of the 4 bytes. The format of Internet addresses will be discussed in Section 6.5.

A node is attached to a network by an interface. If more than one interface is attached to the same physical link, as in a bus or ring network, packets destined to the different interfaces appear on that common link. An interface identifies packets destined to it by comparing the packet destination address with the interface *physical address*. The interface physical address is different from its network address. For example, every Ethernet interface board comes with a different, unchangeable, 48-bit physical address set by the manufacturer. When you install an Ethernet interface board in a computer, the physical address is associated with the board and is independent of where the board is attached to a network and, therefore, of the network address of the node. As another example, the physical address of an interface board for a *ProNet-10* ring—a commercial 10-MHz token ring—is an 8-bit word that the network administrator selects by setting eight switches situated on the board. Thus, there are only $2^8 = 256$ different physical addresses of such interface boards. These addresses can differentiate up to 256 boards attached to the same token ring. As a third example, the physical address of an X.25 node is specified by up to 14 decimal digits. These addresses are similar to telephone numbers.

To deliver information to a node with a known network address on the same LAN, a node needs to know the physical address of that destination. As an example, consider the delivery of information from computer A to computer B on the Ethernet network shown in Figure 6.4. The packets sent by node A to node B must be stamped with the physical address y of B. Typically, node A knows only the network address of B, not its physical address. Consequently, the network address of B must be translated into the physical address y. For Ethernet nodes, as in Figure 6.4, node A must learn the physical address y of B, and the *address resolution protocol* is a commonly used method for doing this. When using the address resolution protocol, node A keeps an address translation table that indicates the physical address of nodes with given network addresses. Node A maintains its address translation table as follows. When node A has packets to send to

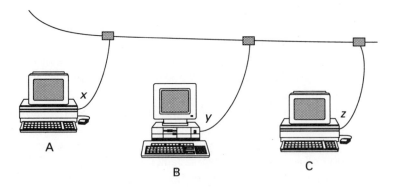

Figure 6.4 Three computers attached to an Ethernet.

Each computer is attached to the Ethernet by an interface board with a
fixed physical address. The interface boards in the computers A, B, and C
have the physical addresses *x*, *y*, and *z*, respectively. The computers
must learn the physical addresses of the other computers.

node B, it first searches its address translation table for the physical address of B.
If the table does not mention node B, then node A sends a special message to the
nodes on the Ethernet. Node A places the message in a packet with the *broadcast
address* 11...11 that indicates that the packet must be read by all the nodes on the
network (see Figure 5.10). The message asks the node with the network address
of computer B to reply by indicating its physical address. These address resolution messages (and their replies) are designated by specific values of the *TYPE*
field of the Ethernet packets (see Chapter 5). When they get that message, the
nodes on the Ethernet compare their network address with the one in the message.
The node that recognizes its network address replies with a message that contains
its physical address. Node A can then add this information to its address translation table. If the address translation table of node A is full, node A removes a
table entry that has not been used for a long time before adding the physical
address of node B. Node A can then send the packets to B with the physical
address *y*.

In most networks, the nodes verify network addresses using a software
procedure which is much slower than the hardware comparison of the physical
address. Therefore, always addressing the packets with the network address of the
destination would require the nodes to perform such a comparison for every
packet and would degrade the performance of these networks. This is why packets in these networks are addressed with the physical addresses. In a few networks, however, the translation of the network address into a physical address is
done by the destination interface board. In these networks, the destination address
of the packets is the network address. This is the case for a ProNet ring on the

Internet. The 32-bit Internet (network) addresses can be chosen so that the first 24 bits are the same for all the nodes on the same ring. When that addressing is used, the last 8 bits of the Internet address uniquely identify a node on the ring. The network administrator selects the 8-bit physical address of the interface to match the last 8 bits of the Internet address.

The network address of a computer is normally stored on a disk so that the information is not lost when the computer is turned off. However, a diskless workstation on a network cannot store its network address when it is turned off. To find its network address upon startup, a diskless workstation sends a packet requesting the *address server* to reply with the network address of the computer. The physical address is contained in the source address of the packet sent by the diskless workstation. The address server is a computer on the network that maintains an address translation table for the network.

So far we know how a node can send packets to another node on the same LAN. What if the nodes are on different LANs? Figure 6.5 shows such a situation. The figure shows three Ethernets *a*, *b*, and *c* connected by bridges B and E. (Ignore node D for the time being.) Packets sent from A to C must go through B. How do A and B know how to reach C? The IEEE 802 working group has defined two routing procedures: *source routing* and *transparent routing*. When source routing is used, the source node, A in our example, maintains a table that specifies the paths to be followed by its packets to their destinations. The node learns about possible paths either from the network manager, who provides routing tables, or by broadcasting *discovery* frames that contain the source and destination address. These frames are repeated by all the other nodes. When the destination receives the discovery frame, it sends it back to the source in a packet with a special field updated by the bridges it crosses. When the source receives these discovery frames, it receives a list of possible paths to the destination. The source can then choose one of these paths, for instance the one with the minimum number of bridges, and place it in its routing table.

When *transparent routing* is used, the bridges learn the paths to the destination. The bridges follow a procedure that we will illustrate on the network shown in Figure 6.5. Bridge B is connected to two Ethernets *a* and *b*. A packet transmitted on *a* is said to be *local* if it is destined to a node on *a*. The same definition applies to packets transmitted on *b*. When a nonlocal packet is transmitted on *a*, B retransmits it on *b*. Similarly, B retransmits on *a* the nonlocal packets transmitted on *b*. To recognize local packets on *a*, B reads all the packets transmitted on *a* and maintains a table of the source addresses of those packets. B maintains a similar table for *b*. The entries of these tables are time-stamped and are cleared after a specified time to adapt the tables to changing connections. When there are different alternate paths, the bridges must exchange some information to prevent packets from being duplicated and looping indefinitely around

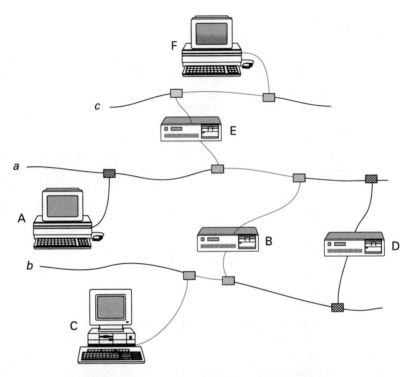

Figure 6.5 Finding a node in interconnected networks.

Three Ethernets *a*, *b*, and *c* are connected by nodes A and B that serve as bridges. When node A sends a packet to C, it sends the packet on Ethernet *a* with destination address *y*. Node B receives the packet and retransmits it on Ethernet *b* with destination address *u*.

cycles. To see this, assume that there is another bridge D between the Ethernets *a* and *b* in Figure 6.5. A nonlocal packet sent on *a* by node A (destined to node F, for instance) is transmitted by B and D on *b*. When D sees the packet sent by B on *b*, it repeats it on *a* since that packet is not local on *b*. Node B then retransmits it on *b*, and so on. The bridges can prevent this infinite looping by periodically exchanging their routing tables and by selecting a loop-free graph of paths. For instance, in Figure 6.5, the nodes could agree that packets follow the paths (F, E, A), (F, E, B, C), and (A, B, C), as well as the reversed paths. With this choice of paths, a packet transmitted on *a* and destined to node C is retransmitted only by node B. A commonly used procedure for selecting such paths is the *spanning tree algorithm* explained in Section 6.2.

The preceding discussion applies also to a general store-and-forward network. When a node A needs to send a packet to a node B not attached to A by a direct link, node A searches a table, called a *routing table*, to find the next node along a path to B. That next node, say C, is attached directly to A. Node A then sends the packet to C with a request to forward it to B. Node C then proceeds in a similar fashion. Eventually, the packet reaches B. In Section 6.2 you will learn how the tables required by the nodes can be updated automatically by the network.

Names are easier to remember than addresses. What if a user knows only the name of the destination, not its network address nor its physical address? To find the address, the user's node consults a directory, as you do to find a telephone number. The organization of an automatic directory service for a communication network is similar to that of telephone directory assistance. Telephone operators are responsible for the information in one area. To learn a telephone number anywhere in the United States, you need only know the area code, say XYZ, of that number and call the directory assistance of that area (1-XYZ-555-1212). Thus, the directory data base is partitioned by area codes. This partition localizes the assistance calls and simplifies the updating of the data base. Similarly, the names in a communication network can be organized by areas called *domains* in Internet. When a node needs the address of some other node, it places a request to a local *name server* process that runs on a computer whose address must be known. This process checks whether the node name belongs to the domain for which it is responsible. If so, the server replies with the requested network address. Otherwise, the name server determines which other name server is responsible for the name's domain, and it forwards the request to that other server.

This decomposition of the set of nodes into domains can be extended further by decomposing the domains into subdomains and subdomains into sub-subdomains, and so on. Such a decomposition is called *hierarchical naming*. In 1988, the CCITT published the first draft of the X.500 naming standards. In X.500, the name has the structure *(country).(organization).(organization unit). (user)*. This hierarchical naming structure is similar to the Internet naming conventions discussed in Section 6.5, except that X.500 provides for the independent administration of the various subtrees of the hierarchy. Gateways can provide translation services between the X.500 names and the local names used by the LANs of an organization. (See box entitled "Names and Addresses," next page.)

We have learned how a node can find the network address and the physical address of a node with a known name. We saw that nodes must maintain routing tables that indicate the next node along paths to destinations. In the next section we will explain how these routing tables are built and updated.

Names and Addresses

■ A network node must have a *name* that designates it. Moreover, the network *connections* of the nodes must have a *network address* and a *physical address*.

■ In most networks the network address of a connection must be translated into a physical address. Nodes on a LAN can use the address resolution protocol to perform this translation.

■ In some networks, the physical address of a connection can be chosen as a fragment of the network address. In such cases, the network address can be used as a packet destination address that is recognized by the connection hardware.

■ Two types of bridges are defined by IEEE 802: source routing bridges and transparent bridges.

■ When node A needs to send a packet to a node B not attached to A by a direct link, node A needs to know the next node along a path to B. This information is contained in a routing table in A.

■ Name servers maintain a list of network addresses of nodes with known names. Usually, the name servers are organized by domains. When a name server gets a request for the address of a node that is not in its domain, it forwards the request to the server of that domain. X.500 is a CCITT naming standard.

6.2 Routing

Routing is the selection of paths for packets. This selection is usually done by the network. The source can also specify the path if it has the necessary information. Before explaining how the network identifies the possible paths to a destination and how it selects a good path among those, let's review the two transport methods used by store-and-forward networks: datagrams and virtual-circuits.

As we discussed in Chapter 2, virtual-circuit transport sends all the packets that belong to the same conversation along the same path, called a *virtual-circuit*. Such a network makes one routing decision per conversation. A datagram transport makes routing decisions for each packet.

We will look at the internal organization of datagrams and virtual-circuits. Specifically, we will explain the information that network nodes must maintain to implement these packet transports and how that information is updated. We start with datagrams.

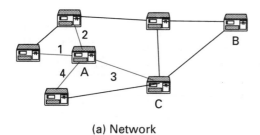

Destination	Link	Fraction
B	2	0.6
	3	0.4
C	3	0.8
	4	0.2

(a) Network

(b) Routing table at A

259

Figure 6.6 Network and routing table in A for datagrams.

The network (a) shows a number of nodes attached in a mesh network. There are multiple paths between nodes. The table (b) is maintained by node A. When a packet arrives at A with destination address B, the table specifies that node A should send that packet along link 2 a fraction 0.6 of the time and along link 3 a fraction 0.4 of the time.

For datagram transport, each node maintains a *routing table* organized as indicated in Figure 6.6. The node routing tables are based on estimates of congestion in the network, as we will see shortly. The alternate links for packets in the routing table in Figure 6.6 enable node A to balance the traffic among its outgoing links. Node A can select among the alternate links at random or according to a periodic sequence. To randomly select the link for a packet destined to B, node A can generate a random variable uniformly distributed in [0, 1]. If that number is less than 0.6, which occurs with probability 0.6, the packet is sent along link 2. Otherwise, it is sent along link 3. We explain a method for generating random variables in Section 10.3. When using a periodic sequence, node A can send successive packets destined to B along the links 2, 3, 2, 2, 3, 2, 3, 2, 2, 3 and continue in this way by repeating the sequence periodically. This sequence is chosen so that a fraction 0.6 of the packets are sent along link 2 and a fraction 0.4 are sent along link 3, as specified by the table. Whereas other sequences can be used, this particular sequence also has the property of spreading out as evenly as possible (for a sequence of length 10) the times when a given link is used while guaranteeing that link 2 is used six times out of ten. Nodes update their datagram routing tables periodically to adapt to changing conditions, as we will explain later.

The routing table for virtual-circuit transport is organized as in Figure 6.7. The table in one node specifies, for each incoming link and incoming virtual-circuit number, the corresponding outgoing link and outgoing virtual-circuit number. For instance, the table shown for node A specifies that a packet that arrives at that node on link 1 and with virtual-circuit number 8 must be retransmitted by A on link 3 with the new virtual-circuit number 2. Node A updates the table when

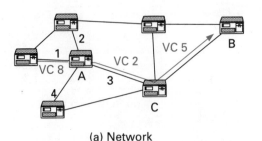

(a) Network

IN		OUT	
Link	VC #	Link	VC #
1	8	3	2
2	5	4	1

(b) Routing table at A

Figure 6.7 Network and routing table in node A for virtual-circuits.

The network (a) is the same as in Figure 6.8. The table (b) is maintained by node A. When a packet arrives at A on link 1 with virtual-circuit number 8, the table specifies that node A should send that packet along link 3 with the new virtual-circuit number 2.

new virtual-circuits are established by using information about network congestion.

We will use the network shown in Figure 6.8 to explain why a node may have to change virtual-circuit numbers. The network first establishes the virtual-circuit ACDE. The network numbers that virtual-circuit as number 1 on each of the links AC, CD, and DE. The network then sets up the virtual-circuit BCDF, numbering it 1 on link BC, 2 on link CD, and 1 on link DF. Let's examine why the network uses that numbering of the virtual-circuits. Virtual-circuits that use the same link must be numbered differently on that link; otherwise, the nodes could not identify the connection to which a packet belongs and they could not handle these packets appropriately. For example, if the two virtual-circuits were numbered 1 on link CD, node D would not know whether to send a packet along link DE or along DF. You will argue that it would be possible to number differently the virtual-circuits on any given link without having to change the number of any given virtual-circuit throughout the network. For instance, the network could have used the number 2 on all the links for the virtual circuit BCDF. However, trying to use such a numbering leads to some complications. In Figure 6.8, a new virtual-circuit on a link is numbered with the smallest number not already in use on that link. If one requires the virtual-circuit number to be the same on all the links, then to number a new virtual-circuit one must identify a number not yet used on any link along the path of the virtual-circuit. This search is time-consuming. Additionally, with the first numbering, a link needs only as many numbers as it can carry virtual-circuits. With the second numbering, you can verify that the set of numbers required is larger.

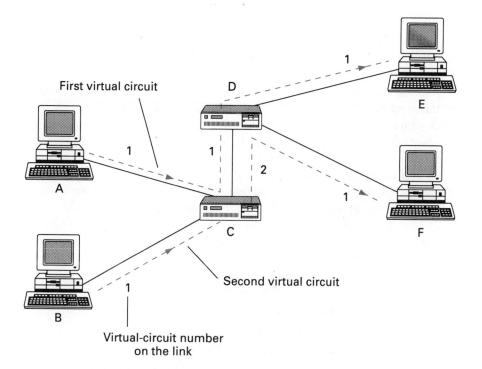

First virtual circuit

Second virtual circuit

Virtual-circuit number
on the link

Figure 6.8 Node C changes a virtual-circuit number.

The figure shows a small network. Initially, there is no traffic in the network. Node A requests a connection to node E. The network sets up a virtual-circuit that goes through nodes C and D. The virtual-circuit is allocated the number 1 on the links AC, CD, and DE. Node B then requests a connection to node F. The network establishes a new virtual-circuit, also going through nodes C and D. That virtual-circuit has number 1 on links BC and DF and number 2 on link CD.

Datagrams and Virtual-Circuits

■ For datagram transport, the network selects the path for each packet individually.

■ For virtual-circuit transport, the network makes one path selection for all the packets of the same connection.

■ The datagram routing tables can specify alternate paths that the node selects randomly or by using a periodic sequence.

■ Virtual-circuit routing tables specify how the node must change the numbering of virtual-circuits.

We have seen the routing tables maintained by the nodes for datagram and virtual-circuit transport. These tables specify the paths followed by the packets. We now turn to the problem of selecting these paths, i.e., to the *routing*. Ideally, the network should select the paths so as to minimize the time taken by the packets to go through the network. To do this, the network attempts to balance the traffic evenly among the links. Typically, the network allocates more traffic to a link with a large transmission rate than to a link with a small transmission rate. However, the ideal balancing of the traffic among the links is never accomplished. Random traffic fluctuations and equipment failures render the traffic allocation less than perfect most of the time. The network adapts the routing to the changing conditions, but these conditions are fluctuating fast enough that the routing decisions are always based on imperfect information.

A *routing algorithm* is a procedure that the nodes follow to select the paths of individual packets or of virtual-circuits. A good routing algorithm has the following properties:

1. *robustness* with respect to failures and changing conditions
2. *stability* of the routing decisions
3. *fairness* of the resource allocation
4. *optimality* of the packet travel times

Robustness

Robustness means that the algorithm must adjust the routing decisions when equipment fails and when traffic conditions change. A robust routing algorithm monitors the network constantly and updates the routing decisions either frequently or soon after a change is detected. The robustness requirement implies three tasks of the routing algorithm: monitoring the network, making routing decisions, and implementing these decisions. The routing algorithm is robust if it rapidly detects changes in operating conditions and reacts fast and appropriately to those changes. How fast should the algorithm react to changes in traffic conditions? Intuition suggests that the routing decisions should be modified before congestion levels increase significantly. We will quantify this intuition in a simple example in Figure 6.9.

Figure 6.9 (see pp. 264–265) shows a hypothetical network with two paths from point A to point B: ACB and ADB. Information arrives at point A at the average rate of 96 kbps. (Recall that 1 kbps = 1,000 bits per second.) For simplicity, we will assume that the bit stream has a fixed rate. A device at point A divides (demultiplexes) the bit stream into two parts that are sent to C and D. The transmitter at C has a buffer that can hold a number of bits waiting for transmission, and the buffer empties at the rate of 2×56 kbps when the bits are transmitted over two 56-kbps links. The transmitter at D empties its buffer at the rate of 56 kbps. Initially, as shown in part (a) of Figure 6.9, the demultiplexer at A sends two-thirds of the 96-kbps stream to C and one-third to D. The buffers at C and D do not accumulate bits since the transmitters are faster than the arrival streams. At time T, one link from C to B fails and the transmission rate from C to B falls from 2×56 kbps to 56 kbps. The arrival rate at C (64 kbps) is now higher than the departure rate. Consequently, the buffer at C starts accumulating bits at the rate of $64 - 56 = 8$ kbps. Define time $T + S$ to be the time at which the routing algorithm implemented at A learns of the failure and modifies the routing by sending half of the traffic to C and half to D. The arrival rate at C is now again lower than the departure rate, and the buffer begins to empty at the rate of $56 - 48 = 8$ kbps. The buffer becomes empty at $T + 2S$. The time S taken by the algorithm to learn of the failure has two related consequences. First, the buffer at C must be able to store $S \times 8$ kbps bits. Second, some bits are delayed when they are stored at C. The bit that suffers the largest delay is the one that arrives at C at time $T + S$ when the buffer contains $S \times 8$ kbps bits. It takes $(S \times 8 \text{ kbps})/(56 \text{ kbps}) = S/7$ seconds for that buffer backlog to be transmitted and for the bit that arrives at $T + S$ to be transmitted. As a numerical illustration, let us assume that $S = 1$ second. Then, the buffer at C must be able to store $1s \times 8 \text{ kbps} = 8,000$ bits and the maximum delay is $1s/7 = 140$ ms. These specific values are not important since our model was hypothetical. However, this simple example illustrates how the reaction time of the algorithm affects the performance of the network.

Stability

A routing algorithm is *stable* if the routing decisions adapt smoothly to changes in operating conditions. That is, a small change in operating conditions should provoke a comparatively small change in routing decisions. Instability could result from the effect of routing decisions on the operating conditions: a change in conditions could modify the routing decisions, which would in turn change the operating conditions, and so on. Such a possibility is illustrated in Figure 6.10. The 96-kbps bit stream is split at A. A fraction of the stream is sent to C, the rest to D. There is a transmitter with a buffer at C and another at D. The transmission rates are equal to 56 kbps. Initially, as shown in part (a) of Figure 6.10, A sends half of the bit stream to C and half to D. The arrival rate at C and at D (48 kbps) is lower than the transmission rate (56 kbps), and no backlog develops in the buffers. The buffer occupancy at C and that at D are measured every second. The algorithm sends all the bit stream to the buffer with the smallest backlog. When the backlogs are equal, half of the bit stream is sent to each buffer. Thus, the situation at (a) persists.

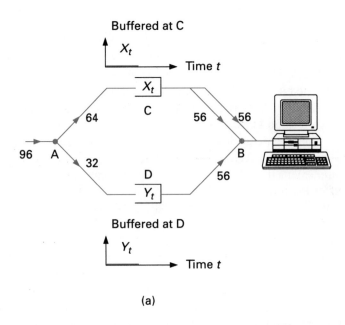

(a)

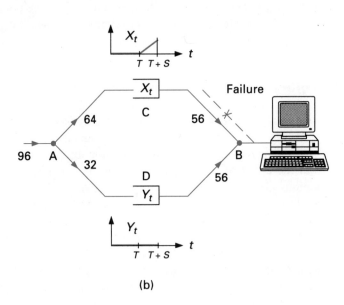

(b)

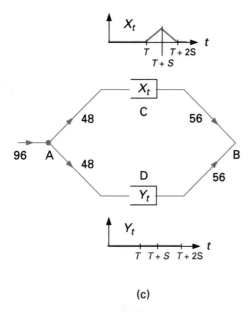

(c)

Figure 6.9 Routing algorithm reacting to failure.

(a) The 96-kbps bit stream is split into a 64-kbps stream, sent to C and a 32-kbps stream, sent to D. The transmitter at C uses two 56-kbps links, whereas the transmitter at D uses only one 56-kbps link. Two-thirds of the 96-kbps stream is sent to C, and one-third is sent to D. The graphs X_t and Y_t show that the buffers at C and D remain empty, which they should since the arrival rates are lower than the departure rates.

(b) One of the links from C to B fails at time T. The figure assumes that it takes S seconds for the routing algorithm to detect the failure. During these S seconds, i.e., between T and $T+S$, the buffer at C builds up at the rate of 8 kbps, the difference between the arrival rate (64 kbps) and the new departure rate (56 kbps).

(c) At time $T+S$, the routing algorithm has learned of the link failure and it modifies the routing by sending half of the bit stream through C and half through D. The graph shows that the buffer at C empties at the rate of 8 kbps, the difference between the departure rate (56 kbps) and the new arrival rate (48 kbps).

Now assume that the transmitter at C fails for a very short time and then recovers. The buffer at C stores the bits that cannot be transmitted during the link failure. This backlog is almost eliminated by the time $t=2$ of the next backlog measurement. However, the algorithm finds out that the backlog in C is larger than that at D. Consequently, the algorithm decides that all the traffic should be sent to D between times 2 and 3. Consequently, a backlog accumulates at the rate of $96-56=40$ kbps in the buffer at D. At time 3, a new measurement is made and the algorithm, finding that the backlog at D is now larger than that at C,

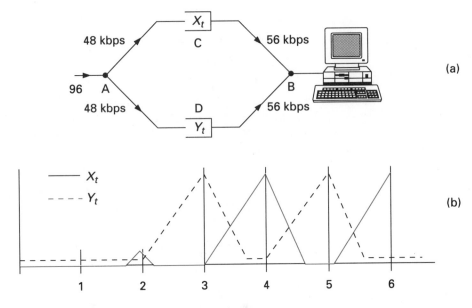

Figure 6.10   Unstable routing algorithm.

A 96-kbps bit stream arrives at A and must be sent to B, via C or D. There is a transmitter with a buffer at C and one at D; the transmission rate of both transmitters is 56 kbps. The routing algorithm at A decides the fractions of the bit stream to be sent to C and D. That decision is based on some information about the backlogs in the buffers at C and D. The figure shows the evolution of the buffer occupancy when the algorithm sends all the bit stream to the buffer that had the smallest backlog at the last measurement time.

decides that all the traffic should be sent to C. During the epoch [3, 4], the backlog at D is dissipated, whereas one develops at C. The occupancy of the buffers continues to evolve as shown in Figure 6.10.

Note that a minute perturbation led to an important change in the routing decisions. According to our definition of stability—a small modification in operating conditions results in a small change in routing decisions—this routing algorithm is unstable. Moreover, this algorithm does not settle on some routing decisions even though the traffic supplied by the network users stops changing. In fact, the algorithm continues alternating between extreme routing decisions that are visibly not appropriate. Consequences of this algorithm behavior are that the buffers must store unnecessarily large numbers of bits and that the bit stream is unnecessarily delayed. How could we modify the algorithm to improve its behavior?

A number of modifications are possible. Note that the behavior of the algorithm improves when it updates its decisions more frequently. A first modification, then, is to run the algorithm with more frequent updates. However, the frequency of updates is limited by the time taken to collect measurements about buffer occupancy. A second modification consists of limiting the changes in the rates being sent to the nodes. You can verify that the evolution of the buffer occupancy at both buffers in our network example is smoother when the algorithm can modify the routing fractions by at most 0.1 in any one step. A third modification is to base the next routing decision on not only the backlogs in the buffer but also some information about the status of the transmitters. For instance, in our example, the routing algorithm at time 2 could decide not to change the routing decisions if it knew that both transmitters were operating at the same rate. The preceding discussions show the compromise between rapidity of adaptation and stability. An algorithm that reacts very fast to changing conditions may become unstable. An algorithm that reacts sluggishly is more likely to behave smoothly, but it may be too slow to adapt. The objective of the network engineer is to design fast, stable algorithms.

Fairness

A routing algorithm is *fair* if it results in similar delays for the packets of different sources and destinations. This definition of fairness should be modified when the routing algorithm is designed to accommodate communication services with different qualities of service. Let's examine the definition of fairness, or the network shown in Figure 6.11. Two streams 1 and 2 of 1,000-bit packets are transmitted to node C. Stream 1 has a rate of 40 kbps, and it is sent through the 112-kbps transmitter at A. A fraction of the 50-kbps stream 2 is also sent through the same transmitter, and the rest is sent through the 56-kbps transmitter at B. The routing is fair if the average delay per packet is the same for the two streams. To derive a fair algorithm, we need to know how the delay per packet depends on the fraction of stream 2 sent through A. Let us assume that the average delay D per packet, in seconds, through a transmitter is given by

$$D = \frac{1}{\mu - \lambda} \tag{6.1}$$

where μ denotes the transmission rate in packets per second and λ the rate of the packet stream, also in packets per second. This formula, justified in Appendix B under specific assumptions on traffic and packet length statistics, shows that the delay D increases without bound when the traffic rate λ approaches the transmis-

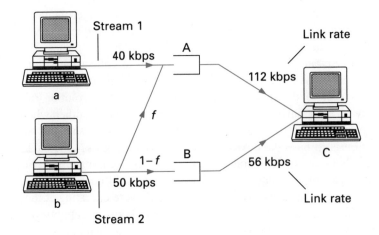

Figure 6.11 A network with two traffic streams.

The two packet streams 1 and 2 must be transmitted to node C. Stream 1 must go through the transmitter A, which has a rate of 112 kbps. A fraction f of stream 2 can also be sent through A, while the rest is sent through transmitter B, which has a rate of 56 kbps. The rate of stream 1 is 40 kbps, and that of stream 2 is 50 kbps. The routing algorithm chooses the fraction f of stream 2, sent through A. That algorithm is fair if the average delay per packet is the same for the two streams.

sion rate μ. Formula (6.1) is commonly used by network designers, even though it is only approximate. Other expressions for the delays are also used. The rate of the stream transmitted by A is equal to $\lambda_A = 40 + f \times 50$ packets per second. The rate of the stream transmitted by B is equal to $\lambda_B = (1 - f) \times 50$. Therefore, the average delay D_A per packet that goes through A is equal to

$$D_A = \frac{1}{112 - \lambda_A} = \frac{1}{72 - f \times 50}$$

and the average delay D_B per packet that goes through B is equal to

$$D_B = \frac{1}{56 - \lambda_B} = \frac{1}{6 + f \times 50}.$$

Since all the packets of stream 1 go through A, their average delay D_1 is equal to D_A. In calculating the average delay D_2 per packet of stream 2, we take into account that a fraction f of those packets go through A and a fraction $1 - f$ through B. The packets that go through A face the average delay D_A, whereas the packets that go through B face the average delay D_B. Consequently, the average delay D_2 is given by

$$D_2 = f \times D_A + (1 - f) \times D_B .$$

To have a fair algorithm, we must choose f so that $D_1 = D_2$. This equality implies that $D_A = D_B$ and therefore that $72 - f \times 50 = 6 + f \times 50$. Therefore, we must choose

$$f = 0.66.$$

Optimality

A routing algorithm is *optimal* if it maximizes the network designer's objective function while satisfying design constraints. A typical choice for the objective function is the rate of revenues for the network when one assumes that the users pay a given cost per transmitted packet. The cost per packet depends on the quality of service provided to the user. The design constraints impose an upper bound on the average delay per packet and on the cost of the network. The bound on the delay generally depends on the quality of the service. Another commonly selected objective is to minimize the average delay per packet. We will illustrate the definition of optimality on the network shown in Figure 6.11.

The model is as before. Assume that our objective is to minimize the average delay per packet by choosing the fraction f of packets of stream 2 sent to A. We first calculate the average delay per packet. Note that 40 out of 90 packets that arrive every second belong to stream 1 and face a delay equal to D_1. Similarly, 50 out of 90 packets belong to stream 2 and face a delay equal to D_2. Consequently, the average delay D per packet is equal to

$$D = \frac{40}{90}D_1 + \frac{50}{90}D_2 .$$

Using the expressions for D_1 and D_2 that we calculated before, we obtain

$$90 \times D = \frac{40 + f \times 50}{72 - f \times 50} + \frac{(1 - f) \times 50}{6 + 50 \times f} .$$

Next, we calculate the value of f that minimizes the delay D. To do this, we calculate the derivative with respect to f of the right-hand side of the above equality and we express that this derivative is equal to zero when f minimizes D. After dividing by 50 the expression giving the derivative, we find

$$\frac{1}{72 - 50f} + \frac{10 \times (4 + 5f)}{(72 - 50f)^2} - \frac{f}{6 + 50f} - \frac{50 \times (1 - f)}{(6 + 50f)^2} = 0.$$

Solving this equation for f gives $f \approx 0.465$.

Note that this value of f, which minimizes the average delay per packet, is not the same as the value that makes the routing fair (0.66). That difference shows that optimality and fairness are not always compatible objectives. In fact, these two objectives are rarely compatible. The network illustrated in Figure 6.12 will provide another example of conflict between optimality and fairness. The figure shows a network with two 56 kbps links used by three packet streams. Stream a uses only link 1, stream b only link 2, and stream c uses both links. Assume that the objective of the designer is to maximize the sum of the rates of the three streams. The design constraint is that each link can carry at most 56 kbps. You can see that the solution to this optimization problem is to permit streams a and b to carry 56 kbps and not to let stream c transmit a packet. This solution achieves a total rate of 112 kbps for the three streams. This optimal solution is not fair to the users of stream c. A fair allocation of traffic would be the same rate, say R kbps, to each of the three streams. The design constraint then requires that the rate carried by link 1, $2 \times R$, be lower than 56 kbps, and similarly for link 2. Thus, the maximum value of R is 28 kbps and the resulting total rate for the three streams is equal to $3 \times R = 84$ kbps. We conclude from the example that a fair allocation is not optimal. Note, however, that this example is somewhat contrived. A more sensible objective for the optimization problem would be the rate of return of the network where each packet is charged in proportion to the network resources that it uses. In our example, a packet of stream c should cost twice as much to transmit as a packet of stream a or of stream b. To see what the optimization problem becomes with this new objective function, let us assume that each packet of streams a and b costs 1 unit to transmit, whereas a packet of stream c costs 2 units. The rate of revenues R, in units of cost per second, for the network is then equal to

$$R = \lambda_a + \lambda_b + 2\lambda_c$$

where λ_a designates the rate of stream a, and similarly for λ_b and λ_c. The optimization problem is to maximize R subject to the design constraints

$$\lambda_1 := \lambda_a + \lambda_c \leq 56 \text{ kbps} \quad \text{and} \quad \lambda_2 := \lambda_b + \lambda_c \leq 56 \text{ kbps}.$$

These constraints express that the rates λ_1 and λ_2 of the traffic carried by links 1 and 2 must be less than 56 kbps. You can verify that this problem admits many optimal solutions. Any allocation that uses the maximum capacity of both links is optimal since the transmission of one packet by any link gives 1 unit of return. In particular, the allocation $\lambda_a = \lambda_b = \lambda_c = 28$ kbps is both optimal and fair.

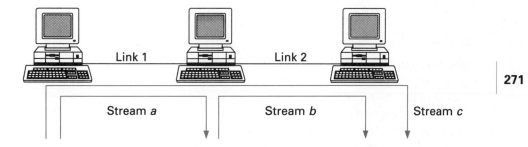

Figure 6.12 Optimality and fairness may be incompatible.

Three packet streams {*a, b, c*} are transmitted over two links {1, 2}. Both links transmit at 56 kbps. The maximum total rate of the three traffic streams is obtained when the rates of the streams *a* and *b* are equal to 56 kbps and when stream *c* carries no traffic. This optimal solution is unfair to the users of stream *c*.

Desirable Properties of a Routing Algorithm

■ A routing algorithm should be *robust* with respect to changing conditions and equipment failures. That is, the algorithm should adapt the routing decisions to such modifications.

■ A routing algorithm is *stable* if a small change in conditions leads to a small modification in the routing decisions. One common cause of instability is the effect of routing decisions on operating conditions.

■ A routing algorithm is *fair* if it results in comparable delays and available transmission rates for the different users.

■ A routing algorithm is *optimal* if it maximizes the network designer's objective function while satisfying the design constraints.

■ Optimality and fairness are not always compatible. Such incompatibility may be caused by an objective function that does not reflect properly the operating cost of the network.

So far, we have learned the desirable properties of routing algorithms. We now turn to a presentation of some examples of widely used routing algorithms.

Flooding

When the *flooding* routing algorithm is used, every node in the network transmits a copy of each packet it receives on every one of its transmission links, except on the link through which it received the packet. To avoid endless retransmissions of copies of the same packet, each node keeps a table with the identity of the packets that it has already transmitted. Alternatively, the network can discard packets that have gone through more than a specific number of nodes. This routing algorithm transmits packets to all the nodes that can be reached in the network. The algorithm wastes network resources because it transmits an excessive number of copies. This flooding algorithm is used mostly to transmit control information that must reach all the nodes when the network nodes are uncertain of the current network *topology*, i.e., of the graph of interconnections between the nodes. For instance, discovery frames initiated by source routing bridges are sent by flooding.

Spanning Tree Routing

Spanning tree routing is the transmission of packets along a tree of paths that leads to a specific destination. Figure 6.13 shows the spanning tree for destination A. Figure 6.13 shows a network with duplex links. The red lines form a *spanning tree* rooted at A, i.e., a set of links along which there is a unique path from A to every other node in the network (i.e., there is no loop in the graph of a tree). When the nodes know a spanning tree to a destination A, the nodes can route packets destined to A along that tree. The advantage of spanning tree routing is that it limits the number of packet transmissions.

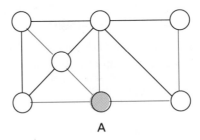

A

Figure 6.13 Spanning tree for destination A.

The circles in the figure represent communication nodes. The nodes are connected by links designated by straight lines. The links are assumed to be duplex, i.e., bi-directional. The colored lines form a tree rooted at A that goes through all the network nodes.

Static Routing

The *static* routing algorithm is the algorithm for datagrams that we described when we explained the utilization of the routing table in Figure 6.6. Each node transmits a packet along a link selected according to some probabilities that depend on the destination. The algorithm is called static when the probabilities do not change in time. Note that successive packets with the same destination may be sent along different paths when the nodes use static routing: successive random numbers are different, even when they are selected with the same probability distribution. We explained one method for calculating the routing probabilities when we calculated the fraction *f* of the traffic in Figure 6.11 that minimizes the average delay per packet. Let us give another example by calculating the optimal routing probabilities in Figure 6.14. Packets are transmitted over three links 1, 2, and 3. Figure 6.14 shows that each transmitter is equipped with a buffer that holds packets waiting to be transmitted. The rates of the links are μ_1, μ_2, and μ_3, in packets per second. The rates of the packet streams arriving at A and B are γ_A and γ_B, also in packets per second. We want to calculate the routing probability p that minimizes the average delay per packet through the network. We will assume that (6.1) is applicable. To use (6.1), we have to calculate the rate of packets transmitted by the three links. The rate through link 1 is $\lambda_1 := p \times \gamma_A$. The rate through link 2 is $\lambda_2 := (1 - p) \times \gamma_A$. The rate through link 3 is $\lambda_3 = \gamma_B + \gamma_A$. Out of the $\gamma_A + \gamma_B$ packets that enter the network every second, λ_1 go through link 1, λ_2 go through link 2, and λ_3 go through link 3. Thus, a fraction $p_1 := \lambda_1/(\gamma_A + \gamma_B)$ of the packets face a delay through link 1, a fraction $p_2 := \lambda_2/(\gamma_A + \gamma_B)$ face a delay through link 2, and a fraction $p_3 := \lambda_3/(\gamma_A + \gamma_B)$ face a delay through link 3. Note that $p_1 + p_2 + p_3 > 1$ since some packets go through more than one link. The average delay D per packet is therefore equal to

$$D = p_1 \times D_1 + p_2 \times D_2 + p_3 \times D_3 , \qquad (6.2)$$

where

$$D_i := \frac{1}{\mu_i - \lambda_i}$$

is the average delay per packet going through line i, for $i = 1, 2, 3$, according to (6.1). Substituting these expressions in (6.2) shows that

$$D = \frac{1}{\gamma_A + \gamma_B} \left[\frac{\gamma_A p}{\mu_1 - \gamma_A p} + \frac{\gamma_A(1 - p)}{\mu_2 - \gamma_A(1 - p)} + \frac{\gamma_A + \gamma_B}{\mu_3 - \gamma_A - \gamma_B} \right] . \qquad (6.3)$$

The *routing optimization problem* is to calculate the value of p that minimizes D. We do this by expressing that the derivative of D with respect to p is equal to zero

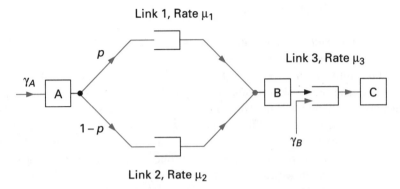

Figure 6.14 Calculating routing probabilities for static routing.

The network has three nodes A, B, and C. The links 1, 2, and 3 have the rates indicated in the figure. The problem is to select the probability *p* that minimizes the average delay per packet in the network.

when *p* minimizes *D*. It may happen that the value of *p* that minimizes *D* does not fall between 0 and 1 and cannot be a routing probability. When this occurs, the value of *p* in [0, 1] that minimizes *D* is either 0 or 1. You should use the approach that we just described to verify that, when $\mu_1 > \mu_2$, the minimizing value is given by

$$p = \min\{\frac{\mu_1\sqrt{\mu_2} - \mu_2\sqrt{\mu_1} + \gamma_A\sqrt{\mu_1}}{\gamma_A(\sqrt{\mu_1} + \sqrt{\mu_2})}, 1\}.$$

Before we leave this example, let us use it to explain the *capacity allocation problem*. This is the problem faced by the network designer who has a fixed budget for buying transmission links. The designer must decide how the budget should be divided among the different links to optimize some objective function. We will solve a version of this problem that concerns the design of the network in Figure 6.14. We use a fixed budget to buy the three transmission links 1, 2, and 3. The cost of buying links with the transmission rates μ_1, μ_2, and μ_3 shown in the figure is

$$C = a_1\mu_1 + a_2\mu_2 + a_3\mu_3 . \tag{6.4}$$

This cost shows that faster transmitters are more expensive. We chose this cost expression mostly for simplicity. The formulation of the problem and the solution that we will explain can be adapted to the actual cost of equipment. We want to find the values of μ_1, μ_2, and μ_3 that minimize *D* subject to $C \leq C_{max}$ where C_{max} is the total budget at our disposal. We will write *D* as $D(\mu_1, \mu_2, \mu_3)$ to recall that it is a function of the link transmission rates. Also, we will write *C* as $C(\mu_1, \mu_2, \mu_3)$. Our problem is then to

minimize $D(\mu_1, \mu_2, \mu_3)$
over (μ_1, μ_2, μ_3)
subject to $C(\mu_1, \mu_2, \mu_3) \leq C_{\max}$.

This is a *constrained optimization problem*. To solve such a problem, we use the method of *Lagrange multipliers*. (See Problem 6.7.) With this method the value of (μ_1, μ_2, μ_3) that solves the problem must be stationary for the expression

$$D(\mu_1, \mu_2, \mu_3) - \beta C(\mu_1, \mu_2, \mu_3)$$

for some value of the Lagrange multiplier β. That is, the derivative of the above expression with respect to μ_i must be equal to zero for $i = 1, 2, 3$. We find that these three conditions imply that

$$-\frac{\lambda_i}{(\mu_i - \lambda_i)^2} + \beta a_i = 0, \, i = 1, 2, 3$$

where the λ_is were defined previously. Solving these three equations for the μ_is, we get

$$\mu_i = \lambda_i + \sqrt{\frac{\lambda_i}{\beta a_i}}, \, i = 1, 2, 3 . \tag{6.5}$$

Substituting these expressions into (6.4) for C gives

$$C = \sum_{i=1}^{3} a_i \mu_i = \sum_{i=1}^{3} a_i \{\lambda_i + \sqrt{\frac{\lambda_i}{\beta a_i}}\} = \sum_{i=1}^{3} a_i \lambda_i + \frac{1}{\sqrt{\beta}} \{\sum_{i=1}^{3} \sqrt{\lambda_i a_i}\} .$$

One then finds the value of β such that $C = C_{\max}$. You can check that this value is such that

$$\frac{1}{\sqrt{\beta}} = \frac{C_{\max} - \sum_{i=1}^{3} a_i \lambda_i}{\sum_{i=1}^{3} \sqrt{\lambda_i a_i}} .$$

Finally, by substituting that value of β into the expressions (6.5) for the μ_is we find

$$\mu_i = \lambda_i + (C_{\max} - \sum_{j=1}^{3} a_j \lambda_j) \frac{\sqrt{\lambda_i / a_i}}{\sum_{j=1}^{3} \sqrt{\lambda_j a_j}} . \tag{6.6}$$

Note that this solution is meaningful only if

$$C_{max} \geq \sum_{i=1}^{3} a_i \lambda_i.$$

276

Indeed, the minimum transmission rate of link i is the rate λ_i of the traffic carried by that link. Consequently, $\mu_i \geq \lambda_i$ for each i and

$$C = \sum_{i=1}^{3} a_i \mu_i \geq \sum_{i=1}^{3} a_i \lambda_i.$$

When $a_i = 1$ for each i, the solution (6.6) is known as the *square root assignment rule* since the excess capacity

$$C_{max} - \sum_{i=1}^{3} \lambda_i$$

is then allocated in proportion to the square root of the traffic through the nodes.

After this digression on capacity assignment, let us resume our discussion of routing algorithms. We have seen that we can calculate the routing probabilities used by the static routing algorithm if we know the traffic rates and the link capacities. The traffic rates change, however. To adapt the routing to the changing traffic rates, the algorithm must collect information from the network nodes. For example, the nodes could monitor the traffic on their links and send estimates of the traffic rates to a central node that would then recalculate the optimal routing probabilities and distribute these values to all the nodes. This approach suffers from the following two limitations and is not used in communication networks. First, the assumption, (6.1), that we used to derive the optimal routing probabilities is only approximately valid. Second, since the nodes would have to report their traffic rates to adapt the algorithm, they might as well communicate their actual congestion levels. You may expect a routing algorithm based on measured congestion levels to be more responsive to random traffic fluctuations than an algorithm based only on average traffic rates.

Bellman-Ford Algorithm

We will now explain an important routing algorithm that attempts to route the packets along the fastest paths to their destinations. This algorithm is the *Bellman-Ford algorithm*. Consider the network shown in Figure 6.15. The circles are communication nodes connected by communication links. Each link corresponds to a transmitter and an associated buffer. There is a delay associated with each link. The delay can be estimated by keeping track of actual delays experienced by packets or by monitoring the occupancy of the buffer. The Bellman-

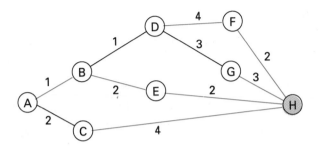

Figure 6.15 An illustration of the Bellman-Ford algorithm.

The circles represent communication nodes. The straight lines are duplex links. The problem is to select paths for packets destined to node H. The links are marked with an estimate of the delay along that link. To simplify the figure, we have assumed that the delay on a link is the same in both directions. The colored links show the fastest spanning tree to H.

Ford algorithm is a method for every node to find out the fastest path to a destination. The number associated with a link in Figure 6.15 is an estimate of the delay on that link. The delay of a packet is its transmission time plus its *queueing time*, which is the time it spends waiting for the other buffered packets to be transmitted. To simplify the discussion, we have assumed that the delays on a link are the same in both directions in Figure 6.15. The procedure that we will describe can be applied without making this assumption. Before explaining how the algorithm determines the fastest path to the destination, we must introduce some notation. We denote by $d(A)$ the minimum time taken by packets sent by A to reach the destination H. By inspecting the figure, you can see that $d(A) = 5$ and that packets take this minimum time to reach H when they follow the path ABEH. Since the routing algorithm cannot inspect the figure as we did, we have to design a systematic procedure that yields $d(A) = 5$. The procedure is based on

$$d(A) = \min\{d(A, B) + d(B), d(A, C) + d(C)\} . \tag{6.7}$$

In this expression, we denote by $d(A, B)$ the delay on the link from A to B and by $d(B)$ the minimum delay to reach the destination H from B. We define the symbols $d(A, C)$ and $d(C)$ similarly. You can verify (6.7) by noting that a packet that goes from A to H must go either first to B or to C. If the packet goes first to B, then its minimum time to reach H is the time $d(A, B)$ taken to go first to B plus the minimum time $d(B)$ to go from B to H. The second term between braces in (6.7) expresses that the minimum time to go from A to H for a packet that goes first to C is $d(A, C) + d(C)$. Since a packet has only these two options to reach H from A, its minimum time $d(A)$ cannot be less than the right-hand side of (6.7). Moreover, if the packet follows the fastest path from B to H or from C to H, then it will take $d(A, B) + d(B)$ to reach H if it first goes to B and $d(A, C) + d(C)$ if it first goes to C. Therefore, the minimum time from A to C cannot exceed the right-hand side of (6.7). Hence, the equality must hold in (6.7).

The relation (6.7) shows how to obtain $d(A)$ from $d(B)$ and $d(C)$. Moreover, the fastest path from A to H must go through B if the first term between braces in (6.7) is less than the second term; otherwise, that path must go through C. Similarly, one can write that

$$d(B) = \min\{d(B, D) + d(D), d(B, E) + d(E), d(B, A) + d(A)\} . \qquad (6.8)$$

In fact, we can write a similar equation for each of the nodes A through G. Solving these equations gives the minimum travel times to H and also specifies the paths with the minimum travel times from the nodes to H. For instance, we saw that (6.7) determines whether the fastest path to H goes through B or through C. Say that it goes through B. We can then use (6.8) to determine whether the path continues through D or through E, and so on. How can we solve these equations? You see that the equation (6.8) for $d(B)$ involves $d(A)$. We have seen before that the equation (6.7) for $d(A)$ involves $d(B)$. How should we start? To explain how such equations can be solved, let us write them in a more general way. Define

$$x = (d(A), d(B), d(C), d(D), d(E), d(F), d(G)) .$$

Thus, x is the vector of minimum times. The equations (6.7) and (6.8) and the equations for the other nodes are of the form

$$x = F(x) \qquad (6.9)$$

where $F(.)$ is the function obtained by putting these equations together. An equation such as (6.9) is called a *fixed-point equation*. A common method for solving a fixed-point equation is the *iterative algorithm*:

$$x_{n+1} = F(x_n), \ n \geq 0 . \qquad (6.10)$$

That is, one chooses some value x_0 and one calculates x_1, x_2, x_3, and so on according to (6.10). The iterative algorithm (6.10) applied to such equations as (6.7) and (6.8) is called the *Bellman-Ford algorithm*. We will explain why the sequence $\{x_n\}$ reaches a fixed value x after a finite number of steps when one chooses $x_0 = (\infty, ..., \infty)$. That value of x is then a solution of the fixed-point equation, and it determines the minimum travel times to the destination H. Moreover, we will show that x is reached after a maximum of N steps, where N is the maximum length of a loop-free path to H.

These properties of the Bellman-Ford algorithm follow from two observations. The first observation is that each component of the vector-valued function $F(x)$ is increasing in each component of x. To see this, observe that the right-hand side of (6.8) increases when $d(A)$ increases. The term $d(A)$ is a typical component of the vector x, and the right-hand side of (6.8) is a typical expression for a component of $F(x)$. Consider then the sequence $\{x_n, \ n \geq 0\}$ that starts with $x_0 = (\infty, \ldots, \infty)$. The next term x_1 cannot be larger than x_0, that is, $x_1 \leq x_0$. Consequently, $x_2 = F(x_1) \leq x_1 = F(x_0)$, since $F(x)$ decreases when the components of x decrease. Continuing in this way shows that the sequence x_n is decreasing.

The second observation is that there is a simple interpretation for the terms of this sequence. The components of the vector x_1 are the minimum times from the nodes to H along paths that use at most one link. The components of x_2 are the minimum times to H along paths that use at most two links, and so on. A component of x_n is infinite if there is no path with n links from the node that corresponds to that component of x_n to H. The sequence is decreasing because there are more paths with at most $n + 1$ links than there are paths with at most n links, and the minimum time among a set of paths decreases when the set increases. This interpretation of x_n shows that the sequence x_n must stop decreasing when n is larger than the maximum number of links in a path to H. Moreover, we need only consider the paths that use links only once since other paths must contain loops that can only add to the packet travel times. Therefore, the Bellman-Ford algorithm converges in N steps at most, where N is the maximum length of a loop-free path to H.

The Bellman-Ford algorithm is implemented by having each node send to a specific computer in the network an estimate of the travel time along its outgoing links. That computer can then run the Bellman-Ford algorithm and communicate the optimal routing decisions to all the nodes.

There is a distributed version of the Bellman-Ford algorithm which proceeds as follows (see Figure 6.15). Periodically, every node sends to its neighbors an estimate of the shortest delay between itself and the destination node. Initially, these estimates are infinite. For instance, at some time, node D may learn that the estimate of F is 10, that of G is 12, and that of B is 22. (These numbers are chosen for the sake of illustration; they may not be possible for the given figure.) Node D computes its estimate of the shortest delay to the destination as the minimum of

$$4 + 10, 3 + 12, 1 + 22 .$$

These correspond to the estimates of delays by going through nodes F, G, and B, respectively. This new estimate (14) is then sent to the neighbors of D (i.e., F, G, B) at some later time. This algorithm can be shown to converge to the correct values of the minimum delays if the nodes continue updating their estimates and transmitting them to their neighbors. An advantage to using a distributed algorithm is that all the nodes execute the same algorithm and no node has a special role. Consequently, a distributed algorithm continues to operate when nodes fail, whereas another algorithm would be disabled when the special node fails. Another advantage of some distributed algorithms is that increased speed is gained from the parallel executions in the various nodes. However, not all distributed algorithms are faster than their nondistributed (centralized) version, as we will see shortly.

One peculiar property of the distributed Bellman-Ford algorithm is that it tends to react slowly to bad news. This undesirable property will be illustrated by example. We will then explain a method called *hold down* that can be used to correct that shortcoming. Consider the network shown in Figure 6.16. Part (a) of the figure shows the estimates of delays on the links of a four-node network. The links are duplex, and we assume, for simplicity, that delays are the same in both directions. That part of the figure also shows the shortest times from each node to the destination D. Assume that the rightmost link fails, as shown in part (b) of Figure 6.16. The table shows the estimates of the minimum time between the nodes and D. The figure assumes that each node takes 1 unit of time to calculate the new estimate and to distribute it to its neighbors. The row of the table marked "step 0" contains the estimates that arrived just before the link failure. The next row is obtained as follows. Station C realizes that it can no longer go to the destination via the link C → D. At that time, node C has an estimate, which B had communicated just after the previous step, that indicates that the minimum time from B to D is equal to 2. C assumes that this estimate is still valid, and it concludes that the minimum time from C to D is equal to 1, the time to go from C to B, plus the estimated time 2 from B to D. Thus, the new estimate of the shortest delay from C to the destination D is equal to 3. The other entries in the table are obtained similarly. The table shows that it takes a very long time before the nodes realize that a failure took place that prevents them from transmitting packets to D.

The *hold down* procedure speeds up the algorithm. When the nodes use the hold down procedure, they continue routing the packets to the nodes they used before the update for a fixed number of steps called the duration of the hold down. This selection is maintained even if the estimates indicate that it would be faster to send packets via another neighbor. Moreover, the node updates its estimated distance to the destination when it routes the packets according to the hold down rule. After the hold down duration, the nodes choose to send the packets to the neighboring nodes that offer the shortest path according to the distance estimates.

Figure 6.17 shows the successive steps of the distributed Bellman-Ford algorithm for the network in Figure 6.16 with a hold down duration of two steps. The row "step 0" of the table gives the estimates of the travel times just before the failure of link CD. The estimate of node C is 1, and node C sends the packets directly to node D. Since the hold down duration is equal to two steps,

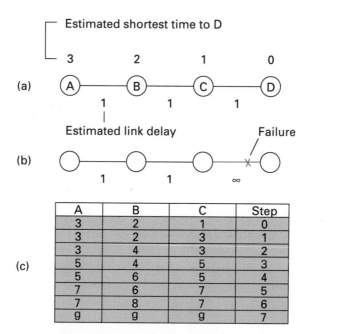

Figure 6.16 Slow propagation of bad news.

Part (a) of the figure shows a network with three nodes represented by circles and the estimates of link delays. The figure assumes that the links are duplex and that delays are the same in both directions. Part (b) shows the same network after the failure of the link between C and D. Part (c) shows estimates of delays to D as they are calculated in successive steps of the distributed Bellman-Ford algorithm.

node C must continue transmitting the packets via node D for the next two steps. Therefore, the estimate of node C is infinite at steps 1 and 2. At step 1, node B compares the two possibilities that is has for sending packets to D. If it sends the packets via C, then node B estimates the travel time as the time from B to C plus the estimated time from C to D. The time from B to C is 1. The estimated time that B has received from C before step 1 is still 1, the estimate that node C had calculated just before updating its estimate at step 1. Similarly, node B estimates that the travel time of packets routed via A would be $1 + 3 = 4$. Therefore, at step 1, node B estimates that the minimum travel time to D is 2 and that it is achieved by routing packets via C. At step 1, node A calculates that the minimum delay is 3 and that it is achieved by sending the packets via B. At step 2, node B knows the updated estimate calculated by node C at step 1. That estimate is infinite. Node B is then tempted to calculate its new estimate by computing the travel time via node A. However, because of the hold down, node B must use its neighbor C for the next two steps. Therefore, at steps 2 and 3, node B obtains an infinite estimate

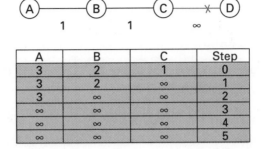

Figure 6.17 Hold down at work.

Step 0 shows the estimates of the minimum travel times to D just before the failure of the link CD. Step 1 is the first update after the link failure. Node C continues routing to D for two steps, the duration of the hold down. At step 1 and step 2, node C calculates an infinite travel time since it must transmit through the failed link. At step 3, when node C is free to transmit to the neighbor that results in the smallest travel time, the estimate of node B is also infinite. After only three steps, all the nodes know that they can no longer reach D.

for the travel time. At step 3, node A also calculates an infinite estimate since it learned the infinite estimate that node B calculated at step 2.

We will now demonstrate that the hold down does not speed up the convergence of the distributed Bellman-Ford algorithm when its duration is too short. Consider the network shown in Figure 6.18. The top left diagram in Figure 6.18 is a network with the delay estimates. The link from C to the destination D fails. The bottom left diagram shows the evolution with a hold down duration equal to 2. The rightmost evolution corresponds to a hold down duration equal to 1. You see that the algorithm with a hold down duration of two steps reaches the correct estimates after seven steps. Continuing the table shows that the algorithm with a one-step hold down takes about 20 steps to converge to the correct estimates.

Hierarchical Routing

We explained the decomposition of the set of nodes into domains and subdomains called hierarchical naming in Section 6.1. We now explain a similar method applied to routing. The advantage of this method, called *hierarchical routing*, is that a node does not have to know different paths to individual remote locations. Instead, the nodes are grouped into domains and a node needs to know only the node to which it should next send the packets destined to the remote

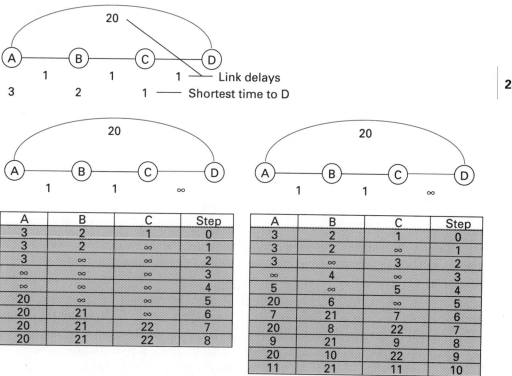

A	B	C	Step
3	2	1	0
3	2	∞	1
3	∞	∞	2
∞	∞	∞	3
∞	∞	∞	4
20	∞	∞	5
20	21	∞	6
20	21	22	7
20	21	22	8

A	B	C	Step
3	2	1	0
3	2	∞	1
3	∞	3	2
∞	4	∞	3
5	∞	5	4
20	6	∞	5
7	21	7	6
20	8	22	7
9	21	9	8
20	10	22	9
11	21	11	10

Figure 6.18 Hold down too short.

The top left part of the figure shows a network with the link delays and the estimated travel times from the nodes to D. The bottom left part shows the successive steps of the distributed Bellman-Ford algorithm with a two-step hold down. This algorithm converges in seven steps. The right table shows the successive steps of the algorithm with a one-step hold down. That algorithm is very slow to converge.

domains. We will explain hierarchical routing in the network shown in Figure 6.19. The network in Figure 6.19 has $N = 18$ nodes grouped into $K = 3$ domains of $M = 6$ nodes each. The values of K and M are arbitrary. Thus, $N = K \times M$. Each node has a routing table that specifies through which neighboring node it should send packets destined to each of the $M - 1$ other nodes in the same domain and to each of the other $K - 1$ other domains. The size of the routing table is then equal to $\{M - 1\} + \{K - 1\}$. Without the hierarchical routing, each node would need an entry for each of the $N - 1$ other nodes. As a numerical illustration, one finds that when $M = K = 100$, each node needs a table of size 198 when hierarchical routing is used and of size 9,999 when nonhierarchical routing is used. Of course, hierarchical routing can be organized with more than two levels by decomposing the domains into subdomains, the subdomains into subsubdomains, etc.

284

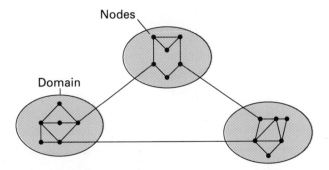

Figure 6.19 Hierarchical routing.

The network nodes are grouped into domains. Each node in a domain has a table that specifies the next node along a path to each other node in the same domain and to each other domain. The tables are much smaller than if there were an entry for each of the other nodes.

Routing Algorithms

- When using *flooding*, a node that receives a packet from a neighbor sends a copy of the packet to all its other neighbors. To avoid sending multiple copies, the node memorizes the packet identification number or discards old packets.

- With *spanning tree* routing, the nodes send the packets along a spanning tree rooted at the destination.

- To implement *static* routing, each node maintains a routing table that specifies a list of outgoing links for each packet destination. A packet is then sent along one of these links chosen according to probabilities also specified by the table.

- The Bellman-Ford algorithm determines the fastest path between nodes from the travel times along individual links.

- In the distributed Bellman-Ford algorithm, the nodes exchange their estimates of minimum travel times with their neighbors. This algorithm reacts slowly to link or node failures, but this shortcoming can be alleviated by using the *hold down* modification.

- The size of the routing tables is significantly reduced by using *hierarchical routing*. The nodes are grouped into domains, and each node keeps a list of the next node for each other domain and for each other node in its own domain.

6.3 Congestion Control

Congestion is defined as an excessive backlog of packets waiting to be transmitted in the buffers of some network nodes. Congestion is undesirable because it increases the travel times of the packets and, therefore, the communication delays between users. Congestion may also increase the number of timeouts experienced by the nodes, and these timeouts further increase the traffic and congestion because they lead the nodes to retransmit copies of packets. Thus, it is desirable to avoid excessive backlogs inside the communication network.

This congestion generating further congestion is not unlike the phenomenon of traffic collapse that you may have experienced on a heavily traveled section of highway. We are referring to the slowing down of vehicles that ends up with traffic crawling to a stall and with vehicles accumulating on a road segment. This effect is caused by the drivers slowing down when they see more vehicles and when the vehicles are closer together. The phenomenon of gridlock is another manifestation of the congestion created when the traffic temporarily exceeds the capacity of the roads.

This analogy shows that it does matter where the backlog occurs. If advanced technology could slow down vehicles that are about to approach a congested section of highway, the onset of traffic instability and collapse could be avoided. One could also advise drivers to follow less congested paths. We will find that congestion control in communication networks employs similar strategies, with the added advantage that, unlike drivers, packets follow directives unfailingly and without delay.

We will use Figure 6.20 to illustrate one method commonly used for congestion control. The figure shows a host, represented by a square, that is connected to a network, represented by a circle. The host has an infinite collection of packets that it wants to transmit through the network. The network is modeled as a buffer attached to a transmitter with rate μ kbps. When should the node transmit if its timeout is equal to T seconds? The answer is that the node can transmit as long as the backlog in the network is small enough for the delay to be less than T. Specifically, say that the node knows that there are now x kbits waiting to be transmitted in the buffer. If the node decides to transmit a packet, that packet will arrive at the buffer when it contains about x kbits. That packet will experience a delay roughly equal to x/μ seconds. This delay should be less than T. Therefore, the node can transmit if

$$x < \mu T.$$

This analysis justifies the congestion control method known as *window flow control*. To implement a window flow control, the nodes need to know the backlog inside the network, or they must be refrained from transmitting when the backlog

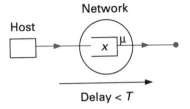

Figure 6.20 Congestion control to limit delays.

The square represents a host that has a set of packets that must be transmitted over the network, represented by the circle. Other hosts are also using the same network.

is likely to become too large. One possible implementation for virtual circuit transport is to limit to C the number of virtual-circuits through each link and to use the selective repeat protocol with window size W on each virtual-circuit. Recall from Chapter 4 that each sender and receiver never stores more than W packets per virtual-circuit. Consequently, with this method, each node stores at most $C \times W$ packets per link.

Instead of using the *link-level* window flow control that we just described, the network can use *end-to-end* window flow control. To implement this method for a virtual-circuit transport, the packets must obtain a permit before they can be transmitted. The permits are released by packets that exit the virtual-circuit. Such a permit is typically transmitted inside a packet that is traveling in the direction opposite to that of the virtual-circuit, i.e., from the destination node to the source node. More generally, it is possible to implement a window flow control for specific subsets of the network.

Some networks control congestion by adjusting the window sizes on the basis of the backlog in the network. For instance, in some networks, *choke packets* are sent by a node that is approaching saturation to inform the source to stop transmitting for a while.

The network layer has to be designed with some care in order to prevent *deadlocks*. Deadlock is the condition of a set of interacting agents when they are all prevented from acting because each agent is waiting for other agents to act. A simple example of deadlock is when two agents wait for each other. In general, a deadlock occurs when each agent in a loop of agents is waiting for the next agent along the loop to act.

Two forms of deadlock are specific to the network layer: the *store-and-forward* deadlock and the *reassembly deadlock*. A store-and-forward deadlock is illustrated in Figure 6.21. Each of the two nodes in Figure 6.21 has a buffer that can hold three packets. The two buffers are full. Node 1 wants to send a packet to node 2, and node 2 wants to send a packet to node 1. Thus, node 1

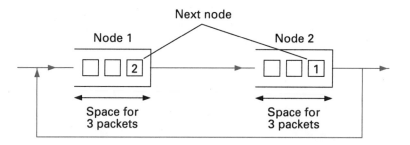

Figure 6.21 Store-and-forward deadlock.

The network has two nodes, each with a buffer that can hold three packets. The packets are marked with their next destinations. The figure shows a situation in which both nodes are unable to transmit and to receive other packets.

waits for node 2 to free space in its buffer to be able to accept a packet. Also, node 2 waits for node 1 to transmit a packet. You should realize that this type of deadlock can occur with arbitrarily large buffers and in more complicated situations that involve many nodes. Let us explain a method for avoiding this deadlock. Assume that the packets in Figure 6.21 move along some loop-free paths in the network. Some of the packets move from node 1 to node 2 and then leave the network. The other packets go from node 2 to node 1 and then leave.

Let us draw the *tree of possible paths* as indicated in Figure 6.22. The graph shows the two paths *a* (from node 1 to node 2) and *b* (from node 2 to node 1) that packets can follow in the network in Figure 6.21. The figure designates the nodes differently when they are visited along the different paths. Node 1 is designated by 1.*a* when it is visited by packets that move along path *a* and by 1.*b* when it is visited by packets that move along path *b*. With this convention, the two paths become (1.*a*, 2.*a*) and (2.*b*, 1.*b*). The graph of possible paths is a tree, as shown in Figure 6.22. Note that the graph is not a tree when the nodes 1.*a* and 1.*b* are not distinguished. To prevent deadlocks, we allocate some buffer space to each of the four nodes in the tree shown in Figure 6.22. For instance, we reserve space to hold two packets in 1.*a* and 2.*b* and space to hold one packet in 1.*b* and 2.*a*. Nodes 2.*a* and 1.*b* can always transmit packets and, therefore, no situation exists in which no node can transmit. We can make the network in Figure 6.21 behave exactly as the network in Figure 6.22 if we keep track of the different paths followed by the packets. For instance, no new packet moving along path *a* can be accepted in node 1 when that node already contains 2 packets moving along path *a*.

The reassembly deadlock occurs when nodes run out of buffers to reassemble out-of-order packets. A simple occurrence of this deadlock is shown in Figure 6.23. The two circles represent nodes that are shared by two virtual-cir-

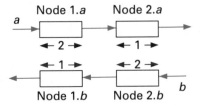

Figure 6.22 Tree of possible paths.

This figure shows the two paths that packets can follow in the network in Figure 6.21: path *a* from node 1 to node 2, and path *b* from node 2 to node 1. Each node appears twice in the figure: once to represent path *a* and again to represent path *b*. Note that one can prevent deadlocks by allocating some buffer space for each of the four nodes in this graph.

cuits VC *A* and VC *B*. Each virtual-circuit uses the selective repeat protocol with window size 2. The buffer in the second node can store two packets. A deadlock occurs when the second node must store one out-of-order packet for each virtual-circuit. This situation is shown in Figure 6.23: The first packet a_1 of VC *A* is lost, and the second packet a_2 must be stored in the second node. Thereafter, the first packet b_1 of VC *B* is also lost, and the node must store the second packet b_2. At that time, the second node is no longer able to accept a retransmitted copy of a_1 or b_1 and this situation will persist forever. The network can prevent this deadlock by accepting virtual-circuits only when the nodes have sufficient free space in their buffers. Specifically, a connection between two neighboring nodes that uses the selective repeat protocol with window size W can be accepted only when both nodes have enough unreserved buffer space to hold W packets. That buffer space must then be reserved for that connection.

Congestion Control

- Congestion, the excessive backlog of some nodes, increases delays and reduces the throughput of a network.

- Window flow control limits the number of packets in some parts of the network, such as virtual-circuits or sets of nodes.

- Nodes can regulate the flow of packets by sending control messages to slow down transmissions.

- Store-and-forward deadlocks and reassembly deadlocks are prevented by reserving buffers.

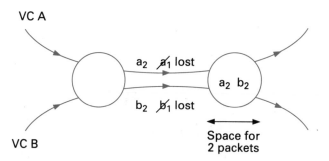

VC A

a_2 $\cancel{a_1}$ lost

a_2 b_2

b_2 $\cancel{b_1}$ lost

VC B

Space for
2 packets

Figure 6.23 Reassembly deadlock.

Two virtual-circuits *VC A* and *VC B* go through the two nodes represented by circles. The node to the right has a buffer that can hold two
packets. The virtual-circuits use the selective repeat protocol with window size 2. A deadlock occurs when the second node must store one out-
of-order packet for each virtual-circuit.

6.4 Network Design

This section reviews methods that network engineers use to design or
to improve store-and-forward communication networks. We will show how the
network engineers select the numbers and the locations of communication nodes
and the rates of the transmission links between these nodes. The objective of the
network designer is to achieve the design objectives at the minimum cost.

The utilization of most wide area networks increases at a fast and
largely unpredictable rate. Users develop new applications when networks become available. Consequently, networks have to be upgraded constantly. Periodically, a new network is proposed to take advantage of new technological developments. When designing such a new network, the engineers attempt to estimate the
data traffic that the network will carry and they select performance objectives,
such as packet delay and network reliability. The engineers then set out to find the
least expensive design that meets their specifications.

A communication network usually consists of a high throughput *backbone network* to which users are connected via a *local access* network. (See
Figure 6.24.) The local access network consists of *concentrators* to which the
nodes of the users are attached. A node may be a mainframe computer that serves
a large number of terminals, as shown in Figure 6.24. It may also be a gateway
that connects a local network to the wide area network.

The network design problem is as follows:

Given:

1. the end users (locations and traffic requirements)
2. the possible locations of nodes

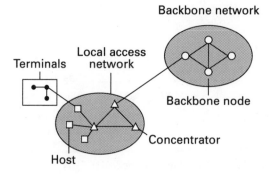

Figure 6.24 Structure of the network.

The network comprises a high speed *backbone* network that intercon-nects clusters of nodes. The nodes in a cluster are attached to a back-bone node via nodes connected to *concentrators*.

3. the possible locations of concentrators

4. the cost of links (function of length, capacity)

5. the cost of concentrators

6. acceptable reliability

7. acceptable delays and throughput

Find:

1. the topology of the backbone

2. the traffic allocation

3. the capacity assignment

4. the local access network

5. the terminal layout

As we stated earlier, the end users and their traffic requirements are never known accurately at the start of the network design process. The network engineers esti-mate these requirements from past statistics and from the observed growth of the demand. The network engineers select a number of candidate locations for the communication nodes and concentrators. For instance, if the network is to be used by universities and research institutions, the candidate locations will be institu-tions that have expressed the willingness to donate adequate space and mainte-nance effort for the network. Most networks lease communication links from telephone and satellite communication companies. The cost of the link, as a func-tion of the length and of the bit rate, is specified by the tariff of the company. The engineers know the cost of concentrators and of gateways. The needed reliability and the acceptable delays depend on the applications that will be used on the network.

Let us consider the problem of designing a new network that will connect N users situated throughout the United States. N is a very large number, of the order of thousands or tens of thousands. The first step is to design the *topology*, i.e., the graph of the interconnections. The number of graphs with N nodes is approximately equal to 2^K where

$$K = \frac{1}{2}N(N-1).$$

We derive this estimate for the number of graphs by noting that there can be up to K links joining N nodes since it takes K links to connect every one of the N nodes to each of the $N-1$ other nodes. The factor $1/2$ in the expression for K is needed when we do not want to distinguish a link from node A to node B from a link from node B to node A. These links should not be distinguished if the communications are duplex, and they usually are as we saw in Chapter 4. A given subset of the K links specifies a graph. If we do not correct for the fact that not all subsets form graphs that connect all the N nodes, we conclude that the number of graphs is the number of subsets of the K links. To find this number of subsets, we note that one subset is obtained by specifying for each link whether it is in the subset or not. Since there are two possible choices for each of the K links, we find that the number of subsets is equal to 2^K. For instance, if $N = 12$, then the number of graphs that could be considered is $2^{12\times11/2} = 2^{66} \approx 10^{20}$. Assuming that we can evaluate one graph every 10^{-8} second, we would need about 10^{12} seconds, i.e., more than 31,000 years, to select the best topology.

The above calculation demonstrates that we cannot consider all the possible topologies and that suboptimal procedures are needed. A first simplification of the topology selection problem consists of clustering the users according to their geographic locations. This clustering leads to considering a *backbone* network to interconnect clusters of users. Usually, the backbone will have a small number of nodes. The possible nodes will be the major metropolitan areas of the country. For instance, ARPANET connected thousands of users, but its backbone had a small number of links. (See Figure 4.38.)

The first step in the design of the network is, therefore, to identify a small set of possible nodes for a backbone network.

The next step is to select a topology for the backbone. For reliability, it is best to require that at least two disjoint paths connect any two nodes of the backbone. We can verify that a given topology satisfies that requirement by using one of a number of algorithms. We can also estimate the reliability of a proposed topology by simulating the possible link failures and by measuring the times when nodes are disconnected by such failures.

After having selected a topology for the backbone, we can choose the routing of the traffic and the capacity of the links. We described these two problems in Section 6.3 using simple examples. Let's review the procedure that we can follow for selecting the routing and the link capacities. First, we can decide to route the packets along the shortest path to their destinations, defining the length of a path as the number of nodes through which it travels. From this selection of the paths, we determine the rate of traffic over all the links. We then formulate the capacity assignment problem as the minimization of the average delay per packet subject to an upper bound on the cost. Using these link capacities, we reformulate the routing selection as the choice of routing probabilities that minimize the average delay per packet. With these new routing probabilities, we solve the capacity assignment problem. We then use the new capacities to solve the routing problem, and we keep iterating between the capacity assignment and the routing problems until we do not notice further significant improvement in the average delay.

The previous steps result in an average delay per packet that is a minimum for the topology that we selected for the backbone. We can go back to select another topology and repeat the procedure until no further improvement appears likely. At this stage, we have completed the selection of the topology, routing, and link capacities for the backbone network.

We now turn to the design of the connection of the nodes and gateways to the backbone network by concentrators. One possible formulation of the problem is as follows. (See Figure 6.25.) Designate a possible concentrator location by j and a typical host by i. Denote by f_j the cost of a concentrator at j and by c_{ij} the cost of a connection between i and j. The problem is to minimize the cost C expressed as follows:

$$C = \sum_i \sum_j x_{ij} c_{ij} + \sum_j y_j f_j$$

over the variables x_{ij} and y_j that take values in $\{0, 1\}$. The interpretations are that $y_j = 1$ if there is a concentrator at location j and is equal to 0 otherwise, and that $x_{ij} = 1$ if there is a connection between host i and location j and is equal to 0 otherwise.

We want the variables x_{ij} and y_j to be such that

$$\sum_i x_{ij} \le K_j y_j \text{ for all } j$$

$$\sum_j x_{ij} = 1 \text{ for all } i.$$

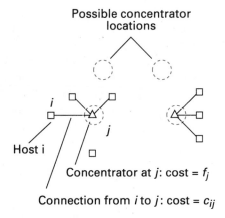

Possible concentrator
locations

Host i

Concentrator at j: cost = f_j

Connection from i to j: cost = c_{ij}

Figure 6.25 Local access network.

Nodes are connected to concentrators. The concentrators are connected
to the backbone network. By buying more concentrators, the network
designer can reduce the cost of connecting the nodes to these concentrators. The local access design problem is to find the best compromise
between buying more concentrators and making more expensive connections to fewer concentrators.

The first inequality expresses that at most K_j sources can be connected to concentrator j, and the second inequality guarantees that every host is connected to a
concentrator.

This minimization problem is an *integer programming problem*
because the optimization variables are integers. Integer programming problems
are known to be computationally hard, and clever heuristics are necessary to
obtain satisfactory solutions with a reasonable amount of computing resources.
The *drop heuristic* is one such heuristic. At each step, the drop heuristic identifies
the concentrator whose removal reduces the cost C by the largest amount. It then
drops that concentrator from further consideration. The algorithm stops when no
reduction in the cost can be found by dropping one more concentrator.

Note that this algorithm may fail to produce the optimal local access
network. Indeed, a design with $N - 2$ concentrators may be less expensive than all
the designs with N concentrators even when the least expensive design with $N - 1$
concentrators is more expensive than that with N concentrators. In such a situation, the drop heuristic would stop at the first step and would declare the least
expensive design with N concentrators the winner, without exploring designs with
$N - 2$ concentrators. It may also be that the first two concentrators removed by
the drop heuristic are not those that are not used in the least expensive design
with $N - 2$ concentrators. Nevertheless, the drop heuristic is widely used, and

experience has shown that it results in satisfactory designs. Let's estimate the reduction in complexity achieved by the drop heuristic. First, we count the number of design problems that the heuristic has to solve in the worst case. The drop heuristic first solves the optimal design problem for N concentrators. It then solves N design problems with $N-1$ concentrators to determine which concentrator should be removed. The heuristic then solves $N-1$ design problems with $N-2$ concentrators, and so on. If we denote the cost of solving an optimal design problem with n concentrators by $J(n)$, then we find that the worst case cost of the drop heuristic is equal to

$$J(N) + N \times J(N-1) + (N-1) \times J(N-2) + \ldots + 2 \times J(1) .$$

The optimization algorithm, without the drop heuristic, must solve the optimal design problem with N concentrators, then N optimal design problems with $N-1$ concentrators. The algorithm must then solve

$$\binom{N}{2} := \frac{N \times (N-1)}{2}$$

design problems with $N-2$ concentrators, since there are

$$\binom{N}{2}$$

ways of selecting two concentrators among N and each of these selections yields a set of $N-2$ concentrators for which the algorithm must find the optimal design. Continuing in this way, we find that the cost of the optimization problem is equal to

$$J(N) + N \times J(N-1) + \binom{N}{2} \times J(N-2) + \binom{N}{3} \times J(N-3) + \ldots + \binom{N}{2} \times J(2) + N \times J(1) .$$

You can see the reduction in cost achieved by the drop heuristic by comparing this expression with the worst case cost of the heuristic.

Assume that the local access network has been designed. We must now design the layout of the connections of the terminals. Thus, given the locations of the hosts and the locations of the terminals, we must find the least expensive layout of the cables to interconnect the terminals to the hosts. The optimal layout depends on the specifics of the hardware. As an example, let us assume that a single cable can be used to connect an arbitrary number of terminals and that the objective is to minimize the total length of cable being used. Equivalently, assume that the cost of installing the cables is much higher than the cost of the cables themselves. The following algorithm, called *Dijkstra's algorithm*, solves the problem:

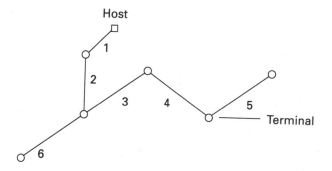

Figure 6.26 Dijkstra's algorithm.

This algorithm determines the connections of a set of terminals to a host that use the smallest total length of wire. At each step, the algorithm connects the closest terminal to the tree of terminals already connected. The algorithm creates the links in the order indicated by the numbers.

1. Find the closest terminal to the host, then connect it.
2. Find the closest terminal to the partial tree produced so far.
3. Repeat step 2 until all the terminals are connected.

This algorithm is illustrated in Figure 6.26. To see why Dijkstra's algorithm requires the smallest total length of wire to connect all the terminals to the host, we can argue that at step n the algorithm has found how to connect n terminals to the host with the minimum length of wires. The details are suggested in Problem 6.8.

6.5 Examples of the Network Layer

In this section we discuss the network layers of ARPANET, SNA, X.25, and Internet.

Network Layer in ARPANET

In 1969, the original *routing* algorithm of ARPANET used the distributed Bellman-Ford algorithm. The algorithm was implemented by having the nodes exchange their minimum delay estimates with their neighbors every 625 ms. The algorithm exhibited oscillations similar to those that we observed in the network shown in Figure 6.10. In 1979, the ARPANET engineers decided to replace the routing algorithm with the centralized Bellman-Ford algorithm. The nodes send their link delays to each other by flooding every 60 seconds. Each node can then run the algorithm to determine the paths with minimum delay to the destinations.

296

The *congestion control* in ARPANET uses end-to-end windows. The initial algorithm accepted up to eight outstanding packets for each source/destination pair. A message consists of between one and eight packets. When the destination received a complete message, it sent a *ready-for-next-message* control packet to the source. This flow control algorithm was modified to accept up to 256 connections between two hosts, with independent windows of size up to 127 for each connection. In this algorithm, the destination packet-switch node reserves needed buffer space when it gets the first packet. If the buffer space is not available, then the packet is discarded. The source retransmits that packet after a timeout, and the connection is eventually set up.

Network Layer in SNA

The *path control* in SNA (see Section 4.6) is comparable to the network layer in the OSI model. The path control supervises the *routing* and the *congestion control*. It also takes care of some OSI transport and session layer functions. In SNA, the network manager can define up to eight paths for any source/destination pair. The network manager specifies these paths in node routing tables. The tables indicate the next node for each path number. The manager updates these tables by sending special control packets to the nodes when the network is modified. When a source establishes a conversation, called a *session* by SNA, it selects a specific path by using information that it has about the status and the load of the network. This information is transmitted to the hosts by control packets. The path is called *virtual route* by SNA.

Congestion control is implemented for each virtual route as follows. When a virtual route is first set up, the destination replies to the source by permitting it to transmit N packets. Typically, N is equal to the number of links along the route. The first packet usually contains a request to be allowed to transmit another set of n packets. The destination verifies that it has enough buffers and replies to the request with an authorization to send $\min\{n, N\}$ packets. The number N of permits is modified to make the flow control responsive to the traffic conditions inside the network. Each packet contains a *congestion field* of 2 bits initially set to 00 by the source. Whenever the packet goes through a heavily congested node, the node sets the congestion field to 11. When the packets goes through a moderately congested node, the node sets the first bit in the congestion field to 1. When a packet reaches the destination with the congestion field equal to 00, the number N is increased by one, up to a maximum value chosen by the network manager. When a packet arrives with the congestion field equal to 10, the number N is decreased by one, down to a minimum value also chosen by the network manager. When a packet arrives with the congestion field equal to 11, N is set to the minimum value.

Network Layer in X.25

We described X.25 and its data link layer in Section 4.6. X.25 uses *virtual-circuit* transport, with up to 4,096 virtual-circuits on any given physical channel. In the X.25 terminology, a user host is called a DTE (data terminal equipment), a PSN attached to a user host is called a DCE (data communication equipment), and the other PSNs are called DSE (data switching equipment).

Three transport mechanisms are supported by X.25:

1. Permanent virtual-circuit
2. Virtual call
3. Fast select call

A *permanent virtual-circuit* is a virtual-circuit that is always set up. Transmissions can take place between DTEs connected by a permanent virtual-circuit without initialization. This is similar to a leased line, except that the virtual-circuit shares transmission resources with other connections.

A *virtual call* is a standard virtual-circuit connection that we described in Section 6.2. To set up a virtual call, the initiating DTE sends a request packet. The answering DTE confirms to the initiating DTE that the virtual call is set up with a special *call accepted* packet.

The *fast select call* is intended for short data transmissions. The call request packet can contain up to 128 bytes of data, and it indicates whether the *call accepted* packet, which can also contain up to 128 bytes of data, must contain a clear request or a call accepted message. If it contains a clear request, then the initiating DTE answers with a clear confirmation packet and the connection is dismantled. If it contains a call accepted message, then the virtual-circuit connection continues until it is cleared.

We saw in Section 4.8 that X.25 uses GO BACK N at the link layer. In addition, a congestion control mechanism is also implemented at the network layer. It is an end-to-end window flow control for each virtual-circuit. The standard window size is equal to 2, but the DTEs can also negotiate different values.

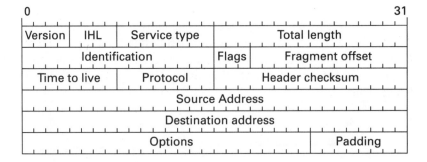

Figure 6.27 IP header.

The IP header has 28 bytes. The information in the header is explained in the text.

Network Layer in Internet

The *Internet protocol* (IP) provides the basis for the interconnections of the *Internet*, which consists of ARPANET, MILnet, NSFnet, the NASA Science Internet (NSI), SATNET, and over 700 other networks, including many university networks. These networks differ widely in size, from a few hosts to thousands, from less than a mile to thousands of miles. The link rates go from 56 kbps for ARPANET to 3 Mbps for some satellite links of the ARPA wideband network. The packet sizes range from 256 bytes for SATNET to a few thousand bytes for LANs.

IP is a datagram protocol. The packets contain an *IP header*. The basic header, without options, is illustrated in Figure 6.27 where each tick indicates a bit position.

The *version* field allows new versions of the IP protocol to be installed while the network is operational. The *Internet header length* (IHL) tells how long the header is on that packet. The *type of service* field indicates the quality of service desired (e.g., low delay, high throughput, high reliability). *Identification, flags,* and *fragment offset* allow reassembly of fragmented datagrams. The *time to live* field indicates how long this packet can remain in the network. It is decremented at each hop, and the packet is discarded when this field reaches zero. The *protocol* field indicates what higher level protocol is contained in the data portion of the IP packet. The *header checksum* is a checksum of the bytes in the IP header only. Higher level protocols must be concerned with error checking of their data. The *source* and *destination* Internet addresses indicate the sending host and the intended recipient host for this datagram.

The Internet addresses have the form "network.host." For instance, the address of the network U.C. Berkeley is 128.32, which corresponds to two successive 8-bit words with decimal values 128 and 32 (thus, 1000'0000'0010' 0000). Similarly, the address of the ARPANET network is 10, and that of U.C. Riverside is 192.31.146. The rule is that small networks have large addresses, since fewer bits are needed to discriminate the few hosts on such networks, while large networks have small addresses; the balance of the address bits are used for the host address. There are three classes of networks: large, or class A (network address = 8 bits, host address on network = 24 bits), medium, or class B (16, 16), and small, or class C (24, 8).

A symbolic address, or *name*, of the form *user@domain* can be used instead of the Internet address. It is translated into the Internet address by directory tables that are organized along the same hierarchy as the addressing. For instance, each host knows the network addresses of the computers connected on the same LAN. Each also knows how to reach the gateways to other networks, or one computer with that information. Typically, the *domain* is of the form *machine.institution.type.country*. The *type* is EDU for educational institutions, COM for companies, GOV for governmental agencies, ORG for nonprofit organizations, and MIL for military installations. The *country* field is omitted for the United States and is a two-letter country code for the other countries (e.g., *fr* for France). For instance, the author's address is *walrand@janus.berkeley.edu*. The *machine* may be further specified as *computer.department*.

A special protocol, the *Internet control message protocol* (ICMP), was designed to take care of packet delivery problems that arise when links or stations are down. The protocol operates by sending ICMP messages to report delivery errors, such as unreachable destinations, delivery rate too high, and changes in interconnections. These messages are then used by the Internet software.

Summary

- The network layer supervises *naming*, *addressing*, *routing*, and *congestion control*.
- Nodes have names, and their network connections have network and physical addresses.
- Nodes use a directory service to translate the name into a network address. The address resolution protocol performs the translation of the network address into the physical address for hosts attached to a common LAN. Nodes on different LANs use source routing or transparent routing.

■ The network engineer can select the routing probabilities for static routing by solving the routing optimization problem. A related problem is the capacity assignment problem.

■ The Bellman-Ford algorithm determines the fastest paths to the destinations. A distributed version of the algorithm reacts slowly to failures but speeds up when it uses the hold down variation.

■ Window flow control is a widely used congestion control procedure, either at the link level or at the network level. Deadlocks are prevented by preallocations of buffers.

■ A network can be designed or improved by choosing a backbone, a local access network, and the terminal layout. A number of heuristics reduce the complexity of the design procedure.

■ ARPANET used the Bellman-Ford routing algorithm and end-to-end windows.

■ In SNA, a source selects a virtual route among those defined by the network manager. A window flow control is used on each virtual route, with a window size adapted to the observed congestion.

■ The X.25 network layer uses virtual-circuit transport with an end-to-end window flow control on each virtual-circuit.

■ The Internet network layer protocol, IP, uses datagram transport. The routing is hierarchical.

Problems

1. Which of the following is an advantage of static routing?
   a. All the packets follow the same path.
   b. The packet travel time is minimized.
   c. The routing is easily implemented.
2. Name three methods for controlling congestion in packet-switched networks.
3. Name two routing algorithms.
4. Consider two transmitters in series equipped with a buffer. The traffic rate through the first transmitter is one packet per second. These packets then go through the second transmitter, as do other packets arriving with the rate of two packets per second. Making the assumption that the delay is given by formula (6.1), find the transmission rates μ_1 and

μ_2 that minimize the average delay through the network subject to $\mu_1 + \mu_2 \le 10$ packets per second.

5. A collection of nodes are interconnected as a mesh network by duplex links. We want to design a *spanning tree algorithm*. That is, we want to design an algorithm that the nodes can execute to construct a tree-like graph that goes through all the nodes exactly once. Propose such an algorithm by finding for each node the path with the minimum number of links to an arbitrarily chosen destination.

6. Describe the sequence of steps of the routing algorithm for Figure 6.10 when the routing fractions can change by at most 0.1 in each step.

*7. This problem will justify Lagrange's multipliers method in a simple case. We want to minimize $f(x, y) = (x - 1)^{-1} + 3 \times (y - 3)^{-1}$ subject to $c(x, y) := x^2 + y^2 \le 15$. The claim is that when (x, y) solve that problem, then

$$\frac{\partial}{\partial x}[f(x, y) - \lambda c(x, y)] = 0 = \frac{\partial}{\partial y}[f(x, y) - \lambda c(x, y)]$$

for some λ. Let us explain an interpretation of this result. Think of x and y as the amounts of two resources, say gold and silver. The function $c(x, y)$ represents the cost of buying x units of gold and y units of silver. The function $f(x, y)$ measures the reward derived from such a purchase. Our total budget is 15. If (x, y) is the purchase that maximizes $f(x, y)$ given our budget, it must be that one cannot increase the reward f by buying ε dollars' worth of more gold and ε dollars' worth less of silver. Buying $\alpha \ll 1$ more units of gold would cost an additional

$$\frac{\sigma}{\sigma x} c(x, y) \alpha$$

dollars and would increase $f(x, y)$ by

$$\frac{\sigma}{\sigma x} f(x, y) \alpha.$$

Thus, ε dollars' worth more gold would buy

$$\alpha := \frac{\varepsilon}{\left[\dfrac{\partial}{\partial x} c(x, y) \alpha\right]}$$

more units of gold and would increase $f(x, y)$ by

$$\frac{\varepsilon}{\left[\dfrac{\partial}{\partial x}\, c(x, y)\right]} \times \frac{\partial}{\partial x} f(x, y).$$

Similarly, buying ε dollars' worth less of silver would decrease $f(x, y)$ by

$$\frac{\varepsilon}{\left[\dfrac{\partial}{\partial y}\, c(x, y)\right]} \times \frac{\partial}{\partial y} f(x, y).$$

As we stated before, the above two expressions must be equal when (x, y) is optimal. Denoting by $\varepsilon\lambda$ this common value yields the optimality equations that we wanted to prove. Use these equations to solve the problem.

*8. Prove that Dijkstra's algorithm yields the shortest spanning tree for connecting terminals to a given host. (*Hint:* Assume that at step $n + 1$, the algorithm does not provide the connections of $n + 1$ terminals to the host with the shortest total length of wire whereas at step n it provides the connection of n terminals to the host with the smallest total length of wire. Derive a contradiction.)

9. Propose a simple algorithm for recovering a spanning tree after a link failure. The algorithm starts when a node finds that its outgoing link along the spanning tree fails. That node sends messages to its neighbors. Provide the details.

*10. Show that the Bellman-Ford algorithm $x_{n+1} = F(x_n)$ converges also to the desired values when $x_0 = (0, 0, ..., 0)$. Conclude that the algorithm converges to the desired values when x_0 is an arbitrary nonnegative number. (*Hint:* The sequence must be nondecreasing. For the second part, note that a nonnegative vector x_0 must be between $(0, 0, ..., 0)$ and $(\infty, \infty, ..., \infty)$ and that the resulting sequence must be between the convergent sequences corresponding to these two initial conditions.)

11. Exhibit a simple example of the layout problem in which the drop heuristic does not construct the best layout.

*12. Consider the network in Figure 6.14 and assume that $\gamma_B = 0$ and $\mu_3 = \infty$. We want to solve the joint routing and capacity assignment problem for this network. That is, we want to find the fraction p and the values of μ_1 and μ_2 that minimize the average delay per packet through the network, subject to $\mu_1 + \mu_2 \leq M$. Propose an algorithm to solve this problem.

*13. We have seen that when the set of N nodes is decomposed into k domains with N/k nodes each, each node needs a routing table with size $k - 1 + (N/k) - 1$. What is the value of k that minimizes this expression? Show that the sum of the sizes of all the routing tables cannot be reduced by choosing domains with different sizes. Formulate the problem with a hierarchical decomposition with n levels; that is, the nodes grouped into domains of level 1 grouped into domains of level 2, and so on. Find the value of n that minimizes the sum of the sizes of all the node routing tables.

14. Consider the network of Figure 6.14. Assume that p has the value that minimizes the average delay per packet. Show that the average delay through the links 1 and 2 are not equal.

*15. Consider the network in Figure 6.14. We want to explore the effect of a routing algorithm based on measured average delays. We assume that p changes slowly enough that the transmitters at the links 1 and 2 can estimate their average delays D_1 and D_2. We want to propose an algorithm of the form

$$\frac{d}{dt} p = \alpha D_1 + \beta D_2$$

where we must select α and β. Exhibit a choice of α and β such that p converges to the value that minimizes the average delay per packet. Discuss the possibility of implementing such an algorithm.

References

The books Bertsekas (1987) and Schwartz (1987) are good sources for more advanced discussions of routing and flow control. Comer (1988) and Stevens (1990) provide commentaries on the implementations of TCP/IP. Chapter 5 in Tanenbaum (1988) contains an informative discussion of interconnecting networks; our discussion of network design borrows from that chapter.

Bertsekas (1987). Bertsekas, D., and Gallager, R., *Data Networks.* Prentice-Hall, 1987.

Schwartz (1987). Schwartz, M., *Telecommunications Networks: Protocols, Modeling and Analysis.* Addison-Wesley, 1987.

Comer (1988). Comer, D., *Internetworking with TCP/IP: Principles, Protocols, and Architecture.* Prentice-Hall, 1988.

Stevens (1990). Stevens, W. R., *Unix Network Programming.* Prentice-Hall, 1990.

Tanenbaum (1988). Tanenbaum, A., *Computer Networks* (2nd Ed.). Prentice-Hall, 1988.

Transport, Session, and Presentation

7

So far, we have learned that the network layer transmits packets between terminal nodes. The packets are transported either as datagrams or as virtual-circuits, and the transmission is either connectionless or connection-oriented. The user applications require end-to-end transmissions of data with a specific quality of service and local syntax. The local syntax specifies the representation of the data used by the application. Different application programs and different computers use different data representations, i.e., different syntaxes. For example, some computers order the bytes in their words with the most significant byte to the right, while others adopt the opposite convention. Thus, the end-to-end packet transmissions are used to implement end-to-end transmissions with specific quality of service (see Chapter 2) and local syntax. The set of tasks required for this implementation is divided into three layers in the OSI model: transport, session, and presentation. Figure 7.1 shows this layer decomposition.

The transport and session layers work together to supervise the end-to-end delivery of data. Figure 7.2 shows some of the communications between the top OSI layers. The figure also shows some examples of these layers and their main functions. In this chapter we will explain the functions performed by the transport, session, and presentation layers. We will illustrate that discussion with TCP, UDP, and TP4.

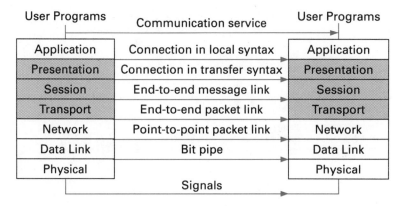

Figure 7.1 The OSI layers.

The network layer provides end-to-end transmissions of packets, either on virtual-circuits (VC) or as datagrams (D). The transport, session, and presentation layers convert these packet transmissions into end-to-end transmissions of data with specific quality of service and syntax.

Section 7.1 discusses a typical scenario and introduces the functions of the transport and session layers. Section 7.2 explains the transport layer. The protocols *TCP*, *UDP*, and *TP4* are examples of transport layer protocols discussed in Section 7.3. Section 7.4 is devoted to the session layer. The functions of the presentation layer include *encryption*, *data compression*, and *syntax conversion*. Encryption makes the information coming from the application layer unintelligible to eavesdroppers. The main ideas of encryption systems are covered in Section 7.5. The concepts of *public key cryptography* and *zero knowledge proof* are explained in Section 7.6. *Data compression* is used to reduce the number of bits that have to be transmitted, so as to limit the communication costs. Some basic principles and examples of data compression are given in Section 7.7. Section 7.8 explains the syntax conversion standards recommended by ISO.

7.1 Sessions

Consider the communication between two hosts. Each host generally has a number of *processes* that are active, i.e., programs that are being executed. For instance, one process may be a "talk" program and another may be a complex distributed data base manipulation. The processes exchange *messages* or *byte streams* with other processes in other hosts.

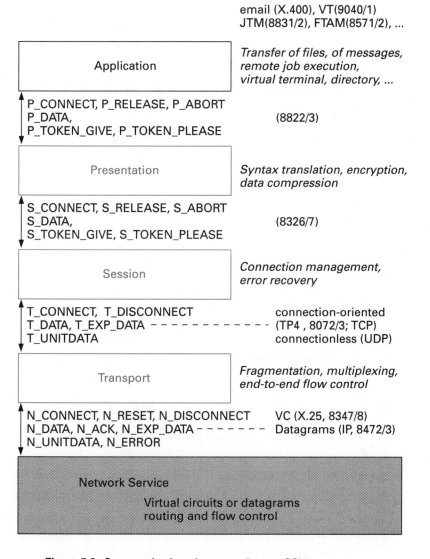

email (X.400), VT(9040/1)
JTM(8831/2), FTAM(8571/2), ...

Application

Transfer of files, of messages, remote job execution, virtual terminal, directory, ...

P_CONNECT, P_RELEASE, P_ABORT
P_DATA,
P_TOKEN_GIVE, P_TOKEN_PLEASE

(8822/3)

Presentation

Syntax translation, encryption, data compression

S_CONNECT, S_RELEASE, S_ABORT
S_DATA,
S_TOKEN_GIVE, S_TOKEN_PLEASE

(8326/7)

Session

Connection management, error recovery

T_CONNECT, T_DISCONNECT
T_DATA, T_EXP_DATA − − − − − − − − − − − −
T_UNITDATA

connection-oriented
(TP4 , 8072/3; TCP)
connectionless (UDP)

Transport

Fragmentation, multiplexing, end-to-end flow control

N_CONNECT, N_RESET, N_DISCONNECT
N_DATA, N_ACK, N_EXP_DATA − − − − − −
N_UNITDATA, N_ERROR

VC (X.25, 8347/8)
Datagrams (IP, 8472/3)

Network Service

Virtual circuits or datagrams routing and flow control

Figure 7.2 Communications between the top OSI layers.

The figure shows the four OSI layers on top of the network layer. The main functions of these four layers are indicated in italics. The numbers, such as 8822, 8823, and 8073, designate OSI protocols. Acronyms, such as TCP, UDP, and FTAM, designate specific protocols that are discussed in the text. The communications between layers are performed through service primitives that are also explained in the text.

Messages are blocks of data with specific boundaries. Streams are sequences of bytes that follow one another without intervening boundaries. For instance, a word processing application on a computer can transmit a text file as a byte stream to another word processing application on a different host. The application process can insert control characters that represent message boundaries in a byte stream, when such boundaries are required. The exchange of messages between processes follows rules that depend on the specific operating system of the computers. For instance, in UNIX computers, this communication is through *pipes*, *FIFOs*, *message queues*, *sockets*, or the *transport layer interface*. These different message exchange mechanisms differ in implementation details, but they are all methods that processes can use to store messages until they are read by another process.

The communication between processes in the application layer is through the presentation layer, which formats, encodes, encrypts, and compresses the data. The session and transport layers supervise the transmission of the data. A typical scenario is as follows:

1. The presentation layer asks the session layer to set up a call; it specifies the destination's name and the type of transmission (e.g., datagram, high priority); the presentation layer translates between the local syntax used by the application process and the transfer syntax; the presentation layer also performs the required encryption and data compression.

2. The session layer sets up the call and takes care of the authentication of the user and of billing; also, the session layer supervises the synchronization (packet numbering) and the recovery in case of failures; the session layer closes the session at the end of the transmission.

3. The transport layer breaks up the messages into packets of acceptable sizes and does the reassembly at the destination; it may multiplex many low-rate transmissions onto one virtual-circuit or divide a high-rate transmission into parallel virtual-circuits; the transport layer controls transmission errors and requests retransmissions of packets corrupted by transmission errors; in addition, the flow may be controlled by some end-to-end window mechanism to prevent one host from sending data faster than the destination host can handle them.

Sessions

- Application processes exchange *messages* or *byte streams* in a specific *local syntax*.
- The presentation layer performs the syntax conversion, data encryption, and data compression.
- The session layer sets up the call and supervises the transfer of data.
- The transport layer performs the fragmentation of messages into packets and the reassembly of packets into messages. That layer also controls the flow of packets and requests retransmissions of corrupted packets. The transport layer multiplexes data streams.

7.2 Transport Layer

As shown in Figure 7.1, the transport layer converts the end-to-end packet transmissions provided by the network layer into an end-to-end message link. That message link is either connectionless or connection-oriented.

An example of the communication service implemented by the transport layer is the connection-oriented service provided by the transport layer in a network with a datagram network layer, such as the *Internet protocol* (IP). Some functions of the transport layer are indicated in Figure 7.2. They include the *fragmentation* of messages into packets, *resequencing*, *flow control*, and *multiplexing*.

Figure 7.2 shows the service primitives of the network layer that are used by the transport layer. When the network layer provides datagram transport, the transport layer asks for the transmission of one unit of data (a packet) by *N_UNITDATA* service primitives. The communication between the layers is through the *request*, *confirm*, and *indication* primitives of *N_UNITDATA*, as shown in Figure 2.23. The *N_ERROR* primitives indicate network failures. For instance, when an Ethernet LLC is unable to deliver packets after repeated collisions (more than 16), the network layer informs the transport layer of this failure by means of an *N_ERROR.indication*. A virtual-circuit network layer offers the service primitives shown in Figure 7.2. A virtual-circuit is first set up with the *N_CONNECT* primitive. The packets are exchanged with the *N_DATA* or the *N_EXP_DATA* primitives. The network layer indicates errors in the transmission that require restarting the data exchange with an *N_RESET*. The virtual-circuit is released with an *N_DISCONNECT*.

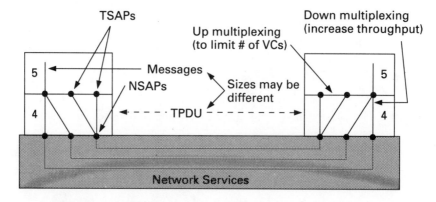

Figure 7.3 Multiplexing at the transport layer.

The figure shows two terminal nodes. The lines represent flows of messages or packets. The flows are distinguished in each terminal node by service access points. These access points are specified at the boundaries between layers. The access points between the session and transport layers are called transport service access points (TSAPs). Between the transport and network layers, the access points are network service access points (NSAPs). The transport layer can perform two types of multiplexing: down multiplexing, which divides a packet flow into different flows, and up multiplexing, which groups different flows into one.

We saw in Chapter 2 that the communication service provided by the network can be connection-oriented or connectionless regardless of whether the transport is by datagrams or virtual-circuits. In terms of the OSI layers, this translates into the transport layer providing connection-oriented or connectionless services on top of a datagram or a virtual-circuit network. Connectionless services are rarely implemented over virtual-circuit network layers, however. As Figure 7.2 shows, the transport service primitive for connectionless services is *T_UNIT-DATA*. This primitive is used to request the end-to-end delivery of a message. A connection-oriented communication service proceeds in three phases: establishing the connection (*T_CONNECT*), exchanging data (*T_DATA* or *T_EXP_DATA*), and releasing the connection (*T_DISCONNECT*).

Figure 7.3 illustrates the *multiplexing* function of the transport layer. The lines represent flows of messages between *transport service access points* (TSAPs). These flows can be divided or grouped into flows of packets by the transport layer. A flow of messages is divided into different packet flows when different transport channels are used to increase the throughput. For instance, the messages between two TSAPs can be transported over the two rings in an FDDI network. Different flows of messages can be grouped into a single virtual-circuit to reduce the number of such circuits and the size of routing tables required in the network nodes.

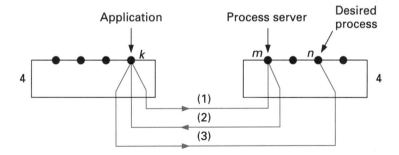

Figure 7.4 Connection to a process with an unknown TSAP.

To connect to a process with an unknown TSAP or to a process which may not be running, the transport layer first connects to a *process server* on a well-known TSAP*m* and requests the desired process (1). The process server creates the desired process, attaches it to some *ephemeral* TSAP*n*, and informs the calling node (2). The transport layer then connects the calling process to the desired remote process (3).

Three problems arise when the transport layer needs to establish a connection. The first problem is to find the TSAP of the process with which the connection must be set up. The second problem is to prevent the nodes from being confused by delayed packets that may reach them at random times. The third problem is to have the nodes agree on the parameters of the connection, such as the initial sequence number and quality of service parameters. We discuss these three problems next.

Consider the situation when an application process wants to establish a connection with a process in another node. If the remote process has a known TSAP number, the calling node establishes the connection to that TSAP. Some frequently used processes have reserved TSAP numbers called *well-known ports*. For instance, the *file transfer protocol* (FTP) uses port 21 of the transport layer protocol TCP (*transmission control protocol*). The *trivial file transfer protocol* (TFTP) uses port 69 of the transport layer protocol UDP (*user datagram protocol*). If the calling process does not know the TSAP of the remote process, or if that remote process needs to be created, some additional steps must be taken. These steps are illustrated in Figure 7.4. The connection to a remote process with an unknown TSAP or to a remote process that may not be running is done with the help of a process server with a well-known TSAP*m*, as shown in (1) of Figure 7.4. The process server creates the desired process, if needed, and attaches it to TSAP*n*. This TSAP is said to be *ephemeral* because it is released when the process terminates. The process server then informs the calling node that the desired process is attached to TSAP*n* ((2) of Figure 7.4). The calling node then establishes the connection to TSAP*n*. Note that the figure assumes that the network

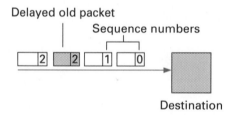

Figure 7.5 Delayed packets arriving at a terminal node.

The figure shows packets that arrive at a node. Some of the packets belong to a new connection, whereas others are delayed packets from a previous connection. These packets may be duplicates transmitted by communication nodes after a timeout.

address of the remote node is known. If it is not, that address can be requested from a name server, as we saw in Chapter 6.

The second problem, preventing terminal nodes from being confused by delayed packets, is illustrated in Figure 7.5. A difficulty may arise when old packets floating around the network show up at a terminal node with sequence numbers that make that node interpret these packets as belonging to a current session. For instance, say that the packets with numbers {0, 1, 2, 3} correspond to a new connection. If a retransmitted copy of a packet from a previous connection with number 2 shows up at the destination, the latter thinks that the packet belongs to the new connection. A number of solutions are possible to prevent possible confusion. We will describe one solution in which the network limits the lifetime of packets to prevent old packets from arbitrarily showing up. Each node decrements a *time-to-live* field in each packet by 1 unit, and the node discards a packet when its time-to-live reaches zero. Since nodes hold packets for some finite time, this procedure limits the time that a packet can spend in the network.

Thus, assume that each packet lives for at most T time units in the network. When a host resumes a transmission upon recovering from a crash, it can avoid confusing its destination with copies of old packets by waiting for T time units before starting the transmission. This guarantees that all the old copies of packets are discarded from the network.

The third problem, agreeing on the connection parameters, can be solved by a procedure called the *three-way handshake*. We illustrate this procedure by showing how it can be used by two hosts to agree on the first number of the packets that compose a message. Assume that host A wants to send a message to host B. Confusion is possible because of old session initialization packets that might be in the network. Suppose that host A wants to start transmitting a packet numbered m. An old packet may arrive at the destination indicating an initial packet number $n \neq m$ for the session. The three-way handshake goes as indicated

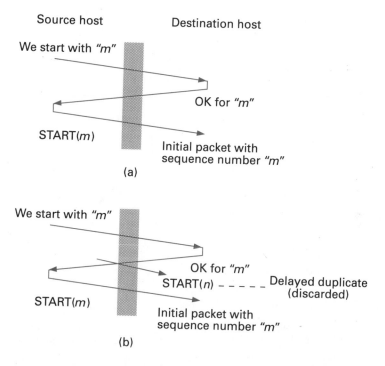

Figure 7.6 Three-way handshake.

Part (a) shows two hosts that agree on an initial number m. Part (b) shows how the protocol reacts when an old packet shows up at the destination node with a different initial sequence number.

in Figure 7.6. The figure shows how the three-way handshake guarantees that the hosts agree on the initial sequence number and, more generally, on the parameters of the connection. Figure 7.6(a) shows the normal exchange of messages: The source host sends a message to the destination host to indicate that the initial sequence number will be m. The destination host acknowledges that message. The data exchange starts when the source host gets the acknowledgement. Figure 7.6(b) shows the sequence of events when a delayed packet shows up at the destination host with initial sequence number n after the source host has requested the initial sequence number m. That delayed packet with initial sequence number n is discarded. Note that errors are possible even with a three-way handshake. For instance, if the delayed packet had the sequence number m, then the destination host would assume that it belongs to the new connection.

Errors can also occur when a host fails. For instance, say that host A is sending packets to host B, using the alternating bit protocol. Assume that host B fails in the middle of the transmission. When B comes back up, it tells A, "I have

314

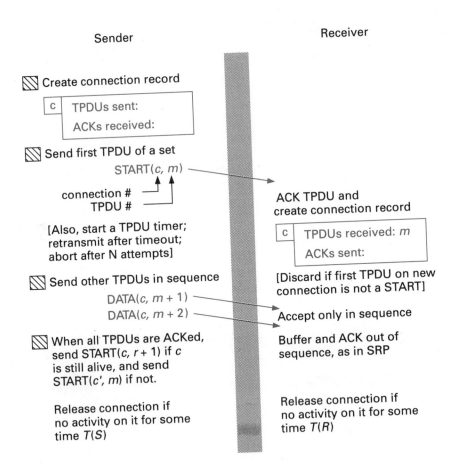

Sender

☒ Create connection record

c	TPDUs sent:
	ACKs received:

☒ Send first TPDU of a set

START(c, m)

connection #
TPDU #

[Also, start a TPDU timer;
retransmit after timeout;
abort after N attempts]

☒ Send other TPDUs in sequence

DATA(c, m + 1)
DATA(c, m + 2)

☒ When all TPDUs are ACKed,
send START(c, r + 1) if c
is still alive, and send
START(c', m) if not.

Release connection if
no activity on it for some
time T(S)

Receiver

ACK TPDU and
create connection record

c	TPDUs received: m
	ACKs sent:

[Discard if first TPDU on new
connection is not a START]

Accept only in sequence

Buffer and ACK out of
sequence, as in SRP

Release connection if
no activity on it for some
time T(R)

Figure 7.7 Timer-based connection management.
The sender starts a connection by creating a record that will specify the
packets (TPDUs) sent and the acknowledgements (ACKs) received. The
sender then transmits the first TPDU that specifies the connection number c and the initial sequence number m. The other packets are numbered sequentially, and SRP is used. The connection is released by the
sender when there is no activity for some time T(S) and by the receiver
when there is no activity for some time T(R).

just recovered from a failure; can you restart after the last packet that I acknowledged?" Two cases are possible. In the first case, B sends the packets to the user
before sending the ACK to A. If the crash occurred between the write and the
sending of the ACK, host A will send a second copy of the last packet and the
user at B will get two copies (by mistake). In the second case, B acknowledges
first. In the situation described before, the user at B will miss a packet.

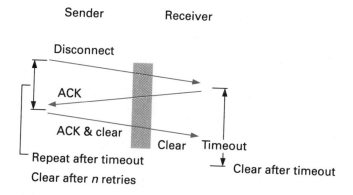

Figure 7.8 Timer-based connection release.

This mechanism guarantees that the connection is released even if failures prevent the connection release messages from reaching the hosts.

Figure 7.7 illustrates an alternative method for handling delayed copies. This method is called timer-based connection management. The figure shows that the sender starts the connection by establishing a record that will specify the TPDUs sent and the ACKs received. The first packet is START(c, m) where c is the connection number and m is the initial sequence number. The packets are then numbered sequentially, and the *selective repeat protocol* (SRP) is used. The connection is released by the sender when there is no activity during $T(S)$ time units and by the receiver when there is no activity during $T(R)$. The packets have a maximum lifetime *max_TPDU_life*. The parameters $T(R)$ and $T(S)$ are chosen so that

$$N \times timeout + max\_TPDU\_life \ll T(R) \ll T(S) \,.$$

This choice guarantees that no delayed packet START(c, k) can appear after the receiver releases a connection. This procedure arranges for the automatic release of connections.

A timer-based connection release mechanism is illustrated in Figure 7.8. To terminate a connection, the sender sends a *disconnect* packet to the receiver. When the receiver gets the disconnect packet, it transmits an acknowledgement to the sender. The sender then terminates the connection and confirms that action to the receiver with an *acknowledge-and-clear* packet. If the sender fails to receive an acknowledgement to its disconnect packet before a timeout, it repeats the procedure. If the sender fails to get an acknowledgement after n retries, it clears the connection. A host clears a connection that has been inactive for a specific time.

Transport Layer

- The transport layer performs the functions of fragmentation, re-sequencing, flow control, and multiplexing.

- The service primitive of a connectionless transport layer is T_UNITDATA. For a connection-oriented transport layer, the primitives are T_CONNECT, T_DATA, T_EXP_DATA, and T_DIS-CONNECT.

- The multiplexing takes place between TSAPs, also called *ports*, and NSAPs.

- Frequently used processes are attached to *well-known ports*. Other processes are attached to *ephemeral ports* by a process server.

- Delayed copies of packets are discarded when their time-to-live reaches zero.

- The connection parameters can be agreed on by means of a three-way handshake.

- Connections can be managed by timers.

7.3 TCP, UDP, and TP4

Transmission Control Protocol (TCP)

The *transmission control protocol* (TCP) is the connection-oriented transport layer protocol designed to operate on top of the datagram network layer Internet protocol (IP). These two widely used protocols are known under the collective name TCP/IP. TCP provides a reliable end-to-end byte stream transport. The fragmentation and reassembly of the messages are done by IP, not by TCP.

TCP uses the SRP with positive acknowledgements and timeout. Each byte sent is numbered and must be acknowledged. A number of bytes can be sent in the same packet, and the acknowledgement then indicates the sequence number of the next byte expected by the receiver. The TCP header is at least 20 bytes long and contains a 32-bit sequence number, the source and destination TSAP (16 bits each), and 16 error detection bits for the data and the header. The error-detection bits are calculated by summing the 1's complements of the groups of 16 bits that make up the data and the header and by taking the 1's complement of that sum. The number of data that can be sent before being acknowledged is the window size, which can be adjusted either by the sender or the receiver to control the flow based on the available buffers and the congestion. Initial sequence numbers are negotiated by means of a three-way handshake at the outset of the connection. Connections are released by means of a three-way handshake.

User Datagram Protocol (UDP)

Some applications do not require reliable, sequenced communication. The *user datagram protocol* is a connectionless transport service that uses the IP network layer. These two protocols are known as UDP/IP. Like TCP, UDP uses 16-bit port numbers.

The UDP header contains 16 error-detection bits which are set to zero when they are not used. UDP adds the multiplexing capabilities to IP and also the possibility of error detections.

TP4

ISO has defined five classes (0 to 4) of connection-oriented transport services (ISO 8073). We will briefly describe class 4, which transmits packets with error recovery and in the correct order. This protocol is known as *transport protocol, class 4* (TP4). It is designed for unreliable networks.

The basic steps in a TP4 connection are described below:

- *Connection establishment*: This is done by means of a three-way handshake to agree on the connection parameters, such as a *credit value* that specifies how many packets can be sent initially until the next credit arrives; the connection number, the transport source and destination access points; and a maximum timeout before acknowledgement.

- *Data transfer*: The data packets are numbered sequentially. This permits resequencing. Acknowledgements may be done for blocks of packets. There is a provision for *expedited data* transport in which the data packets are sent and acknowledged one at a time. Expedited packets jump to the head of the queues. Flow is controlled by windows or by credits.

- *Clear connection*: Connections are released by an expedited packet indicating the connection termination. The buffers are then flushed of the data packets corresponding to that connection.

TCP-UDP-TP4

- TCP implements a reliable connection-oriented communication service on top of the datagram network protocol IP of the Internet. TCP controls errors and the flow of messages by the SRP with adjustable window size.

- UDP is a datagram communication service build on top of IP. It adds multiplexing and error detection to the IP capabilities.

- TP4 is the ISO reliable connection-oriented communication service. TP4 is similar to TCP.

7.4 Session Layer

The session layer supervises the exchange of data and the recovery in case of errors. The main functions of the session layer are the following:

- Connect. Establish the session. Different sessions may use the same transport connection for efficiency. Conversely, one session may use different transport connections for redundancy. Thus, up and down multiplexing are possible at the session layer, just as they were at the transport layer.

- Exchange data. OSI distinguishes four classes of data: regular, expedited, typed (typically used for control), and capability for agreeing on session parameters.

- Release connection.

- Supervise dialogue. This function determines who can talk and when; it is implemented by exchanging a token. The process that has the token can transmit.

- Recover after errors. The recovery is explained below.

Figure 7.9 illustrates the recovery mechanism used by the session layer. The session layer groups the messages into *dialogue units* by inserting *synchronization points* in the transmission. In case of error, the transmission resumes at the beginning of the dialogue unit that was interrupted by the error. The *activities* in the figure are independent tasks.

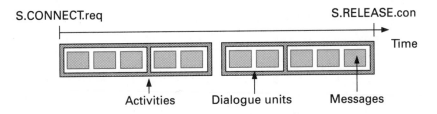

S.CONNECT.req   S.RELEASE.con

Time

Activities   Dialogue units   Messages

Figure 7.9 Grouping of session messages.

The session layer groups the messages into *dialogue units*. In case of error, the transmissions restart at the beginning of the current dialogue unit. The *activities* are independent data transfers, such as different files.

Session Layer

- The session layer performs the following functions: connect, exchange data, release connection, supervise dialogue, and recover after errors.
- The session layer supervises the dialogue by using tokens.
- The recovery after failure is handled by inserting synchronization points that divide the data exchange into dialogue units.

7.5 Encryption

One aspect of security is preventing unauthorized access to files in the computer. Another aspect is making files that are transmitted on the network unintelligible. This is achieved by *encrypting* the files, as we explain below.

In abstract terms, an encryption system works as indicated in Figure 7.10. The text that the sender must transmit in a secure way is the *plaintext P*. The sender converts P into the *ciphertext C*. The receiver converts C back into P. The sender uses a function $E_K(.)$ to convert the plaintext. The subscript K, called the *key*, designates the specific encryption scheme used by the sender. The receiver recovers P from C by computing $D_K(C)$ where $D_K(.)$ is the inverse of the function $E_K(.)$. There must be many possible functions $E_K(.)$. Otherwise, any eavesdropper could learn how to decode C. The different functions correspond to dif-

Encryption   Decryption

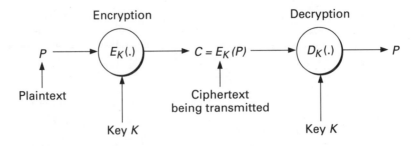

Figure 7.10 Encryption system.

The sender transforms the *plaintext P* into the *ciphertext C,* which is
transmitted. The receiver converts *C* back into *P.* The encryption function
$E_K(.)$ and the decryption function $D_K(.)$ are identified by the key *K.*

ferent codes, or to different parameters of the code. Each code is identified by a
key K that specifies the coding algorithm. The sender and the receiver must agree
on the code that will be used. We next examine a few simple codes and indicate
their weaknesses.

The *letter substitution code* replaces every letter with another one. For
instance, one could have the correspondence $a \rightarrow f, b \rightarrow s, c \rightarrow o$, etc. With this
code, the word $P = cab$ gets encoded into $C = ofs$. The inverse operation converts
$C = ofs$ back into $P = cab$. The key specifies the substitution to be used. This code
is easily broken when used for plaintexts in English by using the relative frequencies of the letters. For instance, the letter *e* is the most frequently used in English.
Thus, by finding the most frequent letter in the encoded text *C*, one knows that it
should be decoded as *e*. One can continue in this way with the second most likely
letter *t*, then the letter *o*, etc.

It is easy to improve the above code by changing the substitution from
letter to letter, according to a periodic pattern. For instance, one could use five
different substitutions and use the first one for the letters number 1, 6, 11, etc.,
use the second one for letters number 1, 7, 12, etc. This code can be broken by
trying different lengths of the period. Once one tries a period of five, by looking
at the first, sixth, eleventh,... letters, one can break the first substitution, and then
repeat the procedure for the other substitutions.

If the number of substitutions is very large, then the code is more
difficult to break. However, it is more difficult to inform the receiver of the
complicated code being used. Transmitting that information must also be done in
a secure way.

Another simple encryption scheme is the *transposition code*. An example of that code consists of writing a text in rows of 10 letters each, and then sending the text column by column. We will use that method to encode the following sentence (the symbol ^ represents a space):

This^is^a^sentence^before^transposition.

You can verify that this sequence encoded with the transposition code becomes:

Tseshefpinoostrs^eeiin^tscti^eroa^an^bn.

This code can be broken by trying various lengths for the rows.

One of the standards adopted for encryption uses a combination of substitution and transposition. In 1977, the National Bureau of Standards adopted the *Data Encryption Standard* (DES) as the official encryption standard for the unclassified information of the U.S. government. DES was developed by IBM. There are inexpensive VLSI chips that perform the necessary encryption and decryption. To perform the encryption of a text, DES first divides the text into blocks of 64 bits. Each block of 64 bits is then encoded separately into new blocks, also of 64 bits. Thus, DES is a mapping $C = E_K(P)$ where both C and P are words of 64 bits. The key K is a word of 56 bits. The first step in the DES encoding of P is to calculate $P_1 = T(P)$ where T is a given transposition. The DES algorithm then calculates successively $P_{i+1} = F(P_i, K_i)$ for $i = 1, 2,..., 16$ where the K_i are obtained from K by applying successive transpositions. The function F is also specified by the algorithm. Finally, the DES algorithm calculates $C = T^{-1}(P_{16})$ where T^{-1} is the inverse of the transposition T.

The key K that is used by the sender and the receiver must be distributed in a secure way. One method to distribute the keys is to encrypt them by using a *master key*. The master key can be hand-delivered. Since the master key is used infrequently, just to change keys, breaking the code identified by the master key is difficult. Another method to distribute keys is to use *puzzles*. Say that two users A and B want to agree on a key. A has a list of N puzzles. Each puzzle contains a number, a key, and a field of zeroes. A then encodes each puzzle with a different DES key and sends all the puzzles to B. To choose a key, B chooses one puzzle at random, solves it, and then sends the number of the puzzle to A. (B verifies that the puzzle was solved by detecting the pattern of zeroes.) A and B then use the key in that puzzle. B has to solve only one puzzle, while an eavesdropper would, on the average, have to solve $N/2$ puzzles before finding the one with the number announced by B.

7.6 Public Key Cryptography

A public key cryptography system requires a collection of encoding-decoding pairs $\{E_K(.), D_K(.)\}$ such that $D_K(.)$ is difficult to discover from knowing $E_K(.)$. The encoding function $E_K(.)$ is then made public. For instance, you might want correspondents to send you confidential messages. You publish an encoding function $E_K(.)$ to be used by those correspondents. You alone know $D_K(.)$, so that the messages remain confidential.

One example of a public key system is based on the difficulty of finding the prime factors p and q of pq when they are large. The system also uses the following lemma from number theory:

Lemma

Let p and q be two prime numbers. Define $n = pq$, $z = (p-1)(q-1)$. Choose d such that $gcd(d, z) = 1$ where gcd denotes the greatest common divisor. Then choose e so that $ed = 1 \ mod \ z$ (i.e., ed is a multiple of z plus 1).

If $P \in \{0,1, ..., n-1\}$ and $C := P^e \ mod \ n$, then $P = C^d \ mod \ n$.

For instance, let $p = 3, q = 11, n = 33, z = 20, d = 7$, and $e = 3$. The lemma implies that if $C = P^3 \ mod \ 33$, then $P = C^7 \ mod \ 33$ for all $P \in \{0,1,...,32\}$. As an example, if $P = 5$, then one verifies that $C = 26$ and that $26^7 \ mod \ 33 = 5$.

The lemma enables us to construct a public key system by making the pair of numbers (e, n) public. To know the decoding function, an eavesdropper needs the pair (d, n). However, finding d from (e, n) is equivalent in complexity to factorizing n into p and q, which is known to be a complex task.

Public key cryptography can be used to construct *electronic signature* systems. Say that A wants to get a signed message from B. We want to construct a system that will make it impossible for B later to deny that it sent the message it signed electronically. One such system is constructed as follows. Say that the pair $\{E(.), D(.)\}$ of encryption and decryption functions is *suitable* if it has the following properties:

1. D is difficult to guess from E.
2. $D(E(P)) \equiv E(D(P)) \equiv P$.

Assume then that $\{E_A(.), D_A(.)\}$ and $\{E_B(.), D_B(.)\}$ are two suitable pairs. Assume also that $E_A(.)$ and $E_B(.)$ are public, but that $D_A(.)$ is private to A and that $D_B(.)$ is private to B. In order to send a signed message P to A, the user B sends

$$C = D_B(E_A(P)) .$$

To decode the message, A calculates $R = D_A(E_B(C))$. You can verify that $R = P$. Moreover, only B could have calculated C since only B knows $D_B(.)$.

Other public key cryptography systems are the *zero-knowledge proof* methods. These methods enable a user to prove that it knows some specific information without revealing any of the information. For instance, suppose that you are using a terminal to access your account on a computer. To access your account, you have to enter a password. There is always the possibility that someone is spying and is learning your password. A zero-knowledge proof is a scheme that allows the computer to recognize that you are a legitimate user, without your having to reveal any information about your password. One zero-knowledge proof system is based on the notion of *quadratic residue*. Let x, y be positive integers that are relatively prime, i.e., that have no common factor other than 1. Say that y is a quadratic residue of x if there is some w such that $y = w^2 \bmod x$. For instance, 9 is a quadratic residue of 10 since $9 = 7^2 \bmod 10$. It turns out that, if x is large, then it is difficult to check whether a given y is a quadratic residue of x. Thus, one can say that it is difficult to produce a "square root" w of a given y. To apply this idea to the password example, let w be that password. The following three steps are then executed:

Step 1: The computer selects a pair (x, y) with $y = w^2 \bmod x$, for some large x, and asks the user to prove that y is a quadratic residue of x, without revealing w.

Step 2: The user chooses some number u that is relatively prime with x and sends $z := u^2 \bmod x$ to the computer.

Step 3: The computer asks the user to reveal either u or $v := uw \bmod x$. In the former case, the computer can check that $z = u^2 \bmod x$. In the latter case, the computer can verify that $zy = v^2 \bmod x$.

An eavesdropper cannot recover w from either u or v alone, and the user cannot make up a value u when asked for a reply since the user does not know whether u or v will be asked. Also, without knowing w, the user cannot produce a v such that $zy = v^2 \bmod x$ since it is difficult to compute square roots.

Encryption

- Encryption is used to make the transferred data unintelligible
  to eavesdroppers.
- An encryption system is a collection of encoding and decoding
  functions designated by keys.
- A key can be distributed by encoding it with a master key. Another
  method is to solve one of many puzzles.
- A public key cryptography system is such that the encoding function can be made public without revealing the decoding function.
  One such system is based on the difficulty to factor a product of
  two large primes.
- A public key cryptography system can be used for electronic signatures.
- The zero-knowledge proof systems enable a user to prove the
  knowledge of a password without revealing it.

7.7 Data Compression

The goal of data compression is to reduce the amount of data that
must be stored or transmitted. This compression must be performed without making the quality of information unacceptable. For instance, a text file must be
compressed so that the full text is recovered when the file is decompressed. A
video signal must be compressed so that, after decompression, the quality of the
images is acceptable.

Data compression is important in applications such as voice, video,
and facsimile transmissions. For instance, transmitting an NTSC video signal
requires, without compression, about 100 Mbps (see Section 3.6). This high bit
rate makes such transmissions expensive. Compression methods can reduce the
necessary bit rate by a few orders of magnitude. Figure 7.11 gives a few examples
of rate reductions achievable by compression methods.

We will examine three basic compression methods in this section: run
length encoding, differential encoding, and predictive encoding. We will conclude
the section by discussing the Huffman encoding and the Lempel-Ziv compression
algorithm.

Run length encoding is the simple but efficient data compression
method used to compress the signal that encodes facsimiles. To transmit a facsimile page, the facsimile machine scans the page line by line and measures the
intensity of the light reflected by points regularly spaced along each line. These
measurements result in a sequence of bits that indicate whether the points along

Examples:

Source	Uncompressed	Compressed
NTSC	100 Mbps	1.5 – 15 Mbps
HDTV	1000 Mbps	6 – 60 Mbps
FAX page	3 Mbits	100 kbits
Telephone	64 kbps	16 kbps
Hi-Fi	1.4 Mbps	350 kbps

Figure 7.11 Bit rates of uncompressed and compressed sources.

The figure lists approximate bit rates for the regular color TV signal (NTSC), for high-definition television (HDTV), for one facsimile (FAX) page, for a phone-quality voice signal, and for a high-fidelity audio signal. The compressed values are typical, but not definitive. Improved compression methods can achieve higher compressions.

the lines are white or black. We will assume that a white point is represented by a 0 and a black point by a 1. If the facsimile machine scans 200 lines per inch and measures 200 points per inch along each page, then the machine represents an 8.5-inch by 11-inch page by $200 \times 200 \times 8.5 \times 11 = 3.74 \times 10^6$ bits. Transmitting these bits with a 9,600-bps modem would require 6.5 minutes. Reducing the number of bits that the machine must transmit by a factor of 20 would bring the transmission time down to about 20 seconds. To achieve such a compression factor, the machine transmits the number of successive 0s between two 1s instead of transmitting a long sequence of 0s. For instance, the string

$$1\,0^a\,1\,0^b\,1\,0^c\,1\,0^d\,,$$

where 0^a represents a successive 0s, is encoded as

$$A\,B\,C\,D$$

where A is the binary representation of a, B is the binary representation of b, and so on. Thus, if $a = 600$ (which corresponds to 3 inches), then $A = 1001011000$ so that 600 0s are replaced by 10 bits. The compression factor, i.e., the reduction in the number of bits, achieved by run length encoding is about

$$\frac{E\{X\}}{E\{\log_2 X\}}$$

where X is a random variable distributed as a typical number of successive 0s between two 1s and $E\{.\}$ denotes the expected value. A compression factor of 20–30 is possible with this method.

The run length encoding of a facsimile page can be combined with the *differential interline encoding* based on the observation that successive lines of a facsimile page are frequently similar. Instead of transmitting the successive lines $L_1, L_2, \ldots$ of the page, the machine can transmit $L_1, L_2 - L_1, L_3 - L_2$, etc. These differences are bit by bit and without carry. For instance, $1001010010 - 0101010001 = 1100000011$. This differential encoding increases the length of the strings of successive 0s and improves the compression achieved by the run length encoding.

326

Differential encoding is also used to compress the bits that represent a voice signal. In order to transmit a voice signal, the transmitter equipment uses a filter to limit its spectrum to a given maximum frequency f_{max}. The transmitter then samples the filtered signal with a sampling frequency $f_s > 2f_{max}$. Finally, the transmitter quantizes the samples and encodes them as binary numbers. This sequence of steps is the *pulse code modulation* (PCM) technique. The telephone equipment performs a nonlinear transformation of the samples before quantizing them to expand the small values and to limit the large infrequent values. This transformation, called *companding*, improves the quality of the sound by using more bits to represent the most likely small values. The *differential* PCM (DPCM) encodes the differences between successive samples. These differences are typically small, and a few bits are sufficient to encode their values. An improvement of DPCM modifies the encoding of the difference between samples adaptively. When the signal changes faster, the differences are divided by a given factor before being encoded. That factor is transmitted to the receiver so that it can decode the differences properly. With this method, called *adaptive* DPCM (ADPCM), an even smaller number of bits is sufficient to encode the voice signal. Excellent quality is achieved with 16 kbps.

Predictive encoding is the name given to a class of methods that use a predictor to guess the next sample value and transmit the difference between the guessed value and the actual value. To illustrate the method, we will assume that we must transmit the sequence $X(1), X(2), X(3), \ldots$. Instead of transmitting these values, we first construct an algorithm that attempts to predict $X(n + 1)$ from $\{X(1), X(2), \ldots, X(n)\}$. Let us denote by $Y(n + 1)$ the predicted value. We then transmit

$$X(1), X(2) - Y(2), X(3) - Y(3), \ldots .$$

If the predictor is accurate, this sequence will contain mostly small numbers that can be represented with only a few bits. The specific predictor that should be used depends on the signal to be transmitted. For instance, the color of a picture cell on a video frame can be predicted from the color of the neighboring points on the previous frames and lines.

There is a general method designed to minimize the *average* number of bits required to transmit a symbol when many independent and statistically equivalent copies of that symbol must be transmitted. This method, called *Huff-*

man encoding, determines how the various values of the symbol should be represented by strings of bits. Huffman encoding can be used with the methods described earlier. To understand the method, assume that we have to send a symbol X that can take any of the N values $\{x_1, x_2, ..., x_N\}$ with different probabilities, say $p_1, p_2, ..., p_N$, respectively. The idea of Huffman encoding is to reserve short code words for the frequent values of X and long code words for the rare values. As an example, say that there are four values $x_1, ..., x_4$ with respective probabilities $0.5, 0.3, 0.15, 0.05$. If one uses the code words $00, 01, 10$, and 11 to represent the values $x_1, ..., x_4$, then it will take 2 bits to transmit the value of X. However, if one uses 0 to represent x_1, 10 for x_2, 110 for x_3, and 111 for x_4, then one finds that it takes on the average $0.5{\times}1 + 0.3{\times}2 + 0.15{\times}3 + 0.05{\times}3 = 1.7$ bits. The code that we used in this example has variable length. However, if we send different values of X encoded as in the example, then no separating symbols are required. For instance, the sequence $x_3x_1x_4x_3x_3x_2$ is encoded as 110011111011010 and this sequence can only be decoded correctly. The reason this works is that one can always tell when a code word ends: no code word is the beginning of another one. A code with this property is called a *prefix code*. The Huffman code is the prefix code that requires the lowest average number of bits per symbol. That code is derived as follows. First, one finds the two symbols x_i and x_j with the lowest probabilities. One then replaces them with $y_i 0$ and $y_i 1$. Then one deletes x_i and x_j from the list and adds y_i with which one associates the sum of the probabilities $p_i + p_j$. One then continues until all the symbols have been exhausted. The construction of the Huffman code is indicated in Figure 7.12 for the example given above.

In the last few years, another method of data compression, the *Lempel-Ziv* compression algorithm, has gained in popularity. This compression algorithm is available as the UNIX *compress* command and as the MSDOS *ARC* utility. The algorithm achieves a compression factor of about 2 on a long file. That is, the Lempel-Ziv algorithm reduces by about 50% the number of data that have to be stored or transmitted. Let us examine how the algorithm would perform the compression of the text of this book. The basic idea of the algorithm is that, instead of repeating a piece of text, the starting location and the length of the first instance of that piece of text should be indicated. For instance, if the string "In the last few years," had been used as the opening of the book, the algorithm would have replaced the beginning of the current paragraph with [1, 22] where 1 points to the first character of the book and 22 indicates the length of the string of characters (including the spaces). More precisely, the algorithm would search the book to find the longest string of characters that agrees with the first sentence of the paragraph. Thus, if the sentence "In the last few years, a bright young researcher..." had occurred earlier in the book, say starting with character 657, the Lempel-Ziv algorithm would have replaced the beginning of the current para-

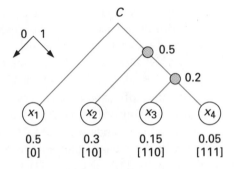

Figure 7.12 Constructing the Huffman code.

The two least likely values x_3 and x_4 are grouped and replaced by a new point A marked with the sum of their probabilities (0.2). We then consider the three points x_1, x_2, and A. The two points with the lowest probabilities x_2 and A are then grouped and replaced by a new point B marked with the sum of the probabilities (0.5). The last two points x_1 and B are then joined to C, as shown. The code is defined by the path from C to each of the original four values x_1 to x_4. The convention is that a downward step to the right is represented by a 1, whereas a downward step to the left is represented by a 0. For example, the value x_3 is reached from C by the sequence of right, right, and left steps; it is represented by the bits 110.

graph with [657, 24]. The algorithm achieves some compression because the pointer and the length indicator require fewer bits to encode than repeating the character strings. Let us illustrate the operations of the algorithm by explaining how it would encode the following sentence:

"the other one is the oldest"

The encoded sequence is

the o[1, 3]r[4, 2]n[3, 2]is[3, 1][1, 5]ld[3, 1][16, 1][1, 1].

The efficiency of the algorithm increases with the length of the text as longer strings are repeated.

The actual implementations of the Lempel-Ziv algorithm differ slightly from those of the original algorithm that we just described. The modification makes the algorithm easier to implement, at the cost of some reduced compression factor. Instead of searching the full text for the longest matching sequence, the modified algorithm maintains a *dictionary* with the character strings already encountered. The modified algorithm searches the dictionary for the longest matching string, and it adds longer strings to the dictionary when it discovers them.

Data Compression

- Data compression reduces the number of bits to be stored or transmitted without deteriorating the quality of the information.

- When run length encoding is used, the number of successive 0s is transmitted instead of all the successive 0s.

- A differential encoding scheme transmits the difference between samples that are likely to be similar. Adaptive versions of differential encoding adjust the encoding of these differences to their typical values.

- Predictive encoding schemes transmit the difference between a predicted sample value and the actual sample value.

- Huffman encoding is the prefix code that minimizes the average number of bits required to transmit a symbol.

- The Lempel-Ziv algorithm is a widely used compression method that achieves a compression factor of about 2 on a typical text file.

7.8 Syntax Conversion

Different applications use different representations of data structures, such as character strings and tables. To enable these applications to exchange data structures, it is convenient to agree on a common *transfer syntax*. The presentation layer then translates between the application specific syntax and the transfer syntax.

To facilitate the translation into the transfer syntax, ISO recommends the *abstract syntax notation one* (ASN.1) for the definition of the data structures. ASN.1 is a grammar for defining data structures, or *data types*. This grammar provides for four classes of data types: *universal*, such as Boolean, integer, and real; *context specific*, which are defined for the local context in which they are used; *application*, defined for the specific application; and *private*, which are defined by the user. Each type is either *primitive*, such as a single integer, or *constructed*, such as a string of integers. For instance, application specific data types, such as tables and forms, can be defined in the ASN.1 grammar. As you might expect, the details of the grammar are as complicated as the concept is elementary. A useful analogy is the definition of data structures in a high-level programming language, such as C or Pascal.

The *transfer syntax* is defined by specifying how the different data types are encoded. The encoding starts with a *tag* that specifies the type of data. Each type has a specific encoding rule. To decode this *tagged data element*, the presentation layer examines the tag and invokes the decoding procedure that corresponds to the data type indicated by the tag. You should consult the ISO specifications if you need the precise syntax of the grammar and the rules of encoding.

330

Syntax Conversion

- Applications use different representations of data types.
- To facilitate the exchange of data between different applications, ISO recommends describing the data types in ASN.1.
- The ASN.1 data types are encoded by means of procedures that depend on the data type. The encoded ASN.1 data types define the transfer syntax.

Summary

- The transport layer implements a connection-oriented or a connectionless communication service by using the end-to-end packet transmissions service provided by the network layer.
- The transport layer performs multiplexing, error control, fragmentation and reassembly, and flow control.
- The session layer establishes a reliable exchange of messages by implementing error-recovery procedures.
- The presentation layer converts the syntax, encrypts and compresses the data.

Problems

1. What is the role of the three-way handshake in the transport layer? Is it used to:
   a. detect and correct transmission errors in the initialization process of a new session?
   b. prevent old packets from creating confusion in the initialization process?

2. Describe two reasons why the three-way handshake may fail to work correctly.

*3. Assume that host A is connected to host B via 10 nodes connected in series. Statistical analysis of the traffic shows that the chance that a packet is received incorrectly at the terminal node is 0.1. Each packet spends 100 ms in each node. When host B receives an incorrect packet, it sends a negative acknowledgement to A. That negative acknowledgement takes 300 ms to reach A. To avoid the difficulties created by old duplicates, the nodes kill the packets that have spent more than T seconds in the network. The time T is chosen equal to twice the average time that a packet takes to go from host A to host B. Find the value of T and find the probability that a packet is killed before it reaches B.

4. Host A transmits packets to host B at rate 56 kbs. Each packet consists of 10,000 bits. Assume that the following protocol for disconnection is used: Host B disconnects when it does not receive any packet for T seconds. Each packet has a probability $p = 0.01$ of being lost during a normal connection. Analysis shows that the probability that host B disconnects during the session is $1 - \exp\{-\lambda(1-p)T\}$, where λ is the packet transmission rate. Find T so that the above probability is smaller than 10^{-6}.

5. Which layer is supposed to be responsible for dialogue supervision? How is this supervision implemented?

6. Why is syntax conversion needed? Is it:

   a. To ensure faster transmission rates?

   b. To make connection between incompatible applicatioms possible?

   c. To prevent messages from being intercepted by eavesdroppers?

7. Consider the data encryption scheme. What property should the function F possess in order for the scheme to be decipherable by the receiver? Formulate the decoding algorithm that the receiver should use, assuming that the receiver knows the key K.

8. Assume that if the key K is known, then it takes 100 ms to decipher a message that has been coded using DES. Suppose that an eavesdropper chooses keys at random and tries to decipher the message. What is the average time required for the correct deciphering? (There are 2^{56} possible keys.)

9. The public key cryptography system is based on the idea that large prime numbers p and q (typically over 10^{100}) will be used. (This is why it is important to know many large prime numbers—it is here that number theorists are needed!) If small prime numbers are used, then deciphering is relatively easy. Here is an example: Suppose a user transmits a message which is an integer between 1 and 10, using $n = 15$ and $e = 3$. The coded message yields the integer 8. What number was transmitted?

*10. Show that the public key cryptography system can also be used as an electronic signature. (*Hint:* Check that the encoding function is invertible.)

*11. Assume that, in a text, the number of consecutive 0s, X, is equally likely to be any integer between 1 and n. Derive an expression for the compression factor r_n achieved by run length encoding. Compute r_n for $n = 5$ and $n = 10$. Using Stirling's approximation for $n!$ ($n! = \sqrt{2\pi n}\, e^{-n} n^n$, for large values of n), find an asymptotic expression for r_n. The assumption that X is uniformly distributed is not very reasonable; for instance, in a text one is very likely to find large sequences of 0s due to margins, empty lines, etc. Will that unequal distribution improve r_n?

12. Is it better to use differential interline encoding to transmit a file containing random numbers representing the outcomes of a coin tossing computer-generated experiment or a file containing the binary encoding of a picture of the sunset over Oahu? Why?

13. Construct the Huffman code for transmitting messages constructed by using the symbols A, B, C, D, E, and F occurring with frequencies 0.60, 0.30, 0.05, 0.02, 0.02, and 0.01, respectively. What is the compression factor, defined as the number of bits per symbol in a straightforward binary encoding divided by the average number of bits per symbol of the Huffman encoding?

References

Comer (1988) provides general commentaries on TCP/IP and that protocol suite. Stevens (1990) discusses implementation details in UNIX. Halsall (1988) and Tanenbaum (1988) are useful references for the different layers. Lucky (1989) offers an enjoyable and informative discussion of various aspects of communication. That book contains a nice discussion of encoding and compression of information, including the Lempel-Ziv and Huffman encodings.

Comer (1988). Comer, D., *Internetworking with TCP/IP: Principles, Protocols, and Architecture.* Prentice-Hall, 1988.

Halsall (1988). Halsall, F., *Data Communications, Computer Networks and OSI.* Addison-Wesley, 1988.

Lucky (1989). Lucky, R. W., *Silicon Dreams: Information, Man, and Machine.* St. Martin's Press, 1989.

Stevens (1990). Stevens, W. R., *Unix Network Programming.* Prentice-Hall, 1990.

Tanenbaum (1988). Tanenbaum, A., *Computer Networks* (2nd Ed.). Prentice-Hall, 1988.

Applications | 8

This chapter is devoted to a number of widely used communication network applications. When examining these applications, we will review some of their OSI layers and we will explain the role of the *application layer*, which provides specific information transfer services for the user application programs. As for the other layers, the ISO has catalogued the functions of the application layer and has defined some terminology to designate these functions. We will briefly define this terminology before turning to concrete applications.

The OSI model is recalled in Figure 8.1(a). We learned in the previous chapter that the presentation layer enables hosts to exchange data structures in their own local syntax. The user programs and the application layer are shown in Figure 8.1(a) and in more detail in Figure 8.1(b). The user programs, such as word processing, e-mail, data base, spreadsheet, and calendar programs, require specialized information transfer services. These services are provided by *specific application service elements* (SASEs). For instance, one SASE may provide directory services, whereas another may provide file transfer services.

We will discuss specific SASEs in this chapter. As shown in Figure 8.1(b), the SASEs use the services provided by *common application service elements* (CASEs). A CASE provides generic information transfer services that are used by different SASEs, such as establishing a connection (also called *association*) between SASEs on different machines. A CASE is itself composed of differ-

336

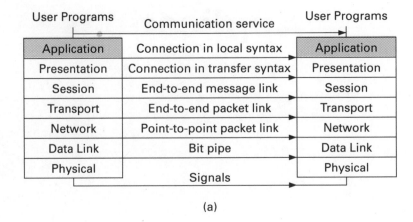

(a)

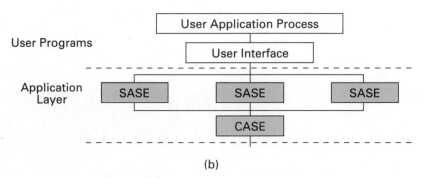

(b)

Figure 8.1 The OSI reference model.

Part (a) shows the seven layers of the OSI reference model and the user programs. Part (b) shows the decomposition of the user programs into application processes and the user interface. The application layer is composed of *specific application service elements* (SASEs) and the *common application service element* (CASE).

ent elements, such as the *association control service element* (ACSE), the *remote operations service element* (ROSE), and the *commitment, concurrency, and recovery* (CCR) element. The ACSE sets up the association between SASEs. The ROSE exchanges commands and results. The CCR decomposes the execution of operations into atomic actions and repeats those that do not complete satisfactorily. The user interface adapts the commands and responses of the user application process to the SASE. This interface enables different commercial application programs to work jointly on a common network.

Figure 8.2 lists some classes of SASEs and gives a few widely used examples of each class. We will discuss these SASEs in this chapter. Sections 8.1 and 8.2 describe the protocol suites for IEEE 802 LANs *TOP* and *MAP*. Section

SASE Class	Example
File access and transfer	Network File System (NFS) File Transfer Protocol (FTP)
Message handling	Simple Mail Transfer Protocol (SMTP) Message Handling System (MHS)
Remote job execution	Remote Procedure Call (RPC) Job Transfer and Manipulation (JTM)
Terminal emulation	Virtual Terminal (VT) X.Window
Directory	Directory Service (DS)
Remote login	rlogin

Figure 8.2   SASE classes and examples.

This is a partial list of widely used SASEs grouped by the class of applications they support. These SASEs are discussed in this chapter. User programs for data bases, load balancing, distributed computing, and other applications have been developed that use these services.

8.3 explains a set of applications that run on top of TCP/IP. They include *FTP, TELNET*, *rlogin*, *rsh*, *rcp*, and *SMTP*. SUN's *Network File System* is discussed in Section 8.4. We examine some features of *NetBIOS* in Section 8.5 and of *SNA* in Section 8.6. The applications of networks to *data base* and *load sharing* are discussed in Sections 8.7 and 8.8, respectively.

Application Layer

- The application layer provides information transfer services for user application programs.

- The user interacts with the application layer through a *user interface*.

- The application layer is composed of *specific application service elements* (SASEs) that use the services of *common application service elements* (CASEs).

- A CASE establishes *associations* between SASEs and may include an *association control service element* (ACSE), a *remote operations service element* (ROSE), and the *commitment, concurrency, and recovery* (CCR) element.

8.1 TOP

Technical and office protocols (TOP) is a *protocol suite*, i.e., a set of protocols at the seven OSI layers. The TOP suite, based on development work done at Boeing in the 1970s, is designed for office automation. TOP is available for both Ethernet and token ring networks. Figure 8.3 shows the organization of TOP.

338

The network layer in TOP is connectionless. It manages the routing of messages between end nodes and controls congestion. The adopted standard is ISO 8473, which is similar to the IP protocol. As we saw in Chapter 6, IP requires a long packet header. This header can be replaced by a special "inactive network layer" when the network has a single segment.

The transport layer is class 4 (ISO 8073, TP4, see Section 7.3), i.e., connection-oriented with error control, flow control, multiplexing for multiple-access points, retransmissions after timeout, resequencing, and recovery from failures. It also permits "expedited data" for urgent messages. Expedited data are not subject to flow control and can be used, for instance, to stop the execution of a program.

The session layer of TOP is known as ISO 8327. It supports full-duplex connections between cooperating session service users. Its basic functions are to establish a connection, exchange data, and release the connection. The session layer creates synchronization points. In the event of an error, the dialogue is resumed at a synchronization point. Synchronization points are of two types: major and minor. Major synchronization points divide the data exchange into dialogue units. One dialogue unit must be confirmed by the destination before

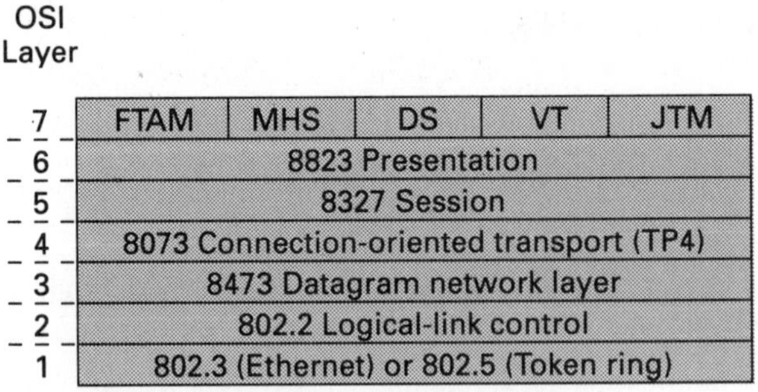

OSI
Layer

7	FTAM	MHS	DS	VT	JTM
6	8823 Presentation				
5	8327 Session				
4	8073 Connection-oriented transport (TP4)				
3	8473 Datagram network layer				
2	802.2 Logical-link control				
1	802.3 (Ethernet) or 802.5 (Token ring)				

FTAM = File transfer and manipulation
MHS = Message handling system
DS = Directory service
VT = Virtual terminal
JTM = Job transfer and manipulation

Figure 8.3 TOP protocol suite.

For simplicity, the figure does not show the CASE used by the SASEs.

more data can be sent. Minor synchronization points can also be used to restart the dialogue after a failure. The orderly evolution of the session is controlled by permits called *tokens*. These session layer tokens should not be confused with the media-access-control tokens that regulate the transmissions of token ring networks. A session service user must own specific tokens in order to create synchronization points or to release the connection. The tokens are exchanged between the users. For instance, if one user wants to terminate the connection, that user must first acquire a specific token from the other user. This guarantees that no data will be lost when the connection is released.

The presentation layer uses the *abstract syntax notation ASN.1* defined in ISO standard 8824. This notation specifies, for each block of data to be transmitted by the application layer (known as an *application protocol data unit*, or APDU), the length of the fields and their data type (Boolean, octet string, bit string, integer, etc.). The APDU is then converted by the presentation layer into a standard format for transmission. The presentation layer at the destination can then perform the conversion from this standard format into the one used by the destination host. For instance, the ANS.1 specifies whether the encoding of symbols is done in ASCII or EBCDIC and the order in which bytes are numbered.

The applications supported by TOP are *FTAM, MHS, JTM, VT,* and *DS*. We will discuss these below.

FTAM

FTAM is the *file transfer, access, and management model* of the OSI (standard ISO 8571). A *file* is a structured set of data with a set of *attributes* which specify the size; the date of creation, last access, and modification; the owner; who can access it; the operations that are allowed (delete, read, modify, change attributes, etc); and its encryption. The general structure of a file is a *tree*, the nodes of which may have data records. A record is specified by the path that leads to it from the root of the tree. A remote access to a file by FTAM is done in the sequence of steps indicated below:

1. Set up connection with remote machine.
2. Select or create a file (*read and modify attributes [if desired]*).
3. Open the file (*delete [if desired]*).
4. Read or write into the file.

The reverse operations are then performed (close, de-select, terminate the connection). In addition, FTAM has provisions for recovering from transmission problems and crashes during the access. One key feature is the creation of checkpoints to avoid losing the entire transaction in case of failure.

MHS

MHS refers to the CCITT's *Message-Handling System* (described in X.400). It is an *electronic mail* service. The basic functions of MHS are the composition of a message (editing), its delivery to one recipient or to a list of recipients, and the notification of its delivery. MHS allows users to place restrictions on the messages that are accepted, and it provides for reply to, storage of, and editing of received messages. Moreover, MHS indicates the reasons why a message could not be delivered (e.g., destination machine down or message not acceptable).

JTM

Job transfer and manipulation (JTM) permits the execution of a job on a remote computer. The computer that will execute the job must collect all the necessary files, check the authorizations, and report on the progress of the execution. JTM also makes it possible to kill a job during execution.

VT

VT refers to *virtual terminal*. This is a method for dealing with the large number of different terminals in existence. The idea is to define a uniform representation of the state of the terminal and of the commands to modify that state. It is then up to each specific terminal to translate those abstract commands into the desired actions.

For instance, different video display terminals may use different inputs to clear the screen. The virtual terminal will define an abstract command, say *clear_the_screen*, that will be translated by each terminal into its own "clear the screen" command.

The parameters of the terminal connected to VT include the size, number of colors, timing characteristics, number of dimensions (1, 2, or 3), and the specific control characters (e.g., line feed, return, clear, home).

DS

DS is a *directory service*. Its function is to translate a symbolic name into a network address. A directory service is usually implemented by having each computer maintain a local directory. The symbolic address is usually hierarchical so that a given computer needs to know only how to get to neighbors in the tree (see Chapter 6). DS allows users to search and modify the directory information, subject to authorization.

TOP

- TOP, the *technical and office protocols*, is a protocol suite for office automation applications using IEEE 802.3 or 802.5 networks.

- TOP's Network layer is connectionless (ISO 8473), its transport layer is TP4 (ISO 8073), and its session layer (ISO 8327) supports full-duplex connections with dialogue control and synchronization points for recovery.

- TOP's presentation layer uses ASN.1.

- The application SASEs are FTAM (*file transfer, access, and management*), MHS (*message-handling system* X.400 for e-mail), JTM (*job transfer and manipulation*, for remote job executions), VT (*virtual terminal*, for terminal emulation), and DS (*directory service*).

8.2 MAP

The *manufacturing automation protocol* (MAP) is a protocol suite used on a token bus network (either baseband or broadband). The development of MAP was started by General Motors in 1982 and continued by the Society of Manufacturing Engineers. The intended applications of MAP are in manufacturing plants where real time constraints are important. The token bus was selected because of its bounded media-access time. The structure of MAP is shown in Figure 8.4.

Note the similarity between MAP and TOP. The main differences are the physical and MAC layers. Also, the application service MMS is provided by MAP and not by TOP. This is the *manufacturing message service*, which is designed to send commands *within* a given manufacturing cell (which may contain robots, numerical machine tools, etc.). Thus, MMS complements the factory-wide communications provided by FTAM. Some basic services of MMS are the following: file transfer, down loading of programs, start and stop commands, and read and write variables. The devices within a cell implement a reduced protocol suite composed of MHS and DS based on 802.2 and 802.4. Cell controllers implement the complete suite.

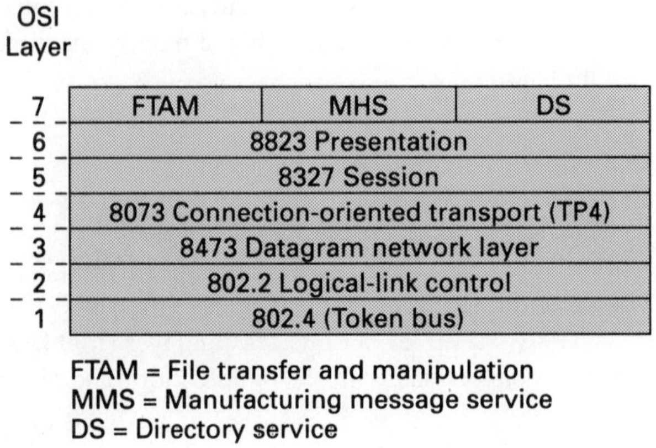

342

OSI
Layer

7	FTAM	MHS	DS
6	8823 Presentation		
5	8327 Session		
4	8073 Connection-oriented transport (TP4)		
3	8473 Datagram network layer		
2	802.2 Logical-link control		
1	802.4 (Token bus)		

FTAM = File transfer and manipulation
MMS = Manufacturing message service
DS = Directory service

Figure 8.4 MAP protocol suite.

MAP is designed for token bus networks, because of their bounded media-access time.

MAP

■ MAP, the *manufacturing automation protocols*, is a protocol suite designed to interconnect work cells in a manufacturing plant with IEEE 802.4 networks.

■ Layers 3 to 6 of MAP and TOP are identical. The SASEs supported by MAP are FTAM and DS, as in TOP, and MMS, the *manufacturing message service*.

■ The services provided by MMS include file transfer, down loading of programs, start and stop executions, and read and write variables.

8.3 FTP, SMTP, TELNET, TFTP, rcp, rsh, and rlogin

Figure 8.5 shows the position of the above seven application layer protocols in the OSI reference model. Note that these protocols are available for most LANs and WANs. Software for these protocols is available for most computers.

OSI
Layer

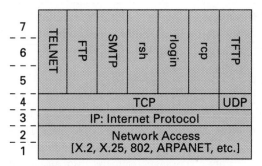

TELNET = Remote terminal protocol
FTP = File transfer protocol
rlogin = Remote login service
TFTP = Trivial file transfer protocol
SMTP = Simple mail transfer protocol
rcp = Remote file copy
rsh = Remote shell

Figure 8.5 The Internet suite.

The applications TELNET, FTP, rlogin, SMTP, rsh, and rcp use the services of TCP/IP. TFTP uses UDP/IP.

FTP

Three basic operations are supported by FTP: a user on a machine can send a file to another computer, get a file from that computer, and transfer files between two remote machines.

FTP is usually used interactively. It provides a large number of options for creating, changing, or consulting a remote directory, deleting and retrieving a remote file, choosing the transfer mode (stream, block, or compressed), and sending files.

The *stream* mode is used by default. The file is sent without modification. The *block* mode partitions the file to be transferred into blocks. This mode is used to simplify recovery in case of an error. Finally, the *compressed* mode is used to avoid sending long strings of repeated characters (e.g., spaces). This is done by the Lempel-Ziv algorithm.

FTP uses two TCP connections: one for the commands/responses and the other for the data transfers/acknowledgements. A host has an FTP process constantly running and ready to process commands. These commands reach the machine on a TCP connection, using a special port number (21). An FTP request from another machine may require the user to be authenticated by a password.

SMTP

The *simple mail-transfer protocol* is used to transfer electronic mail messages between hosts. The transfer takes place via TCP on port 25 of the receiver. A mail server process is always running, ready to handle messages.

SMTP accepts a message from the user along with a list of destinations. A copy is then sent to each destination, except when different users are on the same host. In that case, the message is sent only once, together with the list of destinations on the corresponding host. When the delivery of a message is not successful, SMTP will attempt delivery a number of times on successive days before giving up and indicating failure to deliver it to the user.

TELNET

TELNET is the virtual terminal protocol of ARPANET. It enables a user to simulate a direct connection from a terminal to a remote host.

This function is implemented by defining a standard character code for the network. In TELNET, this is ASCII (the usual symbols plus a set of control codes). This standard code corresponds to a *virtual terminal* that all the hosts are able, it is assumed, to interact with. This interaction takes place by converting the characters sent by the actual terminal into the network standard. Similarly, the virtual terminal input is translated into the input expected by the host.

The transmission is done by means of TCP. Special commands can be sent as expedited data so as to bypass queued data.

The TELNET virtual terminal is a primitive scroll mode terminal. That is, when the end of a line is reached, a new line starts and the others move up, as in most printers. Many screen commands, such as "home" and "clear screen," are not supported. The selection of this primitive terminal guarantees that most existing terminals can support the features of the virtual terminal. The disadvantage is that it limits the capabilities of the terminal. In order to make the connection of more sophisticated terminals possible, TELNET has an *option negotiation* phase that allows users to agree on a set of options to be supported by the virtual terminal. For instance, the *echo* (i.e., displaying the sender's commands on the sender's screen) can be handled either locally or by the remote machine. In the latter case, each character is sent in a separate TCP packet to the remote machine and is then sent back for echoing. In the case of local echoing, the characters can be sent together in one packet. The *sizes* of the output (line length, page size) can also be negotiated.

rcp

The *remote file copy* (rcp) command is used to copy files between machines. It can also be used to copy files from one remote machine to another remote machine. An option allows the user to copy all the files of a subdirectory.

rsh

The *remote shell* (rsh) command is used to execute a command on a remote machine and to see the results on the local output. Thus, *rsh* first connects to the remote machine, then sends the command to the machine, returns the result of the command, and finally terminates the connection when the command is executed.

rlogin

rlogin is the remote log in command. It is used to connect the local terminal to a remote host. The remote host will verify that the user is authorized to log in and will then execute the log in without asking for a password.

The echoing is done by the remote machine. Special commands to control the flow of data (the "stop" ^S and the "resume" ^Q commands) are sent as expedited data.

TFTP

The *trivial file transfer protocol* enables the transfer of files between two processes over UDP. A file to be transferred is decomposed into blocks of up to 512 bytes. Each block is sent as a UDP packet together with a block number to enable the receiver to reassemble the file. The blocks are acknowledged by the receiver. The sender retransmits blocks that are not acknowledged before a timeout.

Internet's SASEs

- The Internet SASEs include FTP, SMTP, TELNET, TFTP, rcp, rsh, and rlogin.

- FTP and TFTP are file transfer protocols, SMTP is the e-mail application, and TELNET is for terminal emulation.
- rcp is used to copy files between machines, rsh is used to execute commands on a remote machine, and rlogin is used to connect a local terminal to a remote machine.

8.4 NFS

NFS is the *network file system* developed by SUN Microsystems, and it is now supported by many other vendors. NFS provides distributed file access and distributed processing capabilities. NFS allows users to create consistent directory and file structures across different machines on a network. A file stored on a remote disk is accessed as if it were on a local device. The tree structure of a local file system is augmented by the remote directories that are *mounted* by the users. As a result, the remote files appear to the local machine as if they were in the local directory.

NFS permits network service, such as *Yellow Pages*, which is a networkwide data base used for network management (indicates configurations, passwords, etc.).

NFS is based on two SUN protocols: *RPC* (remote procedure call) and *XDR* (external data representation). XDR is a set of machine-independent data formats. It permits machines with different data formats to communicate by converting to and from the XDR format. A remote procedure call allows a process to execute a procedure on another machine. To simplify the handling of failures, NFS is a *stateless* protocol. That is, the machine providing the service does not need to keep track of the past requests: all the requests are handled one at a time. If a machine serving the remote procedure call happens to crash, the machine requesting the call will repeat it after a timeout. If the machine serving the request comes back up, it can then respond to the request as if it had not crashed (except for the delay).

NFS

- NFS is SUN Microsystems' network file system.
- NFS provides a global file system across machines on the same network.
- NFS is a stateless protocol based on RPC and XDR.

8.5 NetBIOS

The *network basic input output system* (NetBIOS) is a collection of network communication services for IBM PCs and PS/2s and compatibles on a LAN. Implementations of NetBIOS on TCP/IP and UDP/IP networks are also available. NetBIOS provides four classes of services: name service, datagram service, session service, and general commands.

Name Service

A name is a string of one to sixteen characters that designates a unique process or a group of processes on a LAN. Each node on the network maintains a list of the names of its processes. The name service enables the users to add, delete, and find names. When a user requests to add a name, the service broadcasts a message asking if that name is already reserved.

Datagram Service

This service is used to transmit packets to a unique name, a group name, or to all the nodes. The user specifies the local name under which it receives datagrams.

Session Service

This is a connection-oriented reliable transmission service for messages of up to 131,071 bytes. As in the datagram service, the user specifies the local name under which it receives messages.

General Commands

Three general commands are provided: *Reset* clears the name tables and aborts the sessions in progress; *cancel* aborts a command in progress; *status* returns the name table of the node or of a remote node.

NetBIOS

- NetBIOS is a collection of network applications for IBM PCs and PS/2s and compatibles.
- NetBIOS provides a *name service* for naming processes, a *datagram service*, a *session service*, and a few general commands.

8.6 SNA

In 1974, IBM introduced its *systems network architecture* (SNA) to connect its System/370 mainframe computers to terminals and printers. Most other vendors now provide SNA software. A network user accesses the network by interacting with a *logical unit* (LU) through a *presentation service*. The LU interacts with a *physical unit*. Under IBM's terminology, the *path control* protocol layer implements virtual-circuits between LUs. The network operator sets up sessions between LUs using these virtual-circuits. User processes in the LUs enter into *conversations* that use the sessions. During a conversation, processes exchange *logical records* of up to 32,765 bytes, including a 2-byte identification field. The LU fragments the logical records into *response units* with a negotiated maximum length (typically 256 bytes). The response units are transported by the links using the *synchronous data link control* (SDLC), which is similar to HDLC (see Chapter 4).

The applications developed for SNA include *DIA*, *SNADS*, and *DDM*. DIA is the *document interchange architecture*. It provides for document storage, retrieval, and distribution. SNADS, the *SNA distribution service*, is used to send documents. DDM, *distributed data management*, enables application programs to access remote file systems.

SNA

- SNA is IBM's *system network architecture*.

- In SNA, a user access the network through a *logical unit* (LU). LUs communicate by *sessions* implemented by virtual-circuits. User processes engage in *conversations* supported by such sessions.

- The applications developed for SNA include DIA, SNADS, and DDM.

8.7 Data Bases

A number of network data base application programs are available. A *data base* is an organized set of data. For instance, a university keeps track of information about its students: address, courses, grades, name of advisor, etc. The data base is *distributed* if all the information is not stored in a single machine. A data base may also be *duplicated* if some information is replicated in different machines. It is also common for many users to be able to simultaneously access the information.

The main issues associated with data bases are their structure, how to access information, and how to permit efficient access.

A popular way to structure a data base is as a *relational data base*. In this organization, the information is stored as a set of tables. Each table is a collection of rows with a number of columns. A row corresponds to a given item and the columns to attributes of that item. For instance, a table could contain the name, address, phone number, and student identification number of every student in a given department. The table will have four columns and as many rows as there are students. Another table might contain, for each student, the student's identification number and the number and grade for each of 20 courses (with a special symbol to indicate that the course has not been taken yet).

The objective of the access to the departmental data base could be to list the students with a grade point average (GPA) below 2.8. This is done by accessing one or more tables. In our example, the second table is needed to calculate the GPAs and to find the identification numbers of students with a GPA lower than 2.8. The first table is then needed to find the student names corresponding to those identification numbers. If the tables are in different machines, then the data base program will need to ask for the necessary data transfers.

When the data base is duplicated, it is necessary to keep the different copies identical. Thus, if one copy is updated on a machine, the data base program must take care of updating the other copies.

If multiple users can access a data base, some special care must be taken in order to make the various transactions compatible. For instance, if two administrators want to add a different course each to the record of one student, then the following difficulty may arise. Say that the original student record is R. It is copied by user 1, who transforms it into $R1$. At the same time, user 2 copies R and transforms it into $R2$. Say that user 1 then writes $R1$ in the data base and replaces R. A while later, user 2 writes $R2$ in the data base and replaces $R1$. The final record will show only the update performed by user 2. A number of solutions have been devised to avoid this problem. A simple one is to "lock" the records that one intends to modify. A locked record cannot be accessed by another user. With this method, if user 1 happens to lock the record R before user 2, then user 1 will update R to $R1$ and will then "unlock" the record. User 2 can then copy $R1$ and modify it.

Deadlocks may occur with the locking scheme described above. Say that users 1 and 2 need the same two records, say R and V. Assume that user 1 locks R and that user 2 locks V. User 1 then attempts to access V but cannot since it is locked. Similarly, user 2 cannot access R. In order to break the deadlock, the program must recognize the situation and remove one of the two users.

Data Bases

> ■ A *data base* is an organized set of data. It can be centralized, distributed, and replicated.
>
> ■ A *relational* data base is organized as a collection of tables. The information in different tables can be used to answer queries.
>
> ■ The different copies of a duplicated data base must be kept consistent. Modifications of data base records cannot be interleaved and must be made exclusive, for instance by locking records. Deadlocks may occur and must be detected and broken.

8.8 Load Balancing

Load balancing refers to the sharing of the computational powers of different computers. The basic idea is to execute programs on machines that are less loaded so as to even out the load. For instance, if a large computation has to be performed on a machine which is already heavily loaded, that machine can send the program and data to be executed on another machine.

A number of experiments on load balancing and many simulations and analytical studies of it have been performed. They indicate that load balancing can be very effective. Implementations require the willingness to share computer power.

Most of the load balancing strategies are based on *thresholds*. If a program is added to a machine whose load exceeds a given value, it tries to send the program to another machine. The machine asks other machines a measure of their loads. The program is then sent to the machine with the smallest load measure, if it is less than some other specified value. The strategy may take into account the time taken to send a program.

Load Balancing

> ■ The objective of *load balancing* is to share computing resources by migrating tasks across the network.
>
> ■ Most load balancing algorithms are based on work load *thresholds*.

Summary

■ The application layer is composed of SASEs and CASEs. A CASE may include an ACSE, ROSE, and CCR.

- The TOP suite uses IEEE 802.3 or IEEE 802.5 networks, a connectionless network layer, a class 4 transport layer, a full-duplex session layer with dialogue control and synchronization points; and its presentation layer uses ASN.1. The SASEs are FTAM, MHS, JTM, VT, and DS.

- The MAP suite uses IEEE 802.4 networks. Its layers 3 to 6 are the same as TOP's. The SASEs are FTAM, MMS, and DS.

- Internet's SASEs include FTP, SMTP, TELNET, TFTP, rcp, rsh, and rlogin.

- NFS implements a global file system across a network. It is a stateless protocol based on RPC and XDR.

- NetBIOS is a set of network services for IBM PCs and PS/2s. It comprises a name service, a datagram service, a session service, and some general functions.

- IBM's SNA enables user processes to engage in *conversations* supported by *sessions* implemented by virtual-circuits between *logical units*.

- Data bases can be distributed or replicated across a network. Networkwide data base application programs must maintain the consistency of replicated records, prevent simultaneous modifications by locking records, detect and break deadlocks, and organize data transfers to answer queries.

- Load balancing shares network computing resources by migrating tasks. Most load balancing strategies are based on work load thresholds.

Problems

1. Why is an application layer needed on top of the presentation layer. Is it:
   a. for flow control?
   b. to provide user interface?
   c. for directory assistance?
2. Describe the main elements of the application layer.
3. Suppose you want to transfer a file from remote host B to local host A. Name two different protocols among the Internet applications that you could use.
4. How is TELNET different from rlogin?

5. Suppose you want to execute a program in a remote host. Explain why rsh is preferable to rcp.

6. What is SUN's NFS? Why is it better to have 10 SUN machines connected through NFS than to have them as separate entities which are able to communicate (via, say, a LAN)?

7. What is a relational data base? Propose a mechanism for detecting and breaking deadlocks that occur when different users access a data base.

8. What is the difference between rcp and FTP? Which of these two applications allows more options in handling files before transfer?

9. Suppose that two users, A and B, are connected on the network via different hosts and that they wish to play a fair game of dice (i.e., one that does not allow the possibility for either of them to cheat) over the network. Give one way for such a game to be implemented by utilizing the Internet applications. For instance, if A uses its local random number generator and then announces the result to B by, say, e-mail, then, of course, this allows the possibility for A to lie once in a while.

10. The application layer offers standardization for some commonly used user programs. Describe some of them.

11. Consider two data bases in two hosts on a network, each with a large number N of entries. Entry n of the first data base contains a number A_n, and entry n of the second data base contains a number B_n. We wish to find the maximum value of $A_n + B_n$ over the N values $n = 1, 2, ..., N$. What is the minimum number of items that have to be exchanged over the network?

12. One of the most important services of the application layer is to provide file-handling services. Discuss the need for more than just one file server (that keep and handle copies of the same file). Discuss also the potential complication that might arise when modifying one file (in which case all copies should be modified).

13. In the FTAM model of the OSI, each file has the structure of a tree whose nodes may have labels or data. Think of a specific file type for which the tree structure is preferable to the flat file structure (i.e., an ordered set of records).

14. Electronic mail (e-mail) is a widely used application of computer networks that you are probably familiar with. Currently, the e-mail address of a user consists of the user's login name, the name of the user's machine, the institution, etc. Discuss the possibility of using just the name of the use as the e-mail address.

15. List applications that are better implemented with virtual-circuit packet-switching than with datagrams.

16. What are the differences between TOP and MAP? What kinds of applications do they support?

References

The discussions of the application layer in Halsall (1988) and Tanenbaum (1988) are useful. White (1989) discusses the ASN.1 and remote operations. See also Comer (1988) and Stevens (1990).

Comer (1988). Comer, D, *Internetworking with TCP/IP: Principles, Protocols, and Architecture*. Prentice-Hall, 1988.

Halsall (1988). Halsall, F., *Data Communications, Computer Networks and OSI*. Addison-Wesley, 1988.

Stevens (1990). Stevens, W. R., *Unix Network Programming*. Prentice-Hall, 1990.

Tanenbaum (1988). Tanenbaum, A., *Computer Networks* (2nd Ed.). Prentice-Hall, 1988.

White (1989). White, J. E., "ASN.1 and ROS: The impact of X.400 on OSI," *IEEE Jour. Selected Areas in Communications*, 7, 1061–72, 1989.

Integration of Services | 9

Communication networks provide services to users. Services include the transmission of data, audio, text, graphics, and video. A number of applications are built from these network services. Whereas in the past the transmissions of voice and data were taking place over different networks, new communication networks are being designed to handle both kinds of transmissions. Networks that support the transmission of voice and data, or of video, voice, and data, are called *integrated services networks*.

Video conferencing is an application of audio-video networks. It enables a group of distant users to see one another while conversing. The digital distribution of entertainment video and of high-fidelity stereo are other possible applications of such networks. The interactive access to text and graphics data bases and bulletin boards is already available with public information systems, such as CompuServe and Prodigy. Considerably improved versions of these systems, providing access to audio, animations, and high-quality photographs, are possible with integrated services communication networks.

The transmissions of video, audio, text, and graphics place widely different demands on the communication network. These differences make it difficult to support all the services economically on a single network. However, service integration presents important advantages by making many new appealing applications possible.

Section 9.1 discusses a number of services and their traffic requirements. The integration of services on LANs is addressed in Section 9.2. After
explaining the basic architecture of the telephone network in Section 9.3, we
discuss the *integrated services digital network* (ISDN) in Section 9.4 and the
broadband integrated services digital network (BISDN) in Section 9.5.

356

9.1 Services

Figure 9.1 indicates the transmission rates and durations for a number
of services. These parameters are used by network designers to estimate the transmission capacity required by the different services.

We will discuss some of the requirements imposed by the transmission
of voice, high-fidelity audio, television, facsimiles, voice-response systems, telemetry information (remote measurements), on-demand movies, and teleconfer-
ence signals. We will also mention examples of integrated networks.

The transmission of *voice* signals by the telephone network should not
introduce a delay larger than about 300 ms. Longer delays are disturbing, spe-

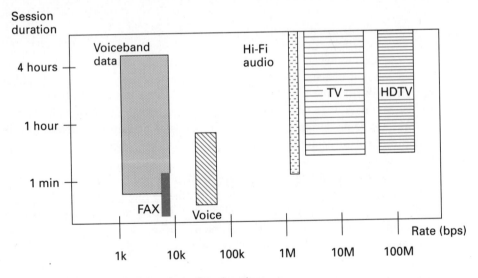

Figure 9.1 Rates and session durations.

The digital transmission of a TV program requires a bit rate between a
few Mbps and a few hundreds of Mbps, depending on the compression
and encoding used. The duration of the transmission can range from a
fraction of an hour to a few hours. The figure shows the corresponding
values for other services. The rate and duration are important parameters for the network designer.

cially in the case of significant far-end echo, i.e., signal reflections caused by equipment at the other end of the communication link. Also, the signal-to-noise ratio should be at least 40 dB, and the bandwidth should be at least 3,000 Hz. A call setup delay of a few seconds is considered acceptable. The bandwidth implies, by Nyquist's theorem (see Section 3.6), a sampling rate of about 8,000 Hz. The signal-to-noise requirement necessitates at least 7 bits per sample (see Section 3.6). A typical phone call has an average duration of 3 minutes. Another important characteristic of a phone conversation is its *activity level*, i.e., the fraction of time that the channel is not silent. A typical value is 25%. (Clearly, it is less than 50% for an average call.) When voice-activity detectors are used, one may assume that the channel is idle for about 60% to 65% of the time. When a good compression technique (ADPCM) is used, it is possible to transmit a voice signal with a bandwidth of 7 kHz and a signal-to-noise ratio of 40 dB as a 64-kbps bit stream.

The transmission of *high-fidelity audio* on a network can be implemented for individual users or as a service for broadcasters. *Teleconferences* may also require high-quality high-fidelity audio. As we indicated in our discussion of compact discs, high-fidelity stereo necessitates (without compression) a rate of about 1.5 Mbps. As we learned in Section 3.6, the rate required by NTSC television is about 100 Mbps, without compression. A video codec (coder-decoder) samples and digitizes the composite NTSC analog signal. Typically, the sampling frequency is 10.74 MHz, and 8 bits per sample are used. This leads to a rate equal to 90 Mbps. Compression algorithms can reduce the necessary rate to 10 to 20 Mbps (e.g., interframe DPCM). Compression to rates of 1.5 Mbps or even lower rates can be achieved for applications that do not transmit rapidly moving images and that do not require a very high picture quality. The digital transmission of HDTV necessitates a rate approaching 1,000 Mbps. Compression methods bring down the required rate to about 64 Mbps or even to lower values.

A *facsimile* machine transmits a typical page (215 mm × 297 mm) in about 1 minute, at 9,600 bps, with a resolution of 7.7 lines per mm, using a compression of 7:1. Run-length coding is an effective compression method for use with facsimile machines, as we explained in Chapter 7. A method called *combined symbol matching* has the potential of achieving compression ratios of 50 to 300. The idea is to attempt to recognize symbols on a page by matching features with a library of stored symbols. If a match is found, the ID number and the position of the symbol are transmitted. This requires many fewer symbols than pixel-by-pixel transmission.

A number of systems provide information in the form of *voice response*, for instance directory assistance, flight information, and stock price quotations. Some of these voice-response systems are based on *speech synthesis*. Instead of storing digitized voice messages, the systems store basic sounds (*phonemes*) that are parametrized in timing, pitch, and volume. In order to store a message, it then suffices to store the time evolution of the parameters needed for the speech synthesis. These systems need about 75 bits per second of speech, as opposed to about 64,000 bits when PCM is used. A number of speech-synthesis VLSI chips are available for such applications. These chips are also found in computer boards and in toys (Texas Instruments' Speak & Spell, for example).

Examples of *telemetry* applications include *burglar alarms* and the *remote control* of lights, appliances, heaters, and air conditioners. For instance, you may wish to turn the heat on at your home when you leave the office. You might also want a home monitoring device that periodically sends information to a receiver at your work place or to the police.

Experiments have been conducted with subscriber-controlled video-disk systems for *on-demand movies*. Instead of renting a videodisk or videotape, the subscribers of video-on-demand can order and receive video programs through the communication network.

In 1984, Nippon Telephone and Telegraph (NTT) started a *tele-conferencing* service. The access to the network is either analog or digital at 100 Mbps. The compression is done in the network down to 6.3 Mbps.

In 1985, the French National Research Center for Telecommunications (CNET) deployed a circuit-switched star network in Biarritz that serves 1,200 homes and 300 businesses. The subscribers can get one or two analog video channels, a high-fidelity audio channel, a two-way 4,800-bps data channel, and an ISDN (see Section 9.4) interface at either 144 or 72 kbps. Similar trials were being conducted in Rennes and in Montpellier.

Nippon Telegraph and Telephone started trials of an integrated information network in 1984. Some 300 subscribers in Tokyo and suburban Mitaka were connected via a 64-kbps digital network with a fiber-optic broadband network. Service included video distribution, video telephony, telemonitoring, high-speed facsimile, and interactive video response. Applications were teleconferencing, medical image transmissions, and seminars. A second set of trials was begun in 1987 with a broadband fiber optic network in central Tokyo. The company plans to deploy 140-Mbps channels to users throughout Japan before the end of this century.

The French government has provided interested telephone subscribers with *Minitel* terminals. The terminal consists of a keyboard and a video display terminal by which alphanumeric text and graphical information can be exchanged. In 1990, about 4 million users were equipped with these terminals and could access services developed by about 5,000 providers. The Minitel services include an electronic telephone directory, transportation and entertainment schedules and reservations, shop-at-home capabilities, restaurant menu information and reservations, weather, traffic route conditions, and dating services. The transmissions to the home are at 1,200 bps. The images are encoded according to an *alpha-mosaic* system. Specifically, pixels are grouped into blocks, called mosaics.

Each mosaic is described by 16 bits. The first 8 bits define the symbol, and the other 8 specify attributes (color and background, for example). Provisions are also made for using dynamically redefinable character sets. The transmissions from the homes to the network take place at 75 bps. The information is transported by the public data network TRANSPAC.

Services

- The transmissions of voice, video, audio, graphics, and photographs place vastly different demands on communication networks.
- The *transmission rates* vary from a few bps to a few hundred Mbps.
- The *durations* of the transmissions range from seconds to hours.
- The *acceptable delays* range from milliseconds to minutes.
- The *acceptable error rates* range from negligible to significant.
- Existing systems demonstrate a wide market for digital communication services.

9.2 Integrated Services Local Networks

LANs, with their high transmission rates and short delays, are well suited for the transmission of voice, data, graphics, and possibly video. This section attempts to identify some design issues that arise during implemention of an integrated services LAN and illustrates these issues with a few examples. We will discuss voice-data integration on a token ring, on a slotted ring, and on a CSMA/CD network. We conclude the section with a brief discussion of video-data integration. We start with some general observations about voice and data integration.

The guiding observations for *voice-data integration* are that voice is more sensitive to delays than data but requires a smaller throughput. These observations lead to systems that give priority to voice and buffer data. Reasonable objectives are that the voice delay should be less than 100 ms (one way) and that the data delay should be less than a few seconds (think of interactive services). If voice is given priority in a station on a LAN, then its delay is the packetizing delay plus the media-access delay plus the transmission delay plus the propagation delay. The *packetizing delay* is the time required to accumulate the samples that constitute a frame. For instance, if the sampling rate is 8 kHz with 8 bits per sample, then it takes about 16 ms to collect 1,000 bits. Indeed, the time taken is the number of bits (1,000) divided by the bit rate ($8 \times 8,000 = 64,000$ bps). If the transmission rate is 10 Mbps and if the cable is less than a few kilometers long, then the transmission and propagation delays are negligible compared to the packetizing time and to the media-access time. Thus, the design objective is a media-access time less than 80 ms. The delay faced by the data is equal to the queueing delay in addition to the media access delay, the transmission time, and the propagation time. That queueing delay is more difficult to estimate than the other delays because it strongly depends on the statistics of the data transmitted by the station.

As a first example, consider a *token ring* that uses the RAR protocol (see Chapter 5) with a cable length of 2,000 meters and with 200 stations, operating at 10 Mbps. Assume that each station originates about ten 3-minute calls in a typical 8-hour work day. Thus, the probability that a given station originated a call that is going on at a typical time during the work day is about (30 minutes)/ (8 hours) $\approx$ 6%. Hence, on the average, $200 \times 6\% = 12$ calls can be expected to be taking place at a given time. Some of those calls are between stations on the LAN, while others leave the LAN through a special station connected to the outside phone lines. It is then reasonable to limit the number of simultaneous calls to 20—these calls involve at most 20 stations—if all the calls leave the LAN. We assume that an average of ten stations are involved in phone conversations at any given time. Say that each station wants to transmit data with an average rate equal to λ bps. The data are sent in frames with an average length of *TRANSP* = 1,000 bits. The stations also transmit voice in frames of 1,000 bits. Denote by *MAT* the maximum time between two successive accesses to the token by one station. Then $MAT \approx K \times \{TRANSP + PROP\}$ where *PROP* is the time taken by a signal to go once around the ring and K is the number of stations that transmit in one "cycle," i.e., between two successive visits by the token to a given. The value of K can be estimated as

$$K \approx 10 + \frac{MAT \times \lambda \times 200}{1,000}$$

since the data frames are 1,000 bits long, on the average. Indeed, in *MAT* time units, about ten stations transmit voice while about $B := \lambda \times 200 \times MAT$ bits of data are transmitted. The data bits are transmitted in $B/1,000$ packets.

For a numerical illustration, we assume that $\lambda = 10,000$ bps. Then we find that $K \approx 10 + MAT \times 2,000$ and $MAT \approx K \times \{10^3 + 200 + 100\} \times 10^{-7}$. To derive the last expression, we observe that the propagation time corresponds to a delay of 200 bits in the stations plus $10 \times 10^6 \times (2,000/2.3 \times 10^8)$ bits on the cable. Solving the above two equations for *MAT* gives

$$MAT \approx 1.75 \text{ ms.}$$

This delay corresponds to the packetizing of 112 bits of voice samples, so that a frame of 1,000 bits suffices.

This design seems fine, but it presents a problem. What if, for some period of time, a large number of stations want to transmit data? This might delay the token to the point that it would get back to the voice transmitting stations too late.

This suggests the need for a *flow-control strategy*. One possible design can be based on the following idea. Say that one wants $MAT \leq 30$ ms, so that the frames contain at most 2,000 bits of voice. One may decide to let a station transmit data only if its token interarrival time is less than 29 ms. The rationale is that this prevents the value of MAT for the next station from exceeding 30 ms. This protocol is essentially the FDDI MAC protocol.

We now turn to a *slotted-ring* MAC protocol. Consider a 10-Mbps and a 20-km-long cable that connects 600 nodes in a ring topology. Each node inserts a delay of 8 bits. The number of bits on the ring at any one time is equal to the propagation time of a signal times the transmission rate plus the 600 delays of 8 bits. This number is, therefore, equal to $600 \times 8 + 10 \times 10^6 \times \{(20 \times 10^3)/(2.3 \times 10^8)\} = 5,669$. We divide these bits into five slots of 1,000 bits, and we assume that a station transmits frames of 1,000 bits of data or voice. A station takes about 16 ms to packetize a voice frame. Thus, we must design the protocol so that every station that transmits voice sees an empty slot at least every 16 ms. During 16 ms, $0.016 \times 10^7 = 1.6 \times 10^5$ bits are transmitted, which corresponds to 160 slots. Thus, each station that transmits voice should get to use one out of 160 consecutive slots.

We assume that the frequency and duration of the calls are the same as in our voice-data token ring example. Consequently, we can limit the number of calls to 60. This number 60 is three times more than the number of calls in the voice-data token ring since there are three times as many stations. When there are 120 stations talking simultaneously, corresponding to 60 calls, then their voice packets occupy 120 out of 160 slots every 16 ms. This leaves 40 slots out of 160 available for data. This corresponds to a data rate equal to

$$\frac{40}{160} \times 10^7 = 2.5 \text{ Mbps}.$$

The average data rate per station can therefore be equal to 4 kbps. When only the average number (36) of calls are taking place, they occupy 72 out of 160 slots, which leaves about 5 Mbps available for data. Thus, the average data rate per station can be of the order of 8 kbps.

We can also consider the integration of services over a *CSMA-CD* network, such as Ethernet. We can implement this integration by giving priority to

voice in each station and by limiting the total number of simultaneous telephone
calls.

The analysis is not very easy, but we can derive some rough estimates
of such an integrated CSMA-CD network. Assume that the cable is 2,000 meters
long, the transmission rate is 10 Mbps, the packets are 1,000 bits long, and there
are 100 stations.

362

Assume also that each station generates data at the rate of 1 Mbit per
minute and voice traffic at 64 kbps about 10% of the time. The load on the
network is then given by

$$\frac{10^6}{60 \text{ sec}} \times 100 + 10\% \times 64 \times 10^3 \times 100 \approx 2.3 \text{ Mbps.}$$

The efficiency of this Ethernet is

$$\frac{1}{1 + 5a} = \frac{1}{1 + 5 \dfrac{2,000/20}{1,000}} = \frac{1}{1.5} \approx 66\%.$$

Hence, the maximum load, or throughput, is 6.6 Mbps. Thus, the load of
2.3 Mbps is less than 50% of the throughput, and we may expect the average
delay to be equal to a few packet transmission times, as simulations and experiments indicate. Thus, the delay for the voice signal is close to the packetizing
delay, which is acceptable.

The main difference between voice and *video* is, of course, the high
bit rate required by the latter. With a good compression algorithm, full-motion
video requires 10 to 20 Mbps, as discussed in Section 9.2. Therefore, the integration of video on a LAN necessitates a basic rate that exceeds that of Ethernet. For
instance, an FDDI network can support a few video channels.

A possible approach to increasing the number of video channels is to
use a broadband network with channels reserved for video. Those channels could
be reserved over a common Ethernet channel. It is also possible to use a broadband network with a few analog TV channels (CATV) in addition to Ethernet or
ring data channels. In such a design, the analog TV channels are switched by the
stations.

Service Integration

■ The different transmission requirements make the integration of
services difficult.

■ We analyzed the voice-data integration of a token ring, a slotted
ring, and a CSMA-CD network.

■ The video-data integration requires high-speed networks.

9.3 Telephone Network

Over the next decade, the telephone network will evolve into an integrated communication network. There are two likely stages of this evolution. One is ISDN, and the other is BISDN, as we will explain in Sections 9.4 and 9.5. This section provides a brief discussion of the main components of the telephone network.

The telephone network is organized as indicated in Figure 9.2. Let us examine the operations of the telephone network. This information is important in itself since the telephone network is the largest communication network. The description will also be useful to help you understand the evolution of the network toward ISDN. The network connects telephones by searching for the shortest path between the caller and the called party. This search is performed with the help of *signaling*, i.e., special signals used to indicate the status of calls and telephone sets. For instance, *dc-signaling* is used to indicate that a receiver is on-hook or off-hook; *tone-signaling* is used for the dial tone, busy indication, etc. For the local loop to the customer's residence, these signals are sent over the same circuit as the voice signals, either in-band, i.e., in the 300-Hz to 3,400-Hz range of the voice, or out-of-band. In addition to the local loop signaling, the network uses special circuits between the switching computers of the central offices for some signaling information. This is called *common channel interoffice signaling* (CCIS). The control information is packet-switched and transmitted using the X.25 protocols.

The transmission is digital, except on the local loop, where it is analog. The encoding is PCM, with a sampling frequency of 8 kHz and 8 bits per sample. The A/D conversion is nonlinear: If the sample value is x, then a circuit computes $sgn(x) \log(1 + \mu \mid x \mid)$ before quantizing that value. This procedure is called the μ-*law compander*.

PCM makes it easy to *time-multiplex* channels. For instance, 24 channels can be multiplexed into frames of $24 \times 8 = 192$ bits, to which an additional bit is added for synchronization. These frames repeat at the sampling rate, i.e., every 125 μs. The resulting composite channel is called DS-1 by the phone industry; its rate is $193 \times 8,000 = 1.544$ Mbps. The transmission system for DS-1 is called the *T1 digital carrier system*. These DS-1 channels can also be time-multiplexed into groups. Channels are standardized into groups of 24 (called DS-1), 48 (DS-1C), 96 (DS-2), 672 (DS-3), and 4,032 (DS-4) voice channels plus the necessary framing and signaling, with bit rates equal to 1.544, 3.152, 6.312, 44.736, and 274.176 Mbps, respectively. The transmission medium is twisted pair cables and radio for the lower bit rates and coaxial cables, fibers, and radio for the higher rates. The signaling in DS-2, DS-3, and DS-4 channels—for example, of on-hook or off-hook information—is done by robbing the least significant bit in

364

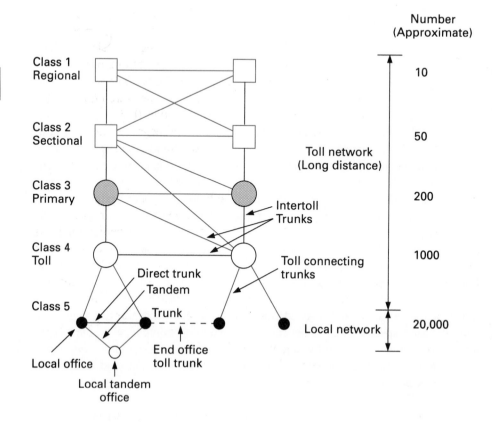

Figure 9.2 Telephone network architecture.

The circles and squares in the figure represent switches. The lines indicate connections between switches. The approximate numbers of
switches of the different classes in the United States are shown. The
telephones are connected to the local offices by the subscriber loops,
which are not shown.

every sixth word of 8 bits representing a voice sample. This adds only a small
amount of noise to the voice signal.

The *synchronization* of the network is needed for the correct time-
division multiplexing of the channels: bit streams can be interleaved only if they
have precisely the same rate. The solution adopted for the North American network is to have a single master clock (in Hillsboro, Missouri) which generates a
signal that is transmitted to all the central offices.

In addition, it is necessary for the receivers to recover the correct timing of the frames. That is, the receiver must locate the starting times of the bits, and also of the frames. The bits are recovered by using a special line code that sends 0s as a constant zero voltage signal and 1s as a positive or a negative voltage, alternatively. These positive and negative pulses that encode the 1s are used by a phase-locked loop. In order to make sure that there are enough 1s to keep the synchronization, every pattern of six consecutive 0s is replaced by a special pattern that violates the sequence of positive and negative pulses so as to be detected. This encoding is the *binary 6-zero substitution* (B6ZS) code used by the DS-2 carrier. Special codes are also inserted in the frames for synchronization.

The *digital switching* used in the phone network is a combination of *time-division* and *space-division* switching. The basic component of a space-division switch is the *electronic crossbar*, which can be viewed as a programmable interconnection matrix C. The interpretation is that $C(i, j) = 1$ if the input link i is connected to the output link j, and $C(i, j) = 0$ otherwise. This is called space division because simultaneous paths are separated in space. The number of necessary "crosspoints" with n inputs and n outputs grows as n^2 for a single crossbar. Crossbars can be combined, with the outputs of some matrices being the inputs of others. A suitable interconnection requires a number of crosspoints of the order of $n\log n$ for n inputs and n outputs.

Time-division switching uses a combination of *time-division multiplexing* and *time-slot interchange*. Time-slot interchange can be described as follows. Consider a switch with n inputs and n outputs. The n input channels are time-division multiplexed, and the samples of channel i arrive in the time slots $\{i, n + i, 2n + i, 3n + i, \ldots\}$. Say that one wishes the output link j to be connected to the input link $a(j)$ for $j = 1, \ldots, n$. One method for doing this is illustrated in Figure 9.3, where $n = 100$. The input samples are stored successively in the memory locations $1, \ldots, n$. The READ line from the memory is connected to the output links in the order $1, 2, \ldots, n, 1, 2, \ldots$, during the successive time slots. That READ line reads the memory locations in the order $a(1), a(2), \ldots, a(n), a(1), a(2), \ldots$. Thus, the output link j receives successively all the samples from the input link $a(j)$, as desired. Note that the samples are delayed by up to $2n - 1$ time slots. Also, the internal bit rate of the switch is n times the input bit rate. As in the case of crossbars, it is possible to combine time-division switches spatially. These switches are commonly used in *private branch exchanges* (PBX) that connect the telephones in a private organization and a number of outgoing lines. The time-slot interchange idea can be used without having to digitize the samples. For instance, PAM (pulse amplitude modulation) is used by AT&T's Dimension PBX.

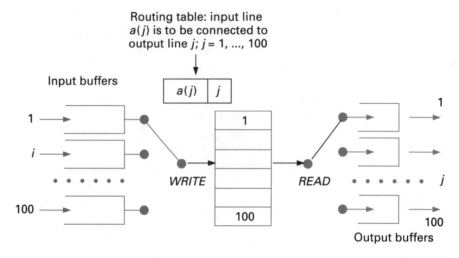

Routing table: input line
$a(j)$ is to be connected to
output line j; $j = 1, ..., 100$

Input buffers

Figure 9.3 Time-slot interchange.

The input buffers are written sequentially on the memory, in the order 1,
2, 3, ..., 100, 1, 2, ... by the *WRITE* line. The memory locations are read,
and their contents are sent to the output buffers in the order $a(1)$, $a(2)$, ...,
$a(100)$, $a(1)$, $a(2)$, ... by the *READ* line. Thus, the output buffer i receives
the contents of memory location $a(i)$, which came from the input buffer
$a(i)$. That is, input line $a(i)$ is connected to output line i.

The selection of the paths for calls, i.e., the *routing* of calls, has a
significant impact on the performance of the network. Two successive switches
along a path are connected by a *segment* composed of a number of *trunk lines*. A
trunk line is an abstraction for a channel that can carry one telephone call. For
example, one DS-1 carrier carries 24 voice signals, and, therefore, 24 trunk lines.
One call along the path occupies one trunk line between any two successive
switches. The most crucial performance measure is the *blocking probability*, i.e.,
the probability that a typical call is rejected because no free path can be found to
route it. A path is free when each of its segments has at least one free line.

The routing strategy used by AT&T is called *dynamical nonhierarchical routing*. Given a (origin, destination) pair, this routing strategy tries a
sequence of paths in order. The call is blocked if all these paths are busy, i.e., not
free.

Routing strategies that take the network congestion into account have
been proposed by a number of researchers. For example, the *dynamical routing*
strategy proposed by Bell Northern Research chooses the path with the largest
spare capacity among the set of paths designated for that (origin, destination) pair.
The spare capacity of a path is defined as the number of additional calls that can

still be carried along that path before one of the segments becomes saturated. That is, the capacity of the path is the minimum number of free lines of its segments.

Telephone Network

- The architecture of the telephone network in the United States is hierarchical.

- The transmission of control information takes place over an X.25 packet-switched network.

- The digital carrier system is a time-division multiplexing hierarchy. The signals are synchronized by a common clock.

- The circuit-switches use a combination of time-division (time-slot interchange) and space-division switching (interconnections).

- A number of routing strategies can be used by telephone networks. Some of these strategies use information about the load of the network.

9.4 Integrated Services Digital Network (ISDN)

ISDN is a concept being developed by the major telephone companies and by the CCITT. ISDN is a likely stage in the evolution of the public phone network to an integrated network.

The ISDN standards specify that the residential subscribers are provided with a *basic access* consisting of two full-duplex 64-kbps channels (called B channels, for bearer) and one full-duplex 16-kbps channel (called D channel, for data). The D channel is used for telemetry and for exchanging network-control information. One B channel is used for digital voice and the other for applications such as data transmission and videotex. Another type of service, called the *primary access*, is made available to larger customers. The primary access consists of 23 B channels (64 kbps each) and one D channel of 64 kbps.

The development of ISDN is stimulated by the following trends:

1. Over the last two decades, digital technologies have been used increasingly in the telephone network for voice transmission and for switching because of the lower life-cycle operating costs of digital equipment. The conversion to digital technology is taking place for most of the network, except for the *local loop*, for which this conversion is not economically justified on the basis of voice-only services.

2. There is an increasing demand for data transmission services. This demand is created by the cost reduction of computers and facsimile machines and the increasing need for residential alarm systems, etc.

These trends justify extending the digital transmission services to the local loop and making them available, together with new services, to customers. A number of field trials have taken place over the last few years. NTT started offering the ISDN service to customers in some parts of Japan in 1988. At the end of 1990, a number of local telephone operating companies in the United States were getting ready to offer ISDN to residential customers.

The B and D rates have been selected mostly because of the structure of the digital services (DS-1, ..., DS-4) of the current phone system. It is rather straightforward to provide a circuit-switched B channel with the existing phone system. A packet-switched B channel for data transmissions that are irregular in rate would have to be created, probably as an extension of the CCIS network discussed in Section 9.3. Are those basic rates justified on the basis of services that could be desirable to customers? This question is difficult to answer. It could be argued that 2B + D does not provide much more than the current phone network: a phone service with a slightly improved quality plus a basic data transmission facility faster than the 19,200 bps now available with voice-band modems, but not large enough to make interesting new applications, such as video transmissions, possible.

The services envisioned by the promoters of ISDN are indicated in the table below. In Table 9.1, BC designates a circuit-switched B channel and BP designates a packet-switched B channel. D designates a D channel.

Possible ISDN Services		
Service	**Bandwidth**	**Channel**
Telephone	64 kbps	BC
Alarms	100 bps	D
Utility Metering	100 bps	D
Energy Management	100 bps	D
Videotex	2.4–64 kbps	BP
Electronic Mail	4.8–64 kbps	BP
Facsimile	4.8–64 kbps	BC
Slow Scan TV	64 kbps	BC

Table 9.1

Note that a number of these services could be provided by the CATV industry, which, in 1990, had a subscriber population of 25 million and had cables passing by more than 45 million residences. Some services could also be provided by the power utilities.

The implementation of ISDN requires:

1. upgrading the subscriber loops;

2. making available circuit-switched 64-kbps channels; and

3. building packet-switched 64-kbps channels.

Subscriber loops were designed to transmit the frequencies from 300 Hz to 3,400 Hz. They are based on two-wire metallic pairs with a mixture of differently gauged cable. In addition, most loops contain cable irregularities, such as bridged taps and gauge discontinuities that induce signal reflections (echoes). A number of approaches have been investigated for achieving the necessary full-duplex 144-kbps transmissions on the existing loops. One promising method combines *echo cancellation* and *time compression multiplexing*.

Echo cancellation is an adaptive filtering technique that can be described as follows. Consider two telephone sets A and B engaged in a conversation. Set A sends the signal x to B, and set B sends the signal y to A. The transmission from A to B is subject to an *echo*. That is, some delayed and attenuated version $e(x)$ of x comes back to A so that A receives $y + e(x)$ instead of y. You may have experienced this echo when placing a long distance call. The objective of the echo cancellation is to reduce the echo $e(x)$. The method used by the echo cancellation circuitry is to subtract a predicted echo value $f(x)$ from the received signal $y + e(x)$. Thus, $f(x)$ is an approximation of $e(x)$. That approximation is calculated by delaying and attenuating the transmitted signal x. More precisely, the circuitry calculates $f(x)(t) = a_1 x(t - 1) + \ldots + a_n x(t - n)$ where time t is measured in milliseconds, for instance, and where the coefficients $a_1, \ldots, a_n$ are adapted by the circuitry so that $f(x)$ is as similar to $y + e(x)$ as possible. More precisely, the circuit attempts to minimize over time the average energy in $y + e(x) - f(x)$ by modifying the coefficients a_i. Since the signals x and y are uncorrelated, the circuit cannot predict y from x. Consequently, the energy in $y + e(x) - f(x)$ is minimized when the circuit is successful at predicting $e(x)$, i.e., when $f(x) \approx e(x)$. As a result, $y + e(x) - f(x) \cong y$, as desired.

Time compression multiplexing can be used to implement a full-duplex channel at 144 kbps by sending data at 324 kbps for T seconds one way, then stopping for $T/8$, then sending data the other way at 324 kbps, then stopping for $T/8$, etc. Of course, data have to be buffered at both ends. This method can be used for about 80% of the subscriber loops. The other loops (which are too long or too ill-conditioned) may have to be improved in order to carry ISDN signals.

Circuit-switched 64-kbps channels require some modification of the DS-0 digital service. (DS-0 is the digitized voice channel.) Indeed, the DS-0 channels rob some of the bits for signaling. As a consequence, only 56 kbps are "clear" for data transmission. One possibility is to use three DS-0 channels per basic access (2B + D), or other similar combinations. The switching facilities are being deployed for the standard phone services. In the early 1990s, almost all the local access lines will be served by digital switches. Also, the toll switches already operate at 64 kbps, and small modifications would make them suitable for 64-kbps clear channels. The *signaling network* CCIS is now system 6. It uses an unlayered protocol which is difficult to upgrade. A new protocol (called system 7) has been developed that allows the users (through their D channels) to control the progress of incoming and outgoing calls.

ISDN

- The basic ISDN access is 2B + D. Each B channel is a full-duplex 64-kbps channel. The D channel is a full-duplex 16-kbps channel.

- The services envisioned for ISDN include facsimile transmissions, access to data bases, videotex, electronic mail, and alarms, in addition to the telephone service.

- The implementation of ISDN requires upgrading subscriber loops, making the 64-kbps channels available, and building packet-switched channels.

9.5 Broadband ISDN

Broadband integrated services digital networks (BISDN) are being designed by a number of research groups. The objective is to provide subscribers with high-speed digital channels that make possible the new services described below. We will explain some ideas that are proposed for the transmission and the switching of these high-speed channels.

Network engineers propose a *basic access* of BISDN that consists of four 150-Mbps channels. (There is no typo; it is 150 *M*bps, *not* 150 *k*bps!) The services that the basic access would make possible include:

1. digital TV (about 100 Mbps, uncompressed)
2. digital HDTV (about 150 Mbps, compressed)
3. digital hi-fi (about 2 Mbps, uncompressed)
4. teleconferencing (100 Mbps, uncompressed)
5. multi-media terminals: videophone + graphics + ...

6. high-speed retrieval of graphics/voice from data bases

7. interconnection of LANs

As an example, consider HDTV. The basic access could be used to provide one video channel that would be connected to some central distribution office. The subscriber would "order" a given movie, and the office would connect the channel to a videodisk player that would deliver the HDTV movie.

These services are limited mostly by the imagination of the designers. The crucial implementation questions are how to estimate the potential demand in the marketplace for such services and how much customers would be willing to pay for them.

The *transmission* of high-speed digital channels will be conducted over optical fibers. As we learned in Chapter 3, optical fibers have very small attenuations and very large capacities. These features enable the transmission of a high bit rate over large distances without repeaters and make the implementation of high-speed networks economically feasible.

At the end of 1987, more than 3.2 million km of optical fibers had been deployed in the United States. Most of these fibers are single-mode fibers that operate in the 405-Mbps to 565-Mbps range, with repeaters every 30 km. Note that 25,000 voice channels can be transmitted on 1 fiber at 1.7 Gbps.

Economic feasibility studies in 1988 showed that fibers would be advantageous in the local loop for customers requiring at least ten channels at 64 kbps. The cost of optical communication equipment is decreasing, and will become economically viable even for lighter users.

The American National Standards Institute (ANSI) has proposed the *SONET* (synchronous optical network) standard for the high-speed transmission of data over public networks. SONET is a time-division multiplexing method associated with a hierarchy of optical interface rates based on a 50-Mbps synchronous transport signal, level 1 (STS-1), containing channel identification, framing, error-checking, maintenance information, etc.

SONET frames can carry BISDN traffic. This traffic contains two types of signals: *synchronous* and *asynchronous*. Synchronous traffic is of fixed rate and long duration, such as a phone call, a video broadcast, or an audio broadcast. Asynchronous traffic has an irregular rate, like most data transmissions.

As we saw in our discussion of digital switching (in Section 9.4), synchronous traffic can be switched without the need for large buffers, because of the regularity of the bit streams. Also, a circuit-switch needs to be configured only when new calls are placed. Thus, the switching of synchronous traffic is easy. However, the switching of asynchronous traffic is more complicated: successive packets may go to different destinations, so that every frame has to be examined before being routed.

As a consequence, it is probably economical to segregate the two traffic types, synchronous and asynchronous, before switching them, and to send the synchronous traffic to a circuit-switch and the asynchronous traffic to an ATM (*asynchronous transfer mode*) switch. We will discuss a possible ATM switch architecture below.

An ATM switch is a device with N input links and M output links. The links are optical fibers, and the rate on each fiber is 150 Mbps or more. Packets of 53 bytes arrive on the input links. Each packet has a header which specifies the output link that it should be sent to.

A number of ATM switch architectures have been proposed and proto- types have been developed. The switches differ in how they resolve "conflicts." A conflict occurs when multiple packets that arrive simultaneously (on different input links) need to be sent to the same output link. Packets need to be stored since they cannot be transmitted at the same time. The packets can be stored in buffers attached to the input and output links, or they can be stored in a large buffer shared by all the links. Therefore, three switch architectures are possible: input buffering, output buffering, and shared buffer.

We will discuss the shared buffer architecture because it is more ele- gant than the others and requires a smaller amount of memory for a given block- ing probability. The shared buffer ATM switch is illustrated in Figure 9.4.

The switch operates as follows. The packets share a large buffer (*BUFFER*) organized as N *linked lists*, one for each output link. A linked list is a set of memory locations that are arranged so that the first location (called the *head* of the list) points to the second one, the second one to the third, and so on, up to the last location (called the *tail* of the list). The tail of the list points to *empty* to designate that it is the last item in the list. The address of the head of the ith linked list is stored in buffer H_i, while that of the tail of the list is stored in T_i. In addition, the free locations are also organized as a linked list. The head of the list of free locations has its address in H, and the tail's address is in T.

Each input link j has a shift register IN_j, and each output link i has a shift register OUT_i. When a packet arrives on input link j, the switch examines its header to identify its output link, say i. The switch then adds the packet to the tail of the ith linked list. This addition is performed by reading the location of the tail of the list in T_i, replacing the content of the *NEXT* field at the address pointed to by T_i by the content of H, and then replacing the content of H with that of the *NEXT* field of the location at the address formerly pointed to by H. The switch then copies the new packet in the *DATA* field at the address indicated by T_i. If no free buffer is available, i.e., when the *NEXT* field of H is *empty*, the arriving packet can either remain in IN_j, where it will be overwritten, or it can use a location that was previously in another linked list. These blocking strategies with priorities require further study.

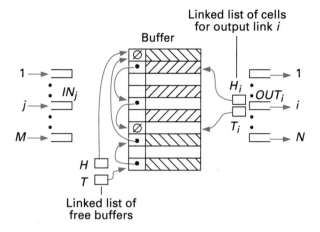

Figure 9.4 Shared buffer ATM switch.

The buffer is organized as N linked lists for the output links and one linked list for free buffers.

When the output link i is ready for a next packet, it finds its address in H_i, then copies the *DATA* field at that address into OUT_i. The content of H_i is then replaced by that of the *NEXT* field at the address formerly pointed to by H_i. The switch then adds the freed buffer at the address formerly pointed to by H_i by indicating this address in the *NEXT* field of the address T and setting the *NEXT* field of the freed buffer to *empty*.

BISDN

- The broadband integrated services digital networks would make 150-Mbps channels available to users.
- The transmission will be over optical fibers.
- The switching may use a combination of circuit-switches and ATM switches.
- The shared buffer ATM switch is one of many designs being explored.

Summary

- Different applications have widely different communication requirements. Flexible transport mechanisms are needed to support such applications on a common network.

- LANs can support synchronous traffic if they use a MAC with bounded media-access time.

- The telephone network transports voice signals by circuit-switched digital carriers. Signaling information is transported by a packet-switched network.

- ISDN provides users with access to the digital carriers. The basic access is 2B + D.

- BISDN would provide users with 150-Mbps channels. The information would be transported by ATM.

Problems

1. Construct a table with the typical transmission rates (in bps) required by different services. The rows should be labeled Voice, Audio, Video, etc. The first column should be Bandwidth (e.g., 3,000 Hz for Voice). The second column should give the rate. Assume that the signal-to-noise ratio is 40 dB. Look throughout the text for needed data. The numbers should be comparable to those of Figure 9.1.

2. Discuss briefly (15 lines maximum) the impact of an integrated services digital communication network on everyday life. What kind of services will be useful? What kind will not be useful? What are the possible dangers? What will be the likely impact on work habits, entertainment, information, and education?

3. It was mentioned, in relation to space-division switching for a telephone network, that in order to connect n inputs to n outputs, we need n^2 crosspoints. It was claimed that if crossbars can be combined, with the outputs of some matrices being the inputs of others, then the number of crosspoints can be reduced. Give an example (graphically) for a specific small value of n to illustrate that claim.

4. Explain why, in the time slot interchange, the internal switching rate should be n times the input bit rate (n is the number of channels). In case the incoming traffic is asynchronous, why is it necessary for the internal memory (buffer) to be significantly larger than when it is synchronous?

5. The proposed access bit rate in a BISDN is of the order of 150 Mbs. Name the expensive network hardware components required because of this high rate.

6. What are the main switching elements of a BISDN? For what type of traffic is each one used?

7. Analyze the delay of signals in a time slot interchange switch.

8. A token ring network contains 100 stations operating at 1 Mbps and uses a 1,000-meter cable. Stations transmit voice and data. Assume that each station transmits voice 15% of the time. Assume also that data are transmitted in frames of length 500 bits at an average rate of 5 kbs. Estimate MAT, the maximum time between two successive accesses to the token by a station.

*9. A section of a telephone network that connects points a and b has n different parallel paths which a call originating at a can use. Statistical observations reveal that λ calls per minute originate at the point a and that λ_i calls per minute use path i ($i = 1, ..., n$). Each call has an average duration of one minute. Each path has L trunk lines. The phone company is about to expand the network and has N additional trunk lines that need to be allocated to the n paths in such a way that the chance that a call is blocked (gets an *all lines are busy* message) is as small as possible. Find a formula for this blocking probability. (*Hint:* Assume that N_i trunk lines are allocated to path i and that the blocking probability of a call that uses this path is given by $B(L + N_i, \lambda_i)$ as in Erlang's formula of Problem 10.14. Argue also that the chance that a call will use path i is the ratio λ_i/λ.)

10. Why is it not efficient to use modems to transmit data between terminals and computers with the traditional telephone network (POTS)? How does ISDN improve that situation?

11. Discuss the differences between time-compression multiplexing and time-division multiplexing.

12. Suppose that at time n node A sends X_n to node B. Moreover, at time n, node A receives Y_n from node B and some echo $\alpha \times X_n$ where α is unknown. Assume that the X_ns and Y_ns are independent. Devise a method that node A can use for estimating α from the received values $Z_n = Y_n + \alpha \times X_n$ and the transmitted values X_n.

13. Consider a 64-kbps link from node A to node B. Two types of traffic will be transmitted by the link. Type 1 has priority over type 2. Type 1 consists of packets of 10 kbytes that arrive as a Poisson process with rate λ_1, and type 2 consists of packets of 1 kbyte that arrive as a Poisson process with rate λ_2. What are the values of λ_1 and λ_2 that can be supported by the link? Find the values of λ_1 such that the average delay (without including the transmission time) for a typical packet of type 2 is less than 1 second. (*Hint:* Consult formula (10.10) for priority queues.)

14. In the previous problem, calculate the average delay per packet, regardless of its class. Calculate the same average delay when the priorities are interchanged. Can you draw any general conclusion about the priorities that minimize the average delay per packet?

376

15. Do you think that real-time video transmission should be implemented by using circuit-switching or packet-switching? Discuss the cost of the switches for both solutions.

References

Integrated services digital networks are described in Bocker (1988) and Stallings (1989). COMM (1991), the January 1991 issue of the *IEEE Communications Magazine*, is devoted to switching.

Bocker (1988). Bocker, P., *ISDN—The Integrated Services Digital Network: Concepts, Methods, Systems*. Springer-Verlag, 1988.

COMM (1991). "Switching in a cooperative environment," *IEEE Communications Magazine*, 29, January 1991.

Stallings (1989). Stallings, W., *ISDN: An Introduction*. Macmillan, 1989.

Performance Evaluation and Monitoring | 10

Implementing a network is a major task that requires the design of specific hardware and software. When designing a new network, it is desirable to be able to predict its level of performance before implementing it. This chapter briefly reviews the methods used by network engineers to predict performance.

These methods can be classified into three groups: *mathematical models, simulations,* and *emulations.* They are discussed in the following sections. In addition to performance prediction methods, we will discuss *performance monitoring* methods, which are an important aspect of *network management.*

Except for the first section, this chapter requires a level of mathematical sophistication higher than that required by the rest of the text. Only the results of the queueing analysis are given here. Derivations can be found in Appendix B.

10.1 Monitoring, SNMP, and CMOT

How can a network administrator evaluate the level of performance of a network? How can such an evaluation guide modifications to the network?

To evaluate the performance of a network, the administrator must monitor its behavior. Some aspects of the behavior can be monitored by adding software to specific nodes of the network. Other aspects require specialized moni-

toring hardware. For instance, a computer on an Ethernet network can be programmed to collect statistics about the traffic of packets it sees on the network.
Such statistics can be used to calculate the load on the network, i.e., the fraction
of the network throughput used by the traffic. The network administrator can use
378   this load information to determine when the network is approaching saturation.

More detailed statistics can also be measured by software. For instance, it is possible to *filter* the packets by examining their headers. Using such
filtering, the network administrator can determine the amount of traffic due to
electronic mail or to FTP, for instance. Traffic can also be classified by pair
(source, destination). Many vendors sell *network analyzers* and network management software that perform this type of monitoring and that provide the network
administrator with a user-friendly interface and tools for computing various traffic
statistics.

By adding specialized monitoring hardware to the network interfaces,
the network administrator is able to collect some information that cannot be monitored by software alone. For instance, some hardware failures, such as cable
rupture or loose connections can be detected and identified with specialized monitoring equipment. Monitoring the number of collisions faced by a packet in an
Ethernet interface requires a specific monitoring of the interface algorithm that is
not possible with all interface boards. Measuring the delay of packets between
nodes makes it necessary to add time stamps to the packets and for the nodes to
synchronize their clocks by exchanging time-stamped control packets.

Hardware failure indications (*alarms*) are clearly valuable. Statistical
monitoring of information is not as straightforward to use. The network administrator can use traffic information to identify when the network has to be modified.
One modification that can relieve an Ethernet network that is approaching its
capacity is to partition it into subnetworks connected by bridges. The subnetworks
should connect nodes that communicate frequently in a way that limits the traffic
between different subnetworks. The network administrator can select the subnetworks by analyzing the traffic statistics for the different source/destination
pairs.

The collection of network information is facilitated when the various
devices use standardized formats and protocols. Two classes of network management standards were emerging in 1990: CMOT (*common management information services and protocol over TCP/IP*) and SNMP (*simple network management
protocol*). In late 1990, a large number of vendors were providing SNMP products, whereas few implementations of CMOT were in operation. These two standardization efforts result from recommendations of the *Internet Activities Board*.

Both SNMP and CMOT maintain images of the network in a data base
called *management information base* (MIB). The consistency between the image
and the network is maintained by exchanging messages. When a management
application modifies attributes of an object in the data base, messages are sent to

the physical device represented by the object to modify its corresponding attributes. Conversely, the data base can learn the attributes of the physical devices by polling the devices periodically or by having the devices send relevant information about selected events.

In SNMP, a management application sends the commands *get, set,* and *get_next* to objects in the MIBs of managed devices. These commands are formatted in ASN.1 and are sent using UDP/IP. Some implementations of SNMP send these commands directly over LLC. This connectionless exchange of commands and responses is used to set and read attributes of managed objects. The managed objects can also signal events to the management application.

CMOT is a protocol suite for the implementation of the ISO *common management information protocol* (CMIP). CMOT provides connection-oriented services between a management application and managed objects. The services are standardized as *common management information services* (CMIS). The application layer contains a *common management information service element* (CMISE) that uses the services of ROSE and ACSE (see Chapter 8). The messages are exchanged over TCP/IP and UDP/IP. CMIP provides more complex naming and applications than SNMP. For instance, CMIP permits management applications to retrieve large numbers of data by linked replies that are not possible under SNMP. Also, CMIP can address multiple objects by type, value, and relative location without having to name them individually, as SNMP requires. Moreover, *system management functions* (SMFs) are being standardized for CMIS. The SMFs provide sophisticated management services that are not available under SNMP.

Monitoring

- A network manager can monitor the performance of a network by using specialized software and possibly some dedicated hardware.
- Alarms identify malfunctions, and traffic statistics can be used to reconfigure the network to improve its performance.
- SNMP is a connectionless management system.
- CMOT is a connection-oriented protocol suite for implementing CMIP.

10.2 Models and Analysis

Some simplified models of computer systems can be analyzed mathematically. The insight provided by the analytical results can be very valuable, even if the methods do not permit the evaluation of detailed models of real systems. The most commonly used models are *queueing systems*. The most widely used results are reviewed in this section.

M/M/1 Queue

Consider a buffer equipped with a transmitter. Assume that packets arrive at the buffer at times $0 < T_1 < T_2 < T_3 < \ldots$ and that the transmission times of the successive packets, which are transmitted on a first come–first served basis, are $S_1, S_2, S_3, \ldots$.

This system is called an *M/M/1* queue if:

1. The random *interarrival times* $T_1, T_2 - T_1, T_3 - T_2, \ldots$ are independent and identically distributed with

$$P\{T_{n+1} - T_n \geq t\} = e^{-\lambda t}, t \geq 0 . \tag{10.1}$$

   That is, the interarrival times are *exponentially distributed with rate* $\lambda > 0$. In that case, the arrival times $\{T_n\}$ are said to form a *Poisson process with rate* λ.

2. The transmission times $\{S_n\}$ are independent and exponentially distributed with rate μ. Equivalently, the packet lengths are independent and exponentially distributed with mean $R\mu^{-1}$ (in bits) where R is the transmission rate (in bits per second). That is,

$$P\{S_n \geq t\} = e^{-\mu t}, \ t \geq 0 . \tag{10.2}$$

Under these assumptions, if one denotes by x_t the number of packets that are either in the buffer or being transmitted at time $t > 0$, it can be shown that, *in statistical equilibrium*,

$$P\{x_t = n\} = \rho^n(1 - \rho), n \geq 0, \text{ if } \rho := \frac{\lambda}{\mu} < 1 . \tag{10.3}$$

By statistical equilibrium we mean that the system has reached steady-state in the sense that the probability that the queue length takes given values does not change with time. This does not mean, of course, that the queue length stops evolving. This situation is similar to what happens when gas is injected into an empty bottle. After a while, the distribution of the gas molecules stabilizes even though the molecules keep on moving. The likelihood of finding a given number of molecules in some section of the bottle approaches some constant value.

If $\lambda \geq \mu$, then the average number of packets in the buffer is infinite. That is, the queue builds up over time, without bound.

If $\lambda < \mu$, we conclude from (10.3) that the average *queue length* is given by

$$L := E\{x_t\} = \sum_{n=0}^{\infty} nP\{x_t = n\} = \frac{\rho}{1-\rho} = \frac{\lambda}{\mu - \lambda}. \tag{10.4}$$

This formula can also be used to derive the *average delay T* per packet through the system. The average delay T is related to the average queue length by *Little's result*

$$L = \lambda T. \tag{10.5}$$

Using this result, we conclude that

$$T = \frac{1}{\mu - \lambda} \tag{10.6}$$

for the M/M/1 queue.

Little's result (10.5) applies to a large class of queueing systems. A simple interpretation of that result can be given for first come–first served queueing systems. If a typical customer spends T time-units, on the average, in the system, then the number of customers left behind by that typical customer is equal to λT, on the average. Indeed, the customers left behind are those who arrived during the T time-units spent by the typical customer in the system. Thus, a typical customer leaves λT customers behind upon leaving the network. This must be the average number L of customers in the system. Thus, $L = \lambda T$.

The result holds for systems that are not necessarily first come–first served, as the following argument explains. Say that each customer pays one unit of cost per unit of time spent in the system. Then the average amount paid per unit of time by all the customers is equal to the average number L of customers in the system at any given time. On the other hand, each customer pays a total of T, on the average, since T is the average time that a customer spends in the system. Therefore, since customers arrive at rate λ, customers pay $\lambda \times T$ per unit of time. Hence (10.5).

Application to Statistical Multiplexing

The above results for the M/M/1 queue can be used to appreciate the gain achieved by statistical multiplexing, when compared to time-division multiplexing.

Consider one transmission line with transmission rate R. A number N of traffic streams of packets, each with rate λ have to be transmitted along that line. Assume that the arrival times of the packets form independent Poisson processes (with rate λ), and that the packet lengths are independent and exponentially distributed with mean L.

Time-division multiplexing consists of dividing the capacity of the transmitter into N channels with rate R/N. Each traffic stream can then be modeled as an M/M/1 queue with arrival rate λ and transmission rate $\mu := R(LN)^{-1}$ (in packets per second). The average delay per packet is given by formula (10.6):

$$T = \frac{1}{\mu - \lambda}.$$

Statistical multiplexing consists of buffering the packets coming from the N streams into a single buffer and transmitting them one at a time. The arrival process into the single buffer now has rate $N\lambda$. (The process can be shown to be Poisson.) This system can now be modeled as an M/M/1 queue with arrival rate $N\lambda$ and with transmission rate $RL^{-1} = N\mu$ packets per second. The average delay is now given by

$$\frac{1}{N\mu - N\lambda} = \frac{T}{N}.$$

Thus, the average delay per packet for the statistical multiplexing system is a fraction $1/N$ of the delay for the time-division multiplexing.

Networks of M/M/1 Queues

In Chapter 6 we used the fact that the average delay per packet in a network of queues is equal to

$$T = \frac{1}{\gamma} \sum_{j=1}^{J} \frac{\lambda_j}{\mu_j - \lambda_j} \tag{10.7}$$

where γ is the average rate of flow into the network, λ_j is the average rate of flow through queue j, and μ_j is the average transmission rate of queue j. All these rates are in packets per second, and the λ_j are obtained by solving the equations that express the conservation of the flows through the nodes.

The assumptions required for the formula (10.7) to be valid are:

1. The arrival streams from outside into the network form independent Poisson processes.

2. The packet transmission times at all the queues are independent and exponentially distributed.

In practice, assumption (1) may be verified. However, assumption (2) cannot be. Indeed, the successive transmission times of a given packet into the various nodes are all proportional to the packet length, and so they cannot be independent. Nevertheless, simulation experiments show that formula (10.7) provides a reasonable estimate for the average delay per packet in store-and-forward packet switched networks.

M/G/1 Queues

Consider once again the M/M/1 queue but assume that the successive packet transmission times S_n are independent and have some common distribution that is not necessarily exponential. The resulting system is called the M/G/1 queue.

We can show that the average delay per packet through the system is given by

$$T = \frac{1}{\mu} + \frac{\lambda E\{S_n^2\}}{2(1-\rho)} = \frac{1}{\mu} + \frac{\lambda(\sigma^2 + \mu^{-2})}{2(1-\rho)} \tag{10.8}$$

where μ^{-1} is the average transmission time, $\rho = \lambda/\mu$, and σ^2 is the variance of the transmission times. That is, $\sigma^2 = E\{(S_n - \mu^{-1})^2\}$.

For instance, if the transmission times are exponentially distributed with mean μ^{-1}, then $\sigma^2 = \mu^{-2}$, so that (10.8) becomes (10.6). As another example, if all the packet lengths are identical, then $\sigma^2 = 0$ and the average delay of the packets is the delay through an M/M/1 queue times

$$1 - \frac{\rho}{2}.$$

Formula (10.8) shows that the average delay increases with the variance of the packet length.

A Word of Caution

The result of (10.8) shows that we must be careful when assuming some distribution for packet lengths. That result shows that the average values of the service times and interarrival times are not sufficient to predict average delays. The variance of the service times has an important impact on the average delay.

A similar caution holds for the packet arrival process. For instance, if we assume that packets arrive exactly every λ^{-1} time units at a queue and that their service times are constant and equal to $\mu^{-1} < \lambda^{-1}$, then every packet arrives after the previous ones have been transmitted, so that no queueing takes place. As a consequence, the delay per packet is equal to a transmission time, i.e., to μ^{-1}. Comparing this to (10.6), we confirm that the distributions of interarrival times and of service times strongly influence delays.

384

One should, therefore, be very wary of hasty assumptions, even when they are convenient. It may be very tempting to assume that some processes are Poisson so as to be able to carry out some analysis. (This is the assumption that we made when analyzing the ALOHA protocols in Chapter 5.) However, network engineers should not trust blindly the results of an analysis based on such arbitrary assumptions. If a more precise analysis is not feasible and if the assumptions cannot be validated, then it is less misleading to admit that fact and to resort to a careful simulation than to make arbitrary assumptions for the sake of convenience.

Queues with Vacations

Consider the following variation on the M/G/1 queue. Assume that once the transmitter has emptied the queue it is turned off for some random time, called a *vacation epoch*. Assume also that the successive vacation epochs are independent, are independent of the past evolution of the system, and have a common distribution.

With these assumptions we can show that the average delay per packet is given by

$$T = T_0 + \frac{v}{2}E\{V^2\}$$ (10.9)

where T_0 is the average delay through an M/G/1 queue without vacations, V denotes a typical vacation epoch, and v^{-1} is the average vacation epoch duration.

Priority Systems

Consider transmission systems with two types of packets: voice and data. Assume that the arrivals of the packets form two independent Poisson processes with rate λ_1 for the voice packets and λ_2 for the data packets. Assume that the transmission times of the voice packets are all independent and are distributed as S_1 and that the transmission times of the data packets are independent and distributed as S_2.

The voice packets are given *priority* over the data packets. That is, whenever a packet transmission is completed, the transmitter starts the transmission of a voice packet if there is one in the buffer, and the transmission of a data packet, if any, otherwise.

One can show that the average delay per voice packet is given by $\mu_1^{-1} + W_1$ and the average delay per data packet is given by $\mu_2^{-1} + W_2$ where

$$W_1 = \frac{\sum_{i=1}^{2} \lambda_i E\{S_i^2\}}{2(1 - \rho_1)} \quad \text{and} \quad W_2 = \frac{\sum_{i=1}^{2} \lambda_i E\{S_i^2\}}{2(1 - \rho_1)(1 - \rho_1 - \rho_2)} \tag{10.10}$$

where $\rho_i := \lambda_i \mu_i^{-1}$ for $i = 1, 2$.

Cyclic-Service Systems

Consider the model of a token ring network illustrated in Figure 10.1. In this model, packets arrive at each station as a Poisson arrival process with the same rate λ. The packet transmission times are independent and are distributed as the random variable S. The token travels around the ring until it is captured by a station that has a nonempty queue. At that time, that station can transmit one packet. After transmission, it releases the token. This is the RAT protocol that we discussed in Section 5.3. The token travel time around the ring, when it is not captured by any station, is equal to R.

The problem is to calculate the average delay per packet. This average delay is known to be equal to $E\{S\} + W = \mu^{-1} + W$ where

$$W = \frac{N\lambda E\{S^2\} + R[1 + \rho N^{-1}]}{2[1 - \rho - \lambda R]}. \tag{10.11}$$

In this expression, $\rho := N\lambda\mu^{-1}$. This formula is valid provided that $\lambda R < 1 - \rho$; otherwise, the system is unstable.

Note that if R (the token walk time) is negligible, then this formula yields

$$W = \frac{N\lambda E\{S^2\}}{2(1 - \rho)},$$

which gives the same queueing time as that in an M/G/1 queue. This result should not be surprising, since the system then behaves exactly as an M/G/1 queue,

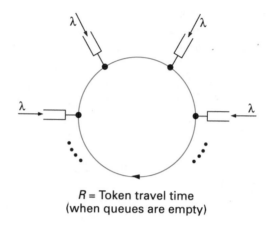

R = Token travel time
(when queues are empty)

Figure 10.1 Token ring network.

except that it is not necessarily first come–first served. This modification cannot change the average number in the system and, therefore, cannot affect the average delay, by Little's result.

The stability condition $\lambda R < 1 - \rho$ can be written as $E\{NS + R\} < \lambda^{-1}$. This condition can be explained by observing that when all the queues are non-empty, the average time between successive visits to a station by the token is $E\{NS + R\}$. This average time should be less than the average interarrival time λ^{-1} at a station.

Models

- The M/M/1 queue is a single-server queue with Poisson arrivals and exponential service times. The average queue length is $\lambda/(\mu - \lambda)$, and the average delay is $1/(\mu - \lambda)$.

- The average delay through a network of queues is given by (10.7).

- The average delay through an M/G/1 queue is given by (10.8). The average delay increases with the variance of the service times. When the server goes on vacation, the average delay increases by the second moment of the vacations divided by twice their mean value.

- We stated the values of the delays in queues with priorities and in a symmetric cyclic-service system.

10.3 Simulation

A computer *simulation* is a process that mimics the evolution of a physical system. By tracing that evolution we can determine quantities about the evolution of the physical system. We will discuss *time-driven* and *event-driven* simulations of an M/M/1 queue. We will then examine the *regenerative simulations* method.

Time-Driven Simulation

Our objective is to simulate the evolution of an M/M/1 queue. Recall that such a queue is characterized by independent and exponentially distributed interarrival times with rate λ and by independent and exponentially distributed .transmission times with rate μ.

Let $\varepsilon \ll 1$ and $t > 0$. Assume that we have simulated the M/M/1 queue up to time t and that the arrival times up to t were $0 < T_1 = t_1 < \ldots < T_n = t_n < t$. The probability that an arrival will occur during the time interval $(t, t + \varepsilon)$ is approximately equal to $\lambda\varepsilon$. Similarly, the probability that a transmission in progress at time t is completed by time $t + \varepsilon$ is approximately equal to $\mu\varepsilon$.

This leads to the following simulation procedure. We divide the time into intervals of duration ε. Assume that we know x_t. We then simulate two independent coin flips. A flip of the first coin yields "head" with probability $\lambda\varepsilon$ and "tail" with probability $1 - \lambda\varepsilon$. A flip of the second coin yields "head" with probability $\mu\varepsilon$ and "tail" with probability $1 - \mu\varepsilon$. The interpretation is that the first coin flip yields "head" to represent that an arrival occurs between time t and time $t + \varepsilon$ and that the second coin flip yields "head" to represent that a service in progress at time t (when $x_t > 0$) terminates between time t and time $t + \varepsilon$. The value of $x_{t+\varepsilon}$ is then given by

$$x_{t+\varepsilon} = (x_0 - C_2)^+ + C_1$$

where C_i takes the value 1 when the flip of coin number i yields "head" and the value 0 otherwise (for $i = 1, 2$). The notation $(a)^+$ means the maximum of a and 0. We repeat this procedure to produce $x_{t+2\varepsilon}$, and so on.

It remains to explain how the coin flipping experiments can be simulated. As you probably know, most programming languages and a large number of pocket calculators have a function "random." When invoked, this function returns a random number that is uniformly distributed in [0, 1], i.e., a random number equally likely to take any value in that interval. Moreover, every call to this function is supposed to provide a new random number that is independent of the previous ones. The computers and calculators usually generate these random numbers by computing a regression of the form

$$U_{n+1} = \frac{X_{n+1}}{M} \text{ with } X_{n+1} = \{a \times X_n + b\} \bmod M$$

where X_0, a, b, and M are well chosen. A suitable choice of these numbers produces a sequence $\{X_1, X_2, \ldots\}$ that is difficult to distinguish from a sequence of independent random numbers uniformly distributed over $[0, 1]$.

Thus, if we choose $0 < p < 1$ and if we define Z_n to be the random variable that takes the value 1 if $U_n < p$ and takes the value 0 otherwise, then the value Z_n behaves almost as independent random variables that take the value 1 with probability p and the value 0 otherwise. This permits the simulation of coin flipping experiments.

The disadvantage of a time-driven simulation is that it may spend a lot of time generating time intervals during which no action takes place. This may result in a very slow simulation.

Event-Driven Simulation

We now describe a different simulation method for the M/M/1 queue. Assume that x_0 is known and let $\{U_n, n \geq 1\}$ be independent and uniformly distributed over $[0, 1]$. Define

$$\tau = -\frac{1}{\lambda} \log U_1 \text{ and } \sigma = -\frac{1}{\mu} \log U_2 . \tag{10.12}$$

You can verify that τ and σ are independent and exponentially distributed with rates λ and μ, respectively. Thus, τ is distributed as the first arrival time T_1 and σ is distributed as the first service time S_1.

The simulation of the queue length x_t then proceeds as follows. If $\tau < \sigma$, we define

$$x_t = x_0 \text{ for } t \in [0, \tau) \text{ and } x_\tau = x_0 + 1 .$$

The interpretation is that the first arrival occurs at time τ before the first service is completed. If $\tau > \sigma$, we define

$$x_t = x_0 \text{ for } t \in [0, \sigma) \text{ and } x_\sigma = (x_0 - 1)^+ .$$

The interpretation is that the completion of the first service occurs at time σ, before the first arrival.

The simulation then proceeds by repeating the previous construction. This simulation method simulates the successive transitions of x_t. It jumps from event to event.

Regenerative Simulation

The evolution of an M/M/1 queue, or of a network of such queues, can be shown to start afresh every time that the system becomes empty. That is, if τ_n denotes the nth time that the system becomes empty, then the evolutions

$$\{x_t, t \in [\tau_n, \tau_{n+1})\}, n \geq 1$$

are independent and identically distributed.

As a consequence, functions of those "cycles" are also independent and identically distributed. For instance, if D_n is the sum of the delays of the packets that arrived during the cycle $[\tau_n, \tau_{n+1})$ and if K_n is the number of packets that arrived during that cycle, then the random pairs (D_n, K_n) for $n \geq 1$ are independent and have a common distribution. It follows that

$$\frac{D_1 + \dots + D_n}{n} \rightarrow E\{D_1\}, \tag{10.13}$$

by the *strong law of large numbers* (see Appendix A), and similarly for the K_n. As a consequence,

$$\frac{D_1 + \dots + D_n}{K_1 + \dots + K_n} \rightarrow \frac{E\{D_1\}}{E\{K_1\}}, \tag{10.14}$$

and this limit is then the average delay per packet. Moreover, we can use the *central limit theorem* (see Appendix A) to construct confidence intervals for the estimates. This idea to decompose the evolution into cycles that are independent and identically distributed is called *regenerative simulation*.

This approach cannot be used for complex systems that take a very long time to "regenerate." Calculations show that a network of 40 M/M/1 queues with $\mu_i = 2\lambda_i$ for each queue and with $\gamma = 200$ packets per second spends 170 years between two successive returns to the empty state. A simulation on a fast computer would require a few weeks between regenerations.

Simulation

- A simulation of a discrete-event system, such as an M/M/1 queue, can be either *time-driven* or *event-driven*.

- A time-driven simulation generates the state of the system every multiple of a small time unit.

- An event-driven simulation generates the successive transitions of the system.

- The *regenerative* simulation method enables us to analyze the output of a simulation by decomposing it into independent and identically distributed cycles.

10.4 Emulation

Mathematical analysis is not possible for realistic models of complex systems, and simulations may be too slow to be useful. These limitations led a number of researchers to turn to the *emulation* of systems. An *emulator* is a physical model that evolves as the system being investigated evolves. In addition, the emulator can be "tuned" to reflect different parameter settings or protocols. Emulation can be much faster than simulation because of the large number of concurrent activities occurring in a real system.

A simple form of emulation is the monitoring of an existing network. This method is useful but usually does not allow one to examine a wide range of operating conditions. Another form of emulation consists of setting up an experimental network that is used only for experimentation. A number of researchers have conducted such experiments with off-the-shelf hardware. This experimentation allows the researchers to compare existing designs.

Another approach is to build an experimental network that can be programmed to use different protocols and topologies. One example is the *magnet* experiment at Columbia University. This is a 100-Mbps slotted-ring network. The allocation of the slots is governed by a protocol that can be modified. Another example is an experimental network built at Berkeley. This network can emulate 10-Mbps LANs in real time with a wide range of topologies (rings, busses, stars, etc.) and protocols (token passing, CSMA-CD, tree, reservation, integrated LANs, priorities, etc.). In addition, time/distance scaling permits the reduced-speed emulation of higher bit rate networks. Moreover, voice and video hardware systems were developed to emulate integrated networks.

Emulation

- Simulations can be exceedingly slow.
- An emulator is a tunable model of a physical system. The emulator may run much faster than a simulation because many activities occur in parallel.

Summary

- Monitoring enables the network manager to evaluate the level of performance of a network. The monitoring information is used to identify corrective actions to be taken and also modifications of the network to improve its performance.
- SNMP and CMOT are management protocol suites being adopted as standards.
- Queueing theory enables one to predict the delays through queues and networks. We discussed the M/M/1 queue and its networks and the M/G/1 queue with and without vacations and priorities.
- Simulations are used by network engineers to evaluate network performance when analytical results are not available.
- Emulators can be built to obtain more accurate estimates of the performance of complex systems.

Problems

1. *Integrated Network.* A communication link is used to send two types of traffic: voice and data. The voice traffic is regular and is made up of a number N of voice channels. Each voice channel has a constant rate equal to α bits per second. The data traffic is modeled by a Poisson arrival process with rate λ. The lengths of the data packets are independent and exponentially distributed with mean L^{-1}. The transmission link has a rate equal to R bits per second. The N voice channels use $N\alpha$ bps of this transmission rate, and the excess of the rate is used by the data traffic.

   Find the maximum number of voice channels when the average delay per packet cannot exceed T seconds.

2. *Little's Formula.* Consider an M/G/1 queue with arrival rate λ and mean service time μ^{-1}. Show that the probability that the queue is empty is equal to $1 - \lambda\mu^{-1}$. (*Hint:* Apply Little's result to the server. The number of customers with the server is equal to one if the queue is nonempty or to zero otherwise. As a consequence, the average number of customers with the server is equal to the probability that the queue is nonempty.)

*3. *Networks.* Consider the network model of the discussion of traffic engineering in Section 6.3. Denote by A_{ij} the average number of visits to node j made by a packet that starts in queue i before it leaves the network. Show that

$$A_{ij} = \delta_{ij} + \sum_k r_{ik} A_{kj}$$

where $\delta_{ij} = 0$ if $i \neq j$ and $\delta_{ij} = 1$ if $i = j$. In matrix notation, this gives $A = I + RA$.

Argue that

$$\lambda_j = \sum_i \gamma_i A_{ij} \, .$$

Relate the above results to (10.6) and (10.7).

4. *M/G/1 Queue.* Consider packets that have B_1 bits with probability $p \in (0, 1)$ and have B_2 bits otherwise. Thus, the transmission times S_n are equal to $B_1 R^{-1}$ with probability p and to $B_2 R^{-1}$ with probability $1 - p$. Calculate the average delay per packet if the packets arrive as a Poisson process with rate λ. (Use (10.8).)

For a given average packet length, what are the values of (p, B_1, B_2) that maximizes the average delay?

5. *Vacations.* Consider (10.9). Assume that the queue is extremely fast, so that $T_0 \approx 0$. It follows that

$$T \approx \frac{\nu}{2} E\{V^2\}.$$

Show that $T \geq E\{V\}/2$. Explain why this is the case, even though one could argue that every packet has to wait for one vacation to complete, so that one might have guessed that T should be equal to half a mean vacation. (*Hint:* A packet is more likely to arrive during long vacations than during short ones. As a consequence, the average delay per packet gives more weight to longer vacations than to smaller ones.)

6. *Priorities*. Using (10.10), compare the average delay per packet in an M/G/1 queue with priorities and in one without priorities.

7. *Simulations*. Show that the random variable τ defined by (10.12) is exponentially distributed with mean λ^{-1}.

8. *Regenerative Simulation*. Derive (10.14) from (10.13).

9. *Regeneration Time*. Consider an M/M/1 queue with arrival rate λ and service rate μ. What is the average time between two successive returns to the empty state? (*Hint:* Denote that time by A. Since the queue remains empty for λ^{-1} units of time, on the average, every time that it becomes empty, the fraction of time that the queue is empty is equal to $\lambda^{-1}[\lambda^{-1} + A]$. Since this is the probability that the queue is empty at an arbitrary time, using (10.3) allows one to determine A.)

10. *Cyclic-Service Systems*. Formula (10.11) shows that

$$W \approx \frac{R}{2(1 - \lambda R)}$$

in the case where $S << 0$. Try to explain this value. (*Hint:* A typical customer has to wait for a residual token travel time (equal to $R/2$ on the average), plus X token travel times, if X denotes the number of customers found upon arrival in the queue. Little's result states that $E\{X\} = \lambda W$.)

*11. Is it better to use one server at rate 1 or two servers at rate 1/2? To address this question, assume that the rate of arrivals in an M/M/1 queue is λ and that the service rate is 1. Show that the mean delay is $T_1 = 1/(1 - \lambda)$. Instead of using one server, use two, but each with half the service rate. The arrival rate remains the same. Compute the delay T_2 for the latter case. (*Hint:* The latter system is an M/M/2 queue. Consult Problem 4 of Appendix B.)

12. Is it better to form one or two lines in a counter with two employees? The second system of the previous problem models the situation in which customers arrive at rate λ in a bank with two employees, each working at rate 1/2, and form one single line and are serviced in an FCFS fashion. Now consider the situation in which there are two lines, one for each employee, and a customer joins one of them at random. Compute the delay T_3 in this case. Make a plot of T_1, T_2 (see Problem 11 above), and T_3 as a function of λ.

13. *Statistical Versus Time-Division Multiplexing*. Argue that the second model of Problem 12 is a model for the time-division multiplexing of two channels and that the first model of Problem 11 is a model for the

statistical multiplexing of the same channels. Conclude that statistical multiplexing is superior to time-division multiplexing even when the arrival streams are random. Compare with the regular (deterministic case) of Problem 15, Chapter 2.

394

*14. Derive the blocking probability formula for an $M/M/N/N$ queue. This is a queue with Poisson arrivals at rate λ, exponential service times at rate μ with N servers, and a buffer of the same size. Show that the blocking probability $B(N, \lambda)$ is given by the Erlang formula:

$$B(N) = \frac{(\rho^N)/N!}{1 + \rho + (\rho^2)/2! + \ldots + (\rho^N)/N!} \quad \text{with} \quad \rho := \frac{\lambda}{\mu}.$$

(*Hint:* Show first that the balance equations (see Appendix B) are $\pi(n-1)\lambda = \pi(n)n\mu$, $n = 1, \ldots, N$. Then solve for the blocking probability $\pi(N)$.)

15. Packets arrive at rate 1 Mbs according to a Poisson process. Each message can either follow path 1, consisting of a single M/M/1 queue with service rate 30 Mbps, or path 2, consisting of two M/M/1 queues in series with service rates 10 and 20 Mbs, respectively. A static algorithm is a controller that sends a packet to path 1 with probability p or to path 2 with probability $1 - p$. (A more sophisticated algorithm would actually look at the queue sizes before taking any decision.) We are given the constraint that the average delay on path 2 should not exceed 0.10 ms. What is the maximum allowable value of p?

16. The interarrival times of packets in a communication link are random variables $T_1, T_2, \ldots$ that are independent with a common distribution, which unfortunately is unknown. For flow control purposes, one is interested in knowing the arrival rate and the standard deviation of the interarrival time. Explain how to estimate these quantities from real-time observations.

References

Ben-Artzi (1990) contains a clear discussion of SNMP and CMOT. Case (1989) is a more detailed presentation of SNMP. Chapter 3 in Bertsekas (1987) is a nice introduction to performance evaluation. Kleinrock (1975) is also highly recommended. Walrand (1988) is a more advanced presentation of the theory.

Ben-Artzi (1990). Ben-Artzi, A., Chanda, A., and Warrier, U., "Network management of TCP/IP networks: Present and future," *IEEE Network Magazine,* 35–43, July 1990.

Bertsekas (1987). Bertsekas, D., and Gallager, R., *Data Networks.* Prentice-Hall, 1987.

Case (1989). Case, J., Fedor, M., Schoffstall, M., and Davin, C., "A simple network management protocol (SNMP)," *Network Working Group RFC 1098*, April 1989.

Kleinrock (1975). Kleinrock, L., *Queueing Systems, Vol. 1.* John Wiley & Sons, 1975.

Walrand (1988). Walrand, J., *An Introduction to Queueing Networks.* Prentice-Hall, 1988.

Probability

Uncertainty affects the operations and the design of communication networks in a fundamental way. The retransmission protocols and the statistical multiplexing strategies used in packet-switched networks are designed to handle the unpredictable traffic and transmission errors. *Probability theory* is one method for quantifying uncertainty. That theory is useful because of its predictive power. Probability theory has been used successfully to predict and to optimize the performance of computer systems, communication networks, manufacturing plants, and many other engineering systems. In this appendix, we explain the few results from probability theory that we need in this text and we illustrate them with examples.

In Section A.1, we define *probability* and *random variable*. The *expected value* of a random variable is defined in Section A.2. Section A.3 explains the definition of *independence* of random variables. The *regenerative method* for computing some mean values is explained in Section A.4.

A.1 Probability and Random Variables

We do not give a formal definition of probability nor of a random variable. Let us just say that a random variable is a function of the outcome of a random experiment and that the probabilities characterize how likely different outcomes are. The following examples illustrate what we have in mind.

A *roulette wheel* has N slots that are equally likely to be selected by spinning the wheel. The N slots are marked with $n < N$ different numbers $\{x_1, x_2, ..., x_n\}$. Number x_i appears on N_i of the N slots, for $i = 1, ..., n$. Thus,

$$\sum_{i=1}^{n} N_i := N_1 + ... + N_n = N.$$

The odds that the number x_i is selected by a roulette wheel spin are N_i to N. We say that the *probability* that the outcome of the spin is x_i is equal to

$$p_i = \frac{N_i}{N}, \text{ for } i = 1, 2, ..., n.$$

Thus, the actual outcome is unpredictable. Let us denote it by X. By definition, X is a function of the outcome of a random experiment. In this example, X takes the value x_i if the outcome of the random experiment, i.e., the slot selected by spinning the wheel, happens to be one of the N_i slots marked with the value x_i. A function of the outcome of a random experiment is called a *random variable*. We define

$$P\{X = x_i\} := p_i.$$

Thus, $P\{X = x_i\}$ is the probability that $X = x_i$. Notice that

$$0 \le p_i \le 1, \text{ for all } i \text{ and } \sum_{i=1}^{n} p_i = 1.$$

For any set A of values that X can take, we define

$$P\{X \in A\} := \sum_{x_i \in A} p_i.$$

This last expression means that the probability that X takes a value in A is defined as the sum of the probabilities p_i of all the values x_i in A. The justification is that if $A = \{x_1, ..., x_k\}$, then a value in A is chosen by the spin if it selects one out of the $N_1 + ... + N_k$ slots marked $x_1, x_2, ...,$ or x_k. The probability that this occurs is equal to $(N_1 + ... + N_k)/N$, which is seen to be equal to

$$p_1 + ... + p_k = \sum_{x_i \in A} p_i$$

since the indices i such that $x_i \in A$ are $1, 2, ..., k$.

The roulette wheel has only a finite number of slots. Our next example examines a random experiment that has an infinite number of possible outcomes. The experiment consists of counting the photons Y that hit a specific photo-detector in a time interval of 1 minute. By repeating the experiment many times, one finds that the fraction of experiments when $Y = n$ is equal to

$$p_n = \frac{\alpha^n}{n!} e^{-\alpha}, \ n \geq 0 \tag{A.1}$$

where α is some positive number. (By definition, $n!$—called *n factorial*—is equal to 1 when $n = 0$ and to $1 \times 2 \times 3 \times ... \times n$ when n is a positive integer.) The number p_n is called the *probability* that $Y = n$. You can verify that

$$0 \leq p_n \leq 1, \ \text{for all } n \quad \text{and} \quad \sum_{n=0}^{\infty} p_n = 1$$

by using the definition of the exponential

$$e^{\alpha} = \sum_{m=0}^{\infty} \frac{\alpha^m}{m!} . \tag{A.2}$$

As before, for any set A, we define

$$P\{Y \in A\} := \sum_{n \in A} p_n .$$

By definition, a random variable with the probabilities (A.1) is called a *Poisson random variable* with parameter α.

So far, our random variables admitted values in a countable set. That is, we could enumerate the possible values as $x_1, x_2, x_3, ...$. The random variable that we examine next takes arbitrary values in $[0, \infty)$. We buy a light bulb and we are told by the manufacturer that the lifetime X of that bulb is such that

$$P\{X > t\} = e^{-\lambda t}, \ t \geq 0 \tag{A.3}$$

where λ is a positive real number. A random variable such that (A.3) holds is said to be *exponentially distributed* with rate λ. From (A.3) we can calculate that

$$P\{X \in (t, t+\varepsilon]\} \approx \lambda \varepsilon e^{-\lambda t}, \ \text{for } 0 \leq t \text{ and } 0 < \varepsilon \ll 1. \tag{A.4}$$

Indeed, since the set $(t, t+\varepsilon]$ is the difference between the set (t, ∞) and the set $(t+\varepsilon, \infty)$, we conclude that the left-hand side of (A.4) is equal to

$$P\{X > t\} - P\{X > t + \varepsilon\} = e^{-\lambda t} - e^{-\lambda(t+\varepsilon)} = \{1 - e^{-\lambda\varepsilon}\} \times e^{-\lambda t}$$

and (A.4) then follows from (A.3) by using $e^{-\lambda\varepsilon} \approx 1 - \lambda\varepsilon$. In general, when X is a random variable that takes values in $(-\infty, +\infty)$ and

$$P\{X \in (t, t+\varepsilon)\} \approx f(t)\varepsilon, \quad \text{for} \quad t \in (-\infty, +\infty) \quad \text{and} \quad 0 < \varepsilon \ll 1,$$

we say that the function $f(.)$ is the *probability density function* (p.d.f.) of the random variable X. Thus, the probability density function of an exponentially distributed random variable with rate λ is

$$f(t) = \begin{cases} \lambda e^{-\lambda t}, & \text{for } t \geq 0 \\ 0, & \text{for } t < 0. \end{cases} \tag{A.5}$$

So far, we have defined a random variable as the outcome of a random experiment and we have examined three examples. We now turn to a more subtle question that is of central importance in probability theory. That question is how we should take available information into account when calculating probabilities. The answer is provided by the notion of *conditional probability*. We will start our discussion of conditional probability with a simple example from which we will derive a general definition. We will then apply this definition to a few more examples.

Consider the roulette wheel discussed at the beginning of this section. We are told that the outcome of the spin is such that $X \in \{x_2, x_4, x_5\}$. We want to find the probability that $X \in \{x_1, x_2, x_4, x_6\}$ given that information. Since we known that $X \in \{x_2, x_4, x_5\}$, the slot selected by the spin must be one of the $N_2 + N_4 + N_5$ slots marked x_2, x_4, or x_5. Also, these slots are equally likely to have been selected and X takes a value in $\{x_1, x_2, x_4, x_6\}$ if it takes one of the values x_2 or x_4, i.e., if the slot selected by the spin is one of $N_2 + N_4$ among the $N_2 + N_4 + N_5$ equally likely slots known to have been selected. Thus, the probability that $X \in \{x_1, x_2, x_4, x_6\}$ given that $X \in \{x_2, x_4, x_5\}$ is given by

$$\frac{N_2 + N_4}{N_2 + N_4 + N_5}.$$

By dividing both numerator and denominator by N, the above probability can be expressed as

$$\frac{P\{X \in \{x_2, x_4\}\}}{P\{X \in \{x_2, x_4, x_5\}\}}.$$

Therefore, if one denotes by A the event $X \in \{x_1, x_2, x_4, x_6\}$ and by B the event $X \in \{x_2, x_4, x_5\}$, one sees from the above discussion that the *conditional probability of A given B* is equal to

$$P[A \mid B] := \frac{P\{A \text{ and } B\}}{P\{B\}} . \tag{A.6}$$

We adopt the above formula as the definition of conditional probability. Let us see how we can apply that formula to two other examples. As a first example, let Y be a Poisson random variable with parameter α (see (A.1)). Then

$$P[Y = 1 \mid Y > 0] = \frac{P\{Y = 1 \text{ and } Y > 0\}}{P\{Y > 0\}} = \frac{P\{Y = 1\}}{1 - P\{Y = 0\}} = \frac{\alpha e^{-\alpha}}{1 - e^{-\alpha}} .$$

As another example, let X be the exponential lifetime of a light bulb (see (A.3)). We want to estimate the probability that a light bulb that has been on for a seconds will survive for at least t more seconds. That is, we want to calculate $P[X > a + t \mid X > a]$. Using (A.3) and (A.6) we find

$$P[X > a + t \mid X > a] = \frac{P\{X > a + t\}}{P\{X > a\}} = \frac{e^{-\lambda(a + t)}}{e^{-\lambda a}}$$
$$= e^{-\lambda t} = P\{X > t\} .$$

This calculation reveals the *memoryless property* of the exponential distribution: a light bulb that has been on for some time is equally likely as a new light bulb to survive for t more seconds. In other words, an old light bulb is exactly as good as a new one (assuming that the lifetime is exponentially distributed).

A.2 Expectation

Intuitively, the *expected value* (or *average* or *mean value*) of a random variable is the arithmetic mean of the values observed when the random experiment is replicated many times. For instance, consider the roulette wheel and denote by X_m the number selected by the mth spin of the wheel. The arithmetic mean of the values selected by one's spinning the wheel N times is

$$\frac{X_1 + X_2 + \ldots + X_N}{N} . \tag{A.7}$$

We expect that the fraction of times that a spin selects the number x_i is close to p_i. That is, we expect that the number x_i is selected about $p_i N$ times during the N experiments. Consequently, the numerator of (A.7) is approximately equal to

$$(p_1 N) \times x_1 + (p_2 N) \times x_2 + \ldots + (p_n N) \times x_n ,$$

so that we expect the ratio (A.7) to be approximately equal to

$$p_1 x_1 + p_2 x_2 + \ldots + p_n x_n \, .$$

We will use this intuitive discussion to define the expected value of a random variable. Specifically, let X be a random variable with possible values $\{x_i, \ i \geq 1\}$. Assume that the x_i are real numbers. (X is then called a *real-valued random variable*.) The *expected value* $E\{X\}$ of X is defined as *the sum of the values of X weighted by their probabilities*, i.e., by

$$E\{X\} = \sum_{i=1}^{\infty} x_i P\{X = x_i\} \, . \tag{A.8}$$

We illustrate this definition with a few simple examples. A random variable X is *geometrically distributed with parameter* $p \in [0, 1]$ if

$$P\{X = n\} = (1 - p)p^{n-1}, \ \text{for} \ n = 1, 2, 3, \ldots \, . \tag{A.9}$$

These probabilities sum to one since

$$\sum_{m=0}^{\infty} a^m = \frac{1}{1 - a}, \ \text{for} \ a \in (-1, +1) \, . \tag{A.10}$$

A simple way to verify (A.10) is to denote the sum by A and to observe that

$$A = \sum_{m=0}^{\infty} a^m = 1 + \sum_{m=1}^{\infty} a^m = 1 + a \sum_{m=0}^{\infty} a^m = 1 + aA \, ,$$

from which (A.10) follows. We use (A.9) and (A.8) to calculate the expected value of X. We find

$$E\{X\} = \sum_{n=1}^{\infty} n(1 - p)p^{n-1} = \frac{1}{1 - p} \, . \tag{A.11}$$

To verify the last equality, denote the sum by S and observe that

$$S - pS = \sum_{n=1}^{\infty} n(1 - p)p^{n-1} - \sum_{n=0}^{\infty} n(1 - p)p^n$$

$$= \sum_{n=0}^{\infty} (n + 1)(1 - p)p^n - \sum_{n=0}^{\infty} n(1 - p)p^n$$

$$= (1 - p)\sum_{n=0}^{\infty} p^n = 1 \, .$$

As another example, let us calculate the expected value of a Poisson random variable x with parameter α (see (A.1)). We find

$$E\{X\} = \sum_{n=0}^{\infty} n \frac{\alpha^n}{n!} e^{-\alpha} = \alpha \sum_{n=1}^{\infty} \frac{\alpha^{n-1}}{(n-1)!} e^{-\alpha} = \alpha \sum_{m=0}^{\infty} \frac{\alpha^m}{m!} e^{-\alpha} = \alpha . \tag{A.12}$$

As yet another example, consider a random variable X that always takes the same value μ (some real number). Thus, $P\{X = \mu\} = 1$. In that case, one says that X is constant and one may denote X by μ. It follows from the definition (A.8) that

$$E\{\mu\} = \mu$$

since there is only one term in the sum (A.8) which corresponds to the value μ and its probability 1.

We conclude our discussion of expected value by examining a random variable that takes values in a continuous set. Let X be an exponentially distributed random variable with rate λ. We want to calculate $E\{X\}$. We argue that, for very small ε,

$$P\{X \in (n\varepsilon, (n+1)\varepsilon]\} \approx f(n\varepsilon)\varepsilon$$

where $f(.)$ is the p.d.f. of X defined in (A.5). Thus, X can be approximated by a random variable that takes the discrete values $\{0, \varepsilon, 2\varepsilon, 3\varepsilon, \ldots\}$ with the probabilities given above. Consequently, using (A.8),

$$E\{X\} \approx \sum_{n=0}^{\infty} (n\varepsilon) \times \{ f(n\varepsilon)\varepsilon \} .$$

This approximation becomes better as ε becomes smaller and the above sum approaches

$$\int_{0}^{\infty} xf(x)dx ,$$

by definition of the integral. We conclude that

$$E\{X\} = \int_{0}^{\infty} xf(x)dx = \int_{0}^{\infty} x\lambda e^{-\lambda x}dx = \lambda^{-1} . \tag{A.13}$$

The above example can be generalized, of course, to a random variable X with p.d.f. $f(.)$ to show that its expected value is given by

$$E\{X\} = \int\limits_{-\infty}^{+\infty} xf(x)dx \, ,$$

(A.14)

404

provided that this integral exists.

In many applications, we are led to consider functions of random variables. You will learn how the expected value of such a function can be calculated. The method is very simple. Let X be a random variable and $H(X)$ a real-valued function of X. Then $Y = H(X)$ is a real-valued random variable. (It is a function of the outcome of a random experiment since X is such a function.) We want to calculate $E\{H(X)\}$. Assume that X takes the values $\{x_i, \ i \geq 1\}$ with probabilities $p_i = P\{X = x_i\}$. Assume further that the function $H(.)$ is such that the values $H(x_i)$ are distinct for different is. Then Y takes the value $H(x_i)$ with probability p_i. Indeed, Y takes the value $H(x_i)$ if and only if X takes the value x_i, which occurs with probability p_i. Hence, by definition (A.8) of expected value,

$$E\{H(X)\} = \sum_{i=1}^{\infty} H(x_i)p_i \, .$$

(A.15)

In general, if the values $H(x_i)$ are not all distinct, a minor perturbation of the function H (after the hundredth decimal place, say) can make them distinct, so that (A.15) must again hold. (See Problem A.2 for another argument.)

We will need to calculate the mean value of sums of random variables. To learn how this can be done, let (X, Y) be a function of some random experiment. Assume that both X and Y take real values. Consequently, $aX + bY$ is a real-valued random variable for arbitrarily chosen real numbers a and b. You will see that

$$E\{aX + bY\} = aE\{X\} + bE\{Y\} \, .$$

(A.16)

To perform the calculation, let us assume that the pair (X, Y) takes the value (x_i, y_i) with probability p_i for $i \geq 1$. By applying (A.15) to the function $H(X, Y) = aX + bY$, we find

$$E\{aX + bY\} = \sum_{i=1}^{\infty} (ax_i + by_i)p_i = a\sum_{i=1}^{\infty} x_i\, p_i + b\sum_{i=1}^{\infty} y_i\, p_i = aE\{X\} + bE\{Y\},$$

as claimed. To derive the last equality, we use

$$E\{X\} = \sum_{i=1}^{\infty} x_i\, p_i$$

as can be verified by applying (A.15) to the function $H(X, Y) = X$. The same method shows that

$$E\{Y\} = \sum_{i=1}^{\infty} y_i \, p_i.$$

A.3 Independence

Independence is probably the most fertile concept in probability theory. Intuitively, two random variables are *independent* if knowing the value of one does not provide information about the value of the other. We will define this concept precisely in this section, and we will explore some of its consequences.

We start with a simple example. Consider two roulette wheels, one in Las Vegas and one in Atlantic City. The wheel in Las Vegas has N equally likely slots, and N_i of those slots are marked with the number x_i, for $i = 1, 2, ..., n$. The wheel in Atlantic City has M equally likely slots, and M_j of those slots are marked with the number y_j, for $j = 1, 2, ..., m$.

Thus,

$$P\{X = x_i\} = \frac{N_i}{N} \text{ and } P\{Y = y_j\} = \frac{M_j}{M}.$$

Assume that both wheels are spun simultaneously. Denote the values selected by the two wheels by X (in Las Vegas) and Y (in Atlantic City). If we consider spinning the two wheels as a single random experiment, then intuition suggests that there are $N \times M$ equally likely outcomes, corresponding to N possible slots selected by the first wheel and to M for the second wheel. To every slot of the first wheel correspond M possible slots for the second wheel. Out of these $N \times M$ possibilities, $N_i \times M_j$ result in $X = x_i$ and $Y = y_j$. Hence,

$$P\{X = x_i \text{ and } Y = y_j\} = \frac{N_i \times M_j}{N \times M} = \frac{N_i}{N} \times \frac{M_j}{M},$$

so that

$$P\{X = x_i \text{ and } Y = y_j\} = P\{X = x_i\} \times P\{Y = y_j\}, \tag{A.17}$$

for $i = 1, 2, ..., n$ and $j = 1, 2, ..., m$.

We adopt (A.17) as a definition of independence. Specifically, two random variables X and Y with possible values $\{x_i, i \geq 1\}$ and $\{y_j, j \geq 1\}$ are said to be *independent* when (A.17) holds. More generally, two random variables X and Y are independent if

$$P\{X \in A \text{ and } Y \in B\} = P\{X \in A\} \times P\{Y \in B\} \text{ for all sets } A \text{ and } B \quad (A.18)$$

and the random variables $\{X_n, n \geq 1\}$ are independent if

$$P\{X_1 \in A_1, X_2 \in A_2, ..., X_n \in A_n\} = P\{X_1 \in A_1\} \times ... \times P\{X_n \in A_n\}, \quad (A.19)$$

for all $n \geq 1$ and all sets A_i.

Note that it is generally not true that the random variables $\{X_n, n \geq 1\}$ are independent if X_i and X_j are independent for all $i \neq j$. In this latter case, one says that the random variables are *pairwise independent*. Thus, pairwise independence does not imply independence of a set of random variables. (See Problem A.3.)

As an illustration of independence, consider the following experiment. One is given a coin that, when flipped, yields *heads* (H) with probability $p \in (0, 1)$ and yields *tails* (T) otherwise. Denote by X the number of times that the coin must be flipped before yielding the first T. We want to calculate $P\{X = n\}$ for $n \geq 1$. In our description of the experiment, we implicitly assume that the successive outcomes of the coin flips are independent random variables. Thus, if one denotes by Y_n the outcome of the nth flip, one has

$$P\{X = n\} = P\{Y_1 = H, ..., Y_{n-1} = H, Y_n = T\}$$
$$= P\{Y_1 = H\} \times ... \times P\{Y_{n-1} = H\} \times P\{Y_n = T\}$$
$$= p^{n-1}(1 - p), \ n \geq 1$$

where the second equality follows from (A.19). This shows that X is geometrically distributed with parameter p (see (A.9)). In particular, $E\{X\} = (1 - p)^{-1}$, by (A.11).

You probably expect that functions of independent random variables are independent. Let us show that this is indeed the case. Let X and Y be two independent random variables and $f(.), g(.)$ be two arbitrary functions. To show that $f(X)$ and $g(Y)$ are independent, we must show that

$$P\{f(X) \in A \text{ and } g(Y) \in B\} = P\{f(X) \in A\} \times P\{g(Y) \in B\} ,$$

for all sets A and B. Now, $f(X)$ takes values in A if and only if X takes values in some specific set C. That set C is the set of values x such that $f(x) \in A$. Similarly, $g(Y)$ takes values in B if and only if Y takes values in some set D. Hence,

$$P\{ f(X) \in A \text{ and } g(Y) \in B\} = P\{X \in C \text{ and } Y \in D\}$$
$$= P\{X \in C\} \times P\{Y \in D\}$$
$$= P\{ f(X) \in A\} \times P\{ f(Y) \in B\} .$$

In this derivation, the first and third equalities follow from the definition of the sets C and D and the second equality follows from the independence of X and Y.

We will need the following result about the expectation of the product of independent random variables. The result states that

$$E\{XY\} = E\{X\} \times E\{Y\} \quad \text{whenever } X \text{ and } Y \text{ are independent} . \qquad \text{(A.20)}$$

We will prove this result when X takes the values $\{x_i, i \geq 1\}$ with probabilities p_i and Y takes the values $\{y_j, j \geq 1\}$ with probabilities q_j. Then (X, Y) takes the value (x_i, y_j) with probability $p_i q_j$ (by independence). Consequently, (A.15) implies that

$$E\{XY\} = \sum_{i,j} x_i y_j p_i q_j .$$

This sum can be computed by first summing over j and then summing over i. We find

$$E\{XY\} = \sum_i [\sum_j x_i y_j p_i q_j] = \sum_i [x_i p_i \sum_j y_j q_j] = \sum_i [x_i p_i E\{Y\}]$$

$$= E\{Y\} \sum_i x_i p_i = E\{Y\} E\{X\},$$

as we set out to prove.

Two very useful results, which we will not derive here, are known for independent and identically distributed random variables $\{X_n, n \geq 1\}$. The first result is the *strong law of large numbers* that states that

$$Y_n := \frac{X_1 + X_2 + \ldots + X_n}{n} \rightarrow E\{X_1\} \quad \text{as } n \rightarrow \infty .$$

That is, for large n, the arithmetic mean Y_n of n independent random variables with the same distribution is close to the expected value of these random variables.

The second result, the *central limit theorem*, states that

$$\{Y_n - E\{X_1\}\} \times \sqrt{n} \approx N(0, \sigma^2) \quad \text{for } n \gg 1.$$

In this statement, $N(0, \sigma^2)$ denotes a Gaussian random variable with mean zero and variance σ^2, where σ^2 is the variance of each X_n. By definition,

$$X = N(0, \sigma^2) \text{ if } P\{X \in (x, x+dx)\} = \frac{1}{\sqrt{2\pi\sigma^2}} e^{-\frac{x^2}{2\sigma^2}} dx \text{ for } -\infty < x < \infty .$$

This theorem says that the difference between the arithmetic mean Y_n and the expected value $E\{X_1\}$ is distributed as a Gaussian random variable divided by $\sqrt{n}$, for large n.

A.4 Regenerative Method

The purpose of this section is to explain a method for calculating mean values of random variables that arise frequently in models of communication networks. The method replaces complicated calculations with elementary algebra.

To introduce the method, we need to develop a preliminary result about a costly gambling experiment defined in two phases. In the first phase, we flip a coin. If the outcome is H (which happens with probability $p \in (0, 1)$), then we go to Las Vegas to spin the roulette wheel X defined before. If the outcome of the coin flip is T, then we go to Atlantic City to spin the roulette wheel Y. We would like to calculate the average earnings ultimately obtained by playing the randomly chosen wheel. To perform this calculation, we denote the final earnings by Z. Additionally, we define V as the random variable that takes the value 1 when the outcome of the coin flip is H and the value 0 otherwise. With these definitions, we can write the ultimate earnings Z as

$$Z = V \times X + (1 - V) \times Y ,$$

since $Z = X$ when $V = 1$ and $Z = Y$ when $V = 0$. Using the independence of V, X, and Y, we conclude from (A.20) and (A.16) that

$$E\{Z\} = E\{V\}E\{X\} + E\{1 - V\}E\{Y\} = pE\{X\} + (1 - p)E\{Y\} .$$

Summarizing, we have seen that if

$$Z = \begin{cases} X, & \text{with probability } p \\ Y, & \text{with probability } 1 - p, \end{cases} \tag{A.21}$$

then

$$E\{Z\} = pE\{X\} + (1 - p)E\{Y\} . \tag{A.22}$$

We will illustrate how the above result can be applied to the analysis of a communication system. A transmitter sends packets to a receiver. With probability $p \in (0, 1)$, the transmission is unsuccessful (contains errors) and it has to be repeated. We want to calculate the expected number of transmissions that are necessary until the packet is successfully transmitted. One way to solve the problem is to calculate the distribution of the number X of necessary transmissions. Using our discussion of the coin flipping experiment, we can verify that

$$P\{X = n\} = p^{n-1}(1 - p), \quad n = 1, 2, \ldots .$$

From this expression we can derive that

$$E\{X\} = \frac{1}{1 - p} .$$

It turns out that this method is difficult to use in more complicated situations. We will explain another approach.

The random variable X is equal to 1 with probability $1 - p$ if the first transmission is successful. With probability p, the number X is equal to $1 + Y$ where Y is distributed as X. Indeed, with probability p, there is a first unsuccessful transmission, and then the problem starts afresh so that the number of remaining transmissions, after the first unsuccessful one, is statistically equivalent to the random variable X. Thus, we can write that

$$X = \begin{cases} 1 & \text{with probability } 1 - p \\ 1 + Y & \text{with probability } p. \end{cases}$$

Note that Y is independent of the outcome of the first transmission. Consequently, using (A.22),

$$E\{X\} = (1 - p) \times 1 + p \times E\{1 + Y\} = (1 - p) + p \times [1 + E\{Y\}] .$$

Now, $E\{Y\} = E\{X\}$ since Y and X are statistically equivalent. It follows that

$$E\{X\} = (1 - p) + p + pE\{X\} = 1 + pE\{X\} ,$$

so that, solving for $E\{X\}$,

$$E\{X\} = \frac{1}{1 - p} .$$

In this example, the economy of the method may not be very apparent. Notice, however, that no complicated summation was needed. The power of the method will be more evident in the next examples.

The simple diagram shown in Figure A.1 summarizes how the random variable X behaves. The figure indicates two points: the "start" and "stop" of the transmission. The arrows are labeled with an expression of the form $[D, P]$. The meaning of D is the duration of the corresponding transition. P is the probability of the transition. Thus, the arrow corresponding to "success" indicates that the transmission takes one unit of time (time is measured here in transmissions) and that it is successful with probability $1 - p$. Similarly, the arrow corresponding to the "error" takes one unit of time and has probability p. If the transmission is a success, then the packet transmission is completed. If not, it restarts. From this diagram, one sees that if X is the total number of transmissions, then

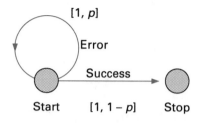

Figure A.1 Transmitter model.

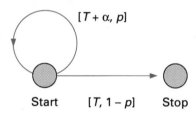

Figure A.2 Transmission durations.

$$E\{X\} = (1 - p)\times 1 + p\times[1 + E\{X\}] \, .$$

Consider now the following variation of the previous problem. A successful transmission takes T units of time. If it is unsuccessful, then it takes $T + \alpha$ time units to realize that the transmission was not successful. (For instance, α could be the time taken to receive a negative acknowledgement.) We want to calculate the average time taken by a successful transmission. The diagram corresponding to this problem is indicated in Figure A.2. To solve the problem, we denote by τ the duration until the first successful transmission. Arguing as in the previous example, we can write that

$$E\{\tau\} = (1 - p)\times T + p\times[T + \alpha + E\{\tau\}] \, .$$

Solving for $E\{\tau\}$ gives

$$E\{\tau\} = \frac{T + p\alpha}{1 - p} \, .$$

The same method applies to more complicated situations. Say that a packet must be transmitted via three successive links. Each transmission takes T seconds and is successful with probability $1 - p$. If the first, second, or third transmission is not successful, then the transmitter finds out that the transmission is not successful after $T + \alpha$, $T + 2\alpha$, or $T + 3\alpha$ time units, respectively. The diagram corresponding to this system is indicated in Figure A.3. Denoting again by τ

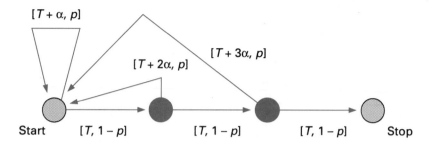

Figure A.3 Multistep transmission.

the total transmission time until the packet first reaches the destination without error, we find

$$E\{\tau\} = p(T + \alpha + E\{\tau\}) + (1 - p)[T + T_1]$$
$$T_1 = p(T + 2\alpha + E\{\tau\}) + (1 - p)[T + T_2]$$
$$T_2 = p(T + 3\alpha + E\{\tau\}) + (1 - p)T.$$

These equations can be solved to obtain $E\{\tau\}$.

Summary

- Probability theory quantifies uncertainty. It is useful because of its predictive power.

- The first step in the definition of a random variable is to consider a random experiment and to assign numbers between 0 and 1 to certain sets of possible values of the outcome. The number associated with a set is called its *probability*.

- A random variable is a function of the outcome of a random experiment. One can define the probability that the random variable takes value in a given set by considering the set of outcome values that correspond to that occurrence. (Recall the roulette wheel example: The probability that $X = x_i$ is the probability that the spin selects one of the N_i slots marked x_i.)

- The independence of random variables embodies the intuition that knowing the values of some of them does not give any information about the others.

- The interpretation of the *expected value* of a random variable is the average value that is to be observed over a large number of replica-

tions of the random experiment. We learned how to calculate the
expected value of (1) a function of a random variable; (2) of the
sum of random variables; (3) and of the product of independent
random variables. We stated the strong law of large numbers and
the central-limit theorem.

■ The *regenerative method* is used for calculating the expected value
of random variables that occur frequently in models of communication networks.

Problems

1. *Card Game.* One is given a perfectly shuffled deck of 52 cards. Four
   cards are drawn out of the deck. What is the probability that they are
   all diamonds? What is the probability that they are four aces? What is
   the probability that they are four consecutive spades?

2. *Expectation of Functions.* Give a derivation of (A.15) without assuming the values $H(x_i)$ are distinct. (*Hint:* Denote all the possible values
   of $H(X)$ by $\{y_j\}$ and let A_j be the set of indices i such that $H(x_i) = y_j$.
   Then

   $$E\{H(X)\} = \sum_j y_j \sum_{i \in A_j} p_i = \sum_j [\sum_{i \in A_j} p_i H(x_i)] = \sum_i p_i H(x_i) .$$

   [The second equality comes from observing that $y_j = H(x_i)$ when i is in
   A_j.].)

3. *Independence.* Consider the following example. Let X and Y be two
   independent random variables with $P\{X = 0\} = P\{X = 1\} = P\{Y = 0\} = P\{Y = 1\} = 1/2$. Define $Z = X + Y(\text{mod } 2)$. (Thus, $Z = 0$ if $X = Y$ and
   $Z = 1$ otherwise.) Show that $\{X, Y, Z\}$ are pairwise independent but
   that they are not independent.

4. *Multiple Access.* In a multiple-access system, N stations compete for
   the time slots of a common channel. The slots have duration T. In any
   given time slot, every station attempts to transmit with probability
   $p \in (0, 1)$, independently of the others. What is the probability that a
   single station tries to transmit in a given slot? What is the expected
   time until a single station transmits?

5. *Reliability.* A physical link consists of N segments. The link is "up" if
   and only if all the segments are up. Moreover, the segments are up

each with probability $p \in (0, 1)$, independently of each other, and are "down" otherwise. What is the probability that the link is up?

Consider now two computers that are connected by two independent links. The first link is as described above, and the second one is similar but is made up of M segments that are up each with probability $q \in (0, 1)$, independently of each other. The connection is working if and only if one of the two links is up. Find the probability that the connection is working.

Generalize to an arbitrary topology (a mesh of independent segments).

6. *Branching.* Generalize the branching result (A.22) to an arbitrary number of alternatives. For instance, say that one first tosses a die. The toss yields i with probability p_i and, in that case, one spins a roulette wheel with some real-valued random outcome X_i. Denote the outcome of the randomly chosen wheel by Z. Show that

$$E\{Z\} = \sum_i p_i E\{X_i\} \, .$$

7. *Random Motion.* Consider a random motion of an object on the set $\{1, 2, ..., N\}$. The rules of evolution are as follows. If the object is in position $i \in \{1, 2, ..., N\}$ at time n, then a die is tossed to determine the position at time $n + 1$. The die tossed in position i is such that the next position is j with probability $P(i, j)$ for $j \in \{1, 2, ..., N\}$. (One assumes that

$$\sum_{j=1}^{N} P(i, j) = 1 \text{ for } 1 \leq i \leq N.)$$

Denote by $A(i)$ the average time that it takes the object to reach the position N starting from position i. Explain why it must be that

$$A(i) = 1 + \sum_{j \neq N} P(i, j)A(j) \, .$$

(*Hint:* Denote by X_i the random time to reach N starting from i and explain why $X_i = 1 + X_j$ with probability $P(i, j)$ with $X_N = 0$. Use the ideas explained in the branching result.)

8. *Regenerative Method.* A packet has to be sent from node A to node D via nodes B and C. The transmission proceeds as follows. First, A transmits the packet to B. This transmission is always successful and

takes T units of time. Second, B sends the packet to C. This is successful with probability $1 - \varepsilon$ and takes T time-units. If the transmission from B to C is unsuccessful, then B finds out that the transmission is incorrect after $2T$ time-units. It then repeats the transmission until the first success. Third, C sends the packet to D. This takes T time-units and is successful with probability $1 - \varepsilon$. If it is not successful, then A finds out after $3T$ time-units and A must then repeat the whole process. Find the mean time needed until D first gets a successful packet.

References

There are many excellent texts on probability theory. Hoel (1971) is an easy introduction. Bremaud (1988) is a more sophisticated, yet very readable, text.

Bremaud (1988). Bremaud, P., *An Introduction to Probabilistic Modeling*. Springer Verlag, 1988.

Hoel (1971). Hoel, P. G., Port, S. C., and Stone, C. J., *An Introduction to Probability Theory*. Houghton Mifflin Company, 1971.

Queues

B

The objective of this appendix is to provide some details on the queueing theory results used in Chapter 10. We will limit our discussion to some of the simplest results of the theory. The reader should consult the references for a more complete exposition.

Queueing theory is the study of models of service systems in which tasks wait to be processed. The objectives of the theory are to predict the *delays* faced by tasks before their processing is completed and also the *backlog* of tasks waiting to be processed. The theory is used to design the telephone network, computer systems, manufacturing plants, and computer networks.

A *queue* is a service facility equipped with a waiting room. Using the standard terminology, *customers* arrive at the queue where they are required to spend some time, called a *service time*, with a *server*. There may be more than one server, and customers may have to wait for an available server. The customers leave the queue once they have received their required amount of service time.

The simplest queueing model is the *M/M/1 queue* defined in Section 10.1. Its analysis is based on the theory of *Markov chains*, which we explain in Section B.1. We analyze *networks of M/M/1 queues* using similar tools in Section B.2. The average delay in many queueing systems can be derived from *Little's result* (10.5). In Section B.3 we will explain how to derive the average delay in an

M/G/1 queue, in an *M/G/1 queue with vacations*, and in *priority systems* using Little's result.

B.1 Markov Chains and M/M/1 Queues

Markov chains are a class of models of random evolution. These models are useful for two reasons. First, they are general enough to model many physical systems. Second, the theory of Markov chains provides numerical methods for evaluating the performance measures of these models.

A *Markov chain* is a random process $\mathbf{x} = \{x_t, t \geq 0\}$ that describes a random evolution in a countable set $\mathbf{X}$. The interpretation is that x_t denotes the *state* of some system at time t. The set $\mathbf{X}$ is called the *state space*. The elements of $\mathbf{X}$ are denoted by $x, y, z, \ldots$, and are called *states*. The Markov chain $\mathbf{x}$ specifies the random law of motion of x_t in $\mathbf{X}$. Given that $x_t = x$ and the values of $\mathbf{x}$ up to time t, the probability that $x_{t+\varepsilon} = y$ is equal to

$$q(x, y)\varepsilon + o(\varepsilon) \ \text{ for } \ y \neq x, \text{ and}$$
$$1 - \sum_{y \neq x} q(x, y)\varepsilon + o(\varepsilon) \ \text{ for } \ y = x.$$

In this expression, $o(\varepsilon)$ denotes a function of $\varepsilon > 0$ such that $o(\varepsilon)/\varepsilon \to 0$ as $\varepsilon \to 0$ and $\{q(x, y), \ x \neq y \in \mathbf{X}\}$ are given nonnegative real numbers with

$$\sum_{y \neq x} q(x,y) \ .$$

We write the above definition succinctly as

$$P[x_{t+\varepsilon} = y \mid x_t = x, \quad x_s, \ s < t] = \begin{cases} q(x, y)\varepsilon + o(\varepsilon) \ \text{ for } \ y \neq x, \\ 1 - \sum_{y \neq x} q(x, y)\varepsilon + o(\varepsilon) \ \text{ for } \ y = x \end{cases} \quad (\text{B.1})$$

where $P[. \mid .]$ denotes the conditional probability (see Section A.2).

Thus, x_t jumps from x to $y \neq x$ with probability $q(x, y)\varepsilon$ in $\varepsilon \ll 1$ time-units. The numbers $q(x, y)$ are called the *transition rates* of $\mathbf{x}$. Notice that the motion of $\mathbf{x}$ after time t depends on its motion up to time t only through the position at time t. That is, the system modeled by $\mathbf{x}$ is *memoryless*: it forgets how it got to its present value. Equivalently, one can consider that x_t contains all the information about the past evolution that is relevant for predicting the future.

One important question about $\mathbf{x}$ is whether it approaches some statistical equilibrium, or steady state. That is, does the probability $P\{x_t = x\}$ approach a constant value (depending on x but not on t) as $t \to \infty$? This question is of interest because if the answer is affirmative, it tells us the likelihood of finding the system in any given state, and that information can be used to derive measures of performance of the system. For instance, if **x** models a communication network, then the limiting probabilities determine how likely it is for the system to be congested. To discuss the evolution of $P\{x_t = x\}$, we first define

$$\pi_t(x) := P\{x_t = x\} \text{ for } x \in \mathbf{X} .\tag{B.2}$$

Using (B.1), we find that

$$\pi_{t+\varepsilon}(y) = \sum_{x \neq y} \pi_t(x)[q(x, y)\varepsilon + o(\varepsilon)] + \pi_t(y)[1 - \sum_{x \neq y} q(y, x)\varepsilon + o(\varepsilon)] .$$

This equation expresses that $x_{t+\varepsilon}$ is equal to y either when x_t is equal to some $x \neq y$ and **x** jumps from x to y in ε time-units or when x_t is equal to y and **x** remains equal to y for the next ε time-units. We can rewrite the above equation by subtracting $\pi_t(y)$ from both sides, dividing by ε, and letting ε go to zero. This gives

$$\frac{d}{dt} \pi_t(y) = \sum_x \pi_t(x)q(x, y)\tag{B.3}$$

where we defined

$$q(x, x) := -\sum_{y \neq x} q(x, y).$$

The equation (B.3) describes the evolution of $\pi_t(.)$. Let us attempt to find an *invariant* solution, i.e., a solution that does not depend on t. To do this, we assume that $\pi_t(x) \equiv \pi(x)$ for $x \in \mathbf{X}$. Then (B.3) becomes

$$0 = \sum_x \pi_t(x)q(x, y) \text{ for } y \in \mathbf{X} .$$

We can also write these equations as

$$\pi(y)\sum_{x \neq y} q(y, x) = \sum_{x \neq y} \pi(x)q(x, y) \text{ for } x \in \mathbf{X} .\tag{B.4}$$

These equations are called the *balance equations*. They express the equality of the rate of transitions leaving y (the left-hand side) with the rate of transitions entering state y from another state. Summarizing, the above calculations show that if the probability distribution of x_t does not depend on t, then it must satisfy (B.4). The system is said to be in *steady state* when the probability distribution of x_t does not depend on t.

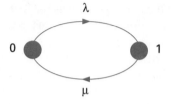

Figure B.1 Transition diagram.

Two questions arise at this point. First, how many solutions do the equations (B.4) admit? Second, if the system is not initially in steady state, can one expect it to approach it as time goes by? The answers are as follows. The Markov chain is said to be *irreducible* when it can reach any state from any other state, possibly by making many jumps. If the Markov chain $\mathbf{x}$ is irreducible, then (B.4) admits *at most* one solution. Moreover, if it has one solution π, then $\pi_t(x)$ approaches $\pi(x)$ as $t \to \infty$, for all $x \in \mathbf{X}$.

Let us examine an example to illustrate how we can use these results. Consider the Markov chain defined by $\mathbf{X} = \{0, 1\}$, $q(0, 1) = \lambda$, $q(1, 0) = \mu$ where λ and μ are two positive real numbers. We summarize this definition by the *transition diagram* in Figure B.1. This diagram indicates the possible states and the transition rates. The balance equations (B.4) are

$$\pi(0)\lambda = \pi(1)\mu \quad \text{and} \quad \pi(1)\mu = \pi(0)\lambda \ .$$

These two equations are redundant and are not sufficient to determine the invariant distribution π. We know that π must satisfy the equation

$$\sum_{x \in \mathbf{X}} \pi(x) = 1 \tag{B.5}$$

since π is a probability distribution. Thus, $\pi(0) + \pi(1) = 1$. Using this equation together with the balance equations, we conclude that

$$\pi(0) = \frac{\mu}{\lambda + \mu} \quad \text{and} \quad \pi(1) = \frac{\lambda}{\lambda + \mu} \ .$$

This is the unique invariant probability distribution. We also know that $\pi_t(0) \to \pi(0)$ and that $\pi_t(1) \to \pi(1)$ since the Markov chain is irreducible.

We are now ready to apply our knowledge of Markov chains to the analysis of the M/M/1 queue that we defined at the beginning of Section 10.2. We will show that the queue length $\mathbf{x} = \{x_t, \ t \geq 0\}$ of an M/M/1 queue is a Markov chain. To do this, we have to show that (B.1) holds. Assume that the queue length has been observed up to time $t > 0$ and that $x_t = n > 0$ (see Figure B.2). The

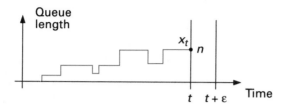

Figure B.2 Evolution of M/M/1 queue length.

probability that, given the observed evolution, $x_{t+\varepsilon} = n + 1$ is the probability that the interarrival time in progress at time t completes in $(t, t + \varepsilon)$ and that the service does not complete during the same interval. By observing the past evolution, one knows when the interarrival time started and also when the service started. Since these random variables are exponentially distributed, they are memoryless (see Section A.1). That is, given the past evolution of the queue length, the probability that the interarrival time terminates in the next ε time-units is equal to $\lambda\varepsilon + o(\varepsilon)$. Also, the probability that the service time in progress at time t terminates in the next ε time-units is equal to $\mu\varepsilon + o(\varepsilon)$.

Consequently, the probability that $x_{t+\varepsilon} = n + 1$ given the evolution up to time t is equal to

$$\{\lambda\varepsilon + o(\varepsilon)\} \times \{1 - \mu\varepsilon - o(\varepsilon)\} = \lambda\varepsilon + o(\varepsilon) .$$

(We used the fact that terms of the form $o(\varepsilon)o(\varepsilon)$, $o(\varepsilon) + o(\varepsilon)$, $o(\varepsilon)\varepsilon$, and ε^2 are all $o(\varepsilon)$.) We write the above result as

$$P[x_{t+\varepsilon} = n + 1 \mid x_t = n, \ x_s, \ s \geq t] = \lambda\varepsilon + o(\varepsilon) . \tag{B.6}$$

Similar arguments (see Problem B.2) enable us to show that:

$$P[x_{t+\varepsilon} = n - 1 \mid x_t = n, \ x_s, \ s < t] = \begin{cases} \mu\varepsilon + o(\varepsilon) & \text{if } n > 0 \\ 0 & \text{if } n = 0. \end{cases} \tag{B.7}$$

This shows that $\mathbf{x}$ is a Markov chain with the following transition rates:

$$q(n, n + 1) = \lambda \ \text{and} \ q(n + 1, n) = \mu \ \text{for } n \geq 0 \tag{B.8}$$
$$q(m, n) = 0 \ \text{for } \mid m - n \mid > 1.$$

These relations can be summarized by the transition diagram shown in Figure B.3.

The M/M/1 queue is an irreducible Markov chain since the queue length can reach any value from any other. Thus, if the balance equations admit a solution, then that solution is unique and is the limiting distribution of the queue length. The balance equations (B.4) become (with (B.8))

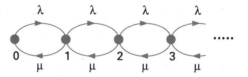

Figure B.3 Transition diagram of M/M/1 queue.

$$\pi(0)\lambda = \pi(1)\mu$$
$$\pi(1)\{\lambda + \mu\} = \pi(0)\lambda + \pi(2)\mu$$
$$\pi(2)\{\lambda + \mu\} = \pi(1)\lambda + \pi(3)\mu$$

and so on. To solve these equations, subtract $\pi(1)\mu = \pi(0)\lambda$ (obtained from the first equation) from the second equation. The result is $\pi(1)\lambda = \pi(2)\mu$. Subtracting $\pi(2)\mu = \pi(1)\lambda$ from the third equation then gives $\pi(2)\lambda = \pi(3)\mu$. Continuing in this way shows that

$$\pi(n)\lambda = \pi(n+1)\mu \ \ \text{for} \ \ n \geq 0. \tag{B.9}$$

These equations imply that

$$\pi(n+1) = \rho\pi(n) \ \ \text{for} \ \ n \geq 0 \ \ \text{with} \ \ \rho := \frac{\lambda}{\mu}.$$

Hence, $\pi(n) = \rho^n\pi(0)$. This shows that the balance equations admit a solution if and only if $\rho < 1$, i.e., $\lambda < \mu$. In that case, normalizing so that the numbers $\pi(n)$ sum to 1 gives

$$\pi(n) = (1 - \rho)\rho^n, \ n \geq 0. \tag{B.10}$$

This is the formula (10.3) used in Section 10.2.

Note that the equations (B.9) admit a simple interpretation. They express the equality of the rate of transitions from $A := \{0, 1, ..., n\}$ to $A^c := \{n + 1, n + 2, ...\}$ and the rate of transitions from A^c to A in equilibrium. (See Problem B.3.)

B.2 Networks of M/M/1 Queues

Our objective in this section is to explain the result (10.7), which formed the basis of the routing and capacity optimization in Chapter 6.

We consider the network shown in Figure B.4. The circles represent queues. Customers arrive from outside as independent Poisson processes, and they follow a random path in the network. There are J queues. For $i = 1, ..., J$, queues i has exponential service times with rate μ_i. When a customer leaves

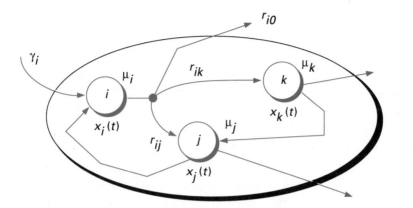

Figure B.4 Model of a network of queues.

queue i, it is sent to queue j with probability r_{ij} for $j = 1, ..., J$ and it leaves the network otherwise, i.e., with probability

$$r_{i0} := 1 - \sum_{j=1}^{J} r_{ij}.$$

Also, customers arrive from outside as independent Poisson processes, with rate γ_i, into queue i for $i = 1, 2, ..., J$.

Denote by λ_i the average rate of flow of customers through queue i, assuming that the network is in steady state. The claim is that these rates must solve the following *flow conservation equations*:

$$\lambda_i = \gamma_i + \sum_{j=1}^{J} \lambda_j r_{ji} \text{ for } i = 1, ..., J. \tag{B.11}$$

To see why the equations (B.11) hold, note that the traffic through queue i is composed of the traffic entering the queue from outside (with rate γ_i) and of the traffic coming from the other queue. For $j \neq i$, node j sends to queue i a fraction r_{ji} of the rate λ_j of traffic going through it. Hence, (B.11).

The network is said to be *open* if every customer eventually leaves. For such networks, it can be shown that the equations (B.11) admit a unique solution for every given vector $(\gamma_1, ..., \gamma_J)$. (For closed networks, see Problem B.6.)

For $t \geq 0$, define $x_t := (x_t^1, ..., x_t^J)$ where x_t^i is the number of customers in queue i at time t, including the one being served, if any. The process

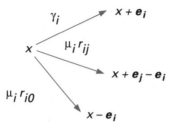

Figure B.5 Transition rates.

$\mathbf{x} = \{x_t,\ t \geq 0\}$ is a Markov chain because the interarrival times and the service times are memoryless. The transition rates are easily computed (see Figure B.5). For instance, let $y = (x^1, ..., x^{i-1}, x^i + 1, x^{i+1}, ..., x^J)$. That is, y is obtained from the vector x by adding one customer in queue i. Thus, $y = x + \mathbf{e_i}$ where $\mathbf{e_i} := (0, ..., 1, ..., 0)$ is the unit vector in direction i in $\{0, 1, 2, ...\}^J$. A transition from x to y occurs when there is an arrival in queue i from outside. Given the past evolution of $\mathbf{x}$ up to time t, this external arrival into queue i will occur with rate γ_i. Hence,

$$q(x, x + \mathbf{e_i}) = \gamma_i \ \text{ for } \ i = 1, 2, ..., J .$$

As another example, let $y = x - \mathbf{e_i} + \mathbf{e_j}$ where we assume that $x^i > 0$ and $i \neq j$. A transition from x to y corresponds to a customer finishing service at node i (with rate μ_i) and being sent to queue j upon leaving queue i (which occurs with probability r_{ij}). Thus, the probability that the transition from x to y occurs in ε time-units is equal to $\{\mu_i \varepsilon + o(\varepsilon)\}r_{ij}$. Hence,

$$q(x, x - \mathbf{e_i} + \mathbf{e_j}) = \mu_i r_{ij} \ \text{ whenever } \ x^i > 0 .$$

Similarly, one finds that

$$q(x, x - \mathbf{e_i}) = \mu_i r_{i0} \ \text{ whenever } \ x^i > 0 .$$

We want to calculate the invariant distribution of $\mathbf{x}$. To do this, we denote by $(\lambda_1, ..., \lambda_J)$ a solution to (B.11). Assume that

$$\rho_i := \frac{\lambda_i}{\mu_i} < 1 \ \text{ for } \ i = 1, 2, ..., J . \tag{B.12}$$

The claim is that a solution of the balance equations of $\mathbf{x}$ is given by

$$\pi(x^1, ..., x^J) = \prod_{i=1}^{J}\{(1 - \rho_i)\rho_i^{x^i}\} \ \text{ for } \ (x^1, ..., x^J) \in \{0, 1, 2, ...\}^J . \tag{B.13}$$

The most elegant known proof of (B.13) is as follows. (You may want to skip this proof on a first reading.) Define, for $1 \leq i \neq j \leq J$,

$$\gamma_i' := \lambda_i r_{i0}, \quad r_{ij}' := \frac{\lambda_j r_{ji}}{\lambda_i}, \quad \text{and} \quad r_{i0}' = \frac{\gamma_i}{\lambda_i}. \tag{B.14}$$

Consider the network with J nodes defined as before except that the parameters γ_i, r_{ij}, and r_{i0} are replaced by γ_i', r_{ij}', and r_{i0}', respectively. Denote by $q'(x, y)$ the transition rates of this new network. They are obtained from the original rates by making the suitable parameter substitutions. For instance,

$$q'(x, x - \mathbf{e_i} + \mathbf{e_j}) = \mu_i r_{ij}' \quad \text{whenever } x^i > 0.$$

One can then verify that

$$\pi(x)q(x, y) = \pi(y)q'(y, x) \quad \text{for all } x \neq y. \tag{B.15}$$

As an example of verification of (B.15), let $x^i > 0$ and $y = x - \mathbf{e_i} + \mathbf{e_j}$. Then,

$$q(x, y) = \mu_i r_{ij} \quad \text{and} \quad q'(y, x) = \mu_j r_{ji}' = \frac{\mu_j \lambda_i r_{ij}}{\lambda_j}$$

where the expression for $q'(y, x)$ is obtained by observing that the transition from y to x occurs when a customer is served in node j and is sent to node i. Thus, for this choice of x and y, (B.15) becomes

$$\pi(x)\mu_i r_{ij} = \pi(y)\frac{\mu_j \lambda_i r_{ij}}{\lambda_j}. \tag{B.16}$$

This equality is verified by using (B.13), which implies that

$$\pi(y) = \pi(x)\frac{\rho^j}{\rho_i} = \pi(x)\frac{\lambda_j \mu_i}{\mu_j \lambda_i},$$

which yields (B.16). The other possible pairs (x, y) in (B.15) are verified similarly.

Moreover, the new network is such that

$$\sum_{y \neq x} q(x, y) = \sum_{y \neq x} q'(x, y). \tag{B.17}$$

To see this, observe that the left-hand side of (B.17) is the rate of transitions out of state x in the original network while the right-hand side is that rate in the new network. Therefore,

$$\sum_{y \neq x} q(x, y) = \sum_{y \neq x} q'(x, y) = \sum_i \gamma_i + \sum_{\{i : x^i > 0\}} \mu_i .$$

The balance equations are immediate consequences of (B.15) and (B.17). To see this, sum (B.15) over $x \neq y$. This gives

$$\sum_{x \neq y} \pi(x) q(x, y) = \pi(y) \sum_{x \neq y} q'(y, x)$$

$$= \pi(y) \sum_{x \neq y} q(y, x) \tag{B.18}$$

where the last equality follows from (B.17). The equations (B.18) are the balance equations (B.4).

It turns out that by proving (B.15) and (B.17), we also proved that the new network behaves as the original network *reversed in time*.

We finally come to our goal: proving the formula (10.7) for the average delay per customer in the network. The key to the derivation is *Little's result*, $L = \lambda T$, which we discussed in Chapter 10 (see (10.5)). Recall that this result states that the average number of customers in a queueing system is equal to the arrival rate multiplied by the average time spent by each customer in the system.

To calculate the average delay T per customer in the network, we will first calculate the average number L of customers in the network and the arrival rate λ. The arrival rate λ is equal to the sum of the arrival rates γ_i. Thus,

$$\lambda = \gamma := \sum_i \gamma_i.$$

The average number of customers in the network is equal to the sum of the average number of customers in the J queues. That is,

$$L = \sum_{i=1}^{J} L_i$$

where L_i is the average number of customers in queue i. To calculate L_i, we use (B.13), which shows that, in steady state, the queue length at node i is distributed as the queue length in an M/M/1 queue with arrival rate λ_i and service rate μ_i. Thus, L_i is equal to the average queue length of an M/M/1 queue with parameters λ_i and μ_i. Using (10.4), we obtain

$$L_i = \frac{\lambda_i}{\mu_i - \lambda_i} .$$

Hence,

$$T = \frac{1}{\gamma} \sum_{i=1}^{J} L_i = \frac{1}{\gamma} \sum_{i=1}^{J} \frac{\lambda_i}{\mu_i - \lambda_i},$$

as we wanted to prove.

B.3 Average Delays

This section explains the formulas (10.8)–(10.11). The derivations are based on Little's result.

Consider first an M/G/1 queue and assume that every customer in the queue pays at rate R when his or her remaining service time is equal to R. A graph of this cost rate is illustrated in Figure B.6. The total cost paid by this customer is equal to the integral of the rate over time, i.e., to

$$SQ + \frac{S^2}{2} \qquad (B.19)$$

where S denotes the service time of the customer and Q his or her queueing delay before the service actually starts. The service time S of a customer and his or her queueing time Q are independent. As a consequence, the expected cost paid by each customer, the average value of (B.19), is equal to

$$C := \frac{E\{Q\}}{\mu} + \frac{E\{S^2\}}{2} \qquad (B.20)$$

where we used $E\{SQ\} = E\{S\}E\{Q\} = \mu^{-1}E\{Q\}$ (see (A.20)). It follows that the customers pay at rate λC since each customer pays C on the average and λ customers go through the queue per unit of time.

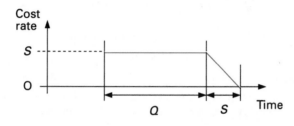

Figure B.6 Cost rate for a typical customer.

At a given time t, the customers pay at a rate equal to the sum of the remaining service times of all the customers in the queue. The queue being first come–first served, this sum is equal to the queueing time of a customer who would enter the queue at time t. Let us denote this "virtual" queueing time by Q^*.

We will show below that Q^* has the same distribution as Q. As a consequence, the average rate at which customers pay is equal to $E\{Q\}$. It has also been shown to be equal to λC. Hence,

$$E\{Q\} = \lambda C = \lambda(\frac{E\{Q\}}{\mu} + \frac{E\{S^2\}}{2}) .$$

Solving this equation for $E\{Q\}$ shows

$$W := E\{Q\} = \frac{\lambda E\{S^2\}}{2(1 - \rho)},$$

and this gives (10.8) since the average delay T is the average queueing time W plus the average service time μ^{-1}.

It remains to show that Q^* is distributed as Q. That is, we want to show that the waiting time of a customer who would enter the (steady state) queue at time t is distributed as the waiting time of a typical customer. This is due to a stronger result which states that *Poisson arrivals see time averages* (PASTA). This statement means that customers who arrive as a Poisson process at a queue in steady state find the queue with its invariant distribution. To show PASTA, we denote the state of the queue by x_t and we assume that the queue is in steady state with $P\{x_t = x\} = \pi(x)$. Denote the arrival times of the customers by $\{T_n, n \geq 1\}$ and assume that these arrival times form a Poisson process with rate λ. We want to show that, given that there is an arrival in $(t, t + \varepsilon)$, x_t has the distribution π. This will show that the distribution just before an arrival is the invariant distribution. To do this, we must calculate

$$P[x_t = x \mid T_n \in (t, t + \varepsilon) \text{ for some } n] . \tag{B.21}$$

By the definition of conditional probability (A.6), this is equal to

$$\frac{P\{x_t = x \text{ and } T_n \in (t, t + \varepsilon) \text{ for some } n\}}{P\{T_n \in (t, t + \varepsilon) \text{ for some } n\}} . \tag{B.22}$$

The numerator is equal to

$$P\{x_t = x\} \times P\{T_n \in (t, t + \varepsilon) \text{ for some } n\}$$

since the Poisson process is memoryless and the occurrence of an arrival in $(t, t + \varepsilon)$ is therefore independent of whatever happened before time t, and in particular of x_t. The preceding equation implies that

$$P[x_t = x \mid T_n \in (t, t + \varepsilon) \text{ for some } n] = P\{x_t = x\} = \pi(x) ,$$

as was to be shown.

      We now turn our attention to an M/G/1 queue with vacations. We will prove formula (10.9). Assume that the server pays the queue at rate R when that server is on vacation with a residual vacation time equal to R. The total cost paid during a vacation with duration V is then equal to $E\{V^2\}/2$. It will be shown below that the rate of vacations is equal to

$$\frac{1 - \rho}{E\{V\}} . \tag{B.23}$$

Consequently, the server pays with the average rate

$$(1 - \rho)\frac{E\{V^2\}}{2E\{V\}} .$$

Assume now that a customer with a residual service time equal to R pays with rate R. The average total cost paid by a customer is then equal to

$$E\{QS\} + \frac{E\{S^2\}}{2} ,$$

as in the M/G/1 queue. As a consequence, the average rate at which the customers pay is equal to

$$\lambda[E\{QS\} + \frac{E\{S^2\}}{2}].$$

It follows that the server and the customers pay with the total rate

$$\lambda[E\{QS\} + \frac{E\{S^2\}}{2}] + (1 - \rho)\frac{E\{V^2\}}{2E\{V\}} .$$

Now, the rate at which the server and customers pay at any given time t is the sum of the residual vacation time and the remaining waiting times of all the customers in the queue. This sum is equal to the waiting time of a customer who would enter the queue at time t. Since Poisson arrivals see time averages, it follows that the average value of this "virtual waiting time" is equal to $E\{Q\}$, as in the analysis of the M/G/1 queue. Hence,

$$W = E\{Q\} = \lambda[E\{QS\} + \frac{E\{S^2\}}{2}] + (1 - \rho)\frac{E\{V^2\}}{2E\{V\}} .$$

Using $E\{QS\} = E\{Q\}/\mu$ and solving for $E\{Q\}$ leads to (10.9).

It remains to show that the rate of vacations is given by (B.23). To do this, we assume that the server pays at a unit rate when serving customers. The server then pays at a rate equal to the probability that the server is serving customers. That rate can be computed as the product of the average cost per customer paid by the server times the rate at which customers are served. This computation shows that the probability that the server is serving must be equal to $\rho = \lambda/\mu$. Thus, the customer is on vacation a fraction $1 - \rho$ of the time. Say that the vacation rate is equal to α. Since the average duration of a vacation is equal to $E\{V\}$, it follows that the average time spent on vacation per unit of time is equal to $\alpha E\{V\}$. Thus,

$$1 - \rho = \alpha E\{V\},$$

which shows that α is indeed given by (B.23).

We conclude our discussion of average delays by deriving (10.10). The first step is to show that if V denotes the residual service time of a customer in service at an arbitrary time, then

$$E\{V\} = \frac{1}{2} \sum_{i=1}^{2} \lambda_i E\{S_i^2\} . \tag{B.24}$$

(The notation is as in (10.10).)

To show (B.24), we assume that a customer pays at rate R when the customer is in service with a residual service time R. The total cost paid by a customer with service time S is then equal to $S^2/2$. Now, S is equal to S_1 with probability $\lambda_1(\lambda_1 + \lambda_2)^{-1}$ and to S_2 with probability $\lambda_2(\lambda_1 + \lambda_2)^{-1}$. As a consequence, the expected cost per customer is (see (A.22))

$$(\lambda_1 + \lambda_2)^{-1} \sum_{i=1}^{2} \frac{\lambda_i E\{S_i^2\}}{2} .$$

Multiplying this expression by the rate $(\lambda_1 + \lambda_2)$ of customers gives the rate at which customers pay. But this rate must be equal to $E\{V\}$, by definition of V. Hence, (B.24).

Consider now a customer of class 1 and denote the waiting time (before service) by Q_1. Then

$$E\{Q_1\} = E\{V\} + E\{N_1\}E\{S_1\}$$

where N_1 denotes the typical number of customers of class 1 in the queue (not in service). Indeed, the customer of class 1 must wait for the residual service time V and for the completion of the service times of all the customers of class 1 upon his or her arrival. Little's result also gives

$$E\{N_1\} = \lambda_1 E\{Q_1\} \ .$$

Hence,

$$W_1 := E\{Q_1\} = E\{V\} + \rho_1 E\{Q_1\} \ ,$$

so that

$$W_1 = \frac{E\{V\}}{1 - \rho_1} \ ,$$

which is the first formula in (10.10).

The case of class 2 is similar. One finds that

$$E\{Q_2\} = E\{V\} + E\{N_1\}E\{S_1\} + E\{N_2\}E\{S_2\} + \lambda_1 E\{Q_2\}E\{S_1\} \qquad (B.25)$$

where Q_2 and N_2 were defined analogously to Q_1 and N_1. To see this, notice that if one calls C the customer of class 2, then C must wait for V, then for the completion of the service of the N_1 class 1 customers in the queue when C arrived, then for the completion of the N_2 customers of class 2 when C arrived, and then for the service of the $\lambda_1 E\{Q_2\}$ customers of class 1 who arrived during the waiting time Q_2 of C in the queue. Combining (B.25), the value of $E\{Q_1\}$ and $E\{N_2\} = \lambda_2 E\{Q_2\}$ gives the second formula in (10.10) for $W_2 := E\{Q_2\}$.

Summary

- A *Markov chain* $\mathbf{x} = \{x_t, \ t \geq 0\}$ is a model of random evolution in a countable set $\mathbf{X}$. The process $\mathbf{x}$ jumps from x to $y \neq x$ at rate $q(x, y)$, independently of how it got to x. If $\mathbf{x}$ is *irreducible* and if the *balance equations* admit a solution π (the *unique invariant distribution of* $\mathbf{x}$), then $P\{x_t = x\}$ converges to $\pi(x)$ as t increases. Thus, $\mathbf{x}$ approaches *steady state*.

430

- The length of an M/M/1 queue is an irreducible Markov chain. It admits an invariant distribution if and only if the arrival rate is less than the service rate. From the invariant distribution, one can calculate the average queue length and the average delay per customer is then obtained from *Little's result*.

- The vector of queue lengths in an *open network of M/M/1 queues* is also an irreducible Markov chain. Its invariant distribution exists if and only if the *flow conservation equations* show that the average rate of flow through each queue is less than the service rate of the queue. Moreover, in that case, at any given time, the queue lengths of the network in steady state are independent and are distributed as M/M/1 queues with arrival rates given by the flow conservation equations. (This property holds even though one can show that the arrival processes at the queues in the network are not Poisson.) From this result, one can calculate the average number of customers in the network, and the average delay is then derived from Little's result.

- The average delay through an M/G/1 queue with or without vacations or priorities can be derived by using Little's result.

Problems

1. *M/M/1/N Queue.* Consider a queue defined as the M/M/1 queue except that it can hold at most N customers (including the one in service). Customers arrive as a Poisson process with rate λ. Customers who arrive when there are N customers in the queue are rejected and never come back. This type of queue is called an M/M/1/N queue.

   Show that the queue length x_t is a Markov chain with the transition diagram indicated in Figure B.7.

   Write and solve the balance equations.

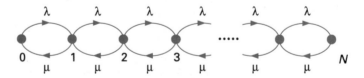

Figure B.7 Transition diagram of M/M/1/N queue.

2. *Exponential Distribution.* Let σ and τ be two independent exponentially distributed random variables with rates λ and μ, respectively. Show that $\min\{\sigma, \tau\}$ is exponentially distributed with rate $\lambda + \mu$. Show that

$$P\{\sigma < \tau\} = \frac{\lambda}{\lambda + \mu} .$$

3. *Balance Equations.* The point of this exercise is to justify the simplification that occurs in the solution of the balance equations of the M/M/1 queue. It turns out, as we will see, that the same simplification occurs for more general systems.

Let $\mathbf{x} = \{x_t, t \geq 0\}$ be a Markov chain with state space $\mathbf{X}$ and with transition rates $\{q(x, y), x \neq y \in \mathbf{X}\}$. Assume that $\{\pi(x), x \in \mathbf{X}\}$ is an invariant distribution of $\mathbf{x}$. Show that if A is a subset of $\mathbf{X}$ and if $A^c := \mathbf{X} - A$ denotes the complement of A, then

$$\sum_{x \in A} \sum_{y \in A^c} \pi(x)q(x, y) = \sum_{x \in A^c} \sum_{y \in A} \pi(x)q(x, y) .$$

The interpretation is that the rate of jumps leaving A must be equal to the rate of jumps entering A when $\mathbf{x}$ is in steady state. (*Hint*: Use the balance equations (B.4).)

4. *M/M/s Queue.* Consider a queue with Poisson arrivals with rate λ and with exponentially distributed service times with rate μ. The queue has $s \geq 1$ servers. Thus, when there are n customers in the queue, $\min\{n, s\}$ of them are being served and the time until the next service completion is, in view of Problem B.2, exponentially distributed with rate $\mu \times \min\{n, s\}$. Conclude that the queue length x_t is a Markov chain with rates

$q(n, n + 1) = \lambda$ and $q(n + 1, n) = \mu \times \min\{n + 1, s\}$ for $n \geq 0$.

Write and solve the balance equations.

5. *Transient Behavior.* In matrix notation, with π_t being the row vector with components $\pi_t(y)$, the equations (B.3) read

$$\frac{d}{dt} \pi_t = \pi_t Q$$

where Q is the matrix whose entry (x, y) is equal to $q(x, y)$. Formally at least, the solution of this equation is

$$\pi_t = \pi_0 e^{Qt} \text{ where } e^{Qt} := \sum_{n=0}^{\infty} \frac{(Qt)^n}{n!}.$$

This solution turns out to be correct when the entries of Q are bounded.

Apply these results to the example of Figure B.1. Show that

$$\pi_t(0) = \pi_0(0)\frac{\mu + \lambda e^{-(\lambda+\mu)t}}{\lambda + \mu} + \pi_0(1)\frac{\mu - \mu e^{-(\lambda+\mu)t}}{\lambda + \mu} \text{ for } t \geq 0.$$

Conclude that $\pi_t(0) \to \mu(\lambda + \mu)^{-1}$ as the general result states.

6. *Closed Network of M/M/1 Queues.* Consider the network of M/M/1 queues of Section B.3 but assume that it is *closed*. That is, no customer can leave and no customer enter. Thus, $r_{i0} = 0$ and $\gamma_i = 0$ for all i. Show that (B.13) is again an invariant distribution with the λ_i's given as a solution of (B.13). (*Hint:* The proof given in the open case still applies without modification.)

References

Elements of queueing theory are introduced in Bertsekas (1987). Kelly (1979) is an excellent reference for product-form networks. Kleinrock (1975) is also highly recommended. Walrand (1988) explains analysis, design, and control methods for queueing networks.

Bertsekas (1987). Bertsekas, D., and Gallager, R., *Data Networks.* Prentice-Hall, 1987.

Kelly (1979). Kelly, F. P., *Reversibility and Stochastic Networks.* John Wiley & Sons, 1979.

Kleinrock (1975). Kleinrock, L., *Queueing Systems, Vol. 1.* John Wiley & Sons, 1975.

Walrand (1988). Walrand, J., *An Introduction to Queueing Networks.* Prentice-Hall, 1988.

Communication Principles | C

This appendix is intended for readers who do not have a background in communication theory. It provides some details about the basic ideas of the theory.

In Section C.1, we explain the concept of *frequency spectrum*. Section C.2 discusses some modulation and demodulation techniques. Section C.3 explains the phase-locked loop used in demodulation and for synchronizing receivers. *Nyquist's sampling theorem* is discussed in Section C.4.

C.1 Frequency Spectrum

Telecommunication engineers usually think about signals in terms of their *frequency spectrum*. Let $x(.) = \{x(t), -\infty < t < +\infty\}$ be a function of t. The function takes real or complex values. In the early 1800s, the French mathematician Jean Baptiste Fourier suggested that almost every such function $x(.)$ can be written as

$$x(t) = \int_{-\infty}^{+\infty} X(f)e^{j2\pi ft}df. \tag{C.1}$$

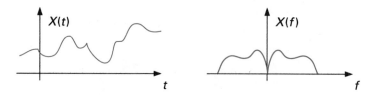

Figure C.1 The function $x(.)$ and its frequency spectrum.

The right-hand side of (C.1) expresses $x(.)$ as a sum of *complex exponentials*
$e^{j2\pi ft}$. Recall that $e^{j2\pi ft} = \cos(2\pi ft) + j\sin(2\pi ft)$. Thus, (C.1) expresses $x(.)$ as a
sum of sine waves. The expression (C.1) shows that $x(.)$ can be described by
specifying the coefficient $X(f)$ of the complex exponential $e^{j2\pi ft}$ for each f. The
values $\{X(f), -\infty < f < +\infty\}$ constitute the *frequency spectrum* (or *Fourier transform*) of $x(.)$. The two equivalent representations of $x(.)$, by specifying the value
of $x(t)$ for each t or the value of $X(f)$ for each f, are illustrated in Figure C.1.

In some cases, the integral in (C.1) gets replaced by a sum. For
instance, if $x(.)$ is *periodic* with period T, i.e., if $x(t) = x(t + T)$, then

$$x(t) = \sum_{n=-\infty}^{\infty} c_n e^{j\frac{2\pi n}{T}t}, \text{ with } c_n = \frac{1}{T} \int_{-\frac{T}{2}}^{+\frac{T}{2}} x(t)e^{-j\frac{2\pi n}{T}t} dt \,. \tag{C.2}$$

That is, a periodic function with period T can be written as a sum of sine waves.

Let us examine a few examples of this decomposition of functions
into sine waves. First, consider $x(t) = \cos(2\pi f_1 t)$. We know the identity
$e^{j\theta} = \cos(\theta) + j\sin(\theta)$. Using this identity, we derive $\cos(\theta) = (e^{j\theta})/2 + (e^{-j\theta})/2$
and, therefore,

$$\cos(2\pi f_0 t) = \frac{1}{2}e^{j2\pi f_0 t} + \frac{1}{2}e^{-j2\pi f_0 t}. \tag{C.3}$$

This expression is a particular case of (C.2). Another example, that we used in
Section 3.3, is the decomposition of the *square wave*

$$q(t) = \begin{cases} 1, \text{ if } \dfrac{2n-1}{4}T \le t < \dfrac{2n+1}{4}T \text{ for some integer } n \\ 0, \text{ otherwise} \end{cases}$$

into sine waves as

$$q(t) = \frac{1}{2} + \frac{1}{\pi}\cos(\frac{2\pi}{T}t) - \frac{1}{3\pi}\cos(\frac{6\pi}{T}t) + \frac{1}{5\pi}\cos(\frac{10\pi}{T}t) - \dots \,.$$

The coefficients $1/\pi, -1/3\pi, \ldots$ are calculated using the expressions given in (C.2) for the c_ns. Another useful example is the identity

$$\sum_{n=-\infty}^{\infty} \delta(t - nT) = \frac{1}{T} \sum_{n=-\infty}^{\infty} e^{j\frac{2\pi n}{T}t}.$$

(C.4)

In this identity, $\delta(t)$ denotes the *Dirac impulse*, which is defined by

$$\int_{-\infty}^{\infty} x(t)\,\delta(t - s)dt = x(s) \quad \text{for} -\infty < s < +\infty$$

(C.5)

whenever $x(.)$ is continuous at s. That is, the Dirac impulse *samples* the signal $x(.)$. The Dirac impulse is the mathematical idealization when $\varepsilon \downarrow 0$ of the function $\delta_\varepsilon(.)$ defined by

$$\delta_\varepsilon(t) = \begin{cases} \dfrac{1}{\varepsilon} & \text{for } -\dfrac{\varepsilon}{2} < t < +\dfrac{\varepsilon}{2} \\ 0, & \text{otherwise.} \end{cases}$$

(C.6)

From this definition you see that

$$\int_{-\infty}^{\infty} x(t)\,\delta_\varepsilon(t - s)dt = \frac{1}{\varepsilon} \int_{s-\frac{\varepsilon}{2}}^{s+\frac{\varepsilon}{2}} x(t)dt$$

is the average value of $x(.)$ in the interval

$$(s - \frac{\varepsilon}{2}, s + \frac{\varepsilon}{2}).$$

As $\varepsilon \downarrow 0$, this average value approaches $x(s)$. This justifies the definition (C.5). To understand the identity (C.4), note that the left-hand side defines a periodic function

$$g(t) := \sum_{n=-\infty}^{\infty} \delta(t - nT)$$

with period T. Consequently, we can use the formula (C.2) to write $g(t)$ as a sum of complex exponentials. Using the formula given in (C.2) for the coefficients c_n, we find

$$c_n = \frac{1}{T} \int\limits_{-\frac{T}{2}}^{+\frac{T}{2}} g(t) e^{-j\frac{2\pi n}{T}t} dt \;.$$

436

Now, for t in the interval

$$\left[-\frac{T}{2}, +\frac{T}{2} \right]$$

of integration, $g(t) = \delta(t)$ since the other terms vanish. Indeed, $\delta_\varepsilon(t - s)$ is nonzero only in a small interval around s, and the same is true for $\delta(t)$. Therefore, all the terms in $g(t)$ are equal to zero in

$$\left[-\frac{T}{2}, +\frac{T}{2} \right],$$

except the term $\delta(t)$. Consequently, we get

$$c_n = \frac{1}{T} \int\limits_{-\frac{T}{2}}^{+\frac{T}{2}} \delta(t) e^{-j\frac{2\pi n}{T}t} dt = \frac{1}{T} \;,$$

where the last equality follows from (C.5) and from $e^0 = 1$. This proves (C.4).

Thus, Fourier tells us that essentially any function $x(.)$ is a sum of sine waves. The restriction *essentially* refers to some mathematical conditions that are satisfied by all the functions that we consider in this text.

C.2 Modulation and Demodulation

Modulation is a technique central to communication systems. One form of modulation, called *amplitude modulation*, is explained next. First, consider the signal

$$x(t) = A e^{\,j2\pi f_1 t}, \;\; t \in (-\infty, +\infty) \;.$$

Since this signal is a single complex exponential with frequency f_1, we can represent its spectrum as shown in Figure C.2.

Now, consider the new signal $y(t) = x(t) \times \cos\{2\pi f_0 t\}$ obtained by multiplying the original signal $x(t)$ by a sine wave. Using (C.3), we find that

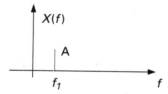

Figure C.2 Frequency spectrum of $x(t)$.

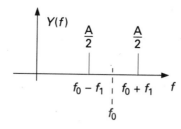

Figure C.3 Frequency spectrum of $y(t)$.

$$y(t) = \frac{A}{2} \times e^{\,j2\pi(f_1+f_0)t} + \frac{A}{2} \times e^{\,j2\pi(f_1-f_0)t}.$$

Assuming that $f_0 > f_1$, one sees that $y(t)$ now consists of two complex exponentials: one at $f_0 + f_1$ and the other at $f_0 - f_1$. The spectrum of $y(t)$ is shown in Figure C.3.

Consider now a signal $x(t)$ that is the sum of complex exponentials with frequencies in the range $[f_1, f_2]$. Arguing as in our previous example, we conclude that $y(t) = x(t) \times \cos\{2\pi f_0 t\}$ is now a sum of sine waves at frequencies in the range $[f_0 + f_1, f_0 + f_2]$ and in $[-f_0 + f_1, -f_0 + f_2]$. In fact, the amplitudes of the various frequencies are half of what they were in the original signal. Figure C.4 illustrates the transformation of the spectrum of a signal when it is multiplied by a sine wave.

The operation of multiplying a signal by a sine wave is called the *amplitude modulation* of the sine wave by the signal. Thus, we have seen that amplitude modulation provides a simple way of shifting the spectrum of a signal.

Some radio transmitters use amplitude modulation. The laws of electromagnetic theory are such that a radio antenna is efficient only when its length is of the order of the wavelength of the signal being transmitted. The wavelength of a signal is equal to the speed of light (3×10^8 meters per second) divided by the frequency of the signal. For instance, a voice signal has a typical frequency of

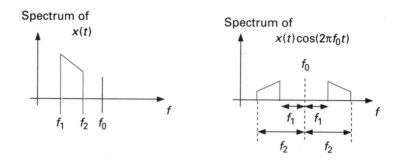

Figure C.4 Frequency spectrum modification.

1,000 Hz. This corresponds to an electrical signal with a wavelength equal to $3 \times 10^8 / 10^3 = 300$ km. Thus, without modulation, an antenna would have to be around 100 kilometers long to be efficient. This is clearly not feasible. If we modulate a sine wave at 100 MHz with the voice signal, the signal to be transmitted will have a wavelength equal to $3 \times 10^8 / 10^8 = 3$ meters. This makes a short antenna efficient.

A few different methods can be used to *demodulate* a signal. We will explain next *synchronous demodulation*. The signals are the same as in Figure C.4. That is, $x(t)$ is a sum of sine waves with frequencies in the range $[f_1, f_2]$ and $y(t) = x(t) \times \cos\{2\pi f_0 t\}$. We will assume that $0 < f_2 < f_0$ and $f_1 = -f_2$. The objective of demodulation is to recover $x(t)$ from $y(t)$. We first compute

$$z(t) = y(t) \times \cos\{2\pi f_0 t\} \ .$$

We then *filter* the signal $z(t)$ to eliminate all the complex exponentials with frequencies not in $[f_1, f_2]$. Denote by $v(t)$ the result of this filtering. The claim is that $v(t) = x(t)/2$. The proof of this claim is as follows. From the definitions of $y(t)$ and $z(t)$, we get

$$z(t) = x(t) \times [\cos\{2\pi f_0 t\}]^2 = x(t) \times \frac{1 + \cos\{4\pi f_0 t\}}{2}$$

$$= \frac{x(t)}{2} + \frac{x(t)}{2} \times \cos\{4\pi f_0 t\} \ . \tag{C.7}$$

The first part in the last expression, $x(t)/2$, goes through the filter unchanged. The claim is that the complex exponentials in $x(t) \times \cos\{4\pi f_0 t\}$ have frequencies larger than f_2. To see this, note that this signal is the sine wave at the frequency $2f_0$ modulated by $x(t)$. The spectrum of that signal is therefore the same as that shown in Figure C.4 with f_0 replaced by $2f_0$. It follows that the second term in (C.7) does not go through the filter and that the output of the filter is indeed equal to $x(t)/2$.

The above synchronous demodulation method requires that the receiver be able to generate $\cos\{2\pi f_0 t\}$. The oscillator that generates $\cos\{2\pi f_0 t\}$ in the receiver must be kept in phase with the received signal $y(t)$. This requirement is achieved by a circuit called a *phase-locked loop*. We explain the operations of that circuit in the next section.

C.3 Phase-Locked Loop

The objective of the phase-locked loop is to match the phase of a local oscillator with that of a received signal. The receiver has an oscillator that operates at a frequency approximately equal to f_0. The oscillator frequency is slightly adjustable by means of an input voltage. To be specific, say that the frequency of the oscillator is equal to $f_0 + \alpha V$ when the input voltage is V. Here, α is a small positive number. Denote by y_t the output of the oscillator and write it as

$$y_t = \cos\{2\pi f_0 t + \theta\}$$

where θ is some phase value.

The signal received is some $x_t = \sin\{2\pi f_0 t + \varphi\}$ where φ is an unknown phase shift due to the propagation delay. Let us compute the average value of $x_t y_t$, i.e.,

$$\frac{1}{T}\int_0^T x_t\, y_t dt \,. \tag{C.8}$$

Calculations show that the average value (C.8) is approximately equal to

$$\frac{1}{2}\sin(\varphi - \theta).$$

We construct a circuit so that V, the input voltage of the oscillator, is equal to this average value. This circuit is illustrated in Figure C.5.

For this circuit,

$$V \approx \frac{1}{2}\sin(\varphi - \theta).$$

The claim is that the circuit will adjust the local oscillator so that $\theta \approx \varphi$ and $V \approx 0$. To see this, assume that $0 < \varphi - \theta < \pi/2$. Then $V > 0$ and the frequency of the local oscillator is slightly higher than f_0. This leads θ to increase, thereby reducing $\varphi - \theta$. A similar argument holds for $0 < \theta - \varphi < \pi/2$.

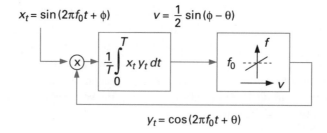

$$x_t = \sin(2\pi f_0 t + \phi) \qquad v = \frac{1}{2}\sin(\phi - \theta)$$

$$y_t = \cos(2\pi f_0 t + \theta)$$

Figure C.5 Phase-locked loop.

Thus, the circuit "locks" the phase of the local oscillator to that of the received signal.

C.4 Nyquist's Sampling Theorem

Nyquist discovered that a signal $x(t)$ with no energy at frequencies larger than f_{max} can be reconstructed *exactly* from the values of its samples $\{x(nT),\ n = 0, \pm 1, \pm 2, \ldots\}$, provided that $T \le 1/2f_{max}$. This fact is called *Nyquist's sampling theorem*.

We explain in Chapter 3 that this result makes *pulse code modulation* (PCM) possible. PCM is the digital modulation used in compact discs, digital audio tapes, and telephone networks.

Nyquist's sampling theorem follows from the identity (C.4). Using (C.4), we see that

$$\sum_{n=-\infty}^{\infty} x(t)\delta(t - nT) = \frac{1}{T}\sum_{n=-\infty}^{\infty} x(t)e^{j\frac{2\pi n}{T}t}. \qquad (C.9)$$

Now, $\delta(.)$ is the limit of $\delta_\varepsilon(.)$ as $\varepsilon \downarrow 0$, and (C.6) shows that

$$x(t)\delta_\varepsilon(t - nT) \approx x(nT)\delta_\varepsilon(t - nT),$$

provided that $x(.)$ is approximately constant in a small interval around nT. Consequently, you can expect, and this can be justified, that

$$x(t)\delta(t - nT) = x(nT)\delta(t - nT).$$

Using this expression, we can write (C.9) as

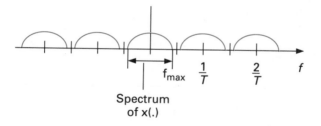

Spectrum
of x(.)

Figure C.6 Spectrum of (C.10).

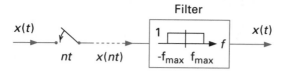

Figure C.7 Recovery of $x(.)$ from its samples.

$$\sum_{n=-\infty}^{\infty} x(nT)\delta(t-nt) = \frac{1}{T}\sum_{n=-\infty}^{\infty} x(t)e^{j\frac{2\pi n}{T}t}. \tag{C.10}$$

We will show that one can recover $x(.)$ from the right-hand side of (C.10) when T is small enough. Since the left-hand side of (C.10) depends only on the samples of $x(.)$ every multiple of T, this will prove Nyquist's theorem. To show that we can recover $x(.)$ from the right-hand side of (C.10), we observe that each term

$$x(t)e^{j\frac{2\pi n}{T}t}$$

has the same frequency spectrum as $x(.)$, except that the frequency spectrum is shifted by the frequency n/T. Consequently, the frequency spectrum of the right-hand side of (C.10) is the sum from $n=-\infty$ to $n=+\infty$ of a copy of the frequency spectrum of $x(.)$ shifted by n/T. That frequency spectrum is shown in Figure C.6. Figure C.6 shows that if

$$\frac{1}{T} > 2f_{max},$$

then the replications of the frequency spectrum of $x(.)$ every $1/T$ do not overlap. It is then possible to recover the frequency spectrum of $x(.)$ by filtering the signal (C.10) so as to keep only the frequencies in the range $(-f_{max}, +f_{max})$.

The diagram in Figure C.7 illustrates the recovery of $x(.)$ from its samples $\{x(nT),\ n=0,\pm1,\pm2,\ldots\}$.

Summary

■ Most signals can be written as a sum of complex exponentials. The coefficients of these exponentials constitute the *frequency spectrum* of the signal.

■ *Modulation* is used to modify the spectrum of a signal. Modulation enables one to transmit electromagnetic waves efficiently with short antennas.

■ The *phase-locked loop* maintains the phase of a local oscillator very close to that of a received signal.

■ According to *Nyquist's sampling theorem*, when a signal has no energy above some frequency f_{max}, it suffices to specify $2f_{max}$ *samples* of the signal per second in order to describe it completely.

References

Couch (1983), Cooper (1986), and Lee (1988) are recommended texts on communication theory.

Cooper (1986). Cooper, G. R., and McGillem, C. D., *Modern Communications and Spread Spectrum*. McGraw-Hill, 1986.

Couch (1983). Couch, Leon W., *Digital and Analog Communication Systems*. Macmillan. 1983.

Lee (1988). Lee, E. A., and Messerschmitt, D. G., *Digital Communication*. Kluwer, 1988.

References

D

We have deliberately limited the references to texts and papers that are directly useful for understanding the material in this book.

In addition to the references listed below, you will find the publications of IEEE very useful to keep abreast of the developments in the field. In particular, the *IEEE Communications Magazine* and the *IEEE Network Magazine* regularly publish very accessible papers on communication networks. The *IEEE Journal on Selected Areas in Communications* publishes papers written at a more technical level, but you should be able to benefit from many of those papers.

The CCITT, ISO, IEEE, and ANSI publish standard recommendations. The CCITT recommendations were published in the *Blue Book* (International Telecommunication Union, Geneva, 1989). The documentation for the Internet is in technical reports called *Requests for Comments* (RFCs) that are distributed by the Network Information Center (NIC) at SRI International and by the NSFNET Network Service Center at Bolt, Beranek, and Newman, Inc. You can obtain copies of these RFCs from NIC by calling 1-800-235-3155. NIC will inform you how to access the RFCs by electronic mail or by regular mail. Books can be, and have been, written just to describe these RFCs.

Ben-Artzi (1990). Ben-Artzi, A., Chanda, A., and Warrier, U., "Network management of TCP/IP networks: Present and future," *IEEE Network Magazine*, 35–43, July 1990.

Bertsekas (1987). Bertsekas, D., and Gallager, R., *Data Networks*. Prentice-Hall, 1987.

Bocker (1988). Bocker, P., *ISDN—The Integrated Services Digital Network: Concepts, Methods, Systems.* Springer-Verlag, 1988.

Bremaud (1988). Bremaud, P., *An Introduction to Probabilistic Modeling.* Springer-Verlag, 1988.

Case (1989). Case, J., Fedor, M., Schoffstall, M., and Davin, C., "A Simple Network Management Protocol (SNMP)," *Network Working Group RFC 1098*, April 1989.

Cohen (1989). Cohen, G., Gaubert, S., Nikoukhah, R., and Quadrat, J. P., "Convex analysis and spectral analysis of timed event graphs," *Proceedings of the 28th Conference on Decision and Control*, 1515–1520, 1989.

Comer (1988). Comer, D, *Internetworking with TCP/IP: Principles, Protocols, and Architecture.* Prentice-Hall, 1988.

COMM (1991). "Switching in a Cooperative Environment," *IEEE Communications Magazine*, 29, January 1991.

Cooper (1986). Cooper, G. R., and McGillem, C. D., *Modern Communications and Spread Spectrum.* McGraw-Hill, 1986.

Couch (1983). Couch, Leon W., *Digital and Analog Communication Systems.* Macmillan, 1983.

Falk (1983). Falk, G., "The structure and function of network protocols," in *Computer Communications, Vol. I,* (W. Chou, Ed.). Prentice-Hall, 1983.

Green (1982). Green, P., *Computer Network Architectures and Protocols.* Plenum, 1982.

Halsall (1988). Halsall, F., *Data Communications, Computer Networks and OSI.* Addison-Wesley, 1988.

Hammond (1986). Hammond, J. L., and O'Reilly, P. J. P., *Performance Analysis of Local Computer Networks.* Addison-Wesley, 1986.

Har'El (1990). Har'El and Kurshan, R. P. "Software for analytical development of communications protocol," *AT&T Tech. J.,* 45–59, Jan/Feb., 1990.

Henry (1985). Henry, P., "Lightwave primer," *IEEE Journal of Quantum Electronics*, QE-21, No. 12, 1862–1879, 1985.

Hoel (1971). Hoel, P. G., Port, S. C., and Stone, C. J., *An Introduction to Probability Theory*. Houghton Mifflin Company, 1971.

Kelly (1979). Kelly, F. P., *Reversibility and Stochastic Networks*. John Wiley & Sons, 1979.

Kleinrock (1975). Kleinrock, L., *Queueing Systems, Vol. 1*. John Wiley & Sons, 1975.

LaQuey (1990). LaQuey, T. (Ed.), *The User's Directory of Computer Networks*. Digital Press, 1990.

Lee (1988). Lee, E. A., and Messerschmitt, D. G., *Digital Communication*. Kluwer, 1988.

Lin (1989). Lin, C. (Ed.), *Optoelectronic Technology and Lightwave Communications Systems*. Van Nostrand Reinhold, 1989.

Lin (1983). Lin, S., and Costello, D. J., *Error Control Coding*. Prentice-Hall, 1983.

Lucky (1989). Lucky, B., *Silicon Dreams: Information, Man, and Machine*. St. Martin's Press, 1989.

Martin (1990). Martin, J., *Telecommunications and Computers* (3rd Ed.) Prentice-Hall, 1990.

Massey (1980). Massey, J. L., "Collision-resolution algorithms and random-access communications," *Technical Report UCLA-ENG-8016*, UCLA, School of Engineering and Applied Science, April 1980.

Meijer (1983). Meijer, A. and Peeters, P., *Computer Network Architectures*, Computer Science Press, 1983.

Palais (1988). Palais, J. C., *Fiber Optic Communications* (2nd Ed.). Prentice-Hall, 1988.

Peterson (1981). Peterson, J. L., *Petri Net Theory and the Modeling of Systems*. Prentice-Hall, 1981.

Schatt (1987). Schatt, S., *Understanding Local Area Networks*. Howard W. Sams & Company, 1987.

Schwartz (1987). Schwartz, M., *Telecommunications Networks: Protocols, Modeling and Analysis*. Addison-Wesley, 1987.

Stallings (1987). Stallings, W., *Local Networks* (2nd Ed.). Macmillan, 1987.

Stallings (1988). Stallings, W., *Data and Computer Communications, Second Edition*. Macmillan, 1988.

Stallings (1989). Stallings, W., *ISDN: An Introduction*. Macmillan, 1989.

Stallings (1990). Stallings, W., *The Business Guide to Local Area Networks*. Howard W. Sams & Company, 1990.

Stevens (1990). Stevens, W. R., *Unix Network Programming*. Prentice-Hall, 1990.

Tanenbaum (1988). Tanenbaum, A., *Computer Networks* (2nd Ed.). Prentice-Hall, 1988.

Walrand (1988). Walrand, J., *An Introduction to Queueing Networks*. Prentice-Hall, 1988.

White (1989). White, J. E., "ASN.1 and ROS: The impact of X.400 on OSI," *IEEE Jour. Selected Areas in Communications*, 7, 1061–72, 1989.

Ziemmerman (1980). Ziemmerman, H., "OSI reference model—The OSI model of architecture for open systems interconnection," *IEEE Trans. Commun.*, COM-28, No. 4, 425–432, 1980.

Index

448

453

DATE DUE

FE 3 '92		
OCT 1 2 1992		
NOV 1 0 1992		
FE 05 '93		
5-14-93		
SE 21 '93		
FE 10 '94		
AP 12 '94		
OC 16 '94		
DE 07 '94		
NOV 21 '95		
FEB 01 '96		

Demco, Inc. 38-293